A HISTORY OF VICTORIA UNIVERSITY

A HISTORY OF

VICTORIA UNIVERSITY

BY

C. B. SISSONS

UNIVERSITY OF TORONTO PRESS
TORONTO · 1952

COPYRIGHT, CANADA, 1952
AND PRINTED IN CANADA BY
UNIVERSITY OF TORONTO PRESS
Reprinted in 2018
ISBN 978-1-4875-8569-3 (paper)

PREFACE

THE first step towards the founding of Victoria University was taken in 1829 at the Conference of the Episcopal Methodist Church of Canada. In 1836 a preparatory seminary named Upper Canada Academy was opened at Cobourg under a Royal Charter. In 1841 the name was changed to Victoria College by an Act of the Provincial Legislature, and university work was commenced at Cobourg the following year, where the first degree obtained in course in the province was conferred in 1845. In 1884, on the absorption of Albert College at Belleville, the name formally became Victoria University, and the President was first called Chancellor. Then in 1887, after much searching of hearts, Victoria pooled resources with the University of Toronto, agreeing if certain conditions were met to hold in abeyance its right to confer degrees in Arts, Medicine, Law, and Science. Removal to Toronto was effected in 1892. Degrees in Theology it continued to grant; and with the union of the Methodist, Presbyterian, and Congregational churches in 1925 a separate college, known as Emmanuel College, was erected within Victoria University to house what since 1873 had been called the Faculty of Theology. Meanwhile, Trinity College and St. Michael's College, under Church of England and Roman Catholic auspices respectively, had joined with Victoria and University (the state) College to form under a federal system the Faculty of Arts in one of the world's largest and best-equipped universities. It is here proposed in telling the story of this growth from small beginnings to depict the actors against the background of the social and political institutions of Canada which they never permitted themselves to forget and thus contributed largely to forming. It is also hoped that now after sixty years it may be possible to assess the worth of the unique attempt to reconcile the claims of church and state in respect of higher education effected in 1892 by university federation at Toronto.

Since the story of Victoria *College*—so he called it—was recorded by Chancellor Burwash nearly forty years ago, a considerable body of relevant historical material has been acquired or made accessible. The voluminous Ryerson correspondence has been set in order and calendared; the Nelles, Carman, and Burwash papers have been secured; and the files of the *Christian Guardian* and *Acta Victoriana* are now ready to hand. In addition to these rich sources, I have perused the Board, Senate, and Faculty minutes of Victoria University and scanned at least the great volumes of minutes of the Senate of the University of Toronto, complete except for the then current volume destroyed in the fire of 1890. Through the courtesy of the authorities of Queen's University their excellently ordered papers have likewise been available.

To lighten this ponderous research, the personal recollections of more than half a century of intimate acquaintance have been freely called upon and supplemented by the sprightly reminiscences of a score of older graduates whose memories extended well into the Cobourg days. The resulting work aims to be accurate and tolerably complete; it is hoped that it may prove to be human as well, being the product of the mind and heart of an ancient and quite human alumnus written with the candour required of one who has so often passed beneath the challenging and cheerful text carved over our portal.

I should like to acknowledge the special debt owed herein to a former teacher, Professor J. C. Robertson, and two former students, Principal Bennett and Professor Ruth I. Jenking; also to thank the Board of Regents for giving me the opportunity for further adventure in a field of Canadian history hitherto only partially explored.

C. B. S.

Victoria University
October 20, 1952

CONTENTS

	Preface	v
	Illustrations	ix
I.	Pioneering in Education, 1829-1836	1
II.	The Embryo Stage, 1836-1842	22
III.	Ryerson's Principalship, 1842-1844	43
IV.	On a Razor's Edge, 1844-1850	67
V.	Salvage Operations, 1850-1859	85
VI.	Of Principalities and Powers, 1860-1867	107
VII.	Left out to Die, 1867-1880	132
VIII.	The Forging of Federation, 1873-1892	158
IX.	"The Good Life" at Cobourg, 1881-1892	191
X.	Pioneering Again, 1892-1913	205
XI.	The Divide, 1913	245
XII.	A Straight Furrow, 1913-1930	265
XIII.	The Second Century, 1930-1952	299
	Appendix	
	The Fallen, 1914-1918	332
	The Fallen, 1939-1945	333
	Index	335

ILLUSTRATIONS
Between pages 180 and 181

Five Founders

The College at Cobourg and its Heads

Faraday Hall and Science Professors

Six Early Graduates

Burwash Hall; The Library

The Massey Family

Reunion Group of 1919

Five Senior Arts Professors of 1913

The Wymilwood of 1926-1952; Gate House from St. Mary Street

Deans and Principals of the Theological Faculty and of Emmanuel College

Victoria College; Emmanuel College

Presidents at Toronto

The Councils of Victoria and Emmanuel Colleges

The Mulock Cup Winners of 1923; the Jennings Cup Winners of 1937-8

The Arts Faculty Cup Winners of 1945; the Campus of 1952

Annesley Hall; the Wymilwood of 1952

A HISTORY OF VICTORIA UNIVERSITY

I. PIONEERING IN EDUCATION
1829-1836

IN 1829 the annual Conference of the Methodists of Upper Canada convened on August 20 in the Union Chapel, now the Bowman Church, on the Ancaster circuit. Having put up their horses and unpacked their saddle-bags at the billets assigned them, the preachers settled down, some forty of them, to discuss the urgent business of saving souls. The harvest was ripe and the labourers, considering the area to be covered, were few—few among the Methodists and fewer still in the other leading denominations. As a means to this end of saving souls, it appeared after deliberation that three practical steps should be taken—the organization of a Sabbath School Union, the publishing of a weekly paper, and provision for a seminary. On November 21, with its first issue as a weekly paper in York, the *Christian Guardian* began a course which within a decade was to make it the most influential journal in the upper province. And Sunday Schools, sometimes as co-operative undertakings of more than one denomination, sprang up everywhere in the centres of population.

The third venture was more difficult and slower of accomplishment, but it was envisaged, and action taken. The minute reads:

"Voted—That a Committee of Five be appointed to take into consideration the propriety of establishing a Seminary and drawing up a Petition to the next Session of the Provincial Parliament for an act of incorporation. The Committee to be nominated by the Chair and appointed by the Conference.[1] The following persons were accordingly appointed: 1. Franklin Metcalf, Wm. Ryerson, John Ryerson, Anson Green, 5. James Richardson."[2]

Two days later the report of the committee was received, considered

---

[1]A nice democratic touch.
[2]Victoria University Archives, Minutes of Conference, 1829, p. 14. The complete minutes in several manuscript volumes from 1824 to 1874 are preserved in the Archives of Victoria University.

item by item, and adopted. It was then filed as No. 17E and lost—an illustration of the imprudence of failing to write reports of committees into minutes. But that was the beginning.

The first editor of the *Christian Guardian* was Egerton Ryerson. He was elected according to a method which became an annual custom, "by ballot without debate."[3] The vote was Egerton Ryerson 16, George Ryerson 15. From the first issue, the *Guardian*, as it was commonly known, kept all three concerns of the Ancaster Conference prominently before the public. Ryerson's first editorial is a ringing call to wider interest in education:

> The present is a most eventful period to the religious and civil interests of this interesting and important portion of the British Empire. The nature of our depending relations—the principles of our foreign intercourse—the complexion of our internal regulations—and the aspect of our literary and religious institutions, are about taking the hue of a permanent character. . . . Education, in every point of view, must be considered of the highest importance—to the comforts of domestic life—the suppression of moral evil—and the stability of good Government. Like the christian religion, of which it is the handmaid, it is designed for every human being—and is suited to the circumstance and adapted to the improvement of the happiness of every human being.[4]

The objection that education tends to lift the lower classes above their sphere and make them dissatisfied with their station in life is next assailed, and the horrors of the French Revolution are cited as a result of mass ignorance. Two months later Ryerson returns to the theme of popular as opposed to exclusive education in the rhetorical periods of the day. "Those literary and ecclesiastical fabrics that were reared in days of superstition and selfishness, still bear the unseemly marks of their bigoted origin—still interpose an impossible barrier against the improving suggestions of more mature experience—still bring the means of entering their halls and enjoying the benefit of their literary favours to comparatively a wealthy few of a particular creed—still leave the most needy portion of the community as ignorant and as wretched as they found them. . . ."[5]

Now what was the stark fact beneath this rhetoric? For some forty years, since 1791, Canada had been governed under the Constitutional

[3]*Ibid.*, p. 17.
[4]*Christian Guardian*, Nov. 21, 1828. Hereafter referred to as *C.G.*
[5]*Ibid.*, Jan. 16, 1830.

Act. That Act had made no provision for education. It is true that a seventh of the Crown lands of the upper province had been set apart for the support of a Protestant clergy, and such was the close connection of the church with education at the time that it might have been thought that a portion of this grant would have been applied to education. Indeed in the special grant sought and obtained by the Rev. Alexander Macdonell, Roman Catholic bishop, for his work in Glengarry, provision for teachers as well as for clergymen was specified. But in 1791 few would have regarded a direct provision for schools or colleges as a concern of government. Anyone so wild as to propose a tax on property for the support of education would have been laughed out of court, or if taken seriously would have been believed a dangerous radical. Even sixty years later the term "communist" was applied by the Rev. John Roaf of Toronto to the advocates of free schools. Education was considered a matter for the individual parent or for the churches as associations of individuals of like mind. However, as a result of representations by Governor Simcoe and his *ad interim* successor, and more with a view to training a ruling class than for any purposes of general education, the Duke of Portland, Secretary of State for the Colonies, issued a despatch on November 4, 1797, which in a beneficent guise was the beginning of many evils for the province. It set aside large tracts of land, some half-million acres, for education. The purpose of the grant was stated as the laying of the foundation for sound learning and a religious education, "First by the establishment of free Grammar Schools in those Districts in which they are called for, and in due process of time by establishing other Seminaries of a larger & more comprehensive nature for the promotion of religious and moral learning, and the study of the Arts and Sciences."[6]

From the plural "Seminaries" it may be inferred that the home government had in mind a situation in which eventually collegiate education would be made available to the widely extended population of the province in several institutions under the control of the leading denominations. What else could it have meant with the stake the churches then had in education? However, that was not the way in which it was interpreted by the ruling coterie of the province. With that peculiar acquisitiveness germane to the capital even when it was

[6]Public Archives of Canada, G 1, vol. 53, pt. 1, pp. 105–6.

muddy York, it was at once assumed that His Lordship meant one provincial university, and at York. And this bland assumption so far prevailed that it would be difficult, indeed perhaps impossible, to find any reference to His Lordship's plural wherever the story of the University of Toronto has been told.[7] Archdeacon Strachan had no doubts on the matter, at least until 1848; there must be one university, at Toronto, and under the control of an Established Church. In 1827 he secured in England a Royal Charter for a seminary of higher learning which embodied his ideas. The University of King's College was to be situated in York; its president was to be the Archdeacon of York; its professors were to subscribe to the Thirty-nine Articles; the system of Divinity taught was to be that of the Church of England—all this for a province of which probably less than a quarter of the population was in active communion in that church.[8]

Meanwhile the more pressing needs of elementary and secondary education were receiving slight attention. Grammar schools for the instruction of the boys of the more respectable families were given priority. The earliest school act, that of 1807, provided decent support for one such school in each of the eight districts into which the upper province was then divided. It was nine years before any public provision was made for common school education. An annual grant of £6,000 was voted by the government towards the salaries of common school teachers; the settlers could see to their buildings and equipment. In 1829 the number of pupils in grammar schools was 372, that in common schools, 10,312. Nor does the situation appear to have improved with the appointment of Strachan to the presidency of the Board of Education for Upper Canada in 1823. He was inclined to

---

[7]At various times it has been proposed to change the name to the University of Upper Canada, or later, the University of Ontario. Indeed it was only in 1946 that the possibility of such change without legislation ceased to exist. Tucked away in the miscellany known as the Statute Law Amendment Act of the province in that year there appeared an amendment rescinding a long-standing provision that a change of name from the University of Toronto to the University of Ontario might be effected merely by a proclamation of the Lieutenant-Governor. No discussion of this little amendment appears to have taken place in the House or in the public press.

[8]The terms of the charter were more liberal than those of the existing English universities in that undergraduates were not required to subscribe to the Thirty-nine Articles. Nevertheless, "although its terms were the most liberal ever granted by the Crown, the exclusively Anglican tenor immediately aroused political and denominational opposition." *A History of the University of Trinity College, Toronto, 1852-1952* (Toronto, 1952), pp. 33–4; cf. ibid., p. 20.

follow in the Simcoe tradition which aimed to build society in Canada on the English model.

While events in England were moving swiftly towards the bloodless revolution involved in the Reform Bill of 1832, progress in correcting such inequalities as that to be found in education in Canada was exasperatingly slow. In spite of the fresh atmosphere of a new society, and the proximity of a neighbouring republic, the advance was more difficult in Canada than in England. Under the constitution not only had the local Assembly and the Council to be convinced of the soundness of any measure, but that measure when despatched by the Governor with his own comments, favourable or otherwise, must meet the approval of the British Houses of Parliament—Commons and Lords—before the Royal Assent made it law. Such were the limitations imposed by a colonial status.

In this long struggle towards freer institutions, the Methodists were the protagonists. It was Egerton Ryerson, an Anglican turned Methodist and son of an officer who had borne arms for the Crown in the Revolutionary War, who first effectively challenged the accuracy and soundness of Strachan's statistics and attitude and in his "Review," published in the *Colonial Advocate* in 1826, shook the province to its foundations. It was his oldest brother, George, missionary to the Indians at the Credit, and bearing on his face an ugly scar received as an officer in the engagement at Fort Erie, who twice, in 1828 and 1831, carried largely signed petitions to Westminster where he pleaded the cause of the non-Anglican interests so cogently that he brought conviction to the Colonial Secretary. Thus "the tide of fortune was now definitely set against the plans to which Strachan was devoting his life."[9]

In 1829 these plans met a rebuff from a rather surprising quarter. The new Lieutenant-Governor of Upper Canada, Sir John Colborne, had become convinced that the charter of King's College was both unpopular and unrealistic. As Chancellor *ex officio* he induced the Council of the College to divert a considerable proportion of its revenues to the establishing at York of a preparatory school to be known as Upper Canada College. This action, as it proved, served to delay the opening of King's College for fourteen years. But Upper

[9]William Smith, *Political Leaders in Upper Canada* (1931), p. 178.

Canada College, with Colborne's brother-in-law, the Rev. J. H. Harris, at its head, was conducted by the Council of King's College on the same exclusive principles as had been contemplated for the more advanced institution. Its establishment accentuated, if anything, the void in general facilities for secondary schools.

It remained for the Conference of 1830 to take definite action on a Methodist seminary. A committee of five was appointed to report on the expediency of the venture and on ways and means. On their report the project was accepted, but the name and site were left to be determined later. This committee was also ordered to select provisional trustees, and a building committee. These matters decided, it was agreed by Conference that each itinerant preacher was to be provided with a copy of the constitution and a subscription book, and was to use his utmost endeavours to obtain funds and scholars. The report of the committee finally stood in four clauses. A fifth clause, which stipulated that each itinerant who had travelled eight years might have one of his family educated free, is marked "rescinded"; no one was to be permitted to say that the preachers were thinking first of themselves.

The constitution for the seminary as adopted on August 23, 1830, provided for nine trustees to be appointed by the Conference, three retiring annually; for five visitors, also chosen by the Conference; and for the appointment of the principal and teachers and the supervision of the "financial and literary state" of the institution by the trustees and visitors jointly. Again a fifth clause is particularly significant—indeed in the account in the *Guardian* and elsewhere it is transferred to first place. It reads:

Resolved, that this shall be purely a literary institution. That no system of Theology shall be taught therein, but all students shall be free to embrace and pursue any religious creed, and attend any place of worship, their Parents or guardians may direct.[10]

Recognizing how ticklish a matter was the choosing of the site, Conference next determined to adopt the unusual plan of having each one of its three districts elect three representatives to a committee to meet at Hallowell (now Picton) on January 27, 1831, at 9 A.M. They were accordingly elected as follows: Niagara District—John Ryerson, Thomas Whitehead, Samuel Belton; Bay of Quinte District—Daniel

[10]V.U.A., Minutes of Conference, 1830, p. 35.

Wright, John Beatty, William Ryerson; Augusta District—Thomas Madden, William Brown, James Richardson. It was ordered that the voting on the site should be by ballot. Open voting, it may be noted, persisted for members of the Legislature until 1871; by so far did the Conference precede the country in the adoption of this necessary instrument of democracy.

Only seven of the nine members of the committee were able to get to Hallowell. Travelling in winter had its difficulties at the time, though usually they were less formidable than those of summer, unless one lived close to the Great Lakes. The two absentees were Brown and Madden, both older men from the back settlements on the Rideau and Ottawa. Their best way of reaching Hallowell would have been by sleigh on the ice of the chain of rivers and lakes which with the help of the Rideau canal were to join the Ottawa with Lake Ontario. But "Father" Whitehead was there, and he had been preaching since 1783. It was he who proposed Cobourg as the site for the Academy, and his nomination finally prevailed by a vote of 5 to 2. The locations considered were six in number and ranged from Brockville to York. The *Guardian* in commending the selection described Cobourg as "one of the most beautiful, healthy, and flourishing villages in Upper Canada, situated on the shore of Lake Ontario, in the centre of the Province, in the midst of a populous and highly intelligent District of inhabitants."[11] The nine trustees, three of them ministers, were chosen by the committee; also a building committee of seven, two of them ministers. It was determined to commence building when £2,000 had been subscribed and £500 collected. The name chosen for the seminary was Upper Canada Academy.

If the whole scheme was ambitious, the mode of securing financial support was nothing less than heroic. With no concentration of wealth in urban centres, with none of the modern means of rapid communication, with a postal system so rudimentary that on grounds of efficiency, as much as economy, correspondents preferred to wait for private emissaries, and with many of the roads mere trails, the founders of the Academy set out to collect subscriptions in almost every settlement of the province. To this end they employed their system of circuits. Ebenezer Perry, a prominent business man of the Cobourg district, was

[11]*C.G.*, Feb. 5, 1831.

appointed treasurer, but all itinerant preachers were expected to collect. Each collector was supplied with a book for the signature of subscribers. The constitution of the Academy was written in each book and the engagement that payment might be made in four annual instalments.

The choice of the Rev. John Beatty as general agent would appear to have been excellent. When he had entered the itinerant work in 1828, leaving his comfortable establishment just west of York, which he had named Meadowvale, he had reached his forty-seventh year. Carroll describes him as "a gentleman of good property, somewhat in years, a zealous Methodist and an able local preacher."[12] His wife was an equally remarkable person. She had followed her first husband, an officer of the British army, in Canadian and European campaigns and had seen Wellington enter Paris in triumph after Waterloo. Most of John Beatty's subscription books are now in the Archives of Victoria University, the only missing records being those of the subscribers from Hamilton Township, including Cobourg, and from the town of York. With their nearly two thousand names, arranged by circuits or townships, these books afford information not elsewhere available as to the names, location, and financial standing of the inhabitants of Upper Canada in 1831. There were two contributors of £100, James R. Armstrong of Toronto, father of Egerton Ryerson's second wife, and Ebenezer Perry, the general treasurer. But very few subscribers gave more than £10, and the average was less than £2. A number of farms of 100 and 200 acres of varying cash value were contributed, and George B. Spencer gave the lot of four acres on the outskirts of Cobourg where the building was to be located.

During the winter months of 1830-1 canvassing proceeded apace. By April 2, a correspondent from Cobourg could report to the *Guardian* that upwards of £900 had been raised in the Township of Hamilton. A week later it was announced that $2,000, that is £500 Halifax currency, had been subscribed in the Niagara District; and by the middle of April Prince Edward County had contributed £700 and 600 acres of land. Of course in most cases only a fourth of the pledge had been paid, but the committee felt justified in calling for tenders for 100 cords of stone and 300,000 bricks, the stone to be delivered by July 1,

[12]John Carroll, *Case and His Cotemporaries* (Toronto, 1867-77), III, 108. Carroll, who modelled his work on Herodotus, was the author of several books on the history of Methodism. His *magnum opus* was *Case*, in five volumes.

PIONEERING IN EDUCATION, 1829-1836 9

and 50,000 bricks by September 1. When the annual Conference met at York on August 31, 1831, it was reported that the amount subscribed had reached £3,954, this sum including 900 acres of land valued at £125. The total cost of the establishment was estimated at not more than £5,000, and the Conference instructed the building committee to proceed with despatch.

Never had prospects for Methodism and its nascent college looked brighter. The Conference year had brought a record increase in membership, 3,553. The three projects conceived in 1829 were all prospering. But a cloud now appeared on the horizon. George Ryerson, again in England, this time as the bearer of a petition originated in York by a "joint committee of Christians," Anglican, Presbyterian, Methodist, Baptist, and Quaker, had seen the cloud and warned Egerton. It was a plan, or more correctly a plot, between the British Wesleyans and the ruling Compact. Missionaries sent out by the English Conference were again to enter the province, from which they had withdrawn under an agreement made in 1820. The London Missionary Committee was to accept a government grant for that purpose and use its influence and that of its "missionaries" to suppress agitation for those measures of reform which the *Guardian* had consistently advocated. The evidence to this effect has been documented elsewhere.[18] All that is required here is to indicate the effect of the scheme on the Academy.

A remarkable incident occurred in 1831. The Conference had sought an interview with Colborne on the subject of certain aspersions which had been cast upon them by the bishop and clergy of the Diocese of Quebec in a petition to the Colonial Secretary. The memorial defending their position, already forwarded to Colborne, said nothing of education. Colborne astonished the deputation by reading them a lecture. He told them that if their preachers had confined themselves to instructing their flocks only in the words of eternal life, and avoided inconvenient attention to secular concerns, a desire for the return of Wesleyan "missionaries" from England would not have been so generally expressed. Then he permitted himself these words:

The system of Education which has produced the best & ablest men in the United Kingdom will not be abandoned here to suit the limited views of the leaders of Societies, who perhaps have neither experience nor judgment to appreciate the value or advantages of a liberal education; but the

[18]C. B. Sissons, *Egerton Ryerson: His Life and Letters*, I (Toronto, 1937), pp. 140–91. Hereafter referred to as *E.R.*

British Government will, I am confident, with the aid of the Provincial Legislature, establish respectable Schools in every part of the Province; and encourage all Societies to follow their example.

A Seminary, I hope, will not be styled exclusive, that is open to every one, merely because the Classical Masters are brought from our own Universities.[14]

Evidently the Governor was forgetting the memorial and taking advantage of the occasion to chastise the *Guardian* and its editor, who was a member of the deputation. As for the indirect reference to Upper Canada College, which Sir John personally, and not the Legislature, had been instrumental in founding, Ryerson had announced its opening, carried its advertisements, and followed its progress in friendly enough fashion. On two occasions only had criticism been included in the paper. In the report of George Ryerson's representations to the Imperial Parliament, a reference occurred to the fact that the people of Upper Canada were so little satisfied with educational facilities provided by the government that forty young people at the time were in seminaries in the United States, and six of these from York. Again when twelve prominent inhabitants of York, including Robert Baldwin and J. E. Small, had petitioned Sir John for a more general and less classical curriculum, Ryerson had printed the petition and given it editorial support. The words "encourage all Societies" may have been intended to suggest that should the *Guardian* mend its ways and follow the good example of the English Wesleyans, renouncing and denouncing those who were given to change, government support might be expected for Upper Canada Academy.

But the sentence about the "limited views of the leaders of Societies" on liberal education was not soon to be forgotten. What manner of men were these of whom the Governor could speak so contemptuously? Take the five who brought in the first report in favour of the founding of the Academy. It would not be difficult to establish a contention that any one of them was in point of intellect equal to and in point of knowledge of the province and its needs superior to his detractor.

Franklin Metcalf was born in 1798, converted in a Methodist protracted meeting in 1812, and after some two years of apprenticeship to a physician was accepted as an itinerant in 1819. Carroll describes him as a little less than six feet in height, straight, symmetrical, lithe,

[14]*Ibid.*, pp. 146–7.

and graceful, with a face clothed with the glow of health and of true and lovely proportions, and the whole countenance lighted up with a genial smile. Green, while less lyrical in his description, is no less free in expressing admiration of his commanding personal appearance, discriminating judgment, and remarkably clear and Methodistic sermons which cost him much time and thought. Carroll tells of a very discerning member of Conference who was accustomed to amuse himself by classifying its members according to their talents. He had his first, second, third, and even fourth classes. But the first class he made to consist of only two men, William Ryerson and Franklin Metcalf; and he was rather inclined to make Metcalf A1. For oratory, William Ryerson was the superior, but for clearness, accuracy, and ability as an expositor, Metcalf stood supreme.

William Ryerson's earlier experiences had left him rough-hewn. The third son of Colonel Joseph Ryerson, he had enlisted at the age of fifteen and served in the War of 1812. Having joined the Methodists, he left his father's roof and pioneered in the woods of Oxford County. In later years he was once tauntingly asked at what college he was educated. "Sir," he replied, "I was educated at the College of Buck and Bright"—common names for a team of oxen which were preferred to horses for clearing land. After serving as a local preacher for some years he was received in the itinerant work, "aged twenty-five, wife and two children, clear of debt."[15] Of a loosely knit but powerful frame, he prided himself on never missing an appointment whatever the effort involved. Carroll remembers his facing a ninety-mile trip against the cutting blasts of winter and discarding his overshoes because he knew that he would have to run beside his horse at times to keep warm. But it is of his other qualities as depicted by Carroll that Sir John might have learned.

We can remember masses of people moved by his word, like forest trees swayed to and fro by the wind.... He is a man of some little learning—of most universal general information—and of a rare order of genius. He has devoured books with perfect voracity. Plan of study he has never had; but, like the ox, he has gulped every kind of edible that came in his way into his capacious reservoir, and ruminated on it at his leisure. He has a mind unceasingly active; hence, if he is not in conversation with a friend, or with book in hand, he is usually pacing backwards and forwards like

[15]*Case*, II, 441.

a chained bear, (he will pardon the figure) working out some of those huge masses of thought which are ever laboring through his intellectual laboratory.[16]

He was always interested in politics, unduly so for a preacher, as Carroll thinks, and in 1861, acceding to the request of a large petition of his neighbours from West Brant, became a candidate for and was elected to the Legislature.

John Ryerson was set in a different mould from his older brother William. Rather slight of frame and delicate in constitution, his high forehead, piercing eye, and sensitive face would mark him as a man of distinction in any company. By reason of his strong determination, ability to grasp a situation, and skill in managing men, for twenty or more years he wielded an influence in the Conference probably greater than that of any other member. His indomitable spirit is indicated by a missionary trip taken at the age of fifty-five from Sault Ste Marie to Fort Garry and Hudson Bay, and thence through the perilous ice floes to England. The account of the trip by canoe and batteau to Hudson Bay,[17] according to Dean H. A. Innis, affords the most accurate description extant of the distances and difficulties of this early trade route. Like William he was a great reader. But it was as keen observer of men and affairs that he excelled. Egerton once remarked that he learned more from a weekly letter of John's than from all the prints, and Professor F. H. Underhill goes so far as to style him "the most wonderful letter-writer that our country has yet produced. . . . What a joy Canadian history would be if we had only more John Ryersons in it!"[18]

The fourth member of the committee was Anson Green. He alone of the five had been born in the United States, but had begun life in Canada as a school-teacher. He was less the student than the man of affairs. Yet after half a century in the Christian ministry, at the request of Conference he expanded his factual diary into a memoir which rivals *Case and His Cotemporaries* as a reliable and interesting account of early Methodism. Chancellor Nelles, in the introduction to this work, notes the eminent place he held as a preacher and the fact

---

[16]John Carroll, *Past and Present* (Toronto, 1860), pp. 271–2.
[17]*Hudson's Bay; or A Missionary Tour in the Territory of the Hon. Hudson's Bay Company* (Toronto, 1855).
[18]*Canadian Forum*, May, 1937.

that he had filled all the highest offices in the gift of his church. Then after referring to his great penetration, his uniform self-possession, his imposing presence, and his dignified and courteous bearing, he adds this observation: "If he had not become a Methodist minister he might easily have risen to eminence as a financier or a diplomatist, and even a Methodist minister is the better of a capacity for both the one and the other."

The fifth name is that of James Richardson. He like the Ryersons had been brought up in an Anglican home. He had sailed the lakes out of Kingston with his father, formerly of the Royal Navy. As a naval lieutenant and master of the *Wolf*, he had lost his left arm at Sackett's Harbour in 1814. Thereafter, settling on a farm at Presqu'Ile with an annual pension of £100 sterling, he was prominent in the community as a collector of customs and a justice of the peace. After joining the Methodists he had acted as a local preacher, but responded to the call to fill a vacancy in York and became its senior minister with Egerton Ryerson as his assistant. This was the year 1825-6 when the latter's famous "Review" shattered the complacency of York and rocked the throne Strachan was building for himself. Carroll has left us no account of Richardson's appearance but describes him as a man of superior education, genteel but easy manners, with an air of unmistakable piety. When the Episcopal Methodists seceded in 1833 he cast in his lot with them, after a year's retirement to the United States, and during his later life served that branch of the Methodists as its bishop.

Such were some of the men whose "limited views" had suggested that they should devote their energies and personal subscriptions from meagre stipends to the founding of a seminary. The feelings of the Methodists and their friends in the other evangelical churches on the publication of Colborne's strictures can well be imagined, and are doubtless pretty accurately reflected in Ryerson's powerful rejoinder in the *Guardian*.[19] The reproof administered by Lord Goderich, the Colonial Secretary, was briefer but severe enough, considering the formality of official correspondence. The despatch is dated April 2, 1832. Sir John is told that he had expressed himself not altogether with that prudence which is necessary on such an occasion. Several

---

[19]*E.R.*, I, 148–51.

expressions are quoted as "calculated to give offence, which could better have been avoided, even supposing the censure they imply to have been deserved, which," Lord Goderich adds, "I confess I am not satisfied to have been altogether the case." He then proceeds:

> ... but there is one part of this reply, which is, I fear, open to a still stronger objection. I allude to the following passage "A Seminary I hope will not be styled exclusive that is open to everyone, merely because the Classical Masters are brought from our own Universities." I agree with you that a Seminary cannot be styled exclusive merely because the Classical Masters happen to have been educated at our own Universities, but if I am to understand that a degree at Oxford or Cambridge was made a necessary qualification for such employment, I cannot refrain from expressing my opinion that as these degrees are only given to Members of the Church of England, the complaint of the Methodists was well founded, to require such a qualification was to adopt the principles of exclusion in a manner which was the more likely to give Offence from the sort of disguise which it assumed.[20]

In leaving this unpleasant incident in Canadian history, it is proper to remark that if the itinerant ministers were without university training they were in good company. Sir John Colborne had none, being a soldier from boyhood with much distinguished service behind him. Nor had the brains of the ruling Compact, John Beverley Robinson.

By June 7, 1832, all was ready for the laying of the corner stone.[21] It would appear that the preachers were not greatly in evidence at this event. In any case, the only extant report, copied by the *Guardian* from the Cobourg *Reformer*, omits any reference even to the presence of the resident pastor, Richard Jones. For the ceremony itself, the building committee took over. In the absence of Dr. John Rolph, who was first invited, the stone was laid by Dr. John Gilchrist, chairman of the committee. He had been practising medicine since 1819, having been the first candidate to secure a licence from the newly organized Medical Board of Upper Canada. Since then he had been doing a number of other things, farming, milling (in both flour and lumber), merchandising, and distilling—the last being the enterprise most frequently mentioned in gossip connected with the laying of the corner stone. Furthermore, he was deep in politics on the Reform side, and

[20]P.A.C., G 1, vol. 69, pp. 90–2.
[21]On the same day William IV affixed the royal signature to the Reform Bill. The coincidence suggests that democracy was advancing more or less *pari passu* in the two countries.

was to be an unsuccessful candidate both in 1834 and in 1836, thus laying himself open to arrest as a Mackenzie man in 1838. He won a seat, however, in 1841 after Durham and Sydenham had changed the face of Canada. A leaden box was embedded in the lower part of the stone containing coins and copies of current newspapers and the following inscription:[22]

UPPER CANADA ACADEMY
by the favor of
ALMIGHTY GOD,
On the 7th day of June, A.D. 1832, and in the second year of the reign of
our most gracious King
WILLIAM THE FOURTH,
The Corner Stone,
Of this Edifice, erected by the *Conference* of the *Methodist Episcopal Church*, in Canada,
was laid by the
COMMITTEE AND BUILDER.
MAJOR GEN. SIR JOHN COLBORNE, K.C.B.
Lieutenant Governor of Upper Canada.
Building Committee.

Messrs. Ebenezer Perry,   Messrs. L. S. Church,
John McCarty,   J. W. Cleghorn,
John Gilchrist,   W. S. Conger.
EDWARD CRANE,
Architect and Builder.

The laying of the corner stone of what was to be Victoria College was an event of some importance. In a real sense it signified the end of exclusiveness and privilege in learning, and the beginning of an idea which made Upper Canada a pioneer in popular education, and in its general diffusion an example to older societies; and it was this

[22]*C.G.*, June 20, 1832 (from the Cobourg *Reformer*). A century later, the then Chancellor of Victoria University, Dr. E. W. Wallace, was impelled by a keen antiquarian interest to endeavour to locate the stone at Cobourg with the purpose of removing it to the present college building. But it was apparently not marked on the outside, and the committee of archaeologists, after working for some time amid ribald remarks from the windows by present inmates, were compelled to retreat vanquished. The building for many years has been a mental hospital for female patients. It is a curious coincidence that a similar fate befell the King's College building in Queen's Park, which became officially known as the University Lunatic Asylum.

general diffusion of education which made possible in Canada the early application of democratic principles to government on the one hand, and on the other hand that unique and peaceful contribution which Canada was able to make to the theory of Empire.

Building operations proceeded rapidly during 1832 and the early part of 1833. In the *Guardian* of July 24, 1833, John Ryerson reported that workmen had just finished burning a kiln of 80,000 or 90,000 bricks which, they said, were of superior quality to anything they had seen in North America; if funds were available the roof should be on the main building by October 1. By May 7 following, the *Guardian* could say that the work was in such a state of forwardness that the building would "be ready for the reception of pupils by the ensuing autumn"; but again the condition—"if a religious and enlightened public will continue to advance the means to prevent the delay of the work." The funds were not forthcoming, and the doors were not opened till June 18, 1836. The reasons for the slackening of effort were two. In the first place the country fell into hard times. This in itself would account for the failure of many of the subscribers to continue their payments to the fourth annual instalment. But it was certainly not the only reason. The union of the Conference with the Wesleyans, broached in 1832 and consummated in 1833, deeply offended and eventually alienated a large section of the Methodist public. The Christian virtue of the act, which was in effect the turning of the other cheek, was regarded by many as a weak surrender of principle to win government aid and approval. Further, it was held that the local preachers and lay members should have been consulted in their quarterly meetings before a change of status and a change of name from Episcopal Methodist to Wesleyan Methodist was effected. And to replace the seasoned Elder Case as Superintendent by an English President, who on his first Sunday in Canada stepped down from his carriage in Hamilton accoutred in knee breeches, black silk stockings, and silver shoe buckles—well, it was quite too much for the youngsters standing by, as Green records, and not good for the pioneer economy of Canadian Methodism. The government grant of £900, although earmarked for Indian work and paid to the London Committee, was loudly proclaimed by the more extreme Reform prints as proof positive that the Ryersons had persuaded the Conference to sell itself to the enemy.

The effect on Academy finances may be inferred from bits of evidence here and there. In the subscription books there are a good many names of men who paid their first instalment and then have "refused to pay" or "no" written where the later instalments should have appeared. No cash entries at all appear after the names of two such notable Reformers as Thomas Parke of Westminster and Peter Matthews of Pickering, who were committed to pay £5 and £4 respectively. It is worth noting, however, that when Matthews stood on the scaffold in 1838, along with Lount, the Rev. John Beatty, who probably had canvassed him for the subscription, stood by his side to afford spiritual consolation. Another piece of evidence is a slighting reference in one of John Ryerson's letters directed against Ebenezer Perry, the treasurer of the fund, and James Lyons, a generous subscriber, as having become furious levellers in matters of church government. Further, at the Conference of 1834, Dr. Gilchrist, who had laid the corner stone, and John McCarty, who had canvassed Cobourg and vicinity for subscriptions, both retired or were dropped from the building committee. And it may be supposed that the contributions from the people of Cobourg and vicinity fell far short of the £1,000 they had boasted of subscribing. McCarty was the son of the early preacher from across the border whose arrest and mysterious disappearance evoked from Chancellor Burwash the title "the protomartyr of Canadian Methodism." John himself was the kind of man who during the heated election of 1844 could mount a waggon in the Cobourg market-place and denounce the Principal of Victoria College for what he considered undue tenderness towards the policies of the Governor. It is not surprising, then, that the *British Colonial Argus* of Kingston was quoted as exclaiming, "What is to become of the Cobourg Seminary which from corner to top-stone was built with the money of Reformers."[23] The *Argus*, to be sure, was more interested in the Reformers than in the Academy, or in complete accuracy, for that matter.

During his brief visit to England in 1833 to negotiate the terms of union with the Wesleyans, Egerton Ryerson had been commissioned

[23]*E.R.*, I, 213 n.

by Conference to inquire as to a suitable staff for the Academy and to explore the possibility of securing financial aid. He had little time to devote to the matter, but managed to collect £111.17.0. sterling, including an unsolicited subscription from Edward Ellice, Secretary of War, of £50, and £5 from Lord Goderich, now Earl of Ripon.

It was only at the Conference of 1834, it would appear, that incorporation of the Academy was considered and the officers of Conference instructed to apply to the Legislature for such an act. The petition was duly drawn up and a bill presented by J. P. Roblin during the session of 1835. The bill was given a first reading and second reading was promised for the next day, but neither the bill nor the record of its fate is preserved. It may perhaps be inferred that the bill was withdrawn in order to avoid the raising of a dispute in the Assembly, with the prospect in any event of rejection by the Council. Either then or later, it was resolved to apply for a Royal Charter instead.

Meanwhile the building itself had been carried far to completion, and considerable additional money had been spent on the grounds and an elaborate fence. The trustees had gone far beyond the cash received and had deeply obligated themselves. Twice the expected date of opening had been postponed. In the emergency Egerton Ryerson was commissioned by the President of Conference, the Rev. William Lord, to leave his congregation at Kingston and lay siege to the British government and people. "Nothing but the alternative, as Mr. Lord deeply feels," he wrote a friend, "of the sinking or success of the Academy could have induced me this year to have undertaken such a task."[24] In the troubled state of affairs during the years 1836 and 1837, little could be expected of the Canadian authorities; Ryerson's mission in effect was an appeal to the foot of the throne. Tedious delay and frequent discouragement awaited him. His absence was protracted to nineteen months. But in the end, sagacity and importunity prevailed. He returned to Canada with the first Royal Charter ever granted to a non-Anglican establishment, and with the promise of funds which, as he then supposed, would satisfy all claims incurred for its erection.

The story of this remarkable achievement can only be summarized here.[25] Evidently Ryerson concentrated his main effort on securing the

---

[24]V.U.A., Egerton Ryerson to Junkin, Nov. 14, 1835.
[25]It has been more fully recorded in *E.R.*, I, chaps. VIII and IX.

Charter, considering that with this in hand finances would follow. At first he made little progress with the Colonial Secretary, Lord Glenelg. But unlike Baldwin with his brief on responsible government, he persisted till he secured an interview. The path was made easier for him with the Cabinet once he had renewed the acquaintance with Ellice made three years earlier. Ellice knew Canada from some years of residence as an officer of the Hudson's Bay Company, and while not a member of the Government at the time yet moved powerfully behind the scenes. For his ultimate success, however, Ryerson had largely to thank the Under-Secretary for the Colonies, Sir George Grey, a man of broad views and simple piety.

The matter of the Charter was referred to the Law Officers of the Crown, that is to say, Sir John Campbell, Attorney-General, later Chief Justice, and Sir R. M. Rolfe, Solicitor-General, later Lord Chancellor. They had several objections to Ryerson's drafting. They did not like the use of "Church" and suggested "Connexion," but yielded on that point. They required that the names of the trustees should be stated, and this was readily done. The main objection, however, was to placing the Academy under the control of a Conference, a term not known, so they said, in law. Ryerson replied that he was not free to change the Charter in this respect; subscriptions had been made out in the name of the Conference, and in its name the whole enterprise had been carried forward. He noted, however, that in the statute giving property rights to trustees of the Methodist Church, reference had been made to the rules and discipline of the Conference of the Wesleyan Methodist Church, also to the term "minister" or "preacher" of that church. Similarly, in the Marriage Act of 1831 Methodist ministers who could produce proof that they had been ordained according to the rites and forms of their church were permitted to perform the marriage ceremony. After a remarkable display of legal knowledge and acumen, Ryerson declared himself willing to accept a change in wording from "The Conference or ecclesiastical Assembly of the Wesleyan Methodist Church at its annual meetings" of his original draft to "the ministers of the said Wesleyan Methodist Church at their regular meetings, held annually according to the rites and ceremonies of said Church." The Law Officers were appeased, and on July 6, His Majesty-in-Council approved of the Charter as drafted. On October

12, 1836, the Great Seal was affixed thereto. One rampart had been scaled.

The securing of financial help was an equally difficult business and thoroughly distasteful to Ryerson. Yet Lord was urging him to "*Beg, beg, beg it all,*"[26] and he was acutely aware of how deeply involved were his brethren personally and in their dearest interests. So he persisted in canvassing London and the prominent towns and in refusing to be daunted by the initial rebuff from the Colonial Office. In the end he was able to convince the Colonial Secretary that instructions should be issued to Sir Francis Bond Head to advance to the trustees of the Academy a sum of £4,100, which at the time Ryerson regarded as sufficient, together with his collections, to meet all obligations. Individual collections amounted only to £1,272.10.6. One of the most gratifying subscriptions would be that of £10 from the Duchess of Kent, whose daughter in a few months was to succeed to the throne and presently to give the College its name. In the total amount was included a promise of the British Conference to donate £100 in books.

The impatient Conference and trustees were not disposed to wait for news of the Charter or of financial relief from England. The *Guardian* of May 11 announced the opening for June 18. In doing so the editor, Ephraim Evans, painted a glowing picture: a salubrious situation, overlooking Lake Ontario; a flourishing village with Methodist, Presbyterian, and Anglican churches; steam communications by water from every part of the province; freedom of the pupils from exposure to the temptations of a larger centre of population. He did not boast of the building, as others did, as being the finest public building in the province. Certainly it makes a splendid appearance and dominates the scene in Bartlett's sketch of Cobourg in 1841.

The weather on June 18 was unpromising in the early morning, but by the time of the opening ceremonies the sun had burst forth with unusual splendour. Evans regarded this as "a delightful omen of the light and effulgence of that day of sanctified science, which is yet to bless this infant country."[27] First a service in the Methodist Chapel, conducted by the Rev. Joseph Stinson, Superintendent of Missions under the British Conference. Next, the procession up to the Academy,

[26]V.U.A., Lord to Egerton Ryerson, Aug. 23, 1836.
[27]C.G., June 29, 1836.

Mr. Edward Crane, the Architect, leading, and in order, the Building Committee, the Steward (the Rev. C. R. Allison), the ministers present, the Principal, the Rev. Matthew Richey (flanked by the two venerable itinerants, Whitehead and Case), the students, the choir, and the spectators. In the Chapel of the Academy Anson Green, who presided as Chairman of the Cobourg District, after telling briefly of the development of the institution, presented the keys to the Principal, who in his academic robes delivered an eloquent inaugural address. Mark Burnham's choir had come from Port Hope, and graced the occasion with appropriate pieces of sacred harmony. At last, after six years of planning, the good ship had spread its sails to the breeze.

II. THE EMBRYO STAGE
1836-1842

THE Upper Canada Academy at Cobourg was in operation for six years, from 1836 to 1842. The provincial statute establishing Victoria College received the vice-regal signature on August 27, 1841; but until October, 1842, work was continued on a preparatory not on a university level. During the first four years of the Academy the Rev. Matthew Richey was Principal, the first three in person and the last by remote and tenuous control from Toronto, where he was pastor of the Newgate Street Chapel. For the fifth and sixth years Egerton Ryerson was Principal, with slight intervention in its affairs at first, but more definite direction as the time approached for university work. The acting head during these three years under a non-resident principal was Jesse Hurlburt, a Canadian and a Bachelor of Arts from the Wesleyan University at Middletown, Conn. During the six years some four hundred students, about a third of whom were girls, or "young ladies" in the speech of the time, were enrolled, for periods of from one term (the year was quartered) to two or three years. Most of the students were in their teens, with a sprinkling of youngsters (Columbus Green attended at seven) and a considerable number of young men in their twenties, some of whom came in for "schooling," as was the custom of the day, during the winter months of slackness in farm operations.

To proceed from small beginnings was only prudent. Queen's leapt at once into college work, and a few months earlier than Victoria. It was to have three professors, Scotch divines, but only two of them were present to examine the fifteen students who presented themselves for matriculation. Six failing or being otherwise discouraged, the College opened on March 7, 1842, with nine students. The Principal within a short time was compelled to admit that he entertained a "decided conviction that a Classical School, attached to the College, is next to indispensable."[1] Thus, the Queen's College School was opened in the fall of 1843. Victoria, realizing the state of education in the province, laid its foundations first.

No record appears to have been preserved of any discussion attending either the decision to make the Academy co-educational, or that which in 1842 effected the relegation of the young ladies to institutions in the town. While boys and girls were frequently educated together in the elementary schools of the province, the ten or twelve grammar schools of 1836 under the Simcoe tradition were exclusive in the matter of sex, as in other regards. Girls may have been admitted at this time to such private secondary schools as the Grantham Academy at St. Catharines, or the Bath Academy of Barnabas Bidwell. At all events, a few years later John Ryerson's daughter attended the former and was actually permitted to study Latin with the boys. But for Upper Canada Academy, the enrolment of girls was doubtless regarded as a concession to modern and American usage, with which the members of Conference had been familiarized in such schools as the Methodist seminary at Cazenovia in northern New York. Ryerson, however, with his strongly British predilections, could hardly have favoured a continuance of the experiment, especially when the Academy was to become the College. He may have known that Oberlin College in Ohio had admitted women in 1833, but, like the strict New Englanders, would have looked upon it as a wild western adventure. Even twenty years later when Horace Mann adopted the same policy at Antioch, abetted by his second wife, one of the famous Peabody sisters, eyebrows were still raised in the East.

It may have ben noted that as the procession wound up the gentle slope from the Chapel to the Academy on opening day Richey occupied a central position between Whitehead and Case. Of the teachers no mention is made. Presumably, if they walked, it was with the students. This failure to give prominence to his assistants is continued throughout the four years of Richey's principalship. In the advertisements only, or in accounts of the annual public examinations by outsiders, do their persons and their labours receive individual notice and

[1]D. D. Calvin, *Queen's University at Kingston, 1841-1941* (Kingston, 1941), p. 50.

commendation. This may have some significance. What manner of man was Matthew Richey? Carroll, whose pen portraits brighten the pages of Canadian history, is less sure of hand with Richey than with many others of his worthies. This is what he says:

He was a native of the North of Ireland, where he was classically educated—if I mistake not—with a view to the Presbyterian ministry. While yet a mere lad, he became converted, and espoused the cause of Methodism. ... He was, at the period of which we write [1835], about 30 years of age, very tall and slender, but straight and graceful, as were all his movements. His hair was very light colored and very curly, surmounting what an American writer pronounced "a comely old country face." For the power and pleasantness of his voice; ease and gracefulness of elocution; ready command of the most exuberant and elevated language, amounting almost to inflation of style; together with rich variety of theological lore, he scarcely ever had a superior, if an equal, in British North America. He was gentleman-like in his manners, Christian in his spirit and demeanour, and soundly Wesleyan in his teachings.[2]

Elsewhere he speaks of Richey as possessing "an unusual fecundity of words, inclining to diffuseness and inflation," and as one who "clothed homely thoughts in a latinized diction."[3] Had Carroll's eye fallen upon certain letters written by Richey in 1844 to Alder defaming Ryerson,[4] they might have suggested even to his broad charity that the words "in his spirit" should be deleted.

Nowhere in the multifarious writings of Ryerson before the break with the Wesleyans in 1840 is there any criticism, expressed or implied, of Richey. His brothers William and John are less favourable—or less restrained. Deploring the effect of union with the Wesleyans on the Academy and on Methodism in general, William says: "As to our English friends, they of course can stand and look on without emotion or concern, while we are struggling for life, and are left to sink or swim as best we can. ..."[5] John is more specific: "Reichy is no economist, he is extravigent,"[6] and again, more fully: "Reichy flounces at some of our Rules for the Academy. Especially that he is not to have the handleing of the money, & that there is no servant allowed him extra. I very much wish Reichy was out of the institution, if he is not,

[2]*Case*, IV, 107-8. [3]*Ibid.*, p. 251.
[4]*E.R.*, II (Toronto, 1947), pp. 83-4.
[5]V.U.A., William Ryerson to Egerton Ryerson, May 18, 1837.
[6]V.U.A., John Ryerson to Egerton Ryerson, Jan. 2, 1837.

I am quite satisfied that he will ruin the institution or else ruin us. We of course can never allow him to have anything to do with the finances of the concern. . . . I think it is indispensible for us to mentain the Laws of the Academy passed by the Board & not allow of any infringement of them whatever."[7]

A few months later Anson Green, who had been closely connected with the finances of the Academy as treasurer and an active member of the Managing Committee, was able to report: "There is a wonderful change in Mr. Richey—He is as tame as a lamb, and is really bringing up his end, manfully—Had he done so from the commencement he would have saved us at least $1000. . . . Should Mr. R. continue to perform his part with promptitude, I am very anxious to know what you think about the propriety of continuing him for another year."[8] It would appear from this that whatever strength Richey may have had in the pulpit, as an administrator and financier he had grave limitations. Indeed, at the end of the first year of operations a committee appointed by the Board to examine the accounts reported that students and parents were in arrears £250.9.2, and found it necessary to ink over certain phrases about the keeping of the books so effectively that only a grave dissatisfaction is evident. Six months later the arrears in collections stood at £456.10.4. In briefly announcing this state of affairs in the *Guardian*, the secretary of the Board remarked, "These facts are trumpet-tongued, and will be weakened by any comments."[9] But it should be said in defence of such slackness that the times were troubled and money hard to come by. Three weeks after the Montgomery's Tavern episode, Richey has this to say of the difficulties confronting the institution:

It is natural for parents, in times of actual, or of apprehended danger, to wish to have their children under their own immediate care. . . . But, whatever grounds there may have existed a few weeks since, to allow the solicitudes referred to, to interfere with claims of such importance and urgency, they are now happily dissipated. Yes, thanks be to God, the storm which suddenly presented its portentious aspect on our sky, and threatened not only to close the portals of science, but to destroy our liberties and lives, and subvert the venerable fabric of our incomparable

[7] V.U.A., John Ryerson to Egerton Ryerson, Aug. 11, 1837.
[8] V.U.A., Green to Egerton Ryerson, March 10, 1838.
[9] *C.G.*, Jan. 31, 1838.

constitution, has been averted in a manner clearly indicative of his vigilant and merciful providence.[10]

It may be deduced from his reference to "our incomparable constitution" that Richey had little sympathy with the Reform movement which claimed the support of a large proportion of the friends of the College. Thus, when two of the older students, James Spencer and Henry Steinhauer, organized a debating society, presumably to discuss problems of current interest, they met with a stern reproof. A minute of the Managing Committee for October, 1837, reads:

Resolved That the Committee decidedly disapprove of the formation of any such Society without a previous understanding of the parties with the Principal and his approval of the questions to be debated—and that it be considered a fundamental principle of such Society that no political question be canvassed by it, in order to preserve inviolate the character of the Acad^y, as a literary and religious Institution.

Of the staff which came to the Academy with Richey, none survived the first year of operation. Mrs. Smith, the Preceptress, with her children and servant and piano and loan of £100 to the Academy, withdrew during the first (summer) term; and H. Baldwin, the Classical Master, apparently at its end, being succeeded by Robert Hudspeth, an Edinburgh man, who resided in the vicinity of Cobourg. The Steward left in the autumn, and after two wives of preachers had been severally drafted for temporary service, a man named Sawyer, and his wife, were finally engaged. The Mathematical Master, James O'Loane, formerly a Roman Catholic, who was appointed at some time during the first year, and for whose family rooms were later found in residence, had greater pertinacity, and served to the end of the second year. He occasionally adorned the pages of the *Guardian* with problems in algebra and geometry, for which solutions were invited and secured, and it is in his beautiful and ornate hand that the book-keeping entries for the dues of parents and guardians are entered.

Of Robert Hudspeth it is to be regretted that so little is known. Several things suggest that he was a man of parts. For two years he taught the Classics and certain other subjects with good success, to judge from the accounts of the public examinations. Unfortunately the text of the Latin dialogue between Masters Hudspeth and Richey, representing Brutus and Cassius, has not been preserved. Master Huds-

[10]*Ibid.*, Dec. 27, 1837.

peth, by the way, later became head boy of Upper Canada College, and one of the early graduates of King's College.

On October 4, 1838, the danger of "hopeless insolvency" produced the following minutes of the Managing Committee:

3. That the Principal has suggested for the consideration of the Com. as the most feasible method of averting such a calamity, and of carrying on the operations of the Academy with the prospect, that Mr. Hudspeth assumed the office of Principal in connexion with his duties of Classical instructor.
4. That Mr. Richey be requested to converse with Mr. Hudspeth on this important change and to ascertain whether for the additional consideration of a house being furnished him, he would be willing to discharge the duties of Principal with those which at present devolve upon him as Classical teacher.
5. After conversing with Mr. Hudspeth, the Principal reports that Mr. Hudspeth will give the matter his serious reflection, and communicate the result to morrow morning.

From the minutes of a committee meeting held two weeks later, it may be concluded that while Richey was ready to vacate, the conditions required by Hudspeth were unacceptable. The minutes reveal the fact that Hudspeth wrote a letter to "the brethren in Toronto," that is to say, the Board; but the changes stipulated by him for the institution were of such a nature as to "render it impracticable to carry that plan into operation at least at present." Here, then, is an intriguing lacuna, which in the absence of Board minutes or correspondence on the matter can only raise questions. Would the Board have considered appointing a Presbyterian trained in Edinburgh to the principalship of a Wesleyan Methodist institution? Was the abandoning of co-education among the changes demanded by this cultivated Scot?

As it was, on October 16 the Managing Committee decided to carry on without any reduction in staff, to ask the present staff to tighten their belts, already far from spacious, to request the chairmen of districts to collect back debts for the Academy, and to urge the preachers in general to drum up attendance. And they were prepared to meet Richey's bill for $95.50 incurred in New York—$50.00 for apparatus, presumably the first science equipment; $20.50 for books; and $25.00 for travelling expenses. One of the teachers was appointed librarian, and one shilling per quarter *in advance* was required of students for the use of library books, but history fails to record whether the £100 worth of books subscribed by the British Conference ever arrived. Not the least significant of the proceedings of the same meeting of the Managing Committee was the following resolution:

That a board of examination be formed consisting of the Principal and teachers to meet weekly to consult respecting the progress of the pupils and on any subject connected with the order and efficiency of the literary department.

This is the first glimmer of a light which, feeble and fitful for ninety years, became a steady flame only in 1928. Then under the new Act of that year the Council of Victoria College obtained a legal status, and proceeded to establish monthly meetings on dates specified in the by-laws.

After two years the Board began to look to men trained in the United States for teachers. In the Academy as in the Conference the pendulum was swinging away from dependence on British connections. William Kingston was in his twentieth year in 1838, when he was brought from a position in a common school in the vicinity of Dundas and placed in charge of the more elementary work of the Academy. Of his early life our information is meagre. An Irish immigrant, he had been educated at Cazenovia and at Girard College in Philadelphia, a charitable foundation of the philanthropist Stephen Girard. From 1838 to 1872 he remained on the staff of the Academy and College, except for a period of three years from 1847 to 1850. His peppery Irish disposition was unable to endure the methods of the acting principal of 1847, Alexander MacNab, and he resigned—as he had threatened to do under Ryerson. During his self-imposed exile he conducted a newspaper called the *Provincialist*, of pronounced Reform stripe. His main interest was in Mathematics, and he was regarded as a thorough and efficient teacher with rigid ideas of discipline. His final leaving of the College in 1872 was not entirely voluntary; it had come to be felt that his training and powers (his degree of M.A. was honorary) were scarcely equal to the requirements of a Mathematics professor in the new age of science. But former students found him a berth in the civil service at Ottawa, where he died in 1887.

Daniel C. VanNorman, who also joined the staff in 1838, as Mathematical Master, was senior to Kingston both in salary and in status.

He was Canadian-born, the son of a prominent and devout Methodist, "Father" Isaac VanNorman of Carroll's story, whose substantial farm was on the Middle Road in Nelson Township. As a youth he had felt the call to the ministry, but desiring the better to prepare himself, according to Carroll, had "studied at Lima, or Cazenovia, perhaps both, and at Hamilton College, and finally graduated at Middletown University, Conn. . . . Mr. V. was a most estimable man, of sincere piety, pure habits, accurate scholarship, as far as he had gone, (one of the best teachers of the elements of language possible), a bold, clear, pointed preacher, rising sometimes to eloquence, who had he been given up to preaching entirely, would have become very able and attractive. He was a sprightly, compact, handsome man, of not thirty years of age."[11] Carroll goes on to explain that his relation with Conference was exceptional; he had no intention of taking a circuit since "his wife was determinedly opposed to the itineracy," and it was with some hesitation that Conference admitted a practice which prevailed in the United States of accepting the membership of teachers in connectional institutions.

In the summer of 1839 the harmony between Richey and Hudspeth, which had suggested the succession of the latter to the principalship—and the association of their sons as Brutus and Cassius in the Latin dialogue—appears to have been disturbed. As early as March 29, the Committee of Management resolved to write Jesse Hurlburt at White Plains, N.Y., and ask him to accept a post, and Richey decided to transfer his eloquence to the pastorate at Toronto, where he could better guard the interests of the British Conference in the growing breach with the Canadians. Hudspeth retired from the Academy after nearly three years of service, evidently in arrears both of salary and of goodwill. At all events, he adopted the course of writing a defamatory letter in the *Cobourg Star*, the contents of which must be judged by replies from Richey and the Rev. Alexander MacNab, the Wesleyan pastor at Port Hope and a member of the Managing Committee. Hudspeth's complaint, apart from delay in meeting salary obligations, had to do with laxity and favouritism in discipline. Children of John Ryerson and the Rev. Joseph Stinson, the General Superintendent of Missions, were mentioned by name. Further, an act

[11]*Case*, IV, 290.

of "indiscretion" between boys and girls was disclosed. This was explained by Richey as an isolated case. A sister had been visiting her brother in his room and had taken another girl along with her. This breach of order was presently discovered, whereupon the two girls took refuge in the closet.

It may be assumed, however, that in general co-education created few difficulties. Actually it was a pretty thin type of co-education. The girls and boys lived in different sections of the building, connected only by the Chapel to which the Preceptress held the key. At meals, while they ate in the same dining hall in the east wing of the building, they were summoned separately by the ringing of the bell and left separately, the girls first and the boys later. The tables were arranged lengthwise in two long rows, one for the boys and one for the girls. During the course of the meal, so a visitor in the winter term of 1837 tells us, it was the custom for young gentlemen to take turns at reading from a work on history or some other cultural subject, a practice which suggests that conversation at table was discouraged. A service was held morning and evening in the Chapel, at which there was prayer, the singing of a hymn, and the reading of Scripture. Here, too, the seating would be separate. And at church we read of the girls sitting apart and marching back to the Academy after the service in close column behind the column of boys. Facilities for recreation are scarcely mentioned for either sex, but the advertisement for the summer session of 1841 states that the playground of the young ladies was entirely screened from public view and that within the enclosure was a botanical garden for students interested in horticulture.

Apparently class instruction was mainly, if not entirely, separate. In fact the curriculum for the girls was largely different from that of the boys. They were not permitted to study Greek and Latin, or Hebrew, after it was introduced in 1839. French, not available to the boys, was the only foreign language offered them. But they had music (at one stage the school had two good pianofortes, and a third in hopeless disrepair), drawing and painting, history, descriptive astronomy, geology and conchology. After American methods invaded the institution with the coming of Hurlburt as well as VanNorman and Kingston, it became the custom to publish in the *Guardian* from time to time Tables of Merit, and in the autumn of 1841 even the names of the cleverest "young ladies" were included. In this list the only subjects in which both sexes were graded were spelling, reading, arithmetic, grammar, and composition. In composition two girls are credited with 8, which was the perfect mark, and another girl received 7½, which was the highest mark attained by any of the boys. The girls were also graded in history, and in some lists in geography. The policy of the Academy is stated in one of the advertisements thus: "In the Female Department, the course of instruction is designed to embrace all the various branches of a complete system of Female Education, both solid and ornamental."[12] The general direction of this "complete system" is exemplified by the subjects of the original papers read by the girls at the annual examinations, such as "Sisterly Affection," "Female Piety," "Character and Improvement of the Indians," "Female Education," "The Heavens," "The Frailty of Human Life," "The Pleasures of Hope," "The Pursuit of Happiness." In Richey's address at the close of the public examination of 1840, the following appears: "It was very properly arranged, in accommodation to that modesty which shrinks from prominent exhibition that the young ladies by whom compositions were prepared were permitted to read them in the Academy, and thus exempted from the embarrassment of appearing on this platform."[13] Richey's whole account ends with the prayer "esto perpetua," which prayer consorts oddly with the capers of comely cheer leaders at rugby spectacles nowadays.

Arrangement of work for the male students must have been difficult. Wide variation in previous education, as well as in age and aptitude, had to be taken into consideration. Only a portion of the whole number, which ranged between fifty and ninety, submitted themselves to the discipline of classics and mathematics required of those who had the learned professions in view. Many, perhaps most, were content to work in what was known as the English department, embracing English grammar and composition, history and geography, arithmetic and book-keeping. Such subjects could most easily be picked up at any time of the year when the student might be free to enter, and their practical value was apparent, however brief the period of exposure to them.

[12]*C.G.*, July 31, 1839. One of the first students, Elizabeth Burr, is still gratefully remembered each year through one of the most valuable matriculation scholarships, that contributed by her son, Dr. J. B. Tyrrell, the eminent geologist and explorer.
[13]*C.G.*, April 22, 1840.

Charles Tolkein of Hallowell and Kingston figured prominently among the youths and young men who pursued a classical training. His original Greek composition and address as Valedictorian marked him as a lad of promise. He was destined for medicine.

Several of the early students made names for themselves in the life of Canada. William McDougall of Vaughan Township entered public life by way of the press and became a Father of Confederation. James C. Aikins of Toronto Township became Secretary of State for Canada and Lieutenant-Governor of Manitoba. William H. Brouse of Matilda took up the practice of medicine at Prescott, and became in turn a member of the Commons and Senate. Oliver Springer of Nelson persevered as a student of the Academy and the College to become the first graduate in Arts of the province, and later passed from a successful law practice to the bench. J. C. Dennis was one of a family of three who came to the Academy from the Humber. He became a land surveyor and rose to the post of Surveyor-General. A mountain on the Canadian Pacific Railway overlooking Field, B.C., is his monument. The two young men who were reproved for unauthorized debating both entered the ministry. Spencer became editor of the *Guardian*, which position he occupied for nine successive years. Steinhauer, a full-blooded Indian, returned to his own people as a missionary. Going west with James Evans in 1840, he served the church as teacher and missionary until 1884, employing his fine mind and training in language in translating the Scripture and hymns into Cree. His son, Robert B., followed in his steps. He attended Victoria College, and after carrying the Senior Stick in his final year, a mark of the highest esteem by his class-mates, graduated in Arts in 1887. With almost a half-century of service as a missionary to his credit, he came east from the foothills of Alberta to receive the Doctorate of Divinity *honoris causa* in 1937. A fine figure he was on the platform that evening (as a student he had excelled at football), tall, erect, and dignified as he told in modest and simple words something of his life-work.

The Indians, however, failed to take the place in the Academy, or the College, envisaged for them. In the appeal for funds, especially to the British public, their claims were always kept prominent; and the argument proved effective with many warm-hearted people like the Duchess of Kent, and such members of the Society of Friends as the

Sturgis family. It would appear that in the six years of the life of the Academy not more than ten natives were enrolled. Certainty is not possible, since hitherto no one—not even Carroll—has been curious enough to inquire. There was Henry Steinhauer, who had previously studied at Cazenovia; William Wilson, a young printer whom Ryerson had brought from the Credit to the *Guardian* as an apprentice, and who won much applause at successive examinations by an oration on "The Importance of Intellectual Culture" and a patriotic poem of some two hundred lines in heroic couplets on "England and British America"; David Wawanosh of St. Clair, whose account for two terms is charged to the Superintendent of Missions; Charles Cobbage from Rice Lake, who stands under Case's account in the Academy ledger; and John Williams and David Whinny from Alnwick, who are probably both Indians. There were at least three Indian girls, one of whom brought her place of origin along in her name, Sarah Rice Lake. Her account suggests that she found it difficult to adapt herself to the amenities of boarding school life; she, or rather her sponsor, stands charged with five shillings for breakages—1/6 for a pane of glass, 1/6 for a looking glass, and 2/ for a pitcher. Two other girls came from the same Indian mission, one named Sally Cow (sometimes spelled Kow), the other Susan Sundy.

The addition of Jesse Hurlburt, A.B. of Wesleyan University, in September, 1839, made for a well-balanced staff, and it is clear that the last three years of the existence of the Academy were its best. He was named Acting Principal, and evidently was free to carry out his ideas independently of Richey, who came from Toronto only to preside at the public examination. Chemistry and Physics, now springing into prominence across the border, were introduced as studies; also Hebrew, another new and intriguing subject. These courses at first appear to have been taught by Hurlburt himself, but he also helped with Classics and Mathematics. VanNorman, however, took over the bulk of the Classics, and Kingston moved up from the work in English to that in Mathematics. A new man was sought for the junior department. The three classes formerly taught by Richey, namely Astronomy, Greek, and Rhetoric, were absorbed by the remaining staff. The female department continued to prosper. Indeed, as we learn from Green, it was the most remunerative, probably because the girls cost less for board and tuition and frequently paid additional fees for extra subjects such as Piano, Drawing, and French.

Of Hurlburt's qualities, appearance, or personality, no clear record has been preserved. We learn from Carroll that "he was exceedingly scholarly, very dignified and gentlemanly, but without the native preaching-zeal and power which characterized the other Hurlburts of the Conference, whose brother he was."[14] While he offered himself and was received on trial in 1841, he did not persist through the three years necessary for ordination. His obituary notice, written by one of his eleven brothers, makes no mention of his earlier association with the Methodists but says that "Religiously, he held to the Catholic faith as contained in the Thirty-nine Articles of the Church of England, and was an ardent Protestant."[15]

The designation of Ryerson to the principalship must have been something of a blow to Hurlburt. He had done quite well as Acting Principal. But such letters as have been preserved would suggest that he lacked the tact and perhaps the culture necessary to signal success in the office, quite apart from his not being a member of Conference. Ryerson was too busy, however, with the pending rupture with the British party and other concerns of Conference requiring his statesmanship to think of taking over the active superintendence. So Hurlburt settled down to another year's work with colleagues who already were becoming restive under his leadership. Strained relations with Ryerson also are hinted at in a letter of October 25, 1840. The routine of the Academy must have been enlivened by the interest of the Acting Principal in Miss Maria Boulter, the Preceptress, and their marriage on November 19, 1840. Indeed, a half-century later, an old student boasted in *Acta Victoriana*, the College monthly, of certain infringements of discipline on the part of himself and one of the girl students rendered possible by Miss Boulter's occupation with the courtship. A few months after the wedding, the Managing Committee felt called upon to intervene, and it was recorded, "The Committee having learned that the Principal & Preceptress do not take their seats regularly at the Table in the Dining Hall, as was anticipated, and that frequent irregularities have occurred, owing as they believe to the want of a proper restraint being kept over the students on these occasions, have

[14]*Case*, IV, 336.
[15]*C.G.*, Aug. 26, 1891.

communicated this to the Principal with a request that a remedy may be immediately applied."[16]

By March 31, 1841, matters had reached a point where Kingston was constrained to pen in his fine and regular hand a remarkable epistle, which VanNorman and he signed and sent to Ryerson. It is written on heavy paper folded in four sheets. The sheets measure sixteen inches by ten inches, and three and a half such pages are filled with the urgent message, in faultless English save for a slip in quoting Shakespeare. The whole boils down to this. They are compelled by a sense of duty to unbosom themselves. There is nothing personal in the matter. On entering the Academy (in 1839), they had found it in a most deplorable condition. For a whole year they had laboured to introduce some regular and efficient system. But they had been driven to the conclusion that a new head was required. Hurlburt had appealed to them as a desirable person. They had known him in the United States and had urged his appointment. A longer acquaintance, however, and especially the experiences of the last winter had convinced them that he too lacked the essential qualifications for the headship of a literary institution. Without the head or hand of another, he could not prepare an article fit for a public journal. They were continually embarrassed by his performance in public. His speech at the centenary of Methodism in Cobourg might have made a favourable impression, but that speech had appeared in whole or in part repeatedly. The disrespect he evoked from the students made for general bad discipline. The situation was critical for the Academy and for Methodism. In Ryerson they saw the one person who could save the day. He could do for Upper Canada Academy what Dr. Fisk had done for Wesleyan University. So far as they were concerned, if he could not come to their aid, then they must transfer their labours to an institution with better prospects. The letter, they say, is highly confidential, but may be shared with the Rev. J. Ryerson. A reply may be sent to either signatory. We have no means of knowing the nature of Ryerson's reply. It may be presumed, perhaps, that it combined admonition and encouragement. At all events, the two complainants settled down to their work, and later they with Hurlburt were prepared to form with Ryerson the four-man faculty of Victoria College.

What of the absentee Principal? When the office had been con-

[16]V.U.A., Committee of Management, Minutes, Feb. 3, 1841.

ferred on Ryerson at the June Conference in 1840, he had no intention of assuming active and personal control immediately. He had just completed his final year as editor. His own bent and circumstances had combined to bring him during this term closely into touch with affairs. He had enjoyed the confidence of Durham, as he was later to win that of Sydenham to a marked degree. Joseph Howe spoke of him as "since our last visit to Canada, upon the list of our cherished and valued personal friends."[17] But these activities had brought him into sharp collision with the British party in Conference. In June, 1841, when the names were called one by one, as was the custom, for the passing of the "character" of each and Ryerson's name was reached, the President presented certain damning documents from a committee of the British Wesleyan Conference. These were read at length. That was on Saturday. On Monday, Richey appeared as the accuser on behalf of the London Committee. The immediate charge was the alleged attempt to deprive the British Conference of its annual government grant, but deeper political issues were involved. After a "lengthened address," Richey moved a resolution, seconded by Ephraim Evans, condemning Ryerson's conduct. Most of Tuesday was taken up with Ryerson's reply, and on Wednesday after considerable discussion the resolution was put to the vote and defeated 8 to 59, with two very junior members excused from voting. The same afternoon Elder Case, of all people, returned to the attack and moved "that this Conference deeply regrets that the resolution passed at its last session for the purpose of securing to the Christian Guardian the character of a properly religious and literary journal has not been duly regarded by the editor during the past year." Again considerable discussion, and again an adverse vote, 19 to 46. In such an atmosphere, then, had one titular principal succeeded another.

During the conference year which followed, plans were laid for the elevation of the Academy into a college. Strachan's restricted views were delaying the opening of King's College, but the Church of Scotland early in 1840 secured the passage of an act by the Legislature for the erection of a college under the name and style of the University at Kingston. The primary purpose was the training of their ministers. Later the Kirk determined to apply for a Royal Charter. Here the

[17]*C.G.*, Nov. 24, 1841 (copied from the *Novascotian*).

THE EMBRYO STAGE, 1836-1842

Law Officers of the Crown imposed their veto; a Royal Charter could not be superinduced upon an act of the Legislature. The act consequently was disallowed, and the Royal Charter was signed only on October 16, 1841, with the permission to use the name Queen's. Stimulated by this action on the part of the Church of Scotland, the Conference applied for and secured by unanimous consent of both branches of the Legislature an act incorporating "Victoria College" at Cobourg with power to confer degrees in the several arts and faculties. The statute received the Royal Assent on August 27, 1841. It is to be observed that while Queen's began with an Act and concluded with a Royal Charter, Victoria began with a Royal Charter and added to it an Act. And the ease with which what had been unobtainable in 1835 was granted by the Legislature in 1841 indicates the change which Sydenham had wrought in Canadian affairs. Supplementing, though not included in, the statute as had been desired, was a provision for an annual grant of £500.

In connection with the terms of the new Act, or Charter as it was called, Hurlburt undertook to make suggestions to Ryerson. This letter perhaps reveals more of his type of mind than any other of his letters—all brief—to Ryerson. His thought is not particularly clear, nor are his words carefully chosen to convey the desired meaning. He writes like a man in a hurry, who has not schooled his mind before putting pen to paper to think again till all the mud has settled. The three points he suggests for examination are (1) whether provision should be made for other degrees than those of A.B. and A.M., (2) whether the President and Faculty should have power to issue warrants to bring back to the institution runaway students, and (3) whether the Faculty should have the nomination of any new members of the Faculty. He appears to recognize that the Board has some rights, but doubts the ability of such a body to choose wisely, impartially, or with a view to harmony in the Faculty.

The opening exercises of the fall term were held on October 21, 1841. Now that the elevation from Academy to College was assured, Ryerson felt free to identify himself more actively with its interests. Leaving his duties as pastor at Toronto, he journeyed down the lake to make his first public appearance as Principal of Victoria College. His words, published in full in the *Guardian* of November 3, are directed to "Gentlemen and young Friends." Evidently the young ladies, whose exclusion from the college had been determined, either were not present in the audience or were included among the "young Friends." It is hardly an inaugural address, the work of the year being regarded as merely preparatory to the opening of the college proper in 1842. The language and thought are simple and unpretentious. The main theme is that education must be useful, and if so should have three characteristics: it must be suited to the individual and the particular society; it must be broadly Christian; it must tend to form habits of industry. He realizes that a type of education proper to a highly advanced and artificial society such as that of England is liable to create attitudes unsuited to a simpler society. He sees before him children of members of several denominations; they are all free to attend such churches as their parents may direct. And in the eight items of advice is included an exhortation to early rising; five o'clock is the hour suggested. Appointment as Principal had been against his own convictions of personal fitness. His studies had been too soon interrupted by "the various duties and cares of public life." He is comforted, however, by Locke's dictum that youth may best be committed to a tutor who is rather a man of experience in the world than of profound learning. He is happy that his own deficiencies will be more than supplied by the gentlemen about him who are fresh from college pursuits. Such in brief summary was the first important address on education by the man who was to lay the foundations of public education in Ontario, indeed to a degree in all Canada westward from the confluence of the Ottawa and the St. Lawrence.

Within a month a storm broke in the Academy circle, which tested the mettle of the absent principal as an administrator and an exponent of the law. Its origin and progress can be fairly accurately recaptured from three sources, minutes of the Managing Committee, another closely written epistle—this time of three and a half foolscap sheets—in the hand of Kingston as secretary but signed by all three teachers, and a draft of Ryerson's long and careful reply. It was over a rather petty matter, but large issues were involved. The Wesleyan Methodist chapel at Cobourg, it seems, was a popular resort of a Sunday evening, and seats were at a premium. The Class Leaders Meeting, corresponding to the Session in the United Church, resolved to permit the young ladies of the Academy to continue to occupy their reserved seats at the front but to dislodge the male students from their block of seats, relegating those under sixteen to a gallery, which would seat about thirty-five, and dispersing the others among the congregation wherever seats were available. The Leaders also proposed to charge ten shillings annually for each seat, or a total of £3.10., although pews were not rented in the chapel, on the ground that the pupils contributed nothing (Kingston says it was because the plate was seldom passed to them). But this charge was a secondary matter, not directly affecting the main issue, which concerned authority and discipline. The Managing Committee instructed the Faculty to accept the plan of the Leaders. The Faculty refused, and appealed to Ryerson.

Their reasons are clearly explained in the letter. Kingston gives a graphic picture of the gallery—a sort of Black Hole of Calcutta. As junior teacher he had been forced for a period to sit there with his flock. The seats were very badly constructed. The ceiling at the front was only seven feet above the floor, and in some parts one could not stand erect. The gallery was situated immediately above a large stove. The heat, the impure air rising from the congregation, and the entire absence of ventilation rendered it "destructive to health." It was impossible to keep awake or at times to remain throughout the service, owing to suffocation. It had been assigned to the singers for a time as a choir loft—evidently the enterprising Cobourg congregation had a choir as early as 1840—but they had been compelled to descend to the body of the church; and now the students (with Kingston and his assistant) were to be returned to this place of torture.

Then there was the question of discipline. The older students, being dispersed through the congregation, would be removed entirely from the control of the staff; and what of getting back to the college after the service on dark winter nights? It was necessary that the male students should go to chapel and return in a body before the young ladies in order to prevent all communication with them, which would now be impossible during the winter evenings at least. All this they, the Faculty, had explained to the Managing Committee, only to be told that by reason of the power delegated to it by the Board, the Committee had "full and entire control over the external and internal affairs of this institution financial and otherwise."[18]

The Faculty's letter to Ryerson requested an answer before the following Sabbath. But he was out of town and did not receive their letter in time to relieve their anxiety. When he did reply on November 29, he left no doubt as to his attitude. His salutation, in the manner of Methodists, was "My dear brethren," and he at once stated: "I perfectly concur with you in the steps you have taken, & in the views you have expressed." Then, after expounding at some length the powers given by the Act to the several bodies, and recounting how at the last Board meeting the powers of the Principal and Faculty had been defined on the basis of passages read from the inaugural address of Dr. Fisk of the Wesleyan University at Middletown, he declared that the Faculty and the Managing Committee were equally responsible to the Board, but that the Managing Committee had no authority whatsoever over the Faculty. Each was supreme, under the Board, in its own sphere, the Faculty in the area of instruction and discipline, seven days in the week, and the Committee in the area of finance, apart from the matter of salaries which were determined by the Board itself. Subject to the authority of the Board, the Committee was everything in the matter of finance, the Faculty nothing; the Faculty everything in respect to teaching and government of the students, the Committee nothing. While he recognized fully the valuable services of individual members of the Committee, it appeared to him "in short just as absurd for the Committee at its meetings to take into consideration the government and discipline of the Institution as it would for the Faculty to examine the Steward's or Treasurer's account or the Butcher's or Carpenter's or Grocer's bills."

On the particular question of the seats and pew rent, he thinks the Leaders ought to have shown a desire to accommodate the students, rather than give them the poorest seats in the chapel. Further, he believes that the circuit gets more support from members of the college than from any other equal number of the congregation, and asserts, descending from the judicial to the personal, "And if I should live to remove to Cobourg, I shall alter my mind much, if I ever preach in the village chapel while that charge is continued . . . unless all the seats

[18] V.U.A., Committee of Management, Minutes, Dec., 1841.

in the Chapel are rented in like manner. Indeed the inconvenience to which, it would appear, the attendance of the students subjects certain members of the Cobourg congregation, impresses upon my own mind more deeply the propriety of having a Sunday Evening Service at the College Chapel." Having written thus at length, in general and particular, doubtless reflecting that he had heard from only one of the three parties involved, he adds, "Such are my sentiments, with the information I possess. I may be mistaken; & when convinced of my error, I will retract it.... I pray God to assist & bless you individually, & to prosper your united labours."

The net result of the flurry was the institution of Sunday evening lectures or services in the college Chapel, and a change of attitude on the part of the Managing Committee which suggested avoidance of faculty preserves. Indeed, except for one instance in the following month, and this may have been before it was apprized of Ryerson's exposition of the Act, the Committee would appear to have confined its interest to matters of finance and property. The minute in question expresses surprise that the Faculty had taken upon themselves the expulsion of three young men "without the consent & contrary to the advice of several members of the Committee."[19]

Letters received late in the year by Ryerson from members of the faculty throw some further light on life at the Academy. A joint letter asks for financial aid for two students, one a carpenter who was trying to support himself and two sisters by working intermittently at his trade, the other a lad who contrary to regulation was living in town and subsisting on a very slender diet. Then Kingston showed concern about the library, and was planning to use the literary society, known as the Philalethic Society, to secure support for it. In the matter of arithmetic texts he took sharp issue with Ryerson. The question was whether an American text by Adams or an English text by Walkingame should be used. Hurlburt preferred the latter. A group of students wrote Ryerson objecting to joining the arithmetic class unless Adams was used. Assuming that Kingston, who was known to have a strong preference for Adams, was the real author of this joint protest, Ryerson replied to him. Whereupon Kingston objected indignantly that he had had nothing to do with the missive, but that he did resent Ryerson

[19] *Ibid.*, Jan. 14, 1842.

and the Board, who were favouring the English text, presuming to set their opinion against that of one who had "taught Arithmetic the greater part of fourteen years."[20]

The single letter presented from VanNorman is very different in tone. It tells something of the difficulties he has had in getting apparatus and materials for his work in chemistry, and in getting dependable help to set up the experiments. Nevertheless in the course of sixteen or seventeen lectures he had carried out all the experiments performed at Wesleyan University. Galvanic electricity, however, he had been unable to handle. He sincerely hopes that there is nothing in the rumour afloat in Cobourg that Ryerson may not come to the College at all. Mrs. Van-Norman wishes to be remembered affectionately to Sister Ryerson and himself, and he too sends his best regards to Sister R. It is clear that from this member of his staff at least, the new Principal might expect the sort of response he had a right to expect from men whom he had addressed as "my dear brethren."

[20]V.U.A., Kingston to Egerton Ryerson, June 4, 1842.

III. RYERSON'S PRINCIPALSHIP
1842-1844

THE constitution under which Ryerson was called upon to work is a curious document. The Act proper of August 27, 1841, runs to less than a page of a modern volume of statutes, and almost half of this consists of the preamble. In plain and simple language it provided that since the Academy had been in successful operation for five years, and since its Board had prayed for incorporation as a College with such privileges as had lately been conferred on the University at Kingston under the Church of Scotland, therefore for the future the Academy should be known as "Victoria College" at Cobourg. Then follow five brief sections stating that all the provisions of the Charter "hereinbefore recited" shall apply to the College; that vacancies in the Board of Trustees and Visitors shall be filled by the Conference; that the College Senate consisting of the Principal, professors, and members of the Board shall have power to confer the degrees of Bachelor, Master, and Doctor in the several Arts and Faculties, so soon as there shall be a Principal and four professors; and that five public officers, namely the President of the Executive Council, the two Speakers and the Attorney-General and Solicitor-General of Canada West, shall be added to the Senate and Board.

That is all in the Act proper. But it stands appended to the Royal Charter, which is recited at length—five full pages in the archaistic lingo of the law, for the drafting of which Ryerson had been forced in 1837 to pay a neat sum after he was informed by the Law Officers of the Crown that a professional draftsman was indispensable. Thus from a wealth of imposing phrases—"divers of our loving subjects," "now know ye and we," "lands, buildings hereditaments and possessions," "these our letters patent or the emolument or exemplification thereof," "notwithstanding any non-recital, mis-recital, uncertainty or imperfection"—from all this the salient and startling facts may be gleaned. A body of Wesleyan Methodist ministers, identified by their right to solemnize matrimony,[1] receive the authority, when assembled at an annual meeting to the number of not less than forty, from His Majesty himself—without assistance of Parliament—to name nine trustees and five visitors to constitute a Board; such Board to have corporate powers to acquire and hold property, to appoint and remove a principal and assistants, and to enact by-laws valid in the courts for the conduct of their business. Nothing was said of the orthodoxy of the principal or his staff, but it was merely stipulated that literature and science should be taught on Christian principles.

Such was the constitution within which Ryerson undertook the principalship of "Victoria College" at Cobourg. The placing of the quotation marks had significance. Almost half a century later the townspeople, not without certain manifestations of resentment, were to learn that the College was not anchored by force of law in their midst. But impressive above all was the fact that His Majesty William IV, beyond all precedent, had freely granted to a body of Methodist preachers the right to establish a religious foundation and on principles so liberal as to startle other churches more devoted to dogmas. Another innovation was the inclusion of five officers of state on the Board. This involved a certain acknowledgment of the right of a government which granted subvention, however small, to have a voice in the administration of the College. As a matter of fact the records fail to show that any one of the five ever exercised the right, although the President of the Executive Council, Robert Baldwin Sullivan, did spend a couple of days at the College in 1843 as the guest of the Principal, either on the occasion of a meeting of the Board or merely in connection with the presence of his son as a junior student.

The status of a provincial act as opposed to a Royal Charter became a subject of debate, when Baldwin's University Bill of 1843 was being considered. At that time the Principal of Victoria College was drawn into public discussion with the Hon. W. H. Draper, late Attorney-General and eventually Chief Justice. Draper as the "agent of others" was heard at the bar of the House in support of the claim that the Legislature had not the power under the constitution to amend the

[1]For the explanation of this curious definition see *E.R.*, II, 299 ff.

Royal Charter of King's College, inoperative since 1827. Ryerson disputed this claim in a convincing argument of some eight thousand words.[2] After dealing at length with the example of Scotch and English universities, although he did not regard Draper's argument on this point as relevant, he examines the case of the Canadian foundations. Strachan had naturally turned to England for his charter in 1827, considering its nature. Eight years later the Methodists were inclined to secure incorporation under an act of the Legislature but, in Ryerson's words, "on account of the prevalence of violent party feeling, which divided the whole Province into two hostile parties, each dominant in one branch of the Legislature," on Colborne's suggestion it was determined to apply to England. Lord Glenelg, however, had hesitated to grant the charter until he "was fully satisfied that such a corporation was in harmony with the views of the Canadian House of Assembly." After another five years, when the Presbyterians wished to incorporate their college, they had applied to the Legislature and received the power in the Act of 1840 to establish a "University at Kingston." Why, then, did they request a disallowment of the Act in favour of a Royal Charter? Not, Ryerson states, because the Act was unconstitutional, as Draper argued, but because they wished to change the name to the "University of Queen's College at Kingston," so that with this name and a Royal Charter they would not be inferior in rank to King's College. Furthermore, it appeared less than decent to add a Royal Charter to a provincial act. To reverse the process was quite in order; and this was precisely what the Legislature did shortly afterwards in an act quoting verbatim the University of Kingston Act, a course which would hardly have been followed had that Act been deemed unconstitutional. Draper's eloquent appeal at the bar of the House failed, and the competence of the provincial Legislature to originate or amend university acts was never again questioned.

The induction of Ryerson as Principal on June 21, 1842, was plain and domestic. Attention was not distracted from the dignity and impressiveness of the spoken word by fanfare or tinsel. No choir from Port Hope on this occasion, no dignitaries of state and church. Doubtless the Trustees and Visitors were well represented, and a goodly number of members of Conference would be there. The audience which

[2]*C.G.*, Jan. 3, 1844.

filled the Chapel was described as "select and respectable" by the Rev. William Hayden,[3] who with three visiting fellow-ministers of the Congregational Church was present. These four were courteously invited by the Principal to dinner afterwards with the Board and ministers. The addresses of Anson Green, Chairman of the Board and also that year President of Conference, and of the new Principal were reported in full in the *Guardian,* and later printed in pamphlet form, along with information as to the staff, curriculum, and rates. Hayden described the remarks of Green in committing the keys to Ryerson as "very happy and impressive." Green congratulated the audience on the period of Canadian history in which their lot was cast. And of the proceedings of the day he predicted that they would be recorded in the archives of the College and referred to with grateful feelings as long as sound literature should find a place in the admiration of men. He briefly recounted the history of the institution, and noted its considerable influence already; everywhere as he travelled through the province, he encountered its former students, ten "in the Lord's vineyard," others in law or preparing for it, and larger numbers in teaching, commerce, agriculture, and mechanical pursuits. But the need for more advanced studies had become apparent; hence Victoria College, which, as he pointed out, was the "first literary institution in actual operation in the province authorized to confer literary degrees." He then proceeded to stress the importance of the faculty in a college, and the particular qualities possessed by Ryerson which fitted him to lead the faculty. Thereupon he addressed the Principal, who rose and bowed to the Board and the audience, which also stood while the keys were presented, with a solemn admonition concluding with the words: "While, therefore, you shall exercise the authority which these Keys confer, never let a teacher with whom you are associated want a counsellor, nor a pupil placed under your care need a *Father or a Friend*."[4]

In an account prepared for the *Guardian* by the Rev. Alexander MacNab, Secretary of the Board, we are informed that Ryerson's address occupied about an hour and a half, but was followed throughout with intense interest. Hayden characterizes it as "a somewhat lengthened synopsis of the course he intended to pursue," and adds, "I

[3]*C.G.,* July 6, 1842.
[4]*Inaugural Address on the Nature and Advantages of an English and Liberal Education, delivered by the Rev. Egerton Ryerson* (Toronto, 1842), p. viii.

cannot but consider the Principal's Address as one of rare merit, and we hope it will be published, that the Church and world may have the advantage of its enlightened and comprehensive sentiments." At the outset Ryerson defines the scope of the education to be offered. There are two types of course in contemplation, the English or Commercial, and the Collegiate. The latter has five branches, Classics, Mathematics, Moral Philosophy, Rhetoric and Belles Lettres, Theology. The contribution made by each of these branches of education to the complete man is surveyed. The emphasis laid on Science and English, embraced in the second, third, and fourth branches, indicates the advanced views on a liberal education held by Ryerson. He would give both a large place in the curriculum, while not in any sense disparaging the Classics unless they "be so taught and studied as to render the English language and the active industry of common life contemptible in the estimation and feelings of the student."[5] In reference to Theology, he actually expresses the hope that the time is not far distant when four years of comprehensive study will be required of probationers before ordination; not that, he hastens to add, he "would make the House of God a philosophical Lecture-Room, or the Christian Minister a literary teacher or metaphysical disputant."[6]

The summer term was already in progress at the date of Ryerson's inauguraton on June 21. Pursuant to notice the young ladies had been excluded, and already in May the enterprising Mrs. VanNorman, with the assistance of the former Preceptress at the Academy, Miss Barnes, had established the Ladies' Seminary, Cobourg, with accommodation for twenty boarders. By autumn a second school known as the Cobourg Female Academy was opened under the direction of Mrs. Hurlburt, with her sister, Miss E. Boulter, helping her. The two professors now lived at home, and each school, as the merry contest for patronage continued, stressed in its advertisements the advantages of home life for the students. Ryerson and Kingston were listed as official Visitors in both cases, and made obvious if not entirely successful attempts to hold their favour in balance.

The work of the College proper began with the commencement of the long winter term on October 20. Matriculants were asked to at-

[5]*Ibid.*, p. 15.
[6]*Ibid.*, p. 29.

tend on October 19 for examination. Kingston was now able to affix to his name an A.M., secured *honoris causa* at Dickinson College, Ohio, then in its ninth year as a Methodist university. Ryerson had received a Doctor's degree at the convocation of Wesleyan University of Middletown, Conn. This was the convocation at which his revered friend, Nathan Bangs, who at the turn of the century had been an itinerant preacher in the wilds of Canada, resigned from the presidency. Ryerson took the departments of Theology and Moral Science. What use he made of the Hebrew which he had studied with a private tutor in Toronto, and which in the infancy of comparative philology he supposed to be the parent language, does not appear. Nor has any clear account of the division of work or the progress made in college studies been preserved. From a letter written by Ryerson to Sir Charles Bagot, the Governor-General, we learn that the attendance was more than ninety, that the combined salaries were £825, and that the staff taught six hours a day.

Something of the spirit and intellectual attainments of the College can be judged from volume I, number 1 of the *Philomath*.[7] It was the production of the Philalethic Society of the College, and, as the foreword tells us, had been established "whilst U.C. Academy was struggling through the vale of obscurity to the attainment of a nobler name and more conspicuous situation in the literary world." The plan was to publish semi-monthly. The first is the only number extant. Its editor was I. B. Howard, a young man of twenty-four. After teaching for three years he had heard a call to the ministry, and attended the Academy during a summer term. For a year he had been Ryerson's assistant at Newgate Street where he had joined his superintendent three times a week in the study of Hebrew.[8] The paper is in manuscript form, the mast-head beautifully lettered, and the articles written in a clear and regular hand. It was published for the students only, being read in the Chapel at the period assigned in the time-table to declamation. The first issue consists of a poem and four articles—"The Believer's Hope," by S. S. Nelles; "Extract from a Traveller's Diary,"

[7] This prized possession was sent (unsolicited) to the College for inclusion in the Archives during the centenary celebration, in 1936, of the granting of the Royal Charter by Mrs. C. Fraser Ritchie, three of whose grandparents were students at Upper Canada Academy: I. B. Howard, his wife Mary Beatty, and William McDougall.
[8] *E.R.*, II, 4.

Wm. Brouse; "The Works of Nature," A. Hurd; and "Our Country," by O. Springer. Apart from a certain inflation of style characteristic of the period the prose items do not differ widely from modern efforts. The poem, however, written by the editor, so nicely catches the spirit of a sensitive and pious student of the period, and is in such marked contrast to a certain fashion of today that it is reproduced.[9]

> FRIENDSHIP
>
> There is a Sweetness in the breeze
> That fans the Summer's early dawn,
> When warblers sing among the trees,
> And nature spreads the vernal lawn.
> The rippling brook, & rolling Stream,—
> And opening flowers so gay & bright,—
> And cloudless sky,—with beauty beam,
> And fill the soul with pure delight.
> But far more beautiful than these . . .
> Are friendship's pure and holy ties.
> The inconstant breeze will cruel prove, . . .
> But friendship's pure undying charms,
> Will sweeten summer's brightest day;
> And even 'mid winter's rude alarms,
> Will shine with clearer purer ray;—
> Will stand 'mid all the shocks of life
> And,—sweetened by devotion's breath,—
> Support the soul in the last strife
> And soften e'en *the bed of death.*
>
> I.B.H.

In 1843 a successor to the *Philomath* appeared under the direction of the Phoenix Association of Victoria College, bearing the name *The Oasis*. In its prospectus we find a note of caution sounded in the words "while fragments of the Philomath surround and indicate the rock on which it split." The new publication appears likewise in manuscript,

---

[9] At the time of writing the author picked up the current issue of *Acta Victoriana* and his eye encountered the following verse entitled "Viaduct Rendevous." The two efforts resemble each other at least in theme and in permitting one error in spelling.

> "She waits by concrete railing, bathed
>   In water colour twilight;. . . .
>   The fragrant flesh of summer leaves,
>   As damp night shadows rise,
>   Intoxicates; while hose-drenched sidewalks
>   grieve
>   Reflecting to the eyes
>   Face-powder clouds in a perfume-ad
>   Blue sky."

with Nelles and Hodgins as prominent contributors, and continues for at least three years, 1843-5. The last and most bulky number extant (vol. IV, no. v) contains in an appendix two petitions to Ryerson for "holy-days" with the names of the signatories, one for June 4, 1841, and the other in 1843 for the whole week between Christmas and New Year's, this on the ground that the term would be longer than usual. Also appended is the statement by twenty-three students in defence of Ryerson in 1844.[10] Last is a list of the twenty-five members of the Victoria College Cricket Club of 1844-5. Its officers were Clegg, president; Springer, treasurer; and Brouse, secretary.

It would not do to suppose that all the students were of the pious type of the editor of the *Philomath*. Certain letters which John George Hodgins preserved from correspondents among his fellow-students bear sufficient evidence to the contrary. And in one of his reminiscent articles in *Acta Victoriana*, Hodgins refers to another type, a young fellow so exclusive in his Episcopalian views that he kept to his room during voluntary services, apparently, though only apparently, Hodgins suspects, unmoved by "the sweet and softened melody of the good old Methodist hymns, wafted up to his quiet room."[11] Hodgins himself, a young Irishman, formerly a clerk at Hamilton, had been converted during his first year at the College in the course of protracted services in the town. I. B. Howard in his diary[12] points to a marked change in the religious tone of the College in 1842-3 from that of the Academy which he attended during the summer session in 1840.

During his first year as resident principal Ryerson was faced with the prospect of extinction for the College by act of parliament. The gravity of the situation has not sufficiently impressed itself on history, because the Government which sponsored the lethal bill resigned in November, 1843, while the measure still awaited its final reading and debate. But the attempt at consolidation involved in the Baldwin University Bill of 1843 merits some attention here as marking the first effort, clumsy to be sure and ineffective, to apply to university work in the province principles which were to attain realization only after half a century of struggle. Victoria had no part in the affair in its

[10]See p. 65.
[11]*Acta*, Dec., 1896.
[12]The property of Mrs. C. Fraser Ritchie, who has kindly made the information it contains on the College available for reproduction here.

earlier stage. Queen's has generally been given the credit—or the blame—for initiating the movement. But the bill was Baldwin's, "with nothing more than a single conversation with each of the parties concerned,"[18] so Ryerson publicly stated. Indeed Baldwin was not a man who readily sought or accepted the opinions of others. While a devout Anglican, he had long disputed the Bishop's theories of church establishment, and church control of education. He well knew how unpopular even in Toronto was the system under which King's College was to begin instruction that very autumn. While the Rev. John McCaul had been transferred from Upper Canada College to act as Vice-President, the Bishop was still President, and Dr. Beaven was still Professor of Divinity, in defiance of the purpose of the Amendment Act of 1837. Hence it was sound statesmanship, and good politics as well, to endeavour to make the provincial university less unpopular.

Queen's, which had opened eighteen months earlier, was already in straits. Without proper buildings, or a decent supply of students, or funds adequate to support their three distinguished professors, as Calvin freely admits, the trustees began to lose heart. The progress of events can be followed in six letters from Principal Liddell. At first no formal approach was made to Victoria, although Liddell's first letter to Ryerson, dated April 21, 1843, opens with the following sentence: "I need not apologize for writing to you on the subject on which we have oftener than once spoken together—the union of all our Colleges as integral parts of our common University, in the Council, or managing Body of which there shall be a just & equitable representation of the various colleges, & thus necessarily of the various leading interests of the country." The letter goes on to say that the Queen's trustees had recorded in a resolution their willingness to amalgamate, and had sent a deputation to Toronto, which had reported the majority to be "unwilling, & *hostile*." Indeed the Bishop went so far in his opposition as to refuse to bring the matter before his Council. Consequently, as the only recourse, Liddell believes that an appeal must be made to the Legislature. His approach to Ryerson is merely private, but he feels assured of Ryerson's "more than readiness" to join in accomplishing an object which is for the real welfare of the country, although it will involve "many sacrifices of a personal, local, and gregarious character."

[18]*C.G.*, Nov. 1, 1843.

Had the lake been open he would have gone to Cobourg and shown Ryerson the several documents in the case, including the correspondence with the Bishop. As it is, he forwards the outline of the plan under thirteen heads—after the manner of a Kirk sermon. There is considerable definiteness in this plan, much also that comports with the scheme rejected by Queen's forty years later: one university "to be styled, for instance, the Univ. of Toronto"; a group of colleges each under its own management; one governing body of the university in which all the colleges should be represented; common access to the splendid endowment (which promises to yield a revenue of £12,000 to £15,000 a year). Definite also is the emphasis on the "notorious fact" that at present King's College is viewed with distrust by the whole community, a distrust "greatly strengthened by the appointment of a Professor of Divinity of the Church of England alone." In two areas, however, the Queen's authorities had not arrived at any very clear position. Nothing is said in the outline about the conferring of degrees, and in the matter of the division of instruction between the university and the colleges there is a certain vagueness of phrasing. It speaks of the "literary and philosophical college," and of other colleges adding "the peculiar species of learning appointed as necessary by their various Bodies & Departments into which it might be the desire of the respective students to enter." From this it may be deduced that Queen's was prepared in 1843 to surrender to the university its Arts work, begun solely with a view to securing an educated ministry, and to confine itself to Theology. In other words, in the very year of the disruption of the parent church in Scotland, Queen's, representing the old Kirk, proposed the adoption of a policy which in the following year the new Knox, representing the dissident Free Church, assumed.

A month later in a second letter the negotiations of Queen's with Victoria became official.[14] Ryerson's reply to Liddell's first letter had been cordial, although it had mentioned certain "practical difficulties." Liddell is still sanguine enough to believe that these would easily be overcome, and states that the government could use the Victoria College building as a normal school. But any such minor considerations, he urges, should not "stand in the way of a great healing measure such

[14]Oddly enough, they are not mentioned by Calvin, who, however, refers to the advances made to King's College.

as that which is contemplated." The main object of this second letter of May 16 is to state that his Board had resolved to confer with the Board of Victoria College and the Methodist body generally in the matter. As a member of the committee appointed for this purpose, he asks Ryerson what he considers to be the "most proper and respectful mode" of proceeding. He asserts that the Government is "exceedingly disposed to move in the matter." If permitted he would be willing to appear before Conference at its annual meeting on June 16.

It is apparent from Liddell's third letter of June 12 that Ryerson advised that the two bodies should move "separately and independently." He also spoke of the proposed plan as "implying the annihilation of Victoria College" and opened Liddell's eyes to the fact that Victoria was primarily an Arts college, for Liddell remarks: "I proceeded upon the supposition that in the erection & establishment of it, your Body had in view chiefly the Theological training of your own candidates for the Ministry—& that your having made it a literary Institution arose from necessity, not from choice—as was the case with the Presbyterians—there being no literary Institution in existence." However, he trusts that both the Conference at its June meeting and the Synod at its July meeting will be found "on the side of Him who is the Prince of the Kings of the Earth."

After Liddell had addressed the Synod, meeting in Toronto, at great length, it went on record as favouring amalgamation. The Conference took no formal action, being preoccupied with dissolving the union with the British Wesleyans. Liddell was ill for some time after returning from the Synod, but on August 1 renewed correspondence with Ryerson, asking what the Conference had done. Commenting on some observation in Ryerson's letter he says he can see no reason why Victoria need be "interfered with at all." The Methodist body might accept the principle of a common university, and at some future time establish a purely theological college, if it should see any advantage in so doing. He wishes to "cooperate & cordially" and thinks his health will now permit his going to Cobourg.

Baldwin introduced his University Bill on October 12, 1843. Sir Francis Hincks in his *Reminiscences* describes it as the most important measure presented to that parliament. The fact that it never became law hardly diminishes its significance. For one thing, it reveals how doctrinaire, or even illiberal, were the policies of the Reform party in respect of education. It also raises a question as to what difference it might have made to the history of higher education in the upper province had Hincks, rather than Baldwin, been in charge of the bill. From Liddell's letters we learn that Hincks was deeply interested in arriving at a solution and entered freely into conversation with the representatives of Queen's. Baldwin, on the other hand, made himself inaccessible to Liddell, and practically so to other interested persons and bodies. The result was a bill which, had it passed, would have failed to satisfy the public conscience even more signally than did his second attempt at a solution in 1849. Hincks, on the other hand, in 1853 produced a measure which in spite of one serious slip in drafting (or was it a slip?) served with only minor amendments for almost forty years.

Just what did Baldwin propose, and how would acceptance of the bill have affected Victoria College? If an attempt may be made to compress in a single paragraph an act of 103 sections—sloughing off archaistic and involved phrasing—the summary would be somewhat as follows. The four existing colleges, King's, Queen's, Victoria, and Regiopolis, were to be deprived of their right to confer degrees; on certificate from any college, however, honorary degrees and degrees in Divinity were to be conferred by the university. The University of Toronto—such was the name chosen—was to assume not only the conferring of all degrees but also such teaching as might be provided for by its own statutes. Statutes were to be initiated in the Council or Caput of about sixteen members, each college being represented by two professors if it had four or more professors, otherwise by one professor. From the Caput a statute went to the Board, a body of about forty members including twenty nominated by the government. The President of Conference was to be a member of this body along with dignitaries of other churches. As approved or modified by the Board the statute would be returned to the Caput, which might send it on to Convocation. This was the final legislative body of the University, consisting of the Chancellor (the governor of the province), the Vice-Chancellor (annually elected by officers and graduates), heads of colleges, professors (of the University, not the colleges), and all graduates in any of the faculties who might keep themselves on the books by paying an annual fee of twenty shillings. That is to say, bodies in all of which the colleges collectively had a minority representation might determine at any time to take over instruction in any subject. The comparative fixity in the division of the subjects of instruction as between university and college, which is the keystone of the arch of our present federal system, was entirely wanting in Baldwin's bill. Equally serious was the control over the internal affairs of the colleges in respect of discipline and appointments, which sections 15 and 29 of the bill gave to Convocation. Furthermore, Victoria College, as well as the other colleges, was deprived of the benefits of previous legislation. The provisions of the Victoria College Act of 1841 repugnant to the new measure were to be "repealed and annulled to all intents and purposes whatsoever." Even the designation was to be changed from plain "Victoria College" to "the Principal, masters and scholars of Victoria College in the University of Toronto." The other three colleges had to bear a similar weight in nomenclature and a similar diminution of power. To sustain them in their new situation the colleges were to be granted an annual sum of £500 from the income accruing from the University endowment.

Few persons could have been much pleased with the bill once the purport of its elaborate provisions was understood. Of course, there would be general satisfaction among members of other denominations at the challenge to Church of England control of a provincial institution; and the blow was not softened by Baldwin's insistence on calling that body the Protestant Episcopal Church in Canada. Moreover the attempt at consolidation of all interests met with approval. But even the Presbyterians, who had the ear of the Government more than had any other religious body, being in Kingston and predominantly Reform in politics, were far from satisfied. They found fault particularly with the absence of even the broadest religious tests for professors, and with the small financial backing required of colleges desiring to join, namely an annual income equal to a thousand bushels of wheat.[15] The Victoria

[15]Wherever, one wonders, did Baldwin get the idea of replacing pounds sterling by wheat? Had it any connection with the fact that a professorship of Agriculture was the one professorship made obligatory on the University? Was this apotheosis of wheat a clumsy appeal for votes of rural members?

Board in addition to the two objections made by Queen's voiced criticism of the control of college affairs by Convocation. No comment from Regiopolis is recorded.

Strachan trained all his guns on the bill. "The leading object of the Bill," he declared in his petition to the Legislature, "is to place all forms of error upon an equality with truth . . . if successfully carried out, it would utterly destroy all that is pure and holy in morals and religion, and would lead to greater corruption than anything adopted during the madness of the French Revolution."[16] Perhaps the most effective part of Strachan's petition was the recital, for the benefit of the French members of the united parliament, of a list of the religious institutions in Canada East, holding property to a total of 2,125,179 acres. He deprecates touching one single acre of these endowments, and feels certain that those whose wish and interest is to preserve them cannot consistently permit any government to lay hands on the 225,944 acres belonging to King's College, equally, in his view, a religious trust. He also sent forward a somewhat milder argument to the Governor, Sir Charles Metcalfe. Draper was briefed to appear before the bar of the House on behalf of King's College. His position was countered by Peter Brown in the *Banner*, Hugh Scobie in the *Colonist*, and by Ryerson in the closely reasoned argument in the *Guardian* referred to above. Ryerson's position, and that of his Board and Church, is summed up in the words: "I argue for no particular University Bill; but I contend, upon the grounds of right and humanity, that Presbyterians, Methodists, and others, ought to participate equally with the Episcopalians in the educational advantages of endowments that have been derived from the sales of lands which, pursuant to an application from the Provincial Legislature, were set apart by the Crown for the support of Education in Upper Canada."[17]

Two cordial letters received from Liddell in November show that the writer, however much he might desire common action, was coming to realize how widely different were the interests of Queen's and Victoria. In his last letter he dwells on the difficulty of seeing Baldwin. As it proved, there was no need to worry about the effect of the bill. Although J. P. Roblin, a Methodist member of the Assembly, informed

[16] J. G. Hodgins, *Documentary History of Education in Upper Canada*, 28 vols. (Toronto, 1894-1910), V, 27. Hereafter referred to as *D.H.*
[17] *C.G.*, Jan. 3, 1844.

Ryerson that Baldwin had the will and the majority to carry the measure, Gibbon Wakefield's shrewder eye saw difficulties in the way. Whatever part these may have had, Baldwin resigned on the eve of the debate on the bill. It is quite possible that the prospect of failure in a measure dear to his heart may have been more responsible for his resignation than historians have admitted. Baldwin was a sensitive man—too much so for comfort, or indeed success, in politics—and it is significant that his resignation nine years later was preceded by a close vote, precipitated by William Lyon Mackenzie, on another favourite project, the Court of Chancery. In any case, the University Bill of 1843, with its obvious merits and even more obvious demerits, never came to a vote. The first attempt at university consolidation had failed for the want of a carefully planned federal system.

While the very existence of the College was in the balance at the capital, the first full year of college work had been brought to a close, a summer session with a slightly decreased attendance had been concluded, and the second year's work was well on its way. It is difficult to assess the change in the institution made by its elevation to the status of a college. Such scraps of information as are available point to the conclusion that Ryerson, with his wider experience of men and affairs, succeeded in infusing a new and more adult spirit into the life and studies. The "collegiate" members, or alumni as they are called, were housed apart in the wing vacated by the ladies and described by a jealous junior as "that earthly paradise." They were given control over the library and the distribution of books to such students as paid the fee of 1/3 per term. Courses of more advanced lectures on Ancient and Modern History, on the Old Testament, and on Christian Evidence were offered by Ryerson himself. The Philalethic Society was officially encouraged, and an opportunity given for the editor of the *Philomath* to read each new number to the students in the Chapel. On the other hand, a new Phi Theta group, of some twenty members with Hurlburt as president, was denied, so its secretary complained, the same privileges of official favour. I. B. Howard in his diary states that before the year was out, the Principal got into some difficulties with his staff and there was a disturbance in discipline owing to his insistence on treating the students as young gentlemen and regarding the schoolmaster methods of his assistants as "over-officious." Howard himself had come to the College under release from the Conference and had been drafted as junior teacher as a result of a serious disruption. During the summer session James Spencer had been in charge of the English department, but had failed to give satisfaction to his class. The result was that all of them—some thirty-five in number, "mostly grown-up men"—declared that they would leave if Spencer were retained. He was permitted to go to Middletown, under the impression that he might return as science master. He was deeply offended with Ryerson when in the following year he was offered a lesser position, and on six months' trial. While Howard took over Spencer's class, he still devoted part of the day to his studies. Although he took the side of the masters in their criticism of Ryerson's type of discipline, in another connection he admits the great improvement in the conduct of the students in the interval of two years since his first acquaintance with the Academy. He says that then "the majority of the students were unconverted and some of them ungodly and profligate," whereas in 1842 "the great majority of the students and all the more influential ones are members of the Church."

A year later Ryerson had occasion to refer to college discipline. His brother John in a letter had mentioned a report of the drinking of brandy in the College by students. Ryerson replies, after taking the matter up publicly and privately with students and staff, that there is not a shadow of truth in the rumour. In fact, he says, those who have known the institution from the beginning declare that there has never been such good order in the student body; he himself has more than once complimented them on their orderly conduct. During the previous year there had been one case of drunkenness, an older student of twenty-two and in the town, but a public confession was required and a public reproof administered. He had heard from the offender, who had left college at the end of term, and could report that he was thoroughly repentant and reformed. Apparently also in dealing with the younger lads his ideas had advanced far beyond the prevailing methods of pedagogy—"*Quis, quae, quod*; bring me the rod." He remarks to his brother that he had not had occasion to use the rod during the term.

The long winter session was brought to a conclusion by the usual public examination. The Hon. R. S. Jameson, Vice-Chancellor of

Upper Canada, Henry Sherwood, M.P., and George Duggan, M.P., were among the visitors. Letters of regret were received from the Hon. Robert Baldwin and the Hon. R. B. Sullivan. The account appearing in the *Guardian* was furnished by "A Spectator," whose identity is not disclosed. The work in the Classical, Mathematical, and Science departments is praised with considerable discernment. Ryerson's own classes in History are described as large and deeply interesting. Of the class in Paley's *Evidences of Christianity*, he says that it "excited the admiration of all present, from the completeness of information, and strength and vigour of intellect, displayed by the young gentlemen who composed it."[18] On the fourth afternoon of the examination eleven original essays were read by senior students in the Methodist church, concluding with the valedictory by Howard on "The Early Propagation of the Gospel." Three other papers were indicative of subsequent interests: Hodgins, "The Educational Prospects of Canada"; Nelles, "The Spirit of Inquiry"; and Springer, "Influence of the Institutions of Moses on the Laws of Nations." The exhibition, as this part of the programme was called, closed with the conferring of prizes by the Principal.

Appended to the account of the examinations is the table of merit for the whole period from October 21, 1842, to April 20, 1843, containing the names of nine students. Several others, we are told, maintained an equal standing during one term. Five of the nine names listed are marked by asterisks to indicate that these students are in the Collegiate department, that is, proceeding to degrees in Arts. All these are studying the Classics, Physiology, and Composition, and all but one, English History. Their other three or four subjects vary. These five were O. Springer, S. S. Nelles, D. Beach, W. H. Brouse, and W. P. Wright. To these students must be added at least one other, W. Kerr. What is described as "the inimitable vein of rich native humour" in his essay at the examinations on the subject "*Egomet*," or "I, Myself," suggests that he may not have regarded his studies seriously enough to warrant inclusion in the list of merit. There would be other older students, such as Howard and Hodgins, whose uneven scholarship excluded them for the present from this narrow circle; we know from a letter how hard Hodgins was working to catch up in the languages.

[18]*Ibid.*, May 24, 1843.

Howard returned to circuit work at the end of the long term, although he states that Ryerson urged him to remain on the teaching staff. An older student, R. W. Young, was pressed into service in the English department. Howard in his diary includes him in the number of young men of ability and promise, each of whom he characterizes. The description of Young reads: "An Irishman about 32 years of age. Has a good English education and some knowledge of the Classics & of French. A warm heart, and a fervid, though somewhat flighty imagination. But diffident, impracticable & despondent. I fear he will never succeed in life unless he has the good fortune to get a commonsense practical wife, who will lead him and help him." From Hodgins' *Reminiscences* we learn that Young was for some years Assistant Librarian and Secretary to the Canadian Institute in Toronto.

At the beginning of the winter session of 1843-4, from a farm in the fertile township of Darlington, a young man of twenty-two named William Ormiston came to the College. Burwash describes him as one whose "natural gifts . . . would have placed him in the front rank in any age and country."[19] He shall be allowed to tell his own story of his first evening in college, a story significant, not only as revealing how strictly Ryerson followed Green's injunction that he should never allow any student to want a friend, but also as affording the only description extant of Ryerson's methods as a teacher.

On the evening of my arrival, while my mind was burdened with the importance of the step I had taken, and by no means free from anxiety about the issue, Dr. Ryerson, at that time Principal of the College, visited me in my room. I shall never forget that interview. He took me by the hand; and few men could express as much by a mere hand-shake as he. It was a welcome, an encouragement, an inspiration, and an earnest of future fellowship and friendship. . . . He spoke of Scotland, my native land, and of her noble sons, distinguished in every branch of philosophy and literature; specially of the number, the diligence, the frugality, self-denial and success of her college students. In this way he soon led me to tell him of my parentage, past life and efforts, present hopes and aspirations. His manner was so gracious and paternal—his sympathy so quick and genuine—his counsel so ready and cheering—his assurances so grateful and inspiring, that not only was my heart *his* from that hour, but my future career seemed brighter and more certain than it had ever appeared before.

Many times in after years have I been instructed, and guided, and

---

[19]Nathanael Burwash, *History of Victoria College* (Toronto, 1927), p. 112.

delighted with his conversation, always replete with interest and information; but that first interview I can never forget, it is as fresh and clear to me to-day as it was on the morning after it took place. It has exerted a profound, enduring, moulding influence on my whole life. . . .

As a teacher he was earnest and efficient, eloquent and inspiring, but he expected and exacted rather too much work from the average student. His own ready and affluent mind sympathized keenly with the apt, bright scholar, to whom his praise was warmly given, but he scarcely made sufficient allowance for the dullness or lack of previous preparation which failed to keep pace with him in his long and rapid strides; hence his censures were occasionally severe. His methods of examination furnished the very best kind of mental discipline, fitted alike to cultivate the memory and to strengthen the judgment. All the students revered him, but the best of the class appreciated him most.[20]

But Ryerson's life as teacher and principal was destined to be brief. On December 18, 1843, he was informed that Sir Charles Metcalfe would be happy to have some conversation with him on the subject of the University question at his convenience. They had previously conversed once at least; the Governor had paid a short visit to the College on September 12, been duly received with evergreens, bunting, and a loyal address, and had duly replied with words of encouragement and the boon of a holiday. It was the second week in January before Ryerson responded to this invitation. In the meantime he had been busy studying the history of royal foundations in Great Britain, and had clarified his views on the Canadian problem in the preparation of his reply to Draper's appeal on behalf of King's College at the bar of the House. The second interview with the Governor was extended to three and a half hours. Its results were momentous, both to Ryerson and to Victoria College. The conversation ranged beyond the provisions of a sound university act to the means of securing advisers to introduce and implement such legislation. Here after three years of abstention Ryerson found himself once more deep in politics. Not less so, when Metcalfe renewed the suggestion which Sydenham had first made, that he should undertake the superintendence of common school education in Canada West. The present incumbent, the Rev. Robert Murray, was admittedly not quite the man for such a work. Ryerson, of course, would not allow that such an appointment was political, but he could hardly have failed to realize that others would regard it as

[20]J. G. Hodgins, ed., *Ryerson Memorial Volume, 1844-1876* (Toronto, 1889), pp. 121–2.

such. The resignation of the Baldwin-Lafontaine ministry in December ostensibly had been on the issue of "Responsible Government," a term which they, and particularly Lafontaine, were inclined to identify closely with the right to advise the Governor on all appointments (even that of his aide-de-camp) and have their advice accepted.

For the present, however, Ryerson returned from Kingston to his desk with good hopes for the College. The solid ground, as it then appeared, for such hope was embodied in the following letter of January 20, 1844, from the Governor's Secretary, J. M. Higginson:

> I am desired by the Governor General to acknowledge the receipt of your letter of yesterday's date, and to convey to you the thanks of His Excellency for that obliging communication, and to say in reply that His Excellency does not see any objection to your stating through the Press his continued approval of the general principle & objects of the late University measure; these he conceives to be the abolition of exclusiveness and the extension of the benefits of the Institution to at least all Trinitarian Churches, either by amalgamation or by separate endowment. The only difficult question appears to His Excellency to be the legal one of property in the present endowment. If that legally belongs to King's College and cannot be taken away without the consent of the present proprietors, that consent must either be obtained, or other means found for additional endowments for other churches, either in union with the University or separately as may be most convenient and practicable. If there be no legal objection and consequently no robbery, then the matter is much simplified; but in either case, the same principle & objects ought in His Excellency's opinion to be kept in view and carried into effect.
>
> I am to add that the Governor General placing great reliance on your judgment is very happy to perceive that you think it probable that a majority of the present House of Assembly would be disposed to support an Administration based on the views which His Excellency had the pleasure of discussing with you, when you were so good as to wait upon him.

Early in March rumours of Ryerson's prospective appointment began to seep through, and they must have reached the College. However, work appears to have proceeded as usual. The long term ended on May 8 with the usual public examination, together with the publishing of the tables of merit—28 students being named for proficiency in class work, 41 for good conduct. The account of the examination itself was furnished to the *Guardian* by one "Candidus," evidently a member of the newly organized Free Church. "Presbyterian though I be," he says, "I should, as I am now impressed, a great deal rather see a young man I wished well enrol himself in Victoria College than in Queen's College, to be under the chilling influence of *Residuarism*."[21] He had nothing to say about the Mathematical or Science classes, but he had high praise for the work in Classics and in Philosophy. In the former he was pleased with the accuracy in translation and syntax; in the latter with the degree to which the students seemed at home in the analysis of Dugald Stewart's "justly celebrated work." "I have witnessed many examinations," he avers, "of the *Alumni* of Edinburgh and other Scotch Colleges in the same science, but never witnessed more accuracy or readiness than at those which this Canadian institution displayed." He has a word also for the ten essays at the public exhibition in the Methodist chapel, all of them creditable and some "evincing genius"; also for Mrs. VanNorman's young ladies, whose essays indicated an even more marked regard for revealed truths than the productions of the College.

During the summer the College suffered a severe loss in the illness and death of its Steward, Robert Webster. Born in Ireland in 1800, he had migrated to Canada in 1833 and engaged with indifferent success in business before coming to the College. He died at Canandaigua, N.Y., where he had gone seeking medical aid. Ryerson was desperately busy at the time (it was August, 1844), but he showed his regard for this faithful servant of the College by travelling to Canandaigua to conduct the funeral service. Webster's name was commemorated by a prize in English established by John George Hodgins, a nephew. Ryerson wrote an obituary, in part as follows: "He was, I think, without exception, the favourite of the College family. The fineness of his person was but an index to the still nobler kindness of his heart, which was manifested by his affectionate cheerfulness as a companion, his attentive sympathy to the afflicted, and his obliging conduct to all. During the protracted illness which terminated his life, the Students almost emulated each other in affording him every assistance in their power; and when it pleased God to remove him, they, with myself, felt that we had lost a brother and a friend."[22]

Throughout the summer session Ryerson was deeply involved in the

[21]*C.G.*, May 22, 1844.
[22]*Ibid.*, Jan. 28, 1846. The date is to be noted. On returning from his long tour of Europe, Ryerson discovered that the customary obituary notice had not been furnished the *Guardian*, and hastened to correct the omission.

Metcalfe controversy. He had undertaken to defend the Governor against the charge that he had violated the newly accepted, but little understood, principle of responsible government as upheld by Baldwin and Lafontaine. Refused access to the *Guardian* earlier in the year for a letter on the University question favourable to Draper, who had undertaken to give effect to Metcalfe's views in university legislation, Ryerson had recourse to the *British Colonist*, a moderate journal ably conducted by Hugh Scobie, for a series of letters which when reprinted in pamphlet form were to extend to some three hundred pages. The Reformers had chosen the Hon. R. B. Sullivan as their champion and the *Examiner* for their organ. For a short time Sullivan was able to conceal his identity under the name of "Legion, for we are many." In the choice of his *nom de plume*, this versatile Irish-Canadian appears curiously enough to have had no qualms about accepting a name first associated with an unpleasant incident among the Gadarenes. Nor did he choose to recall his fervent words when he had sent his "little Willie" to Cobourg: "In asking these things of you, I place myself under no common obligation. There is no man in Canada of whom I would ask the same. My doing so of you arises from a respect and regard for you personally, which has grown as we have been longer acquainted, and which no prejudices on the part of those with whom I have mixed and no obloquy heaped upon you by others have ever shaken."[23]

As the contest proceeded through the spring and summer months, the country was divided into rival camps with much personal and party bitterness. The town of Cobourg was no exception. Burwash tells of hearing as a lad how John McCarty, one of the founders of the College, had denounced the Principal, with a waggon in the market-place for a rostrum. And it was said that students were invited to tea at a certain Reform home with a view to indoctrination. Controversy came to a head on September 12, 1844. This was the anniversary of Metcalfe's visit, and in accordance with the decision of the Board at that time, it was to be observed as a holiday. It would appear that a section of the students regarded this honour to the Governor as rather a matter of political partisanship than of loyalty to the Crown. Thus when they found the Union Jack flying over the College early on the morning of September 12—certain Metcalfe partisans among the

[23]V.U.A., Sullivan to Egerton Ryerson, July 20, 1843.

students had flown it before daylight—they proceeded to take it down. In the scuffle the flag was slightly damaged. The Metcalfe partisans thereupon made a flag of their own and proceeded to fly it.[24] This precipitated another scuffle, and the banner was torn to pieces. Neither "scrap" was of such proportions as to disturb the Board, which was meeting at the time, and the Principal learned of the incidents only later. But news of them spread about the town, and two other flag episodes resulted. On the night of the 16th an American flag was hoisted on the wall in front of the College. The suggestion was that the College politics were of that stripe. Next morning the students tore the flag to shreds. The following night, just before dawn, a group of townsmen were detected carrying a flag in front of the College. They were hidden by the wall, and the character of the flag (which proved to be a Union Jack) was not discernible in the uncertain light. Five students sallied forth and one of them received a serious blow on the back of his head from a club. The rumpus awakened Ryerson who appeared in night attire to order the intruders off the premises.

The press of the province made much of the incident, and Ryerson found it necessary to give a full account of the whole matter[25] in order to correct quite misleading news items and letters by students, or professed students, masking under the names "Jonathan Swipes" and "Rhoderick Scissors." Twenty-three students also signed and published a statement in rebuttal. A letter from H. A. Hardy of Mount Pleasant to Hodgins probably represents prevailing student opinion. He was a member of a family prominent to this day as Reformers, or Liberals to use the current term. He had remained out of college during the summer term and was teaching school. Now on September 21, 1844, he writes his class-mate that he regrets having been absent from the College in view of the events of September 12 and their sequel. He continues: "Political discussions run high in this part of the country. All of those old friends of Dr. R.'s are now his bitter enemies. I assure you that I have had many warm rounds, and why I can scarcely tell. Certainly no one can be more directly opposed to the Doctor's course than

---

[24]It probably bore some legend like that of the banner unfurled at a Conservative meeting by students of the Ontario Agricultural College during the hot campaign of 1896, with the slogan "Laurier, Mowat and Victory," which caused quite a riot in Guelph.
[25]*C.G.*, Oct. 16, 1844.

I am. Yet my love for the man, the splendor of his talents, his social character & all that list of excellencies which are found in him induce me not to be silent when I hear motives attributed to him which I cannot suppose actuate him."

With such mingled manifestations of favour and hostility did the first Principal of Victoria College lay down his work. Although the appointment as Superintendent of Common Schools had been foreshadowed in February, it was not formally proffered until the Governor had finally completed his Executive Council in September, nor accepted until in October Ryerson had the satisfaction of knowing that the electors of his native province by an overwhelming majority had approved of the policies he had advocated. So far in this instance at least did Sir Charles Metcalfe and his defender exhibit in practice the application of the principle of responsible government which they were charged with flouting, or at best, failing to understand. And Ryerson in his office could regard himself as responsible not merely to the party in power but to the sovereign burgesses.

It was late in the summer when Ryerson concluded that he could not attempt to superintend the common schools of the province until he had studied the best systems of Europe. He did not resign the principalship. Had the province accepted the views of the Reform party, he would probably have remained at Cobourg, that is, unless the members of Conference whom he had shocked by his "meddling with politics" had made further tenure of the College principalship impossible. As it was, both the College Board and the Executive Committee of Conference gave him leave of absence. The Rev. Alexander MacNab was appointed Acting Principal; by the government he was gazetted as Deputy Superintendent in Ryerson's absence. Thus Canada West for some two years was to accept educational edicts issuing from an office in Victoria College.

IV. ON A RAZOR'S EDGE
1844-1850

THE withdrawal of Ryerson, in the circumstances attending it, was a severe blow to the College. He must have realized that it would be so. But he could not refuse the opportunity offered by his new office. It was much greater even, and more vital to his country, than the important work he was doing at Cobourg. Nor could he be insensible to the honour done his church in his being entrusted with the first considerable office of emolument under the Crown given to a Methodist.[1] Being a man of faith, and constitutionally sanguine, he fancied he could rely on the working out of some policy favourable to the College by the Governor and the new Executive Council with Draper at its head. Either a division of the endowment, if that were legally possible, or some other source of revenue had been promised by Metcalfe, and he was a man of his word. The influence of the Governor in matters of education, in spite of the theory of responsible government, continued to be great for some time. There was no Minister of Education in the united Canadas, or indeed in Ontario after Confederation until 1876. Formally under the department of the Provincial Secretary, education was even more dependent upon the Attorney-General; but an active interest by the Governor was not resented. In fact to Sir Edmund Head more than to anyone else University College is indebted for the magnificent pile which almost a century later proudly does service. But there were two factors upon which Ryerson could not have reckoned sufficiently. Fixed of purpose and indomitable of will Metcalfe might be, but there was that malignant growth on his cheek which already had invaded one eye and which the

[1]The emolument to be sure was not to be boasted of. Five hundred pounds was promised, the sum allowed to the corresponding but less onerous position in the lower province; but for some years Ryerson received only £375, whereas his predecessor, the Rev. Robert Murray, was translated at a salary of £548 to King's College, where history records that the students toasted him thus:
"Here's to the professor of dull Mathematics,
He knows more about steaks than he does about statics."

best medical care of the day was unable to arrest. And Draper was not just the man Ryerson took him to be. He was much more interested in law than in public life, and it was only when he became Chief Justice that his fine qualities of mind and character were fully exhibited. For the politics of the time he had no heart, and he lacked both the resolution and the finesse—either might have served—to carry a sound University bill for Canada West through a House in which the members of one province were largely apathetic while those of the other were divided, often bitterly so, on the basis of sectarian or local interests.

The result was a period of nine weary years of dispute and uncertainty for Victoria and the other colleges. In his evidence before the Commission of Inquiry into the affairs of King's College University in 1848, Dr. McCaul used the words, "Action has been impeded in this, as in other important matters, by the constant expectation of extensive changes being made in the constitution and management of the University."[2] If this was true of King's College, with its buoyant revenues, what must have been the case with Victoria? It had been threatened with annihilation by the abortive University Bill of 1843. Draper's two attempts in 1845 and 1846, both dealing more generously with the two religious colleges—Regiopolis is not mentioned—than the Baldwin bill of 1843, likewise never came to a vote in the House. John A. Macdonald next took the question in hand with a measure of out-and-out partition. The succeeding general election, in the upper province at least, was contested largely on this issue. There the vote was indecisive, with a slight advantage to the administration, but the opposition swept Canada East.[3] Thus Baldwin was able to carry his University Act in 1849; but it so little satisfied the public conscience of the province that four years later it was supplanted by the Hincks Act. The agitation attending these successive measures made any planning for the future by the Board of Victoria College next to impossible. They were ground between the upper millstone of an unstable governmental policy and the nether millstone of inadequate financial support. In this respect their situation was worse even than that of Queen's, which could depend with reasonable assurance on a grant of £300

[2]*D.H.*, III, 28.
[3]Party lines were not so strictly drawn nor party names so definitely established at the time that majorities could be exactly calculated. The returns are announced in this election (January, 1848) under the heads *Ministerial, Opposition*. In 1844 they were announced under *G.G.* (Governor-General) and *L.E.C.* (late Executive Council).

from the Kirk in Scotland and another of £500 from the Clergy Reserves, £125 for each of the four ministers on its staff. For Victoria the general situation during the six years covered by this chapter was precarious indeed.

At the time Alexander MacNab took a sputtering torch from Ryerson's hand, he was thirty-five years of age. Carroll describes him when he first presented himself for circuit work in 1831 as "of Scottish descent, tenderly brought up by a widowed mother and do[a]ting sisters, . . . now fresh from Cazenovia Seminary, in the State of New York. He was tall, sandy complexioned, and fair to look upon, but too frail to stand so laborious a Circuit [just west of Toronto]; and the fall rains and cold of commencing winter sent him home an invalid."[4] John Squair who knew him well as rector of Darlington also emphasizes his fine appearance: "He was a typical English Church Parson, the *Person* of the parish, of handsome build, of fine carriage, dignified, scholarly, friendly with all, whose presence in a locality is a benediction."[5] From a letter by Dr. John Beatty in the *Cobourg Star* of September 20, 1848, we have the information that he had studied the Classics in Belleville under the Rev. John Greer, M.A. of Trinity College, Dublin, and had spent some time in the study of law in the office of James H. Sampson of that town. Although vanquished by the hardships of autumn circuit-riding, MacNab, "after being recruited from his illness, imbibed on the Toronto circuit,"[6] assisted for a time on the Hallowell circuit, and at the Conference of 1832 was received on trial. Evidently his health was considered in the circuits to which he was sent during his probation and ordained ministry. In 1842-4 he was assigned to the City circuit and the office of Book Steward. At the Conference of 1844 he was given a light charge at the Credit and the collection of funds for the library at Victoria College. In this latter mission little progress appears to have been made apart from a subscription of £50 by Metcalfe. When Ryerson took over his new position with leave to investigate school systems in Europe, MacNab had already moved to Cobourg and was prepared to assume the duties of Principal as well as those of deputy in the Educational Office.

The prospect when the winter term opened late in October was

[4]*Case*, III, 331.
[5]John Squair, *The Townships of Darlington and Clarke* (Toronto, 1927), p. 310.
[6]*Case*, III, 341. Is "imbibed" a *lapsus stili*? The "Toronto" circuit lay to the northwest of the city, largely in what is now Peel County.

gloomy enough. VanNorman's resignation in the spring had meant the loss of the steadiest, most efficient, and most co-operative member of the staff. Kingston had his strong points, but he was difficult, and Hurlburt was even suspected of being the author of some of the anonymous letters against Ryerson at the time of the flag incident. Ormiston, however, agreed to combine teaching of the Classics with study for his degree, and his vitality and force of intellect would largely counterbalance any deficiencies of knowledge. Many of the former students failed to return, among them Nelles, who transferred to Middletown to take his degree. The total enrolment was only forty-nine. In May, Green reported that the College was going behind at the rate of £400 a year. At the annual examinations, however, the usual questioning of students took place, and the usual display of talent. The outstanding features were a Latin oration by J. Campbell of Hamilton, a Greek oration by W. P. Wright of Cobourg, a poem ("My Country") by S. P. Morse, a paper on "Christianity" by W. Ormiston, and the Valedictory by O. Springer on "Portraiture of Character." The enrolment during the short summer term was given by G. S. Playter, the editor of the *Guardian*, as less than fifty, a number, he remarked, equal to that of King's and exceeding that of Queen's. He contrasts "the heavy, gloomy, massive, lumpy style" of the old King's College building just being erected, with "the light and blithesome aspect" of Victoria. The value of the College he places at £12,000.

The summer session appears to have proceeded without event. On September 12 the second anniversary of Metcalfe's visit was celebrated with the Union Jack proudly flying. On October 1, statutory notice having been given a month earlier in the official *Gazette*, a meeting of the Victoria College Senate, consisting of Board, Visitors, and Professors, was held for the conferring of degrees. Oliver Springer, who was entering law, was the only candidate. He had been in attendance at the Academy and College since 1840, with the exception of one summer term, and had successfully met the regular biennial examinations. Now on this first day of October, 1845, he was given a special examination on part of his work—twelve books of Homer, Horace, Differential Calculus, and Astronomy. From 10 A.M. to 5 P.M., with a short intermission, he faced his inquisitors in the presence of a number of outsiders as well as the students. Having conducted himself in a highly creditable manner, he was presented for the degree of Bachelor of Arts by one of the oldest senators. Thereupon, MacNab delivered to him the diploma, accompanying the act with "the usual Latin charge," followed by an address in a "dignified and pleasing" manner. Such was the simple ceremony, as described in the *Guardian* of October 15, 1845, by the resident minister, the Rev. W. McCullough, at the conferring of the first Arts degree earned by study in course in the province.[7] McCullough goes on to say of Springer: "During his residence in Victoria College, he has uniformly sustained an irreproachable moral and religious character. Steady in his habits—pleasing and kind and gentle in his manner—diligent in the prosecution of his studies— and faithful in the discharge of his religious duties, he was loved and respected by all who knew him." In fact, this young man of twenty-three, with qualities that were solid if not brilliant, set a very fair standard for the long succession of graduates, now numbering some 9,000. In course of time he became County Judge of Wentworth County.

An incident in connection with this first diploma occurred some six months later, which if it had not been bruited abroad so widely in the province might well have been omitted from this chronicle; it reflects little credit on the College and less on the detractors of the College. The diploma was borrowed from Springer by young John Roaf, also a law student, who had just graduated at the age of eighteen from King's College—his youth may serve to excuse his act. He copied the Latin of the diploma for the benefit of the Toronto *Globe*, which had run about ten years of its exciting course. Now the *Globe* was desperately keen on one provincial university at Toronto and equally scornful of all claim to countenance on the part of the other colleges. It published to its little world the news that the authorities of Victoria College did not know enough Latin for the purposes of a diploma. MacNab replied to the attack in an unconvincing letter to the press, claiming hurry and careless work by the engraver in Toronto as an excuse. The *Globe* returned to the attack on April 14, with three columns under the caption MARCH OF INTELLECT—VICTORIA COLLEGE AS IT IS IN 1846. This article was copied in the *Banner*, edited

---

[7]In 1844 the Bachelor's degree had been conferred by King's College on F. W. Barron, then Principal of Upper Canada College, and on W. Ramsay. The latter was described as graduated "ad eundem," and the former could well have been; if Barron had taken lectures at King's College, which is doubtful, it could only have been for one session. Queen's conferred its first Bachelor's degrees in 1847.

by Peter Brown, father of the editor of the *Globe*. Three letters were included in the article, one by Ormiston, who had prepared the text of the diploma for transmission to Toronto, one by John Gouinlock, the engraver, who declared that the fault was not his, and MacNab's letter excusing the College and castigating the *Globe*. The charge, in brief, was that Victoria College had plagiarized the Yale degree, and in adapting it to local use had been guilty of four clear mistakes and four additional inelegancies. The fact was that Victoria had turned to Wesleyan University for the text, not knowing that Wesleyan had borrowed from Yale, and that four slips occurred in the copying or engraving—an "a" for an "e," and "a" for an "ae," and "ss" twice for "s." The alleged examples of "inelegancies" need not be spread here. They were not serious, and one of them appears on the parchments of today. In any case, both in medieval and in modern Latin, what passes as elegant is largely a matter of fashion, and of course a current fashion had not yet been established in Canada.

But only a small proportion of the students of Victoria College in 1845 were to win degrees; many indeed had no such aspirations. One such was Hart Almerin Massey. He was present in 1892 at the formal opening of the present main building of Victoria University, when Dr. John Potts read the following letter:

My dear Sir,—

The citizens of Toronto and the Methodist Church of Canada will rejoice this day in the completion and opening of a magnificent new Victoria building in this city. There can be no more suitable time for all her friends to rally round her, forgetting those things which are behind and reaching forward unto those things which are before, rendering her their united support by giving her that aid which will place her on a proper basis. I herewith enclose my check for $40,000 to endow a chair in the theological department of Victoria College. Sincerely yours,

H. A. Massey.

The report in the *Guardian* continues:

"I should be glad to receive a few more letters like that," said the Doctor, when the great burst of applause had died away.

"Thank you, Mr. Massey," said Dr. Carman; "long may you live to see the fruits of your offering" . . . and he called on Mr. Massey to speak a few words.

Mr. Massey came forward, and he was once more cheered to the echo by the undergraduates. He told in simple, touching language of a time

ON A RAZOR'S EDGE, 1844-1850

fifty years ago when he attended two sessions at old Victoria, and paid for his tuition by chopping and drawing wood seven miles. Those were days, he said, in which poor lads prized education, and the students once more broke into applause.[8]

One of the old account books salvaged from the Beatty home at Cobourg in 1931 tells a more complete tale, with an eloquence rarely achieved by figures. The account stands not as usual in a parent's name, but in that of the young man himself. It is to be noted that his connection with the College was for three short periods, not two as he recalled, that in the third period while himself in residence he provided for a brother who lived at home, and that beef, not cordwood, was bartered for this more leisurely third spell of "schooling."

Mr. Hart Massey
Dr.

1842			
Nov.	To Tuition, 1 term		1.
	Books		.6
	By 4¾ cords Wood @ 6/3		
1843			
Novbr. 2	To Board & Tuition, 8 weeks.		4.14.8
	1 Arith. 4/ 1 Philo 6/3		10.3
	1 reader		3.9
	By 16 Cords Wood @ 6/3	£5.0.0	6. 9.2
		1.9.0	6. 9.2
1845			
Novbr.	To Board & Tuition 8 weeks		4.14.8
	Tuition for Br.		1.10.0
	1 Gram 3/ 1 spelling book 9		3.9
	1 arithmetic		
	Cr.		4.
			£6.12.5
1845	By Beef Rendered the College		
	Account signed by Mrs. Webster	£3.7.8	
	Balance	3.4.9	6.12.5
Oct. 10	To Balance due		3. 4.9

[8]*C.G.*, Nov. 2, 1892.

The loyalty of Hart A. Massey to Victoria College at Cobourg, which prompted opposition to federation, was later freely transferred to Victoria College in the University of Toronto. He himself died in 1896, but his family continued a succession of benefactions. First Annesley Hall, then the Household Science building, then Burwash Hall, and finally the incomparable Hart House stand as monuments to an idea which had its germ in those three brief periods of study at Cobourg.

The general situation in university affairs in 1846 was far from favourable. Both of Draper's bills had held out encouragement for Victoria and Queen's. They recognized the stake of religious bodies in higher education, would have provided substantial financial support, and might eventually have worked out a system for what they designated as the University of Upper Canada which would have reasonably satisfied the claims of both church and state. But in June, 1846, Baldwin was able to carry an amendment to the effect that it was inexpedient to proceed with the University bill during that session. Thus the struggling institutions at Cobourg and Kingston learned that Draper had not the power to give form to his ideas. Then at the autumn convocation of King's College, with MacNab on the platform, McCaul announced that King's College was prepared to give no less than seventy-two scholarships. Twelve provided both board and tuition, and three offering tuition only were assigned to each of the twenty districts of Canada West. This marked a new phase of the contest. Students were now to be attracted from other colleges by financial inducements.

Draper resigned from office on May 28, 1847. The succeeding Sherwood-Daly administration was Compact and Tory in its character, but included one man of talent from Draper's ministry, namely John A. Macdonald. Undismayed by Draper's failure, he determined to try conclusions with the University question. His plan was simple and definite, the direct opposite to that of Baldwin. Where Baldwin would consolidate and secularize, he would divide the endowment among several separate church colleges. Representing Kingston, as he had since 1844, he was well acquainted with the claims of Queen's and Regiopolis. He wrote Strachan and secured his approval on behalf of King's for his new policy. He wrote MacNab also, and saw Ryerson. They were satisfied. That was his method; even at the age of forty-two he was not the man to conceive legislation in a rare and detached atmosphere. The bill was introduced on July 9, 1847. It proposed to divide the revenue from endowment, which was estimated at £10,000 and likely to increase, among the existing colleges, and grammar schools, with the anticipated balance funded for any colleges which might later be set up. King's College (Anglican) was to receive £3,000 and its buildings, library, and equipment; Queen's (Presbyterian) £1,500; Victoria (Methodist) £1,500; Regiopolis (Roman Catholic) £1,500; and each of the district grammar schools an additional £125, which would have made a total grant for each of £500. The endowment was to be placed in charge of a board of five, one member named by the government and one by each of the four colleges specified. Thus the intention of the royal grant of 1797 was at length to be realized, Macdonald argued, by laying education, so to speak, on every man's hearthstone. But before the House divided on the question, Strachan made it known through a private member friendly to the Government that he had come over to the view of the King's College Council that the terms were inadequate. At this turn of events Macdonald decided to withdraw the bill, and make it an issue at the approaching general election.

The autumn months were devoted largely to campaigning, with the pace quickening as voting approached in January, 1848. In the upper province the University bill appears to have been the main issue— apart from the general effectiveness of a party led by statesmen so mediocre as Sherwood and Daly. The three churches whose colleges would have benefited passed resolutions favourable to the measure. Never was the *Guardian* more decided in its political pronouncements. The *Church*, however, was inclined to be hostile although it failed to carry all the members of the Church of England with it. Many of the shrewder supporters of that church must have foreseen that it might well prove to be a case of the boy and the filberts. Knox College, recently founded by the Free Church, which had already nestled in the bosom of King's College and was having its Arts teaching done at no cost to the church, issued a series of six resolutions opposing the bill, the most impressive of which is number three,

That the proposed scheme of partition would necessarily stamp the Education of the Country with a sectarian character, and by needlessly separating the ingenuous youth of Canada, in their educational career, would destroy one of the most wholesome means of harmonizing the heterogeneous, and, in some respects, discordant elements of which Canadian Society is composed.⁹

In resolution five Knox deprecated the fostering of declining and impoverished institutions at the expense of a great common foundation. When the polls had closed, it was found the lower province had rejected the ministry by a majority so overwhelming that Macdonald's first essay in statesmanship was abandoned and all prospect of direct state endowment for denominational colleges was shattered.

The vitality of Victoria was shown in a gradually increasing attendance, in spite of the sense of insecurity which must have attended these attempts at legislation. During the year 1847 the staff was on the whole strengthened by the appointment of John Wilson, B.A. of Trinity College, Dublin, as Professor of Classics, and William McK. Paddock, A.B. of Harvard, as Professor of Mathematics. Hurlburt after almost nine years of service had resigned in June, withdrawing with his wife's Academy to Toronto, and Kingston in the autumn had abandoned teaching to edit a Reform newspaper, the *Provincialist*, in Cobourg. He carried on a running battle with the *Star* for a year, when he retreated to Hamilton under cover of a joint stock company. John Wilson was a scholar and a gentle and devout soul who had laid aside all worldly ambition. For more than forty years, with a brief interval in 1850-1, he gave freely of his learning and his skill as a teacher to the College. Although not ordained, he preached occasionally, and in later years he lectured on the New Testament to students in Theology. Judge Dean says that Paddock was a son of the Rev. Dr. Paddock, who was a man of mark in the American church. "I have pleasant recollections," he adds, "of this professor, but have been unable to learn anything of his subsequent career."[10]

In July, 1847, a bill which gave to the degrees in Arts of Victoria and Queen's the same standing as those of King's for entry into law passed the Legislature. This act assisted Springer, and may indeed have been a *privilegium* passed for his benefit. In a letter to Hodgins, Ryerson referred to it as "the bill in which Mr. Springer is interested."[11]

[9] *D.H.*, VII, 58.
[10] *Acta*, Dec., 1904, p. 155.
[11] In commenting on this (*E.R.*, II, 144) the writer fell into error in connecting this statement with an earlier statement by Ryerson that he did not think the diploma legal according to the provisions of the Charter. I supposed that the bill

In the same month Strachan resigned the presidency of King's College, opening the way for McCaul to succeed. It had become evident to the old warrior that the dream of an established church fed by a provincial university had become forever impossible. The choice now lay between the partition of the endowment and a position at best of *prima inter pares*, as proposed by Macdonald, or Baldwin's policy of stark secularism. After fifty years of endeavour he had no relish for either alternative.

During the summer or early autumn of 1847 Ryerson formally resigned from the principalship, and MacNab was duly appointed Principal. He retained the position for some two years. But his tenure was never quite secure. In May, 1846, he had stated in the *Guardian* that he was about to leave the College. At the annual Conference some charge had been made against him by the Cobourg District Meeting, but his explanation satisfied, and he was continued in good standing with the minute in the District journal expunged. In September John Ryerson wrote from London, where he and Green had been negotiating terms of reunion with the British Wesleyans, that Richey might be reappointed to the College, if the Board approved. On May 25, 1847, the *Canada Christian Advocate*, published by the Episcopal Methodists in Cobourg, in commenting on the prominent place given Sir Allan MacNab, other Anglican laymen, and several Anglican clergymen at the late public examinations used these words: "But the secret of the whole matter is simply this—the Church people confidently expect the 'Rev. Principal' to join their ranks when the fullness of time has come. This is no secret in Cobourg." On July 3, 1847, Egerton Ryerson wrote to President Olin of Wesleyan University stating that Richey had been offered the principalship and that he was prepared to accept it if

---

corrected some informality in the diploma, although disturbed by the fact that I could find no confirmation either in the Journals of the House of Assembly or in the printed Statutes. A closer perusal of the files of the *Christian Guardian* (whose great value as a source of Canadian history is only now coming to be recognized) has revealed the truth of the matter. The only question which now remains is the nature of a certain irregularity in the diploma, which Ryerson supposed to exist. Two of the three requirements of the Charter (or Act of 1841) were certainly met. The College had a principal and four professors, and the month's notice of the Senate meeting had been given in the *Gazette*. Ryerson, who was absent in Europe, may have learned that the quorum of half the members of the Senate required by the Act was wanting; that is the only possible irregularity. In any event, I do not find that criticism on this point was ever publicly raised. Springer's degree was honest and well earned.

financial support, for which John Ryerson and Richey were at the time negotiating in Montreal, could be obtained. He requested for the Principal-designate a D.D. from Wesleyan. The degree was forthcoming, but not the finances; and MacNab continued at Cobourg as Principal, or as he sometimes designated himself, President. The statement was made in 1850 by Ryerson that it was with the express understanding, however, on all sides that he would resign at any moment Richey could take over, and that the members of the Board never looked on him as more than a locum tenens.

In spite of this anomalous position, MacNab's administration was creditable, and the attendance increased each year. If one may judge from his one extant address, there was nothing particularly inspiring—and certainly nothing essentially Methodistic—in what he had to offer his students. This appears in the Catalogue, or Calendar as we now call it, for the year 1848. It consists largely of a homily on proper conduct for students, together with some analysis of the process and purpose of education. It is difficult to conceive how more advice, and tolerably sound advice, could have been vouchsafed at one sitting. An item which would particularly shock Victoria undergraduates of a century later is the exhortation to early study (the College hour of rising was still five) and the observation that "a great part of the *immoralities* of young persons proceed from the baneful custom of sitting up after midnight." Also disturbing is the frank avowal that education is desirable as "one of the most important requisites of obtaining a respectable standing in society." "You cannot reasonably expect to rise above the rank you now occupy," he tells his young friends, "without a diligent application to the enlightenment of the mind." He has much to say on the advantages of having a mind well furnished, and tells how society is elevated by the sympathy of kindred minds and "degraded by the prevalent custom of making good eating, or good drinking, the main concern in a social visit." The address concludes with an admonition to emulate Solomon in his pursuit of wisdom; indeed there is little in the whole twenty-eight pages that transcends the Old Testament.

Of the closing exercises in May, 1848, we have an excellent account. The Rev. George R. Sanderson, editor of the *Guardian* since 1846, himself reported them at some length in the issue of May 10. He witnessed the examination of the students during Tuesday and Wednesday, missing Monday, and was greatly impressed with the whole performance and particularly with that of Master George M. Meacham of Belleville.[12]

Tuesday evening was given over to an address by the Chief Superintendent of Education on "The Obligations of Educated Men." Having concluded the main part of his address, Ryerson did a surprising and significant thing. It had always been his custom to emphasize the broadly Christian character of the institution as Academy and College. Now he undertook to address especially those who were members of the Wesleyan Methodist Church, and he hoped that in doing so it would not be considered improper for him to adopt the Wesleyan mode of extemporaneous speaking. He said that among the sectional and sectarian divisions in the Christian world there appeared to him to be substantially but two classes, the disciples of an *external* and those of a *spiritual* and *vital* Christianity. The prevalent religion when Wesley commenced his career was external. The object Wesley aimed at was the diffusion of a spiritual, or, to use the current term, "evangelical" Christianity; the difference was not one of forms of worship or church government, of terms of communion or articles of faith; the Wesleyan emphasis was on "the power of God unto salvation to every one that believeth." This attitude was not exclusively the property of Wesleyans or even Protestants; in the Greek and Romish churches he had met with persons whose Christian experience was as clear as anything to be found in a Wesleyan class meeting. But it was the *special* character of the Wesleyan body, and not least in Canada, to uphold this doctrine to society at large and extend the message to the heathen tribes. A person might spend the greater part of his life in investigating disputed questions of theology and litigated points of church polity, and terminate his research in greater doubt than when he began; but "being justified by faith he has peace with God," and carries in his own heart the "antidote for the symbolism of Italy, the rationalism of Germany, the Arianism of the North of Ireland, the

[12]The name is still honoured in Victoria in the George M. Meacham bursaries for students preparing for the mission field. It was 1860 before Meacham took his degree. After some twenty years in various home charges, he went to Japan in 1876, three years after the Canadian Methodists had opened their first mission in the Far East.

Unitarianism of New England and the Puseyism of England." He rejoiced that, so far as he knew, in Victoria College questions of ecclesiastical controversy had never been mooted, and he hoped that it would ever maintain this scriptural and catholic character. While ending on this note, he intends, it is clear, in this appendage to his address to elevate Methodism as his ideal before his young hearers. It is difficult to account for his doing so, had he not felt that this ideal was in some danger under the present administration.

The following evening was the Commencement, as it now began to be called, and Sanderson is at some pains to explain this strange "denomination." It began at 7 o'clock and was held in the College Chapel. Hundreds were unable to get within hearing of the speakers, so Sanderson was informed. MacNab in his address stressed the point that sectarianism was not emphasized in the College and cited as proof the fact that nearly twenty of the eighty students had recorded themselves as members of the Church of England, and about ten as Presbyterians. Again, the character of the education at Victoria College he declared to be "truly British." "While mere *party politics* are never mentioned within these walls," he averred, "sentiments of true patriotism and sound loyalty are constantly inculcated."

After the applause had subsided, no less than thirteen original essays in prose or poetry were presented, including the usual Latin and Greek orations, the latter by A. J. Broughall, later Canon Broughall. Sanderson briefly characterizes each performance, criticizing the delivery of one student and noting that another on "The Tender Passion" was received with unmeasured applause. Wesley P. Wright's valedictory on "The Past and the Present" was described as "the gem of the evening." Now occurs an intriguing paragraph in the account. "At a subsequent period, Mr. Silverthorn,[18] of Toronto, we believe, delivered an original poem. Subject, Victoria College. This was written by request, and afforded some amusement." Is the poem hopelessly lost?

After a lapse of three years, Victoria College was ready again to confer degrees. They were two—to Wesley P. Wright of Hamilton, who had he not left to help his sister, Mrs. VanNorman, and brother-in-law, could have graduated in 1846, and to William Ormiston, whose

[18]The name N. Silverthorn of Meadowvale appears in the Calendar.

winning of the degree had been retarded by teaching in the College. Ryerson presented them to the Principal who with "some most appropriate and eloquent observations," presented the diplomas. Then the benediction.

The year 1849 was to prove an eventful one in the history of the College. It began with good promise. The combined attendance for winter and summer terms reached 140. There was still the difficulty with finances and the uncertainty as to what a government under the leadership of Baldwin would do. In fact it failed to do one thing which other governments had done promptly at the end of the session, namely forward the grant of £500. This led to a report that the work of the College was to be suspended. Dr. Beatty, as secretary of the Board, denied the rumour in a letter to the *Star* of October 17, 1849, and called on friends of the College to send "a household of students with cash in hand" to meet the shortage. The annual examinations were held from April 30 to May 2, while the "godless" University Bill was being advanced through the House and the country was still reeling under the news that the Parliament Buildings had been burned in Montreal and the Governor-General made the target of missiles.

To judge from the *Guardian*, it would be difficult to say which event was regarded with more concern by the friends of the College. Baldwin's bill of 1849 carried the principle of his bill of 1843 to its logical conclusion. Higher education was to be centralized and secularized. The university endowment was to be reserved exclusively for the use of the University and Upper Canada College. There was now no mention of any subvention to the denominational colleges. All that was said of them was that if any of them wished to surrender its degree-conferring powers other than in Divinity, it might claim one seat on the Senate, and thus become equal in influence to a single university professor, since all professors were members of the Senate. But it was against clerics in particular that the bill showed its teeth. Not only were all religious tests barred for staff and students, but it was stipulated that no "minister, ecclesiastic or teacher under or according to any form or profession of religious faith or worship" was eligible for election as Chancellor by "the voices in open convocation," and of the six members appointed by the government to the Senate, none could be a "minister, ecclesiastic," etc., according to the above formula.

Further, the teaching of Divinity was to be excluded from the University. However, section 48 provided that special cases of hardship among former professors might be inquired into; and under this section, as it proved, Dr. Beaven, Professor of Divinity, found a cushion in Metaphysics and Ethics. Baldwin might be doctrinaire, but he was not inhuman.

With ostracism on the part of the government impending—the Act was to take effect only on January 1, 1850—the third ceremony of conferring of degrees was carried through at Cobourg, after the usual preliminaries of examining classes and listening to original papers. On this occasion, Richey was present and delivered what Green described as "one of his happiest efforts," on "The English Language." The degree of B.A. was awarded to J. Campbell of Hamilton, and C. M. D. Cameron of Addison; the M.A. to Oliver Springer, Barrister, of Hamilton, and William Brouse, M.D., of Prescott; and a D.D. to the Rev. John Scott of London, England. He was to be Victoria's first Doctor of Divinity. The astonishing sequel shall appear in the prospective recipient's own words, addressed to Richey on October 6, 1849.

You are a Doctor, and your generous nature leads you to wish that your friends may be raised to an elevation similar to your own. I duly received your kind letter, informing me that the *Senatus Academicus* of the University of Victoria College, at its recent commencement, had conferred on me the degree of Doctor in Divinity, offering to me your congratulations, and reminding me that some time since you had foretold the event. I most gratefully appreciate your kindness and that of your friends, who have deemed me not unfit for so high a distinction, and I offer to you my sincere thanks. On a full consideration of the matter however, I have written to say, that I cannot leave my less elevated ground and take a position so high; I should not ornament your class, and I will not detract from its importance and high consideration. Though I have thus decided, I shall ever retain a lively sense of your disinterested kindness.

At the end of the summer session of 1849 MacNab tendered his resignation in a letter to Richey, who was chairman of the Board. No account of his leave-taking appears to have survived. He immediately went over to the Church of England. For a short time he remained in Cobourg, after which he transferred to the rectorship of Darlington, a stipend augmented by £100 from the ingeniously contrived commutation fund of the Clergy Reserves,[14] and a respected old age in a stately home at Bowmanville.

[14]See *E.R.*, II, 283–4.

The last minute of the Managing Committee, September 19, 1849, records a difference of opinion between MacNab and Dr. John Beatty on the question of whether the appointment of a successor to Paddock should be made by the Committee or left to the Board. For some time Beatty had been coming to have an increasingly influential place in the affairs of the College. Born in New York in 1810, he moved with his family to Meadowvale nine years later. As a lad he had taken his part in the clearing of his father's farm, but had returned to the United States for his academic and medical training. He had received his degree in New York in April, 1833, and in July added a provincial licence from Dr. John Rolph's office. He began his practice in Cobourg, where his father was agent for the Academy, but moved to Toronto in 1835 and continued in practice there till 1844, when he returned to Cobourg. His services as superintendent of the Sunday School at Newgate Street were warmly recognized on his leaving Toronto. He had married a daughter of J. R. Armstrong, merchant of Kingston and Toronto, and was thus a brother-in-law of Egerton Ryerson. The *Christian Advocate* states that he was less than friendly to MacNab, but the editor was likely to magnify anything unpleasant at the College. Certainly, when Kingston attacked MacNab in the *Provincialist*, Beatty came promptly and strongly to the defence of the College and its Principal in a signed letter to the *Star*.

When the winter session of 1849-50 opened on the last Thursday in October, Richey was set down as President and Professor of Theology, both new titles. The Rev. Conrad Van Dusen was named Governor and Treasurer. Wilson retained the chair in Classics and Beatty, probably without entirely abandoning his practice of medicine, undertook the work in Science. Two tutors and an instructor completed the staff. But Richey was not to come to Cobourg. The issue of the *Guardian* which announced his appointment described also a serious accident he had suffered. Returning from Quebec he was proceeding home from the wharf in his carriage when his horse bolted on Wellington Street and dashed off at a furious pace. Richey tried to leap from the carriage but was thrown to the street and received serious injuries. It was several months before he recovered, and by that time the state of the College was such that he had no heart for the position. On December 19, 1849, Van Dusen wrote of the financial stress and the fact that the grant of

£500 had not yet been received, and from Hamilton the *Provincialist* continued to prognosticate the sale of the College.

Something of the character of the work and life of the College during this winter term can be learned from Judge Dean's account written fifty-four years later.

Prof. Wilson, B.A., T.C.D., who had taken the chair vacated by Prof. Hurlburt in the spring of 1847, became Acting Principal. Those who remember Prof. Wilson fifteen or twenty years later—and in that time he had grown no less active or executive—will readily understand that he was designed by nature to adorn the classic shades of Parnassus, rather than to shine as the guide and governor of a body of tempestuous youths. However, things did not go badly; as larger democracies have done before and since, the boys resolved themselves into a committee of safety. They were at heart very loyal to "Old Trinity"; besides disciplining other unruly ones, they formally expelled one boy and sent him home.

There was no summer session in 1850. Prof. Wilson accepted the mastership of a private classical school, and it seemed for a time that the doors of the dear old house would never more open.[15]

[15] *Acta*, Dec., 1904, p. 156.

V. SALVAGE OPERATIONS
1850-1859

IN 1850, after a lapse of nine years, the affairs of Victoria College once more became the subject of legislation. On August 10 assent was given to a brief bill, of one sentence in fact. It was provided that the Board of Trustees and Visitors, if at any time they deemed it expedient, might remove the site of the College from Cobourg or its vicinity to Toronto or its vicinity. The reason stated in the Act was that it had been represented to the Legislature that the objects and usefulness of the College would be greatly promoted by such removal. On the same day assent was given to a bill amending the University Act of 1849. This amendment, less remarkable perhaps in its terms than in its preamble, serves to explain the Victoria College Act. The preamble states that whereas the Act of 1849 had "originated in a sincere desire for the advancement of true religion, and a tender regard for the conscientious scruples of all classes of professing Christians," its object, which was to keep the government of the University free from all denominational bias, had been misunderstood. The purpose of the new measure, then, was the satisfaction of all whose minds "might have been disturbed by such doubts." It was therefore provided that each affiliated college might prescribe religious requisites for its students, and that the Senate of the University should be bound to recognize such requirements before admitting the student to its degree. Further the Senate was pronounced competent to pass statutes requiring on the part of students attendance at public worship and religious instruction according to their respective forms of religious faith. Thus did Baldwin, himself a deeply religious man, recant and seek to allay the suspicions he had raised that he was creating a "godless" university.

It has sometimes been stated that the attitude of the Victoria College

Board in asking for legislation to permit removal to Toronto was determined by financial considerations. These were involved, to be sure; and had a purchaser been found for the buildings at Cobourg, as appeared probable, the removal of Victoria to Toronto might have taken place forty-two years earlier than it did. But the decision to transfer the site in certain contingencies was based on broad educational policies as well. In September, 1850, after the decision to remain at Cobourg, the trend of events was explained in a joint letter to the *Guardian* by John Ryerson and Enoch Wood, as Visitors of the College and officers of the Conference. The statement recalls how in 1843, 1845, and 1847 the authorities of Victoria College had shown "a disposition to co-operate in any just and practical arrangements, by whatever party proposed," with a view to an efficient Christian system of university education; how the Act of 1849 had left them no alternative but to remain separate; and how in the early part of 1850 hope had been revived of a modification of the law which would "place the Toronto university upon a foundation that would render it worthy of the confidence and support of all religious denominations." The College authorities had decided that in such an event it might appear their duty to remove to Toronto and exercise three functions only: elementary instruction in English, Classics, and Mathematics; supervision of the religious and moral interests of students attending the University; and a more thorough training in Theology of candidates for the ministry. This step would involve the surrendering of the power to confer degrees except those in Divinity. During the summer, however, it was finally determined—the comparative weight of financial and higher considerations is not assessed in the joint letter—that for the present the College would remain at Cobourg.

For the work of resuscitation two members of Conference were selected, the Rev. Lachlin Taylor with the title of Pastoral Governor and Professor of Moral Philosophy, and the Rev. Samuel Sobieski Nelles as Professor of Classics. Taylor was a native of Argyllshire, of attractive personality, with "a zeal and faith which nothing could hold back or daunt."[1] After ten years in the itineracy he had burned himself out and was resting for a year on his father's farm. He felt unequal

[1] *Case*, V, 264.

to the responsibility of the College, and Nelles had to bear the whole weight.

Nelles was born at Mount Pleasant near Brantford on October 17, 1823, so that he was only in his twenty-seventh year when he took up the work which was to be his life for thirty-seven years. He may justly be called the saviour of Victoria College. At his graduation from Middletown in 1846, Ryerson had written him about joining the staff, but he had replied that he felt called upon to preach. However, he would not refuse, he adds, to comply with the Board's wishes, although "Ichabod would seem to be enstamped on the very walls."[2] After a year spent in teaching at the Newburgh Academy he entered the ministry "on trial." For a year he preached on the Port Hope circuit and for two years at Toronto East with John Ryerson as superintendent. The Conference of 1850 assigned him to London under Carroll. He had barely settled in his new charge and was "giving great satisfaction to his fellow-laborer and the people"[3] when the imperious call came. The manner of the man, and the spirit in which he entered upon his new duties, are best told in the words of his diary.[4]

July 4—Felt melancholy sensations on leaving Toronto. Two years of my life have gone in that city. And yet I was struck with the fact that people in cities become dulled to the tender scenes & occasions of life. Custom seems to harden the heart. I myself do not seem to feel so deeply as formerly. Alas life wears away the soul's freshness. . . . In going to London—my new field of labor—I have only one aim—to sustain a true ministerial character—to be a faithful steward of the manifold Grace of God. I must be more pastoral—less loquacious—more natural and conversational in the pulpit and more *systematic* in my studies. Life is passing away with me—and how different from my earlier fancies! I begin to think now that my life will amount only to this—a plain Methodist preacher—for a few years—in Western Canada. Well let it be so. . . . Fame is the shadow of a shade.

July 12—Mr. Lavell left this morning for Montreal. His departure made me both sorry and glad. Sorry because he is a cheerful companion—and glad because his society kept me from study. . . . Commenced this morning using Tinc. of Gentian as a tonic.

July 13—Health poor—Unable to study—Lay on sofa—read Carlyle—wonderful style & mind. Full of great truth & great error.

[2]V.U.A., Nelles to Egerton Ryerson, Sept. 21, 1846.
[3]*Case*, V, 68.
[4]This diary is in the Archives of Victoria University.

Aug. 13—Began about this time to get juster views of the Second Coming of Christ. Feel much profited thereby.

Sept. 26—Came to Victoria College—as Professor. Greatly tried in this thing.

Oct. 2—Students are coming in. No Profs but me. L. Taylor has refused to come. The chief care is likely to devolve on one little prepared for it. I am as yet hearing all the classes in the several branches. Never needed more grace. Feel the doctrine of Providence to be one most precious. I have not sought my present position. Resisted as much as seemed meet—in a Wesleyan minister, acting under his superiors. Feel the importance of sustaining our literary institution as a place of preparation for young ministers. Don't know what is to be the end of the matter. Must stay where I am for the present. May God guide me and keep me pure in motive.

Oct. 25—We have about 2 doz. students. I do not dislike the work. Health much better. I am giving more attention to Natural Science.

May 23, 1851—Have been dipping into Boswell's Johnson. A book at once very *silly* and very valuable. . . . I am unwell. Took cold playing ball.

May 30—Resolved to be more practical in my studies. Read less poetry and more of science. Note. Have wonderfully improved of late in my religious views and inward peace.

Half a century later the Rev. Dr. E. B. Ryckman thus described the situation at that anxious time as it appeared to a student:

My memory goes back to September, '50. It was then I entered the halls of glorious "old Vic." It was a critical period in her history. At that time the Calendar provided for two "sessions" in the year. The winter session of '49–'50 had been a fizzle on account of the bolting of the Rev. Principal. He said a curt farewell to Methodism and went to *the* Church. The summer session of '50 had dropped out. The College had come to what physicians call "the intermitted breathing." Even then there was hope of recovery. Announcement was made that the College would re-open on a certain day in September. I reported myself on the very day—I only. (Pretty low water for the College.) In two or three days three others came in. (The waters began to rise!) Of the three, one was His Honor Judge Dean, County Victoria; another was James H. Beatty, Esq., Thorold; the third was—better not be named in such company; the only respectable thing about him was his ability; he remained two or three years, acquired a bad reputation and made an inglorious exit. For fully two weeks we four constituted the whole body of students. For two weeks no classes were organized. The Professor of Classics was the only one of the staff on the ground. The Principal, who had just been ordained to the ministry, was yet lecturing to his flock in London. The Professor of Mathematics was still in his printing office in Hamilton, where he was, or had been, editor and proprietor of a newspaper. The delay was most annoying. The wonder is that we did not go home. But we were boarded for nothing and detained by assurances of better things "to-morrow." We spent much of our time in various discussions, philosophical, ethical, political, in which His Honor generally led, and always came out ahead.

When about a dozen students had gathered (waters still rising!) we were set to work in classics and mathematics. In another week or two the principal arrived (the waters took a leap up!) and soon the college machinery was all in operation—the classes all organized, though several of them contained only two students, and some only one! However, we went through all the motions of college life. The tide of prosperity rose until thirty-nine students had been enrolled! There the proud waves were stayed! That was the whole number for that year, though, of course, not so many were ever present at any one time.

Our instructor in classical languages was the late Rev. Wesley P. Wright, M.A., a pains-taking and successful teacher. The Professor of Mathematics was the late Wm. Kingston, Esq., M.A., whose pet-name, "Old Dot," the etymology of which cannot now be traced with certainty, would sound very irreverent to strangers' ears, but was uttered with profoundest respect by all the best students in his classes. Last, not least, the Principal was the late Rev. Dr. Nelles, who began his brilliant career as an educator at that time.

The feeble but convalescent session of '50-'51, in which I was the first student, i.e. first on the ground, and Dr. Nelles was installed as Principal, was epochal in the University's life and mine also. It changed my whole life by changing my purpose from merely getting a fair education by spending two or three years at college, to taking a full university course, i.e. full for that day. It is fuller now. It certainly changed the life of the College by placing at its head a man whose sagacity, eloquence, energy and other notable gifts placed the institution for which he lived on an up-grade, towards the top of which she is still speeding under the yet unexpired impulse that he gave her. . . .[5]

Operations were continued with slowly increasing numbers during 1850-1 and 1851-2. In the first autumn Kingston returned from the barren field of publishing, and W. P. Wright joined the staff, teaching mainly the Classics. On November 22, 1851, Nelles wrote Ryerson that they had "but few students—about forty-five." By the autumn of 1852 the College was well filled. Nelles could record in his diary under date of November 29: "The winter session has opened prosperously. We have about 110 students—a large number for us. What a contrast with the opening two years since! Then we had but four or five at first whom Mr. V. [Van Dusen] and I detained from the States by the argument *a posteriori*, that is, by holding onto their coat-tails." Pro-

[5]*Acta*, Dec., 1899, p. 290.

fessor Wilson had now returned, and the staff was at full strength with Nelles as Principal and Professor of Moral Science and Rhetoric, Kingston as Professor of Mathematics, Beatty as Professor of the Natural Sciences, Wilson as Professor of Latin and Greek, John Campbell as Classical Tutor, Thomas A. Ferguson as English Teacher, and Thomas H. Robertson as Teacher of Music. At the head of the list stands the name of Ryerson as President. The Calendars for 1850 and 1851 are not available, but it may be assumed that when Nelles took charge in 1850 he did so only on condition that Ryerson should stand by.

On July 3, 1851, with Ryerson officiating, Nelles married Mary Bakewell, eldest daughter of the Rev. Enoch Wood, President of Conference. From their suite of rooms at the College, and later from their residence in the town, they afforded to successive generations of students a most gracious hospitality. Nelles had early developed ideas on the subject of home life which he disdained to hide under a bushel. It is recorded that at a missionary meeting at Thornhill eighteen months before his marriage he "gave the ladies a very interesting lecture on domestic comfort and happiness as induced and promoted by Christianity." "He did well on the subject," the *Guardian* continues, "notwithstanding his being a young man."[6] His future father-in-law was speaking at the same meeting, and one wonders whether the eldest daughter had come along.

The main problem of these years was financial. Nelles, however, was fully occupied with matters which he considered more fundamental. The Rev. Conrad Van Dusen, who had served in MacNab's day, was continued as Agent, and the far from buoyant revenues of the College were, under the Board, his particular concern. From June, 1848, to June, 1849, the receipts were £3,251.13.6; from June, 1849, to June, 1850, £1,603.3.9. As attendance increased the revenues rose, but not enough, especially since the experience of 1849 proved that the government grant could not be relied upon. Endowment was essential, and with this in view Van Dusen persuaded the Board to adopt from the United States an ingenious plan of "scholarships." The goal was modest enough, by present standards. $50,000 (£12,500) was to be raised by the sale of 500 "scholarships." Each purchaser secured the right to

[6]*C.G.*, Jan. 30, 1850.

educate his own son, or any other youth whom he might designate, at any time during the next twenty-five years without tuition fees. The term of study was not specified, merely due submission to discipline. Under the bond with good behaviour a beneficiary might claim instruction indefinitely. The whole scheme was a natural product of a decade of speculation in railway and other ventures. It mortgaged the future to satisfy the demands of a hungry present. It meant that for twenty-five years many, perhaps most, of the students would be claiming free tuition on the strength of such interest as $100 would beget. Even if all the "scholarships" had been sold and cash paid within the four years given for payment, with interest included during these four years, and if the whole had been invested safely at the high rates of interest prevailing (some of it was in fact invested at 10 per cent)—given all this, it was rather flimsy financing, as Ryerson and Nelles appear to have recognized, although both purchased "scholarships," Ryerson two of them. However, meetings were held through the province and something over 600 subscribers secured on paper. But treasurers were changed, and books were badly kept, and the hey-day of high finance in the province was shortlived. After a decade two separate investigations examined the wreckage to discover that the total received in principal was only $27,326. Of this amount $9,597 had been sunk in the current expenses of the College, while $13,803 was invested, with a revenue from interest of $1,187. In fact during the fifties the annual deficit of the College amounted to some $3,000, or, if improvements were charged, some $4,000. Meanwhile all "scholarships" not cancelled by attendance of a designated student continued (even into the seventies) to be a liability. Two advantages, however, flowed from this grandiose scheme: it paid certain immediate and pressing debts, and it contributed to an increase in the attendance.

While Van Dusen was floating his "scholarships," Ryerson as titular President was working on finance from another angle. The year 1851 saw the end of what is sometimes known as the Great Ministry of Baldwin and Lafontaine. Baldwin retired first, sorely wounded by shafts directed against his Court of Chancery Bill by the pesky William Lyon Mackenzie, and Lafontaine followed a few months later. This left Hincks the leading figure in the administration. On the University question he was not a rigid voluntaryist like Baldwin, but was prepared to concede to the denominational colleges a substantial share of public support. In 1852 it appeared likely that funds from the university endowment or from the impending settlement of the ancient Clergy Reserves dispute, or from both, might be available for Victoria College. The details of the interesting exchange of views between Ryerson and Hincks on the subject need not be given here.[7] As it proved, Hincks' mind was too much occupied with railway finance to persevere with his friends and prevail over his opponents sufficiently to secure such a settlement of either question as he would have preferred.

His University Act of 1853, in spite of curious inconsistencies, is not without merit. And it set the general pattern of higher education in the province for a generation. The Baldwin Act of 1849 was repealed. The principle of state control was applied with thoroughness. The endowment and property were vested in the Crown. The Chancellor was appointed by the government, as were the members of the Senate (other than the representatives of the affiliated colleges) and the teaching staff. All statutes of the Senate became valid only on receiving the signature of the Governor. No religious test (or indeed profession of religious faith) was required of staff or students, but regulations might be made for the moral conduct of students and for their attendance at worship at their respective churches. The state withdrew from the teaching of Medicine and Law, so that the training of doctors and lawyers, like that of ministers, was left to private enterprise. For Arts work a new state college was set up and named University College, with a President or Vice-President and such professors as might from time to time be appointed by the government to hold office during its pleasure. These constituted the College Council, which was empowered, apparently quite independently of the Senate, to pass statutes which became valid with the Governor's signature. The University itself became merely an examining body, after the manner of the University of London, on which it was specifically modelled. Its duty was to maintain standards equal to those of the University of London, to assign scholarships to students for proficiency shown in examinations in any of the affiliated institutions, and to regulate by statute the examination of candidates for degrees from all colleges within the province.

[7]See *E.R.*, II, 260–3.

But what inducements were there for other Arts colleges to affiliate? Never perhaps has the promise of the preamble of an act been more signally belied in its terms and effect. The preamble announced:

Whereas the enactments hereinafter repealed have failed to effect the end proposed by the Legislature in passing them, inasmuch as no College or Educational Institution hath under them become affiliated to the University to which they relate, and many parents and others are deterred by the expense and other causes, from sending the youth under their charge to be educated in a large City distant, in many cases, from their homes; And whereas from these and other causes, many do and will prosecute and complete their studies in other institutions in various parts of this Province, to whom it is just and right to afford facilities for obtaining those scholastic honors and rewards, which their diligence and proficiency may deserve, and thereby to encourage them and others to persevere in the pursuit of knowledge and sound learning; And whereas experience hath proved the principles embodied in Her Majesty's Royal Charter to the University of London in England, to be well adapted for the attainment of the objects aforesaid, and for removing the difficulties and objections hereinbefore referred to. . . .[8]

To this end in earlier drafts of the bill specific sums had been suggested for the support of University College and of other colleges which might affiliate. As finally amended, however, section 54 of the Act read as follows:

Any surplus of the said University Income Fund remaining at the end of any year after defraying the expenses payable out of the same, shall constitute a Fund to be, from time to time, appropriated by Parliament for Academical Education in Upper Canada.

In accepting the clause thus amended Hincks had been led to adopt an illusory formula. No surplus for distribution was ever permitted to exist. When ordinary means for preventing a surplus seemed certain to fail, recourse was had to a building programme which at a cost of £95,000 placed in Queen's Park the fine building of University College, far beyond the needs of the time.

In the event, then, the Hincks Act of 1853 provided no statutory support for Victoria College. Nor do we hear of any scholarships or degrees in the University being sought or held by its students. Until 1854 there was still hope that the Methodists might have a share in the final disposition of the funds set apart for the support of a Protestant clergy and that their share might go to the College, as appa-

[8]*Statutes of Canada*, 1852-3, p. 313.

rently was the intention; but this hope proved vain. Nelles must have been disturbed, but he was far from discouraged, by the financial plight of the College. Witness an address of good cheer which he delivered to the "young gentlemen" of the College on October 29, 1853.

The paper unless expanded in delivery would not consume more than a half hour. Unlike his great mentor, Nelles was an apostle of brevity. In the course of these remarks, timely yet timeless, something may be gathered of the ideals which this young man of thirty was holding before the students. First it is to be noted that no important public occasion was selected for the address, just an hour usually assigned to a class in elocution. He begins by raising for consideration the question as to how long they propose to continue their studies at college. He will not attempt a positive or decided answer. That must depend on individual circumstances. He will put them on guard, however, against a probable error. They are likely to make their academic career too short and consequently their attainments superficial. It is the error of most young men. He compares youth to the courser of untamed mettle and unwearied nerves, standing at the door of his stable, champing his bit and spurning the earth under his feet. This natural impetuosity is augmented by the nature of the age in which they are living, one of hot haste, of high stimulus and rapid accumulation, an age in which patience and perseverance, profound thought and independence of intellectual discipline have become secondary virtues, quite behind the times. Some may have come to college later in life and the tardy mark may rest upon them, urging them to a premature conclusion of their studies. Again, there is another influence more melancholy than all, the injudicious advice of friends (Vocational Guidance as a profession was still of the future). Some of these not having had the advantage of full culture themselves and having achieved some success in their way are wont to pronounce much schooling quite unnecessary and practical talent all that is required, and to add much more such advice equally inconsiderate and equally fallacious. Thus unless on their guard they are likely to be hurried away into the business and bustle of the world. In the face of such pressure he would have them in no haste to try the world; they will probably be weary of the trial before they have done with it. But it occurs to him that someone may imagine that in offering such advice he himself has an ulterior motive. He does not deny that he has experienced much gratification in seeing so large and interesting an assemblage of young men before him. But he has never yet urged a student to come to the institution. It is not his habit to use such persuasions at all, although he has sometimes dissuaded students from coming, and others from remaining when it seemed that they were not likely to gain any advantage. It is not numbers he wants, but students who will do credit to their instructors and be a blessing to their country.

He asks them to examine their object in coming. Is it to be useful? Is it to achieve happiness? Only by the cultivation of the mind is either attainable. Christianity itself brings happiness to men only in so far as it rectifies their disordered natures and brings peace to the conscience, purity to the heart, and light to the understanding. The gospel has never been truly received either by an individual or by a people without some sort of intellectual melioration. And whether the search is for usefulness to others or happines to oneself, or both together, neither will be found in the highest degree without a full and symmetrical cultivation of all one's powers. This requires time. The growth of the mind cannot be forced. There is no railway passage to the hill of science.

He then proceeds to examine a recent observation of the President of Harvard University that the leading feature of the age is intellectual anarchy. He notes certain symptoms of this: the want of fixed and well-defined views; or a certain sickly irresolution, the result of a conscious blindness; or perhaps a rampant and headlong dogmatism; or a certain impatience of investigation or incapacity for it; or perhaps a feverish spirit of search without any sure method or any discernible progress. The only means of checking this intellectual anarchy is by learning to think clearly and for oneself. It may be said that we are to derive our principles from the Bible. But how is this possible without study? We are not called to choose between study and prayer. Study without prayer is arrogance, prayer without study is fanaticism; and neither arrogance nor fanaticism will find true wisdom.

Becoming more specific, he considers the preparation required for the several occupations. These he discusses in the following order: law, medicine, farming, trade, politics, and the mechanical arts. It is to be noted that he makes no mention of the ministry—presumably regarding it as *sui generis*, not to be entered by personal choice or from ambition. For all six occupations he postulates the same qualities: patience, perseverance, a passion for excellence. Referring particularly to law, medicine, and politics, he declares that the stream will not rise higher than its source. *Nihil ex nihilo fit*; without a full intellectual discipline they will become pettifoggers or quacks or political nigglers. The race is not to be won by premature starting; indeed it may almost be said that the sooner one starts the longer one will be in reaching the goal. The term "learned professions" is becoming a palpable misnomer in the hands of unlearned tyros. Crowded they may be, but, as Daniel Webster puts it, there is always room above. To those who are the sons of farmers and intend to return to the farm, he has words of encouragement. It is an independent and noble calling. Nothing but ignorance and vice can degrade the farmer. The soil itself, the oversight of cattle, the homespun garb, the heavy tread and sun-burnt visage and brawny hand do not degrade him, only the failure to become intelligent. No one has a better opportunity than the farmer to study the works of man and of God. Those, again, who will enter trade are urged to seek resources other than the till and the ledger in order to be saved from a grovelling spirit of accumulation and the insufferable vacancy and weariness of old age which is the punishment for a youth spent without intellectual improvement. A similar warning follows to those who aspire to legislative halls. Sometimes the want of moral honesty is observed among politicians, yet there is another deficiency nearly as common but not generally noted—an absence of almost anything like a true political or social science. He urges them to avoid adding to the misdirection of effort of those for whom the stars are hidden as they try to guide the ship of state. Without an enlarged and well-disciplined intellect, no amount of patriotism or integrity will avail in politics. Those who will follow the mechanical arts (the engineers of today) are reminded that yonder illiterate man carrying the hod might with a more active intellect have been the mason, yonder untutored mason with more education the architect. Any who may feel their proverty an insurmountable barrier to a complete education, he advises to work until they can realize their ambition: life may be all the richer for the delay. His final admonition is: "Keep our rules; consult our wishes; respect our office and respect yourselves.

Scorn everything low, everything dishonorable, everything that is unworthy of you as gentlemen and as Christians; and so apply yourselves to the important work now in hand that you may hereafter review these hours without regret and return to your parents and your homes without the blush of shame."

It must not be supposed that every student who heard Nelles' words that morning in October was able consistently to behave as a gentleman and a Christian. Many of them were young men fresh from the farm or their trade, without having had even the advantage of training in one of the scattered and frequently inefficient grammar schools of the province. Others were lads in their early teens, like Nathanael Burwash, who at the time was in his second year of attendance. The variation in ages would add to the difficulties of discipline in residence life. Burwash gives a graphic account of the breaking up of a prayer meeting held one evening in a class-room by the "heavy rhythmic march of many well-shod feet ascending the stairs and coming along the third hall east"[9]—of the candles of the worshippers, pinned to the blackboards by jack-knives, being made the targets of irreverent marbles and sticks of pine kindling—of the kneeling group coming to their feet while their leader begged the intruders not to disturb the worship of God—of utter darkness and a dislodged blackboard—of a disorderly retreat, but no tales told. Evidently the member of the staff who had been assigned to visit the rooms that evening was not on hand; all members took their turn at such visitation, the Principal with the rest. It was delegated, moreover, to the two junior members to see that the students were wakened at five and ready for work at five-thirty. The minutes of the Faculty meetings, preserved from 1853, indicate that as the term advanced the restiveness increased. On December 12, 1853, it was necessary to name five students whose "connection with the institution should cease at the Christmas recess." The following week another was charged with threatening to "injure the College buildings." He was forthwith expelled, and "bound according to law to keep the peace." Evidently the problems of discipline were lessened by a "revival" during the winter in Cobourg, which at the end of six weeks brought conversion to all but a half-dozen students. In the spring term a single case of discipline came before the Faculty, one

[9]Nathanael Burwash, *History of Victory College* (Toronto, 1927), p. 180.

of improper conduct in the College Chapel. The culprit was suspended for an indefinite period, and the verdict sustained on his appealing it. Further, we are informed that Thomas A. Ferguson, the Steward, was required to "dismiss from his employment his colored servant girl, on account of her unruly conduct among the students."[10]

By May, 1854, the College had sufficiently recovered from the *débâcle* of 1850 to present candidates for degrees. The recipients were W. W. Dean, destined for law and the bench, and R. I. Hickey, who continued in medicine. The summer session was curtailed to permit extensive repairs to the boarding hall of the College. In the autumn two important changes were made. First a better classification of students was effected. Those who were not prepared for collegiate work were henceforth taught separately under William Kerr in what was now known as the Grammar School, and very young students were excluded from attendance. The more mature students were divided into two classes, those properly matriculated and proceeding to a degree, and those taking a partial or general course in undergraduate subjects. Many of the classes were now transferred to a cheaply constructed frame building euphemistically known as the Chapel, but by the undergraduates called "the Barn." The second change was the institution of a medical department. The Toronto School of Medicine had been founded by Dr. John Rolph in 1843 and was being conducted in Toronto by an able staff consisting at that time of Rolph himself as Dean, Jno. Joseph Workman, William T. Aikins, Michael Barrett, and Henry H. Wright. In 1854, after the discontinuance of medical teaching at the University of Toronto, Rolph's school turned to Victoria for its degrees and was known as the Medical Department or Faculty of Victoria College. No instruction was given at Cobourg, and there was but slight oversight of either the curriculum or the rather troubled business affairs of the Faculty. A portion of the fee for the degree was retained by Victoria and applied strictly to the purchase of books for the library.

From 1854 to 1859 the administration of the College was divided. Ryerson retired from his titular presidency in 1854, with a warm resolution of appreciation for his willingness to assist during these critical years, and Nelles succeeded to the title. Apparently the Conference and

[10]Victoria College, Minutes of the Faculty, April 3, 1854.

the Board, however, regarded Nelles, who was pre-eminently the scholar and teacher, as unequal to the business management of the College. Hence the appointment of the Rev. S. D. Rice to the office of Moral and Domestic Governor. Rice, born in New England, son of a physician, but brought up in New Brunswick, had been educated with a business career in view till his conversion at the age of nineteen. He was prompt and energetic, notably devout and not without talent as a preacher. But he was the type of minister who built churches rather than filled them. As Agent for the College he spurned buggies, then coming into general use, and mounted his horse to visit every part of the province to canvass for scholarships and drum up students. As Domestic Governor he had charge of the residences and the newly equipped boarding hall. It was as Moral Governor that his sharing of authority with the Principal must frequently have created difficulties in spite of the pacific disposition of Nelles, poles removed from the dictatorial or imperious. However, for three years the rather absurd arrangement appears to have worked tolerably well. The numbers increased, and Rice's business capacity, while not removing the financial pressure, eased it considerably. Nelles moved his residence from the College, and discipline was largely in Rice's hands. The minutes of the Faculty meetings reveal something of the problem created by overcrowded residences and scattered rooming houses tenanted by boys and young men of various types and classes. Indeed, after Kingston became secretary in 1855, the details of misdemeanours are recorded much after the fashion of a police court reporter, and quite subordinate the references to time-tables and curricula and examinations, or even merit and demerit marks—these latter, evidently, much in favour with the secretary.

Rice withdrew from the College in 1857, and the resignation of Dr. Beatty also was involved. Apparently with the rapid development of science Nelles felt that he should take the opportunity of adding to the staff the Rev. G. C. Whitlock, M.A., LL.D., one of his own teachers at Lima. He had a many-sided intellect and a great soul, according to Nelles. Burwash tells us that he was over fifty years of age, but "retained the brilliant imagination of youth; and his kindly hazel eye flashed with enthusiasm as he forgot the work of the drill-master, so much the order of the day at that time, and carried us away in a brilliant survey of some new field of science."[11] He had studied in earlier days in Paris, and had kept in touch with the scientific literature of Europe. It would be difficult to assess the influence of this remarkable man on education in Canada, through the students he inspired during his eight years at Victoria, and particularly through Burwash, whose interest in science he awakened. But Beatty resented his appointment. For some eight years he had served the College both on the Board and on the teaching staff. As a lecturer he was both methodical and interesting. It may well be that, in addition to the expansion of science, the extent of Beatty's financial and political connections may have had something to do with the invitation to Whitlock. But as a man Beatty was highly regarded by the students, and his resignation roused the student body. They prepared a "public address" to him "expressive of their regard for him personally and of regret at his separation from the College,"[12] and certain of their number burned Rice in effigy. Beatty's place was filled, and ably filled, by Elijah P. Harris, an American by birth and a Ph.D. of Göttingen, the first Doctor of Philosophy from a German university, Burwash believes, to be appointed to a chair in a Canadian university. He remained on the staff till 1866. His work is described as thorough, but without the brilliant discursiveness of Whitlock. In addition to his science teaching, he gave instruction in language and sometimes appears as Professor of Modern Languages. The students of the day were thus afforded the opportunity of contrasting French and German methods in the field of science.

The upshot of the address and effigy was the indefinite suspension of three students, and other lesser penalties to several seniors. Two interesting documents, in addition to the Faculty minutes, have survived in connection with the incident. One is a letter from President McCaul denying, somewhat curtly, the accuracy of a report forwarded by Nelles that he had given encouragement to the application of two of the suspended students to enter University College. The second is an

[11]*History of Victoria College*, p. 184.
[12]Victoria College, Minutes of the Faculty, Sept. 24, 1856. After a brief abstention, attended by a protest against clerical domination in the Board, Beatty resumed his place on that body, and continued a member until 1878. The composition of the Board was altered in 1858 from nine ministers and five laymen to twelve ministers and twelve laymen. Beatty's science lecture notes, carefully written out, are in the possession of his grandson, Dr. E. S. Ryerson.

appeal from the culprits drawn up in legal form, declaring that the Faculty, since the name does not appear in the Act, had no right to suspend them from the College and (doubtless without his consent) appointing Dr. Beatty their attorney in the matter. For some months an unusual number of misdemeanours, punishments, prayers for remission of penalties, and public apologies appear in the minutes. Altogether it is evident that the incident created quite a stir in the college community.

The place of Rice was taken by John Ryerson, now the elder statesman of Canadian Methodism. He came directly from a pastoral charge at Quebec, the seat of government, and was serving for his eighth year in the highest office within the gift of his brethren, that of Co-Delegate or Vice-President, the presidency still being reserved for appointees of the English Conference. Rice's title had been Moral and Domestic Governor; that of John Ryerson was Governor and Treasurer. In this latter capacity his fourteen months of tenure failed to sustain his considerable reputation as a man of business and finance. The dropping of "Moral" from the title probably indicates that the College Board was aware of an awkward division of authority. Certainly from this time the control of discipline was unified under Nelles as President.

But such vagrant squalls as the burning of the Moral Governor in effigy touched only the surface. The process of education flowed steadily forward. The graduating group of 1855 were to be remarkable for both the length and the distinction of their subsequent careers. Fifty years later they were all prominently engaged in their several professions. Dr. Moses Henry Aikins was practising at Burnhamthorpe with a far more than local reputation—today he lives in the gratitude of scores of students who have benefited by the series of scholarships endowed in perpetuity; the Honourable William Kerr, eminent alike in legal and in political circles, had been for many years Vice-Chancellor of Victoria University; Dr. Albert Carman had become General Superintendent of the Methodist Church; and Dr. E. B. Ryckman had long been one of its most distinguished ministers. Dr. Ryckman's first year after graduation was spent as tutor in Mathematics at the College. Only one Bachelor of Arts was created in 1856, but he too rose to eminence in his profession—Byron M. Britton, Judge of the High

Court of Justice for Ontario. In this year four M.A.'s were granted, and two English brethren were granted—and accepted—D.D.'s. In 1857 B.A.'s were conferred on R. A. Montgomery and J. W. Kerr, and M.A.'s on Principal Robertson of the Normal School and Professor Wilson. The number of M.D.'s conferred each year was usually about twenty.

In the autumn of 1856 the Hon. John Rolph, Dean of the Medical Department, received one of the greatest shocks of his long and eventful career. One morning he found himself with classes on his hands but no lecturers. The resignations of all four had been written on the previous day. One of these letters must have caused Rolph particular pain, that of Dr. Henry Hover Wright. He would reflect how young Wright had been his special messenger to Mackenzie at Montgomery's Tavern, had facilitated his escape by horse, as if he were proceeding on a professional call, along Dundas Street and across the Niagara, and for some time had shared his exile at Rochester and profited by his great skill as a medical teacher. While his dissident professors were setting up for themselves and assuming the old name, Toronto School of Medicine, which had fallen into disuse in favour of the Faculty of Medicine of Victoria College, Rolph appealed to the students, and they remained with him. For a few days he lectured on all the subjects, it is said, but shortly was joined by Drs. Walter Geikie, John Reid, C. B. Berryman, and E. A. Ogden, so that the work was carried forward much as usual. At the end of the year Rolph was able to report a successful term and all expenses paid. It should be said that Victoria College failed to prevent by process of law the dissidents using the name "Toronto School of Medicine" and was compelled to pay the costs of an action in Chancery.

During the session 1856-7, a Literary Association was organized at the instance of the tutor in Classics, John Campbell, who was its president from its founding to his retirement from the College in 1860. Burwash says that Campbell was an effective and thorough teacher, especially in grammar, but neglects to describe the Literary Association meetings, which doubtless contributed to that proficiency in debate for which he himself was justly famous in later years. Campbell was of a quiet and retiring disposition, and the founding of the Literary Association was his special achievement. He transferred shortly to high school teaching. On July 7, 1858, an appeal for funds for the Association, signed by W. R. Parker and seconded by Nelles, appeared in the *Guardian*. Parker explained that the Association consisted mostly of undergraduates, but some other students were admitted; that it held weekly meetings for the discussion of a subject previously announced and for the hearing of readings and essays, and that the money was being collected for a library for the use of Association members. Nelles and Campbell headed the list with $20 each.

For some time in the *Guardian* the question of changing location had been agitated. The inadequacy of the building in view of increasing attendance and the insistent claim for a better provision for the education of young women had matured a suggestion that the College should be removed to Hamilton and the present premises turned into a ladies' college. An additional reason was that in twenty-five years population in the province had shifted westward, and Cobourg no longer held the central position it could claim in 1830. Hamilton friends were already pledging money for a new building, when Cobourg in alarm busied itself. Five acres of land contiguous to the College grounds were purchased from Dr. Beatty for $1,500 and offered by the municipality to the Board, together with necessary street improvements. The proposal was that in view of this gift the College should bind itself to Cobourg in perpetuity. The matter was considered at a full meeting of the Board on March 25, 1857. But the Board was not to be caught with small bait. They passed the following resolution, from the cultivated pens of Ryerson and Carroll, which the town authorities accepted in lieu of more explicit promises:

That the Board is willing to accept the offer of the Municipal Council of Cobourg with the understanding & assurance that efforts be made by the Board as soon as practicable to improve & enlarge the present buildings for the accommodation of a larger number of students. The Board regards the soliciting & collecting of public subscriptions & the expenditure of large sums for the erection of additional College accommodation a sufficient guarantee of its intentions to continue the establishment & operation of the College at Cobourg.

In years to come the careful phrasing of this last sentence was to prove the College's salvation.

When Anson Green became Treasurer in 1858, without the added title of Governor, Nelles' presidency entered a new phase. Up to that time he had taken no responsibility for the financial policy of the College. Now he assumed leadership in every area. In the summer of 1858 plans were set afoot to liquidate the debt and at the same time to secure subscriptions for a building expansion rendered necessary by the increased enrolment. Nelles explained the situation in two letters to the *Guardian*, stating that there need be no difficulty in carrying forward both campaigns. In the first and more general of these letters, he stressed rather more than was his wont the vital relation of the College to Methodism. "We shall err most sadly," he declares, "if we look for this result [the maintenance of a devoted ministry] from the efforts of other denominations, or from the secular and secularizing Colleges of the state. . . . If we allow others to sow the seed, we must allow them also to reap the harvest. . . . And why should Methodism subject herself to such disadvantages? . . . It has been hers to convert the ignorant and the poor, let it be hers also to convert the rich and the learned, and to pour the influence of her earnest Christianity through every channel of life."[13] In the second letter he places the debt of the College at £8,000. He notes that McGill in spite of an endowment of £15,000 was running behind at the rate of more than £1,200 a year, while Victoria had no endowment and a legislative grant of only £750. Greater financial support he regards as essential. "Without bigotry," he concludes, "and without latitudinarianism we must stand by our connexional interests."[14] That his practice did not belie his precept is shown in the fact that he subscribed $200 to the Agent's fund. Ryerson and Thomas Dumble were the largest subscribers, with $400 each; but it would appear, in spite of Hodgins' statement to the contrary, that the appeal was not particularly successful. 1858 was a year of financial depression, and it was followed in 1859 by what Nelles describes as "the failure of the harvest, and unexampled scarcity of money."[15] Attendance, however, remained satisfactory. The Arts enrolment was 59, that of occasional and preparatory classes 153, and that of Medicine 73.

On November 30, 1858, the College was the scene of a remarkable leave-taking. The gold rush to the Cariboo created a call for missionaries. Ebenezer Robson, who had been a student for two years, was one of the four volunteers accepted. A group of twelve fellow-students,

[13]*C.G.*, Aug. 11, 1858.
[14]*Ibid.*, Sept. 8, 1858.
[15]*Ibid.*, July 6, 1859.

Burwash being one of them, arranged a complimentary address and breakfast for him at the College, and the professors joined in the farewell. There was no set order of speeches, but each spoke as the spirit moved him. It was an affecting occasion. "The emotions and impressions enkindled by the interview, are not likely to soon die away—many a young man of the company is preparing himself to respond to the next appeal which the Wesleyan Church must, in the order of Providence, make for the reinforcement and extension of her Missionary work."[16] This was the first of a long series of farewells to departing missionaries, with its climax almost half a century later when the Student Volunteer Movement swept through the College. Robson was joined at the Pacific Coast by his brother John, who as an editor became the foremost champion of constitutional government in British Columbia and in 1889 Premier of the province. The writer has always liked to think—against other explanations which have appeared in print, some of them absurd—that one of these two gave the name to the great peak at the head waters of the Fraser River, whose conquest forms one of the most romantic stories in mountaineering. Ebenezer Robson's parish extended well up the Fraser, and Professor A. P. Coleman, who made three early attempts on the mountain, was inclined to the view that the heroic missionary work of Ebenezer Robson was commemorated in this manner, as was that of Robert Terrill Rundle in the south by the massif which looks down with lofty disdain on the palatial Banff hotel at its foot.

As the fifties drew to their close, and still greater sacrifices were demanded on the part of the members of Conference if the College were to prosper or even survive, and the extravagance with which the business of the University of Toronto was conducted was increasingly obvious, a rankling sense of injustice could not be restrained. The situation was so ridiculously at variance with the avowed intent of the University Act that it could no longer be tolerated. The whole matter was set forth in a series of nine resolutions spread on the pages of the Conference minutes of 1859. A month after Conference, at the Board meeting of July 5, the following resolution was carried.

That this Board has listened with much interest to the reading of the late University Act and being of opinion that the intentions and spirit of the said Act are not at present carried into effect in the administration of

[16]*Ibid.*, Jan. 12, 1859, signed "J. B." (probably Dr. John Beatty).

University affairs, earnestly requests the Revd. Dr. Ryerson to prepare for publication a series of articles on the subject, for the information of the public and for the vindication of our own educational claims and that the Editor be respectfully requested to publish the same *editorially* in the columns of the *Christian Guardian*.

Thus, Ryerson, and the College, and presently the other colleges of the province, embarked on a contest which was waged with great vigour, even bitterness at times, and with varying fortunes on either side for three full years. In the end the colleges failed to achieve their object, and the victory for the University of Toronto was driven to a point where in 1868 the colleges were completely cut off from state support. But that is the story of the next chapter. Subsequent chapters will reveal how the state has gradually modified a policy of restricting aid to one provincial university with no religious affiliations. So time has had its revenge, and the claims of Victoria and Queen's and Trinity in 1860 have at length been recognized as not without foundation.

VI. OF PRINCIPALITIES AND POWERS
1860-1867

THE agitation of the University question which stirred Canada during the sixties was begun by Victoria College. At a later stage Queen's joined the crusade, and most effectively, under its new principal, the Rev. William Leitch. The support of Trinity College was never whole-hearted; indeed Bishop Strachan in the Synod of 1861 refused to have any part in what he was pleased to call "the present raid."[1] Regiopolis and the Roman Catholics only rarely appeared as more than interested spectators.

The first impulse was given in the series of nine resolutions carried by the Conference at its annual meeting in Hamilton in June, 1859. The resolutions protested "the exclusive application of the Legislative provision for superior education to the endowment of a College"[2] whose non-religious principles were not in harmony with the conscientious convictions of a large proportion, if not a large majority, of the inhabitants of Canada. To these resolutions the *Globe* and the *Leader* took prompt and strong exception. And throughout the whole struggle the Toronto daily press received the consistent support of the Montreal *Witness*, which had already acquired something of the reputation among English-speaking and Protestant Canadians for courage and rigidity of principle which under the Dougalls, father and son, gave it wide influence in Canadian affairs for eighty years. Outside Toronto the press of the province was divided, with considerable, perhaps majority, opinion favouring the colleges. Nelles undertook to reply to the *Globe* and explain the reasons for the Conference resolutions in a series of letters. In one of these, dated Cobourg, July 11, 1859, he summarized the position of Victoria College in these words: "We wish it to be distinctly understood that we are not opposed to the

[1] *C.G.*, July 10, 1861.
[2] V.U.A., Minutes of Conference, 1859, p. 63.

existence of one Provincial University, provided that University be properly constituted and administered. But we are opposed to the narrowing down of that University into one solitary College, and that College one whose basis does not commend itself to the majority of the Christian people of this Province. We are willing that the one secular College should remain and be handsomely endowed to meet the case of those who prefer that kind of Institution."[3]

Such was the beginning of what W. Stewart Wallace describes as the "most determined and dangerous attack"[4] in the history of the University of Toronto. The attack was sustained and formidable, it is true, and it accumulated bitterness as it proceeded, as is the manner of such quarrels; but the ugly terms "raid" and "spoliation" as applied to the demands of the outlying colleges have little justification in fact. The minutes of the Senate of the University of Toronto, John Langton's frank letters to his brother, correspondence in the archives of Victoria and Queen's universities, the proceedings of the Select Committee of the Legislature in 1860, and the report of the Royal Commission of inquiry published in 1862 all combine to prove that there was much justice in the claims of the outlying colleges as against those of what they designated the Toronto College monopoly.

The term "monopoly" was not inappropriate to the position of University College as it developed between 1853 and 1860. In effect the University had become the College. The Act of 1853 had relegated Law and Medicine to private corporations. Divinity was outlawed. Other professional schools were still of the future. The one Arts college had assumed and continued to dispose of the munificent endowment. By 1860, when the issue was joined, its position had been consolidated through the management of the Senate and the support of the Toronto press.

The opening of Trinity College in the western suburbs of the city in 1852 had been at first a severe blow to the state university. A considerable proportion of the students of Upper Canada College, which had been intended as a feeder for the provincial university, preferred the new Church of England college. Indeed, in the year 1853 there was no class to graduate in the University of Toronto, and for several

[3]*D.H.*, XIV, 211.
[4]*A History of the University of Toronto* (Toronto, 1927), p. 78.

years only by counting non-resident students could the statistics show a respectable comparison with Queen's and Victoria. Even the government appeared to have forgotten its child; the new King's College erected at a cost of $55,000, more than that of the Normal School which still does service,[5] was alienated in 1856 for the purpose of what was called the University Lunatic Asylum and the University compelled to find sanctuary, first in the old Parliament buildings, and finally, when the government was moved to Toronto for its biennial term, in the old Medical School.

The reorganization of the University of Toronto under the Act of 1853 had given the heads of each of the affiliating colleges a place on the Senate, which, subject to government oversight, was in control of finances as well as curriculum. But from the outset the business of the Senate was conducted in such a way that the representatives of Victoria and Queen's could not take their full share in its deliberations. The minutes show that Nelles started bravely enough. In the first month after the reorganization, however, there were meetings on thirteen days, in the second month meetings on six days, and the total for the year was thirty-seven. It was plain enough that residents of Toronto were to manage the affairs of the University. The addition of three professors of University College to the Senate in 1856 meant that four members of the teaching staff of that college sat on a body which had a quorum of five. There was little to encourage even occasional attendance from Cobourg or Kingston.

The Chancellor was appointed by the government, but every two years the Vice-Chancellor was elected by the Senate from its members. In practice he became the leader of the Senate, with less dignity but more influence than the Chancellor. Thus when President McCaul was replaced as Vice-Chancellor by John Langton in the election of 1856, the University dispute entered upon a new phase. Langton was a Cambridge man, endowed with energy and a keen mind. Coming to Canada in 1833 he had pioneered in the Lakefield district and been elected to the Legislature for Peterborough. He resigned his seat to become Provincial Auditor in 1855. Experience had given him a

---

[5]Its appearance greatly impressed Daniel Wilson on his arrival in Toronto. He wrote in his diary: "It has a normal school of great extent, and a much handsomer building than those of Edinburgh and Glasgow, and highly ornamental to the town."

humorous if somewhat cynical outlook on life.⁶ As Vice-Chancellor he proceeded to press for a revised curriculum and a new home for University College, being convinced that capital expenditure was the only way to save the university endowment from the College despoilers. "Every stone that goes up in the building," he wrote his brother, "every book that is bought is so much more anchorage and so much less plunder to fight for."⁷ The need of reform within University College, if its appeal was to be widened, he fully admitted. Thus the strictly classical tradition, which McCaul favoured, was mitigated by the lowering of matriculation requirements, the permitting of options, and the offering of honour courses.⁸ In all his policies he relied much on the assistance of Professor Daniel Wilson in the Senate and on that of George Brown of the *Globe* with the public.

Daniel Wilson merits some word of introduction. For thirty years he played a prominent part in the life of the University of Toronto, and during his last five years was its President, adding this office to the presidency of University College, which he had held for the preceding seven. A Scot by birth, he had taken lectures, without graduation, at Edinburgh. Before coming to Canada in 1853 he had acquired some reputation both in literature and in archaeology, and considerable proficiency in etching. He was a clever writer and speaker, with wide interests, but was not in the modern sense a scholar. His title was Professor of History and English, subjects which had still to make a place for themselves in a university. Differences between Wilson and President McCaul soon developed. Langton speaks of the "holy hatred with which he regards McCaul, a hatred most religiously returned."⁹ The result was that he attached himself to Langton and seconded, where he did not initiate, many of the "reforms" which the Vice-Chancellor carried through the Senate.

When the corner stone of the new University College was to be laid—the cost sanctioned by Order-in-Council was $300,000, with $80,000 added for library and museum—there was no public ceremony. Langton and Professors Wilson and Croft were the only wit-

---

⁶See the charming sketch of how the yacht *Calypso* and shillelaghs and refreshments won an election, in his *Early Days in Upper Canada* (Toronto, 1926).
⁷*Ibid.*, p. 297.
⁸William Mulock could graduate in 1860 in Honour Moderns with no Latin or Mathematics after his second year—a revolutionary proceeding.
⁹*Early Days in Upper Canada*, p. 290.

nesses. Two years later at the ceremony accompanying the laying of the coping stone Wilson, turning to Sir Edmund Head, offered this explanation: "We did not then invite Your Excellency to aid us in that work. We rather proceeded in it like the returned captive Jews of old, with the sword in one hand and the trowel in the other. Secretly, as though it had been a deed of shame, we laid that stone; full of hope; yet not without apprehension. Perhaps it was well and wisely that it was so done."[10]

Meanwhile the three colleges which by the Act of 1853 were regarded as affiliated were carrying on as best they could in an isolation that was far from splendid. The severe depression which descended on Canada in 1857 following the end of the Reciprocity Agreement added to their financial difficulties. Already Trinity was in straits. The Medical Faculty had resigned in 1856 and enrolment and fees were "considerably reduced."[11] Victoria's enrolment was maintained, but fees were reduced and subscriptions were hard to come by. The finances of Queen's were more buoyant. Like Victoria, Queen's had an annual grant from the government of $3,000, but in addition could count on $1,440 a year from the General Assembly and $2,000 a year from the avails of the Clergy Reserves. Interest from an endowment fund of $3,200 and fees of $600 made a total revenue of $10,240, a sum sufficient, if not ample, for the six professors, since the then principal, having a church in Quebec, served without charge.

But the lavish expenditure on buildings and scholarships at Toronto was not to be endured. Thus the Queen's authorities and the General Assembly gave ready support to the petition of the Wesleyan Conference in 1859. At the next session of the Legislature a committee of nine was set up to study the question. Nineteen sittings were held during March and April, 1860. Five witnesses appeared on behalf of Victoria, two for Queen's, two for Trinity, and Langton and Wilson replied for Toronto. The proceedings, fifty copies of which were printed for the use of the committee, run to 249 generous pages.[12] While occasionally marred by personalities, they constitute a valuable document in the history of higher education. Several of the witnesses were men of broad

[10]Wallace, *History of the University of Toronto*, p. 75.
[11]*A History of the University of Trinity College, Toronto, 1852-1952* (Toronto, 1952), p. 59.
[12]See *E.R.*, II, 402–20 for a fuller analysis of the proceedings.

culture and experience. Ryerson called upon his wide observation of the systems of the United States, the British Isles, and the Continent. Langton proved himself not only adroit in argument, but also a careful student of current trends in university education. The inquiry went far beyond the exposure of the financial policies of the defendant university in comparison with those of the complainants, and made an exhaustive study of the merits of options at various stages of the new honour system at Toronto, and of certain subjects which were then invading its curriculum. The outlying colleges appeared as champions of a stiff matriculation examination and the standard disciplinary courses in the Classics and Mathematics, with Philosophy and the Natural Sciences added in moderation. The argument on the other side, ably presented by Langton and less ably or objectively by Wilson, was that the University of Toronto was simply applying ideas which were stirring in the universities of the old world, shaking off as they were the shackles of the classical tradition; and that lower standards of entrance (and by inference, of undergraduate studies) were required if the university was not to be "practically closed to the bulk of the people,"[13] as King's College had been.

On the financial side the colleges made good their case against the University, or rather against University College. They would have been justified in laying the blame on the government, which had permitted such extravagant and indeed illegal expenditures, had prudence suggested such a course as desirable before a parliamentary committee on which the present Government was strongly represented. And there was less criticism of the Act of 1853 than of its abuse by the University Senate. Wilson, however, was inclined to excuse the financial policy on the ground that it was invited by the Act, and observed: "At present, it is provided, that if we save any money, it is only that thereby it may pass away for ever from the funds of the institution to which we belong. We are men, and that must be an unwise system to place us under, which provides that the more we economise, the more we lose."[14]

Perhaps the general conscience of the complainants in 1860 was fairly well interpreted in a suggestion—he demurred at calling it a

[13]*Proceedings and Evidence of the Select Committee* (1860), p. 82.
[14]*Ibid.*, p. 17 n.

mature plan—outlined by Dr. John Cook, the Principal of Queen's. He would separate University College, the non-denominational college, from the provincial university, which he would call the University of Upper Canada. Any institution incorporated by Royal Charter or provincial act and employing a staff of not less than five competent professors and admitting students without regard to religious persuasion would be permitted to affiliate with the provincial university, on agreeing to hold its university powers in abeyance and submit to common examinations for degrees. After making liberal allowances to the colleges for libraries and museums, the income from the consolidated fund would be divided, University College receiving not more than twice the sum allowed the other colleges. The Senate would consist of a fixed number, twenty-four, half designated by the affiliating colleges and half by the government, the government appointments not to give the preponderance to any one college or neighbourhood. It is interesting to compare this proposal with the solution actually arrived at in the Federation Act of 1887.

"The next move," says Calvin, "by Victoria and Queen's, late in 1860, was to secure the election of a sympathetic Vice-Chancellor at the University of Toronto, in the person of James Patton, M.L.C."[15] No evidence is adduced in support of this statement, and none is to be found. On the contrary, it is quite clear, from evidence presented elsewhere,[16] that Patton, himself an alumnus, was quite acceptable to the partisans of Toronto in 1860 and even two years later at the time of his re-election, and that it was only after the report of a commission of which he was a member had been published in 1863 that his popularity waned and his loyalty was suspect. Queen's and Victoria had no part in a conspiracy to influence the elections of 1860.

The next important move in fact was a request for the setting up of a commission. When it became evident that the committee could not report, at least in time for any action in 1860, Ryerson wrote to Macdonald on April 20 suggesting the appointment of a commission which might come to Parliament in 1861 with a "measure simple, just, comprehensive and practical, which would secure the approbation of the country generally." After consultation with the parties concerned and

[15]D. D. Calvin, *Queen's University at Kingston, 1841-1941* (Kingston, 1941), p. 70.
[16]See *E.R.*, II, 420–2.

annoying delays—Macdonald's natural tendency to procrastinate was aggravated by the uncertainties of government during the last years of the Union—the Commission was finally gazetted on October 28, 1861. The members named were the Hon. James Patton, the Vice-Chancellor of Toronto, and Dr. Beatty and John Paton, who were members of the boards of Victoria and Queen's, respectively.

Meanwhile the cause of the denominational colleges was much strengthened by the coming to Canada late in 1860 of the new Principal of Queen's, the Rev. William Leitch, D.D. A graduate in Arts and Divinity of Glasgow, he had run a close second to Caird for the chair in Divinity in that university. For eighteen years he had served Monimail Church, Ladybank, Scotland, but had maintained his scholarship and done considerable writing. Wide intellectual interests, a capacity for affairs, the manners of a Christian gentleman, and an unselfish devotion to his work, marked him as in every way destined to be a great university president for Queen's and for Canada. On his arrival he addressed himself to the study of the University question, and was largely responsible for the organizing of a public meeting convened by order of the Mayor in the City Hall at Kingston on March 6, 1861. The *Whig* described it as the most influential meeting of inhabitants that had ever been held in Kingston. The whole room, perhaps the finest civic assembly hall in Canada, then or now, was densely filled. The leading citizens were present in force, including the Venerable Archdeacon Stuart, who in seconding one of the resolutions noted that he had been a teacher in the first grammar school in Kingston; also Dr. Machar, an equally venerable figure in the Church of Scotland. Ryerson and Nelles were present by invitation. The Mayor took the chair at seven o'clock and the speaking continued until after eleven. Leitch moved the first resolution:

That it is desirable that the system of higher education established in Upper Canada be rendered more national in its efforts and results than it has hitherto been, and that these objects can be best obtained by means of collegiate institutions established in different parts of the Province; and that the apportionment of the University endowment should be made so as to grant a fair share of public aid to such Colleges.[17]

[17]*University Reform: Report of the Resolutions adopted at a great Public Meeting of the inhabitants of Kingston, Wednesday Evening, 6th March, 1861, with the speeches delivered on the occasion*, pp. 5–6. Subsequent quotations from speeches made at this meeting are also taken from this report.

His speech in support is an excellent statement of the whole issue, both as to fact and as to principle, all the fresher and more effective as from a newcomer. He begins by a general statement on the development in society of a national and patriotic feeling from the earlier selfish attitude of local aggrandizement. Then he proceeds to a definition of certain terms: "university," "college," "degree," and "student." Using the University of London as an example, he observes that a university needs no imposing buildings; it can conduct its business in an ordinary office. The college, on the other hand, must have buildings and teachers. The natural significance of a B.A. or M.A. degree is not to certify that a man is wiser or more learned than others, but to certify that he has received a college education. The definition of "student" is handled in lighter vein:

According to the natural meaning of the word, a student at a university is one who regularly attends classes during the day, and spends his nights in study. This is by no means the meaning of the word at Toronto. The student may never hear a single lecture, never perform a college exercise. He may be all the year round a store-keeper in some distant town. He has only to put his name in the University books, go through an examination, receive probably a sum of money in hand, called a scholarship, and he ranks as a student. If he is an industrious young man the $30 may be useful in adding to his stock in trade; if he be a fast young man it will aid him in leading a gay life, but there is no obligation whatever to submit to any college attendance or discipline. There is still another novel meaning attached to the word student. Dr. Williamson, as part of the obligation of the college to the Corporation of Kingston, will deliver a short course of lectures on astronomy to the public, and it is to be hoped that hundreds of the people will attend. Now if Queen's College imitate the example of Toronto you will be all returned as occasional students, our Institution will be proved to be in a most flourishing condition! The real test of the state of a University is the number of *bona fide* students going through a regular course of college instruction and proceeding to a degree in one of the faculties, and not the number of *quasi* students which may be exhibited by novel definitions. (p. 9)

The two essential requisites of a national system of higher education, he continues, are, first, one university with a number of colleges, and second, equal religious rights in the endowment and affiliation of these colleges. He notes old world experience: France with its single university and twenty-six affiliated colleges; England studded with colleges, some fifty having affiliated with the University of London; Scotland with its four colleges; and the recent endowment in Ireland of three colleges in different localities. The inconvenience of having only one college in Canada would be very great. Further, a plurality of colleges is essential for healthful competition. If there is room for twenty-six competing colleges in Oxford, surely there is room for three or four within the 200,000 square miles of Upper Canada.

Turning to the second point, he declares that by its whole history and constitution Canada is pledged to religious liberty. If the colleges meet the requirements of secular education, they should not be proscribed for their religion. The state demands that there be no religious tests for admission, for degrees, or for professors in Arts. "Now, if a district college agrees to all this," he observes, "would it not be the worst kind of sectarianism to say—No, you are an Episcopalian, Methodist or Presbyterian; you belong to a denomination, and therefore we cannot accept your services" (p. 12). He continues:

But the public have to do, not with the denomination of the men who offer the article wanted, but with the quality of the article itself. Suppose the government advertised for tenders for government stores, and that the offerers appeared with samples of their goods, would it be just to say to one man: Your flour is certainly of the best quality, but you are an Episcopalian, and we don't want denominational flour; to another, your broad-cloth is unexceptionable, but you are a Methodist, and we don't want denominational broad-cloth. But a third man comes, and being asked his denomination, says that he is Episcopalian and Methodist, Jew and Mahommedan; that all creeds are alike to him; he is pronounced to be the right man, and a liberal, honest fellow. His non-denominational flour and broad-cloth are passed without inspection, and he is told to charge his own price. Every man would condemn such practice as exclusive sectarian dealing. . . . Let the endowment be solely on the ground of doing the work required, and let the same test of efficiency be applied to all. (pp. 17–18)

The whole advantage of a munificent fund—or so much of it as has been saved from wasteful expenditure on "a vast pile of ornamental buildings" and a policy which has cost the country $10,000 for each graduate or $17,200 if the capital is reckoned—has been confined to one college, one-half of whose students belong to the single body of Presbyterians. "He did not find fault with this, he was naturally proud of the sagacity of his countrymen in getting the lion's share and in turning this endowment to the gratuitous education of their ministers while other bodies have to expend large sums for the support of Colleges" (p. 19). But Queen's College is by no means so denominational;

only a fourth of its students (excluding those in Divinity Hall) belong to the Church of Scotland, and the proportion of Roman Catholics at Queen's is four times greater than at University College. In concluding he commends the teaching at Toronto as "the great redeeming feature of the whole matter" (p. 20), and he is sure that the professors would be the ultimate gainers by being placed in a position of fair and honourable rivalry with the other colleges.

After the "loud and continued applause" had subsided, Leitch's resolution was seconded and carried with much cheering. It presages exactly the situation which has been accepted as public policy ninety years later, if "provincial grants" be read for "university endowment." Not only is public aid extended to the three denominational colleges which have entered federation through the free provision of teaching to their students in rather more than half of the Arts work, but five other colleges or universities, two of them denominational, receive substantial grants from the Province of Ontario (for 1952 appropriations totalling $1,500,000 and supplementary appropriations of $1,400,000 on capital account).

Five other resolutions were presented, one by Nelles and the others by prominent citizens of Kingston. Nelles' resolution advocated the maintenance of a uniform and efficient type of university education under an impartially constituted board. In an eloquent speech, which compares favourably with that of Leitch, he pointed out that the people of the province had evinced their preference for denominational colleges; that in spite of the fact that University College had been "nursed in the rich soil of $100,000 a year," and the several denominational colleges were set in "the rugged soil of poverty" (p. 37), these were far stronger and more popular than they had been in 1853. In seconding the resolution, the Archdeacon advocated the diffusion of high literary and scientific education throughout the province. Ryerson had not been asked to move a resolution, but late in the evening was called upon to address the meeting. He responded with a brief and excellent speech. He first congratulated Kingston and Queen's upon the accession to the community and university of a gentleman "noble in sentiment, of high scientific and literary attainments, with largeness of heart, Christian in character, and philanthropic in spirit" (p. 41). His argument centred on the need for a recognition of

"Christianity as the soul of intellectual growth" (p. 43). He contended that state assistance should be distributed to those religious bodies who had provided themselves with proper buildings and teachers, under the same principle as that by which the common school system co-ordinated local effort and government support. He had strong hopes of the future of Upper Canada, but not with a low standard of religious principles or an absence of all religious feeling. "What is the history of a country," he asks, "but the history of the religious denominations of that country?" (p. 44).[18] Furthermore, Ryerson thought it well frankly to meet a point of view often whispered in the Lodges and talked about in homes in which the Montreal *Witness* and the Toronto *Globe* were read.

> It has been said if the state grant aid to denominational Colleges, the Roman Catholics must get a share, or it would be an injustice. I think I may appeal to the history of the past in proof that I am the last man to yield to unjust Roman Catholic pretensions; but I hope I am the last man to do injustice to Roman Catholics or any other class of citizens. If the Roman Catholics do the work done by Protestant Colleges they are entitled to aid as well as others. . . . That, Sir, is the true way to cherish equal rights of all classes, and to respect the true feelings and principles of all classes of the community. (p. 45)

Macdonald, although he represented Kingston in the House, was inclined to evade the issues raised by the meeting. Two weeks later he wrote Ryerson that he scarcely thought it politic to legislate on the University question at present, that they were "on the eve of an Election Contest which may determine the future of Canada—and whether it will be a limited Constitutional Monarchy or a Yankee democracy."[19] Late in May, the elections being called for June, he stated that it was time to appoint a University Commission; he was proposing Patton for one member, and he asked Ryerson to send a good name or a series of names. "The reasons for hurrying the elections are 1st that Brown is hors de combat & the Grits disorganized 2nd unless the elections come off before 12 July, the Orangemen & R.C.'s will be breaking each others heads. At present we have *both* those bodies all right and we

---

[18]It was in 1874 that John Richard Green noted in his preface to the *Short History of the English People* that he was not disposed to let his work sink to the level of a drum and trumpet history; consequently, for example, he would give more space to the Wesleyan revival than to the battle of Cressy.
[19]V.U.A., Macdonald to Egerton Ryerson, March 18, 1861.

only want the Wesleyans to carry Upper Canada. . . ."[20] Before the elections Macdonald let it be known confidentially that he proposed the Hon. James Patton, Dr. John Beatty, and John Paton as the three commissioners and also "£10,000 apiece for Victoria, Queen's and Trinity and a like sum to be divided among the R.C. Seminaries."[21] The correspondence during these months shows clearly enough how the attempt to arrive at a reasonable settlement of the question was impeded, as it was in the end frustrated, by the exigencies of party politics.[22] Voluntaryists like the Baptists were not without an argument.

The Commission, when finally it was appointed, got to work at once and in six months issued a report of 205 pages with an index added. It was a workmanlike document which revealed in sufficient detail the past disposition of the endowment of 226,000 acres including a park of about 150 acres within the city of Toronto, and the present situation of the University finances. The Commission found little to criticize in the handling of investments and records by the Bursar's Office. It was, however, impressed with the Bursar's statement that actually there were "no limits to the demands which the authorities of the University and of University College might make upon him,"[23] and the imperfect control of such expenditures by Orders-in-Council when the seat of government was so far removed from Toronto. It noted for instance that the excess of current expenditures over income in 1859 was $18,569.36, while that of income over expenditures in 1854 (the first year under the Act of 1853) had been $12,148.26. Four items of policy were censured as improvident or extravagant by reason of which the annual income had been reduced by an amount estimated at $39,562 to a sum of about $61,000.

But the Commission was not content to stop at the exposure of extravagant expenditure and certain suggestions for retrenchment. Its members reasoned thus: "So long as the University and University College have no inducements to practise economy, there will, from the nature of things, be large expenditure without corresponding results;

---

[20]V.U.A., Macdonald to Egerton Ryerson, May 29, 1861.
[21]V.U.A., Macdonald to Egerton Ryerson, June 6, 1861.
[22]See *E.R.*, II, 428 ff.
[23]*Report of the Commissioners appointed to enquire into the expenditure of the funds of the University of Toronto, and into the state of its financial affairs, and to enquire into the annual expenditure of the appropriations for University College, and the general state of its financial affairs* . . . (1862), p. 16.

and so long as the other Colleges, having University powers, can see no advantage from affiliation, as is undoubtedly the case under the present system, they will not only decline to unite, but will inevitably continue to occupy a position of rivalry and of remonstrance."[24] Hence the Commissioners determined to seek the opinions of the several colleges on the broader question. Replies to the series of questions submitted were received from the heads of University, Queen's, Victoria, Regiopolis, and Trinity colleges. All agreed that the present provision for affiliation was unsatisfactory. A comparison of the suggestions of remedy offered by the heads of the four denominational colleges is instructive, but McCaul's reply is so extraordinary—in view of what had happened and was to happen—that it cannot be passed over. It is dated March 29, 1862, and consists of one sentence: "In reply to the questions proposed to me by the Commissioners of enquiry relative to one University Board, and different systems of affiliation, I beg to state that I concur in the answers to these questions by the Senate of the University of Toronto."[25]

What had happened was this. McCaul had submitted a report on the questions to the Senate at an unusually full meeting on March 14. Of the twenty-one members present no less than fourteen sponsored one or other of the several resolutions which comprised the Senate's opinion. The minutes do not reveal that there was any difference in point of view. The Senate declared the present system of affiliation unsatisfactory, as practically inoperative. It placed itself on record as favouring one university board to be designated the University of Upper Canada, whose several colleges would adopt a common curriculum, submit themselves to simultaneous examinations, and have the right to confer degrees on students who had passed the prescribed examinations of the University of Upper Canada. As to funds, while University College should have "a first claim to a fixed endowment amply sufficient to its support in its present state of efficiency"[26] and should be permitted to re-establish faculties of Law and Medicine with grants equal to that afforded the other colleges, the other affiliated colleges should receive such funds as the Legislature might see

[24]*Ibid.*, p. 28.
[25]*Ibid.*, p. 157.
[26]*Ibid.*, p. 156.

fit to set apart for them, in three parts, two of these to be distributed equally and one "in proportion to the beneficial results effected." The number of the Senate should be fixed in relation to the number of affiliated colleges: one-third to be heads of the colleges, one-third elected by the graduates of each college, and one-third appointed by the provincial government. It was further suggested that in the new university a Convocation be created, consisting of its graduates, with such other powers as the Legislature might confer and especially that of electing the Chancellor.

Such was the action of the University Senate on March 14, 1862. At length virtual unanimity had been attained among the colleges, so it would seem. A week later Parliament assembled. Two months passed without legislation in the matter. Then on May 20 the defection of Lower Canadian supporters on his Militia Bill forced Macdonald's resignation—just eight days before the Commissioners signed their report. Again the settlement of an ancient dispute, which had never seemed nearer, had been delayed. The issue would depend on the new Government of John Sandfield Macdonald and Louis Victor Sicotte.

In December, 1862, when the election for Vice-Chancellor was pending, the prospect still held hope. Patton's re-election was moved by McCaul and Crooks and was not opposed. Possibly the fact that only eighteen members were present, not twenty-six as two years before, may be regarded as evidence that a contest was not expected. Leitch, however, excusing himself from a Board meeting, did come up from Kingston to vote for one "who has been of so much service in the University question and who may be of great service if elected."[27] The trouble began only when the report of the Commission became available to the public, early in the new year. Other suggestions would not fail to sting, such as that for the exclusion of university professors from the Senate, but one clause struck deeply. It recommended that the annual appropriation of King's College (the old name was to be restored) should not exceed $28,000. Again the *Globe* and *Leader* took the war-path. The undergraduates rallied to the cause. They called an indignation meeting in St. Lawrence Hall on March 5. Crooks as President of the University Association was asked to take the chair.

[27]Queen's University Archives, Leitch to Hamilton, Dec. 17, 1862.

The resolutions, one of which was proposed by young William Mulock, excoriated the report, and the meeting closed with three cheers for the Queen and three groans for the Commissioners.

The Government now began to show its hand. Five new members were named to the Senate, including Dominick Edward Blake, the brilliant son of the former Chancellor. All were known to be hostile to the claims of the denominational colleges. It became clear that the Vice-Chancellor could no longer carry the Senate with him in implementing the report of his Commission, or indeed hold them to the decision of March 14, 1862, to co-operate with the other colleges in a common policy of reform. The circumstances surrounding this tergiversation may be omitted; they have been recounted and documented elsewhere. *Semel satis*.[28]

Any reforms which resulted from the work of the Commission were in the matter of retrenchment. Larger questions of policy were left untouched. All the efforts expended on devising a settlement between 1860 and 1863 appeared in vain. Victoria and Queen's had once more made a definite attempt to work out a provincial system and again had failed. After 1863 their representatives never took their places in the Senate of the University of Toronto. Nor did Ryerson, although an *ex-officio* member as Superintendent of Education till 1876. Indeed here was the one great failure of his life. Leitch's abstention was a matter of resolve, but in any case ill health would have made attendance difficult. His four years at Kingston were further troubled by the necessity of dealing with a long-standing feud between two members of his staff which resulted in the resignation of one and the dismissal of the other, followed by a suit in chancery; and when he died of heart disease on May 9, 1864, the Kingston *News* was thinking of this difficulty at Queen's when it wrote: "That his heart should have been almost broken by finding himself dragged down from all his high sacred endeavors to the petty arena of local and meaningless squabbles is one of the saddest events with which we have ever become acquainted."[29]

The five years after 1863 were comparatively uneventful for Victoria. Disappointed in securing any sort of permanent endowment

[28]*E.R.*, II, 438–46.
[29]Quoted by *C.G.*, May 18, 1864.

from the state for their university, the Methodist people redoubled their own effort. For some years they had been going into debt at the rate of almost $3,000 a year. An heroic measure was adopted: for two years the ministers by Conference resolution authorized a deduction of 1¼ per cent from their gross incomes, and for a third year of 1 per cent. This produced an amount sufficient to cover the annual increment of debt, until the principal ($30,000) could be cleared off. The man mainly responsible for this financing was the Rev. Isaac Brock Aylesworth, M.D. An extraordinary man he was by any count. In the successful practice of medicine he had acquired a competence before heeding a call to the ministry. When assigned this new task by Conference he addressed himself to it with his usual zeal. For three years he travelled the circuits, with assistance towards the end from the Rev. Charles Fish in eastern Ontario and Quebec, and was able finally to secure the whole amount with a sum added for bad subscriptions. At the beginning he had advised, and it had been stipulated, that the first half of the subscriptions should be payable only when the whole had been subscribed, and John Macdonald, already becoming something of a merchant prince in Toronto, had applied a stimulus by agreeing to pay the last thousand. By May, 1867, it could be announced at Conference that the College was free of debt. But of the sacrifices necessary to this end, none could have been so great as those in many a parsonage in meeting the 1¼ per cent assessment.

On the fly sheet of Sir Daniel Wilson's diary the following words appear: "Sir John A. Macdonald's *mot* was the advice 'to put the university endowment into a building—even a Methodist can't steal bricks and mortar.'" Wallace quotes the saying with a charitable dash where "Methodist" stood. Perhaps this is the place to complete the quotation, with the suggestion, however, that it represents less the sober judgment of Macdonald than the accumulated animus of Wilson. And it may not be inopportune to add that another thirty years had to pass and federation be consummated before any supporter opened his purse for the benefit of the University of Toronto. Only then did Edward Blake by his magnificent endowment of matriculation scholarships break the evil tradition of leaving all that sort of thing to the state.

During this same period of five years Victoria extended its field in three directions. In 1860 the addition of a Faculty of Law was first mooted, and the Board minutes of February 15, 1862, tell of the drawing up of a curriculum and the appointment of examiners. In 1863 the first LL.B. degree was granted, to William McCabe of Whitby, with Lewis Wallbridge, Q.C., M.P.P., and Robert A. Harrison, Esq., as examiners. In 1864 William Kerr, M.A., was added as examiner. In that year there were eleven students. By 1867-8, Byron M. Britton, B.A., had replaced Harrison, and the number of students at Cobourg was only six. But a new group from Montreal had attached itself to Victoria. Its staff appeared not as examiners but as professors. There were six of them, including the Hon. A. A. Dorion and C. A. Geoffrion, and their students numbered thirteen. The "Montreal Branch" disappeared from the Calendar after the issue of 1871-2, but the Cobourg faculty was continued until federation. By 1890 the examiners had become ten, and the undergraduates twenty. William Kerr was Dean of the Faculty, three of whose members later became high court judges. Degrees of LL.B. and LL.D. were conferred. To obtain the former four annual examinations after matriculation were required, but a graduate of Arts of three years' standing was eligible. For the LL.D. a period of ten years after the M.A. or LL.B. was required, an examination two years before the degree, and eight months before the degree "a printed thesis, containing at least thirty-two octavo pages on a subject approved by the Examiners which afforded satisfactory evidence of literary and scientific attainments." Among the requirements for the preliminary examination, the classical tradition was represented by the *Commentaries of Gaius*, Books I-IV, and Book IV of the *Annals of Tacitus*, with Aristotle's *Politics* I and II, together with Plato's *Republic* I and II as an option. The fee was $50. Nothing was said of lectures. Apparently the Faculty was mainly, if not exclusively, an examining body, and its students merely "read" law in a lawyer's office.

During the sixties the Faculty of Medicine continued to present candidates for degrees at the rate of about twenty each May, although in 1866 the number reached forty. The College took no responsibility for the payment of salaries, but a considerable part of the Board's time and thought was taken up with composing disputes in the staff. The venerable Dean, Rolph, who in 1863 reached the age of seventy, excelled as a teacher, but was not so successful in handling either his staff or the financial affairs of the institution. Indeed in 1868 the Faculty of Medicine ran into such difficulty that the College waived its right to any part of the examination fees, the regular arrangement being that it received two-thirds while the Faculty retained one-third. In 1866 the medical connections of Victoria University were extended to Montreal. Two representatives of a French School of Medicine in that city, Doctors Peltier and Beaubien, appeared before the Board at Cobourg, and as a result the "Faculty of Medicine of the University of Victoria College in Montreal" was instituted. The same arrangement for fees as at Toronto obtained, and a certain oversight of standards was provided for through visitorial rights accorded representatives of Victoria. The reasons for this connection with French Canada, which persisted to federation, are nowhere explained. They could not have been merely financial, since the fees amounted to only a few hundred dollars a year. Broadly national considerations may have been involved; and it is significant that the advances appear to have come from French Canada. It may be that facilities for practice beyond the Ottawa after Confederation were principally in mind.

Another important advance was made in 1867. For twenty-five years a preparatory course had been conducted as a necessary concomitant of the Arts work. But at length the grammar schools in the province had responded to public demand and in 1865 had been brought fairly into the educational system of the province. The Board of Victoria was now convinced that it could turn over the instruction of non-matriculants to the Cobourg Grammar School. Arrangements were made to merge the Collegiate department with the local school. A certain degree of superintendence of both studies and discipline was retained by the Victoria College faculty, at whose meetings the members of the grammar school staff were assessors. The first staff consisted of Abraham Robert Bain, a Victoria graduate of 1856, as Classical Master, and David Ormiston, a brother of William and a graduate of Toronto, as Mathematical Master.

The life of the College during this period must be discussed briefly. In default of a college publication, other than the Calendar, and of an editor of the *Guardian* who was much interested in such matters, little remains by way of record. Games were doubtless played, religious activities maintained, and social events occasionally held. Of the Literary Association occasional brief news items appear. Nelles himself took John Campbell's place as President, and open meetings were held with debates and public contests for a prize between rival proficients in elocution. In 1862 the Association made a departure which hardened into custom and persisted for fifty-odd years. It held a "conversazione" at which "about four hundred of the elite of the town partook of refreshments furnished by the young gentlemen of the Association, and engaged in pleasant conversation till late in the evening."[30] Late in the evening may have meant eleven o'clock. At all events, that was the time a year later. At this second affair, to the conversation and refreshments of the first party, promenading and a soda fountain and speeches were added. Various innovations were introduced from time to time, such as experiments by the Professor of Chemistry, recitations or musical numbers by local or imported artists; but the constant factors were a popular chairman, an entertainment of some sort, a number of promenades arm in arm to music, and refreshments. Victoria did not become officially light of foot till 1932.

The curriculum remained fairly constant during the sixties. One notable change, however, first appears in the Calendar of 1862-3. Additional courses in each subject were added for honours. But the Toronto system of options was avoided, and honours did not mean specialization. The announcement of the change is made with the following confession of faith to which Victoria in the main adhered until federation:

The Curriculum is constructed on the principle of encouraging a well-balanced and varied culture, and not with the view of stimulating extraordinary proficiency in particular departments. It will be seen in another part of the Calendar that there are a few *prizes* awarded to special excellence, but all candidates for honors are required to pursue the same course, and the estimate of merit will be based on an aggregate of all the subjects of the curriculum, including pass-work as well as honor-work. For pass-men the course is also uniform, with the exception of the two terms in which the option is allowed of French or Mathematics.

Thus all the graduates of Victoria in the sixties had Latin and Greek and some science in all four years, Mathematics in the Freshman and Sophomore years (so the years are named in the Calendar) and

[30]*Ibid.*, May 28, 1862.

Philosophy (Logic, Ethics, and Metaphysics in order) during the Junior and Senior years. Of the modern languages, French appears in all years at first, but by 1866-7 German has taken its place in the Senior year. In 1867-8 Hebrew also appears, as an optional subject, in the Senior year. Lectures in English Literature formed no part of the course until 1868-9, but English Composition was demanded in all four years. Elocution was added for the first two years until 1865, when it disappears. Such was the general scheme of studies, and they were continued throughout two equal terms for a full eight months from the last Thursday in August to the first Wednesday in May. The fees were uniform, $12 a term or $24 a year, whatever studies were pursued. Room and board in the College, washing and lights extra, were provided for $2 a week, and it was announced that the cost for the whole year need not exceed $100. There were no scholarships, merely two medals and three prizes. Gold and silver medals for the best degrees had been endowed from the £200 given the College by the Prince of Wales during his visit to Canada in 1860, and after 1861, three prizes from a gift of $635 by Hodgins—the Ryerson prize in the first year for "the best knowledge of scripture history," and the Webster and Hodgins prizes in the Junior and Senior years respectively for English essays.

The faculty was less constant than the curriculum. It was in this decade that the practice of appointing graduates with training abroad to the permanent staff first developed. When Whitlock resigned in 1864 "for domestic reasons"—so the Board minutes state—to retire to his farm in Iowa (where he died in November), no successor was appointed. His work in Science was divided between Harris and Kingston. This meant a vacancy in Modern Languages, which the Board filled temporarily by the appointment of a Frenchman; but a committee of five was named to seek an occupant for a new chair to be established in Modern Languages and English Literature. The search in this and other cases, as Burwash broadly hints, was restricted for reasons of economy, but finally two years later the Board was able to announce that the Rev. Alfred Henry Reynar, B.A., had been appointed to the chair, with the understanding that he spend twelve or fifteen months in Europe at his own expense to qualify himself more fully for his duties, at a salary of $800 "on his return, i.e. from the commencement of his labors in the college." After Reynar's graduation in 1862 as Silver Medallist, he had served successively as Tutor in Classics and Instructor in French, and had occupied briefly a pastoral charge in Lower Canada. His stay in Germany and France was extended to two years, and a fine natural taste in literature was thus further cultivated. The story is told that when Professor Bell some years later was planning a similar mission to Europe, he went to Professor Bain to inquire about the cost. Bain directed him to Reynar, as more travelled and better acquainted with Germany. Reynar suggested ten dollars a day as a proper amount. Disturbed by such a formidable outlay, Bell reported back to Bain, and was thus consoled: "Don't mind Reynar; he always wants the best, and what's more he gets it." Reynar's aestheticism was exhibited in the fact that when he was asked to address the Alumni at their annual meeting in Convocation week after his first year as professor he chose as his subject, "The Relation of the Beautiful to the Good." Forty years later, although some of his colleagues might have been inclined to hold that he took his duties both as Dean of Arts and as lecturer rather lightly, on the testimony of one of the most brilliant professors in the University of Toronto, a member of University College, his lectures were still outstanding. And who can ever forget his reading of the first canto of *In Memoriam*? He was not without a sense of humour, subtle withal, at times tending to irony. Passages from letters written to Nelles in 1866 will serve to illustrate:

Will you be so good as to let me know your views on the subject [of his staying a second year abroad] as soon as convenient; and at the same time excuse the way I *mix things up* in addressing you, one end of a sentence being directed to the President of the College and the other, directed to one whom I take to be my friend: can you not make both ends meet?

I often feel anxious to know how things are going on at the College. . . . And I pray for the peace of Jerusalem. With the help of imagination in the last word of the wish I say "peace be within thy walls & prosperity within thy palaces."

Give my kindest remembrances to the members of the faculty,—especially to Rector Bain. Tell him to answer my letters immediately, whether he receives them or not.

. . . I add a few things in harmony with the nature of the day. The strict notions of Sabbath observance in which I was brought up still cling to me, and I am grateful for it. I may not be able to defend my views of Sabbath observance from the letter of the law, much less can I enforce them as legally binding on others; but as a matter of spiritual *expediency*, I may say of *necessity*, I must avoid anything like secularizing the sacred hours of this day. I pity the man who has no memories of childhood's sabbaths spent in a godly home, even if it was a humble one. The holy stillness, the brighter sun & balmier air, the extra dressing, after the extra washing of the previous day,—the pleasing awe of the House of God,— the satisfaction in going to Sunday School, and the satisfaction on getting out again,—the comfort of being spoken to by kind, good men & women,— the rest from everyday sport,—the pictures in the huge old family Bible and in other books examined with new interest every Sunday,—the Scripture lessons, catechisms, & collects,—the story-books and stories and singing,—and the little sweet additions to the table,—I would not exchange the pictures which these memories contain for the finest paintings that adorn the galleries of Europe.[31]

In 1866 the Rev. Nathanael Burwash was summoned to the chair of Natural Science, also at $800. He had graduated in 1859 as Valedictorian, the highest honour attainable before the founding of the medals, and after a year as Tutor of Mathematics had entered the active ministry. On his third charge, at Hamilton, he had achieved some notoriety by accompanying the troops as a volunteer chaplain in the Fenian raids and by criticizing the bungling at Ridgeway in the *Guardian* of June 23, 1866. Such boldness did not deter the Board from preferring him for the chair (probably on grounds of economy) to Dr. John Beatty, who was an applicant. The appointment was made on September 26, and Burwash was already at Yale brushing up his science.

Although the Calendar of 1866 does not include his name, but gives Burwash as Professor of Natural Science, Harris remained and taught at Victoria during the greater part of the academic year. After assuming his new position at Beloit, Wisconsin, he returned to Cobourg for Convocation to renew friendships and receive the gift of a silver tea service. Among the references in Nelles' diary to one who was evidently respected as a colleague and friend, the following suggestive entry appears: "Junior class applied for permission to take German instead of Optics. Prof. Kingston gave way, after some discussion. Harris pretty strong, but *restrained*. Said there was no science in England, or

[31]The first three passages are from a letter dated November 8, 1866; the fourth is from a letter dated November 17, 1866.

words to that effect. Kingston 'regretted very much to hear any one say so.'" Harris' loss must have been a severe blow to the College. He was broadly cultured, efficient, and popular. In addition to his other duties, for a time he was Dean of Residence. His cabinets of some four thousand geological specimens were much spoken of, and when he left were purchased by the Board for $800, payment being made by cancelling his $500 subscription towards the debt and an agreement to pay $100 a year for three years, for which subscriptions were invited from alumni and friends. From Beloit after two years he was called to the chair of Chemistry in Amherst College, his *alma mater*, where he remained till retirement.

Certainly Burwash, who admits that his own primary interest was in theology, must have felt himself at a disadvantage in succeeding men of such broad scholarship and wide experience as Whitlock and Harris. But while no estimate of Burwash's work during his seven years as Professor of Natural Science has been preserved, it is safe to say that native intelligence, strength of will, capacity for hard work, and remarkable memory would combine to overcome many of the disadvantages of inadequate preparation. As to memory, on one occasion he told the writer, who had been complaining of the damaging effect on memory of note-taking in lectures, how he had contrived to improve his own even at church. By concentrating on the words of the preacher he eventually acquired the power to reproduce sermons almost exactly on returning home.

The third young graduate to be pressed into service was Abraham Robert Bain. He had taken his degree in 1858. In 1860-1 he appears in the Calendar as English Tutor, and there remains until the affiliation of the Cobourg Grammar School, when he is set down as its Rector and Classical Master. Meanwhile dissatisfaction with Kingston's work had reached a point where members of the Junior and Senior classes laid their complaints before the Board. The result was that Kingston was reduced in rank to an Adjunct or Associate in May, 1867, and a committee was appointed to seek a new professor. A year later Bain was appointed Professor of Mathematics with the understanding that he should spend one or two years in Europe at his own expense. Twenty-five years later, when federation relieved the College of Mathematics, and no berth was found for Bain on the University staff, he again took two years overseas, this time at Oxford, and returned to become Professor of Ancient History. And at the turn of the century, this most versatile of teachers—English, Classics, Mathematics, and Ancient History—was regarded by students as by no means the least effective and admirable of the professors in Classics in the University of Toronto. Further, as College Registrar for many years, he preserved the tradition begun by Wilson (and continued to this day) that the office sits better on the shoulders of a kindly and considerate man.

The qualities of these three men, indigenous to Victoria but with training abroad, were built into the life and work of the College for forty years. After Nelles' death Burwash took the central place, buttressed by his two friends and confidants. It could not be said that he leaned heavily upon them; it was not in his nature to depend greatly on others. Especially was this the case after removal to Toronto. While they did not see eye to eye with him on federation, once the question was settled they worked agreeably under him within the Faculty of Arts in Toronto.

VII. LEFT OUT TO DIE
1867-1880

THE University question, as has been noted, receded into the background during the period immediately preceding Confederation. In the new Dominion education became the concern of the provinces. Sir John A. Macdonald, as Prime Minister, was thus able on July 1, 1867, to transfer a troublesome question, with which he had first become involved twenty years earlier, to the knees of the Ontario Premier, John Sandfield Macdonald. Now Sandfield, or "Sandy," as he was commonly called, was not disposed to procrastinate as John A. had latterly been inclined to do. His Government, to be sure, was a loosely knit coalition—the *Globe* called it a "conspiracy"—and probably lacked a common conscience on the matter. But the Premier himself had two principles which combined to give him a firm opinion. He was a Glengarry Scot, addicted to economy, and he objected to clerical interference in matters of state. In fact, he was the type of Roman Catholic who did not like Separate Schools. Within a few months he had made up his mind, and that of his cabinet. By December 20, 1867, information reached the *Globe* that the grants to the colleges were to be discontinued. And when the estimates were presented in February, a sum one-half greater than usual was set down for the several colleges, accompanied by the explanation that the extra amount was to "lessen the inconvenience," in other words give six months' notice, of the cutting off of the grants.

The estimates precipitated a debate on University policy. The speeches indicated that considerable opposition existed to the system of annual grants, but in taking this position some of the members assumed that subvention would take some other and more permanent form. Indeed, the Rev. Wellington Jeffers, the editor of the *Guardian*, admitted that he himself had never liked annual grants. His failure to press for another and better method, however, was a disappointment to the friends of Victoria and a source of weakness to the cause.

With the rumour of stoppage, Queen's and Victoria had conferred on the matter. On January 14 at Toronto, Nelles and Ryerson met Principal Snodgrass and Dr. John Barclay, the veteran Kirk minister who had come out from Perthshire in 1821. The correspondence indicates that the two colleges were working closely together. On January 30, Ryerson wrote Snodgrass:

The ground I have taken in conversation with Members is, that the Grants should be made this Session as usual, but that voting for them should not be considered as committing the Government or any member on the question itself, which should be considered in the course of the year the same as the Grammar & Common School system, & the future policy of U.C. be decided upon.

Again on February 17, and less hopefully:

I have this moment received yours of the 15th inst. I have not seen any member of the Government, & know nothing more than you do respecting the "stringent" resolution with which it is said the estimates for the Colleges are to be accompanied. Mr. Beatty, one of the Members of the Assembly, called upon me Saturday evening on the subject. He proposed to try & get the Government (and S. Macdonald) to modify the resolution so as to read in the *present form* or until the subject shall have been investigated. In this I concurred but whether he could succeed or not, he felt uncertain, as Sandfield was very obstinate, & seemed determined to try & get the House committed to some expression of opinion against the continuance of the Grants. I have written to the Atty. Genl. very strongly on the subject. I propose to call upon him in the morning. I wish to keep Members, if possible, from committing themselves until the whole subject is thoroughly "ventilated." Whatever you can do in that direction is, I think, very important. It is clear the whole question will have to be fought on the field of public discussion & agitation. It will be necessary for the advocates of Christianity, of right & of liberty to buckle on their armour & by prayer & faith & courage to challenge & meet the enemy in open combat. Had I the vigour of former years, I might do something; but the weight of the contest & its success, must chiefly rest upon younger and more vigorous men. I know of none on whom more dependence can be justly placed than yourself, but all should do what they can.

Nelles on March 18 outlined to Snodgrass what he considered the best tactics:

We deemed it better first of all to confer among ourselves as we agree in all essential points and then we can determine what may be the best attitude to assume toward Trinity, Regiopolis, etc. Not that we wish to ask for any narrow scheme, but because the exclusiveness of Trinity etc. hampers our movements and prejudices our cause. What may be the best way of neutralising this evil and of carrying through a general measure, is the question.

Let us therefore meet as soon as practicable. Would some day after next week do you. Say Wednesday April 1st or Thursday 2nd? We wish to meet at *Toronto* for greater privacy. Anything done in Cobourg, as your arrival etc. would be known to everybody. In Toronto we would be unperceived and could if necessary confer with Trinity College.

Besides I think we should be more likely to secure the attendance of Dr. R. in Toronto.

The conference took place on April 8, 1868, at Elm Street Methodist Church in Toronto.[1] Nelles' diary reads:

April 4
Began to devise scheme for endowment of denominational Colleges. Think I have hit on true plan for meeting two main objections, viz. undue multiplication of feeble colleges and 2nd employment of public funds for ecclesiastical or sectarian uses.

Tuesday, 7.
Left for Toronto to attend meeting of friends of Queen's & Victoria to lay plans for securing endowment. Took tea at Mr. Rose's.

Wednesday, 8.
Com. met at Elm St. at 10 A.M. Present Drs. Ryerson, Green, Snodgrass, Taylor, Prof. McKerras, Dr. Rice, A. A. Lauder, J. H. Dumble, R. Jones, S. S. Nelles. Talked all day about affiliation, etc.[2]

Thursday, 9.
Dr. Ryerson, Snodgrass & self a subcommittee to work up details.
Reported at 3 P.M. Adopted.
Dr. Snodgrass, Barclay & self appointed to see Provost of Trinity. He generally concurred in scheme. Saw Dr. Ryerson. All pleased.

Friday, 10.
Saw Drs. Green & Taylor. Also Dr. Barclay.
Could not see Bishop (Catholic) it being Good Friday—which as Dr. B. said was worse than Sunday.
Home train at 12.37. Arrived at 8 P.M.

The proposal of Snodgrass and Nelles would have set up a provincial university named the University of Ontario and embracing all institutions capable of giving a full collegiate course and willing to come in. The conditions of affiliation were to be: the holding in abeyance of the

[1]Burwash follows Hodgins in the error of placing the conference at Kingston.
[2]Hodgins (*D.H.*, XX, 213) has Senator Donald McDonald and Mr. James Michie also present at the conference.

power to confer degrees in Arts, Law, and Medicine; the adoption of a matriculation and curriculum determined by a Board or Senate on which the contracting colleges and the government would have equal representation under the chairmanship of a Chancellor appointed by the government; the maintenance of a staff of at least five competent professors in Arts over whose appointment the government should possess the power of veto; the submission of annual reports to the government; and the erection, equipment, and maintenance of suitable buildings backed by public securities deposited with the government.[3]

During the summer at Conference and Synod, through petitions and counter-petitions, the question was kept before the public, but with slight impression on the inertia of the Government and the obstinacy of the Premier. When the Legislature met in November and it became apparent that the Government had not devised any substitute for annual grants and was adopting a purely negative attitude, the friends of the outlying colleges in the House determined to force the issue by introducing a resolution. On December 2, 1868, it was moved by M. Clarke of Grenville and seconded by A. Fraser of Northumberland,

> That in the opinion of this House, it is necessary and expedient, in the interest of Collegiate Education, that some comprehensive scheme be devised and adopted for giving effect to the objects, and for extending the operation of the Act 16 Vict., cap. 89, in the establishment of a Provincial University, and the affiliation of Colleges to be supported in connection therewith.[4]

Twelve private members engaged in the debate. The Government did not show its hand, apart from interjections by the irrepressible Provincial Treasurer, the Hon. E. B. Wood, and an expression of satisfaction by the Premier after the vote. The outstanding speech was that by F. W. Cumberland, architect and engineer, then member for Algoma. It must rank as one of the most finished and impressive arguments ever presented in the Ontario House. Blake's effort by comparison was insignificant, but he scored heavily on Cumberland by branding him as the spokesman for Trinity College; its position was particularly vulnerable, since membership in the Church of England

[3]*Ibid.*, XX, 212–15. The original minutes I have not been able to find.
[4]"The College Question," being the debate in *The Legislative Assembly of Ontario on December 2nd, 1868* on "The Outlying Colleges" and "Sectarian Grants," reported by J. K. Edwards, title-page.

was required as a condition of receiving a degree. This imputation Cumberland repudiated, and indeed in his speech he had stipulated as a condition of affiliation of any college that no theological tests should exist. The member for Lincoln, J. C. Rykert, warmly defended the University of Toronto, and throughout a long speech smote the supporters of the claims of denominational colleges hip and thigh, going so far as to include a barbed sentence about "the lobbies . . . crammed with these white-chokered gentlemen."[5] For this he was severely taken to task by J. Coyne of Elgin, who pleaded with the Government not to attempt to evade their responsibility to work out a permanent solution of the question. But his appeal fell on deaf ears. Clarke's handling of the debate, if courteous, was inept; and in the end he withdrew his resolution and accepted an equivocal amendment by Blake which merely affirmed the willingness of the House to consider any good scheme which might be laid before it, while at the same time adhering to the view that denominational colleges should not be supported by the state.

But neither the Government nor any private member was prepared to work out a plan to lay before the Legislature in the form of a bill. The statesmanlike scheme of the conference of April 8 and 9—on which Victoria and Queen's were prepared at the time to agree—thus fell to the ground. The record of the groping in the sixties towards a provincial system broader than one subsidized college at Toronto may be concluded by quoting excerpts from two letters. On December 19, 1868, after a meeting of the Queen's Board, Snodgrass wrote to Nelles,

There is amongst us hardly a dissent from the conviction that it is useless to attempt by agitation or otherwise to obtain a reversal of the determination of the Legislature to give no assistance to any Institution having a denominational character and connection. . . . I fail to see any course upon which the Colleges can now unite, and must therefore proceed in future on the ground that it is the duty of each to set itself in order after its own fashion and with its best endeavours to fulfil its own mission. We have been fighting side by side in the same righteous cause. We shall cherish the same deep sympathies which a common struggle begets in the hearts of Companions in arms, and as we pursue our respective ways the associations of the past will keep alive within us a fraternal interest for the future.

On December 21 Nelles concurred, not without a touch of sadness:

[5]*Ibid.*, p. 49.

Opinion among us will I presume be divided. Our people are numerous and may perhaps by their liberality determine us to go on as before. Unless however their donations should be of unusual magnitude, so as to secure Victoria an *adequate permanent endowment*, it will be of doubtful expediency to attempt any longer to do the work of an *Arts* course.

I have come to your conclusion as to Government. It is I think useless to struggle any more—at least at present. The concessions we should have to make would leave nothing worth contending for. . . .

Be assured I shall cherish very peculiar sympathies toward you and your College from the associations we have had together in this righteous though not successful contest.

For yourself personally I entertain feelings of high regard and shall always be glad to cooperate with you in any enterprise that may invite united action.

It may be asked whether Nathanael Burwash, one of the central figures in the final settlement, played any part in this earlier attempt. He was then in his second year as Professor of Natural Science and was the junior member of the permanent staff. However, his fondness for statistics suggested a study of the occupations of the graduates of Victoria from the beginning, which was included by the Board in a memorial to the Legislature of January, 1868. Its purpose was to show that the work of the College was not narrowly denominational or sectarian, as opponents argued. Of the 108 graduates in Arts only 29 had become Wesleyan ministers, and these during course had paid fees like the other students. Law had taken 22, teaching 20, and medicine 12. Later in the same month, the circulation of a petition among the alumni was undertaken; but on January 31 the following entry appears in Nelles' diary: "Prof. B. reported difficulty in carrying on the petition of alumni. Telegraphed Dr. Potts to give up the matter." Now Burwash on his appointment had at once taken an interest in the Alumni Association and had become an officer. It may perhaps be inferred that he discovered that amongst the alumni there were Reformers who had accepted the voluntaryist doctrines which prevailed in that party and objected to pushing for grants.

Another personality whose influence on the issue may have been greater than was generally recognized must also be mentioned. Late in March, 1868, the Rev. William Morley Punshon, one of the great preachers of the age, arrived in Canada. His coming had been at Ryerson's persuasion, and it was planned to offer him the presidency of the Conference in June. A professorship of Theology at Victoria was also mentioned as a possibility. His remarkable gifts at once gave him wide popularity and influence. It was as if a new planet had appeared in the religious firmament. Among the Methodists there had been nothing comparable since Ryerson's emergence in 1825. And everywhere Punshon stressed the need of an educated ministry and the place of Victoria College in supplying that need. It was not surprising, then, that the *Globe* caught at his plea as a proof that Victoria College was not so broad in its policies as it would have people believe.

The failure of the effort to secure a truly provincial university in 1868 was due to a combination of untoward circumstances. Certain of these have already been suggested. The inertia of the Legislature merely reflected, however, a fairly widespread apathy with respect to university education. When T. Swinarton, member for Cardwell, during the debate in December professed to find Cumberland's argument unintelligible and declared that the honourable member would be better employed in advocating two or three common schools for Algoma, he was speaking the thoughts of a considerable section of the people of the province. Just as Law and Medicine had been driven from the University of Toronto in 1853 as merely training for lucrative professions which could best be paid for by those who were to profit from them, so the claims of Arts were considered by many to be negligible as compared with other needs in a new country. On the part of the friends of University College, including the Free Presbyterians and the Congregationalists, who had Arts training at their command without expense, a lack of interest is readily understood. But the downright hostility of the Premier—and of a large number of members and their constituents—requires further explanation. Possibly those who like to trace such attitudes to schools of thought in other lands might prefer to look across the Atlantic to Hume and Roebuck and thence across the Channel to the philosophers of the French Revolution. But there is no need to go so far afield; in Canada itself there had been cause aplenty for hardening of feeling. The policies advocated, not without success, by Strachan before Union and by de Charbonnel and other ecclesiastics after Union had left a train of bitterness. "Is he a cleric, then he's fond of power," was a pertinent aphorism; and men called a plague on all clerical meddling in matters of state. Even Burwash, who was nothing of a bigot, in dealing with this agitation notes the effect on the popular mind of the fact that the Separate School concessions which were embodied in the British North America Act were carried in the face of an Upper Canadian majority opposed to them.[6] And the province was not disposed to regard with equanimity any movement which looked like a concerted attempt on the part of the churches to dictate to parliament. The dangers appeared to outweigh the advantages of securing the co-operation of the several religious denominations in a comprehensive scheme of higher education.

One further impediment to a solution at this time must be mentioned. Until 1876 there was no Minister of Education in the province, no member of cabinet who devoted his time to working out details of administration. The difficulties inherent in any such proposal as Queen's and Victoria had favoured at their April conference would have imposed a heavy burden on the Attorney-General and the Provincial Treasurer, the ministers most directly concerned. But administration would have been easier had the two colleges alone been involved; it was rendered much more complicated by the extension of the grants to a number of smaller, less well equipped, and more definitely religious foundations. The appropriations for 1867 included $5,000 for Victoria, $5,000 for Queen's, $4,000 for Trinity, $3,000 for Regiopolis, $2,000 for St. Michael's, $1,400 for Ottawa, and $1,000 for L'Assomption; while Albert College under the Episcopal Methodists at Belleville, and St. Jerome, a Roman Catholic college at Waterloo, were asking to be included. All of which gave force to the argument that the grant system was being exploited by the churches to the detriment of university standards. The simplest and easiest solution had been adopted by the Legislature in 1868.

The rebuff from the Legislature had the effect of stimulating the movement for an adequate endowment both at Queen's and at Victoria. Already in November, 1868, a "drive" for $100,000 had been inaugurated in a meeting at Cobourg, where some $13,000 was subscribed. The projected theological department was specifically mentioned in the appeal, indeed emphasized by Punshon, who contributed $750 and promised to make the total $3,000 within two years—a task not too difficult in view of the popularity of his lectures, one of which, for instance, at Clinton, Iowa, netted $1,000. John Macdonald again

[6]The desperate struggle in which Ryerson was compelled to engage in order to keep these concessions to a minimum and ensure the right of the individual parent to determine whether or not his child should attend a common school has been described in *E.R.*, II, 465 ff.

contributed liberally, this time $2,000, and Ryerson from his salary (he had no other resources) $1,000. By February, the total had reached $40,000. Even so, the Victoria effort was outdistanced by that of Queen's, whose constituency, it should be said, had not been so frequently combed. Indeed, a persistent canvass of some four years and the Jackson bequest, of which more hereafter, were required to carry the Victoria campaign past the objective.

In the meantime, penury and the disturbing publicity attending the proceedings in the Legislature combined seriously to affect the enrolment. The number of Bachelors of Arts declined to 7 in 1869 and then to 3 in 1870, but sprang back to 14 in 1871.[7] The loss of Whitlock and Harris and the necessity of filling their places by young men who could be secured for $800 a year must have caused deep concern in the student body. And Kingston was slipping badly. The extent of the dissatisfaction can be realized when Nelles thought it well to permit the Junior class to lay a petition against him before the Board, backed as they were by the Seniors. If the students had known that George Paxton Young had been approached to become his successor and had considered the offer and declined, as we learn from Nelles' diary, the discontent would not have been lessened. Young at that time was acting as high school inspector, and the salary available from Victoria would have little attraction. It is interesting to reflect what changes the association of this remarkable teacher with Victoria rather than with University College might have effected. Kingston finally retired in 1870. The unpleasantness he had with the Board over financial arrangements in connection with a mortgage then held by the College against his house and on which at one time he had paid 10 per cent interest was softened by the presentation at Convocation of a gold-headed ebony cane containing about $125 in sovereigns. One of his old students, the Hon. J. C. Aikins, so Burwash tells us, found him a post at Ottawa. And as the three younger men, with their widely differing excellencies, settled down in the College and the community, tak-

[7]Nelles' diary of November, 1869, contains the following extract: "During early part of this Session some two or three students left for University of Toronto, partly from fear lest our College endowment should not be secured. One has since returned being dissatisfied at Toronto, another also of them has gone to our Medical School at Yorkville. The return of Mr. Dingwall has done much to raise our institution in the estimation of our students." This was Kenneth Dingwall, who became Valedictorian and Punshon prizeman in 1872, entered law, and married Nelles' oldest daughter.

ing to themselves wives—Reynar, a daughter of Punshon; Burwash, Miss Margaret Proctor of Hamilton; and Bain, Miss Martha L. Dumble of Cobourg—the College could look the province in the face in an appeal for students. The serious drawback always encountered in the fact that only rarely did a Methodist home in Toronto send a student to Cobourg was more or less offset by the development of the Cobourg Grammar School as a feeder for the university. The responsibility assumed by the faculty of Victoria for finding suitable homes for Grammar School students and otherwise supervising their conduct added not a little to Nelles' cares.

The reduced number of graduates at the Convocation exercises of 1869 did not prevent carrying through all the regular features, including the conversazione. This was described in the *Guardian* by "an outsider" in a manner which indicates the tug between the more modern ways of life and the puritanism of older Methodism.

Although not remarkably to my taste, or adapted myself to figure very much on such an occasion, I paid my dollar and went to the Conversazione in the evening. I found the great hall crowded with well-dressed (although some of them a little too gaily for *Christians*) and well-behaved people, who walked about and chatted with each other in the best of spirits. I tried to improve the occasion in renewing and extending acquaintances. A gathering of that kind may do very well, once a year, but not oftener, if we mean to keep our General Rules, which prohibit the "singing of those *songs* which do not tend to the knowledge and love of God," to avoid the frivolity in dress and manner disallowed in the same formula, and to escape the imputation of holding a "Methodist ball." But lest I should run into censoriousness, I hasten to subscribe myself, with every sentiment of reverence for the college, *Rusticus*.[8]

Four years later, at the College meeting during Conference, the Rev. J. E. Sanderson said that duty compelled him to raise a question; he was afraid an influence went forth from the conversazione which was damaging to the spirituality of all concerned. He received some support from the floor. Nelles defended the college function, and was supported by Ryerson and Burwash; he said that it was not more objectionable than many evenings spent in basements of churches and in private homes, but added that he would much prefer if it were not held.

In 1870 it became necessary for Rolph to give over the deanship of

[8]*C.G.*, May 19, 1869.

the Medical department. During the previous year the staff had joined in asking for the appointment of an assistant dean, but Rolph at the age of seventy-six had stoutly maintained that he was capable. Matters came to a head the following summer and both he and Dr. Geikie resigned. Dr. William Canniff assumed the deanship, which he held amid increasing difficulties for four years, when the students went over in a body to the Toronto School of Medicine. The Calendar of 1875 carried the following notice: "The Lectures in Victoria Medical School having been discontinued, Students intending to graduate in Victoria University are recommended to attend lectures in the Toronto School of Medicine, from which school certificates will be accepted by this University." The names of the seventeen lecturers and their departments follow, with Dr. W. T. Aikins as President. It was well that Rolph did not live to see the victory of the group who had suddenly deserted him in 1856. In his long and crowded life he had experienced enough of the "slings and arrows of outrageous fortune." He survived his retirement only two months. History has yet to do justice to his remarkable powers and achievements.[9]

Victoria College had been honoured by the selection of its head as President of the Ontario Teachers' Association, and Nelles' presidential address was delivered at the Normal School buildings on August 3, 1869. The subject was homely enough, "The Importance of the Teacher's Calling," and nowhere throughout the address is there a shadow of an impression that he was speaking down to the teachers from the loftier eminence of the professor's lectern. Pithy observations intermingle with deeper religious sentiments. In speaking of the difficulties confronting the teacher he remarks: "While the iniquities of the fathers are visited upon the children, the iniquities of both fathers and children are visited upon the teacher."[10] The wide diffusion of education he regards as "the glory of our age"; also the fact that "the light which once illuminated only the mountain peaks now floods the plains and finds its way into the valleys." Of Christianity, he observes

---

[9]When his son Thomas died in Toronto in 1949, *Saturday Night* carried an editorial in which it was noted that the lives of the two men, father and son, covered a span of 156 years and that twelve instances of like vigour and longevity would carry the race beyond the manger of Bethlehem.
[10]*D.H.*, XXI, 288–94.

that "she alone of all religions demands and creates the schoolmaster, she alone does not fear him when he appears."

The year 1871 witnessed the first definite step towards theological teaching at Victoria—a full thirty years after the provincial act which elevated the Academy into the College. On July 18 the Board decided to appoint a tutor to assist Burwash and Wilson so that they could give "some additional classes more especially adapted to the case of theological students." The Calendar for the year 1871-2 announced a theological course. Nelles was responsible for Ethics, Evidences of Natural and Revealed Religion, and Homiletics; Wilson for Biblical Antiquities and New Testament Exegesis; Burwash for Hebrew, Biblical History, and Theology; Reynar for Rhetoric and Church History. The sum of $100 had been secured by Punshon from H. W. Brethour of Brantford for prizes to theological students, and this was also announced. A year later the course was enlarged into a department, and the Calendar announced a two-year course for such candidates as were "allowed by Conference to spend two years of their probation at College." In addition a full four years' course was advertised leading to the degree of Bachelor of Divinity. Graduates in Arts possessing the required knowledge of Hebrew were admitted to the examination of the third year in this course. It was further announced that while the course was intended more especially for candidates for the Wesleyan and other branches of the Methodist Church, it was open to all who might wish to avail themselves of its advantages. The third and final stage was taken in 1873, when the department was elevated to the rank of a faculty, with Nelles as President and Burwash as Dean. In addition to the four members of the faculty mentioned above, Richard Worral Wilson (son of Professor Wilson) who had graduated in 1871 with the gold medal, is listed as Classical Tutor, and the Rev. James Roy, Principal of Cobourg Collegiate Institute (the new name of the Grammar School adopted in 1871), as Lecturer in Elocution. In establishing the new Faculty, it was stipulated by the Board that the Dean should preside in the absence of the President and that the finances, including the endowment, should be kept separate.

The chair in Theology was endowed by Edward Jackson of Hamilton and his wife, Lydia Ann Sanford. He had made provision in his will for that purpose, but had left the final arrangements to his capable wife; and on her death in 1875 the sum of $30,000 became available to establish a chair in Theology. This was the first of the endowed chairs at Victoria; and as benefactors as well as for other reasons Edward and Lydia Ann Jackson merit some special notice. They were both born at Redding, Conn., he in 1799 and she in 1804, the Sanfords having been Wesleyans before migrating from England, and the Jacksons being Episcopalians. They were married in 1826 and immediately moved westward into Canada, settling first in Ancaster and later in Hamilton, which was in fact a sort of outpost of Ancaster. By 1832 he had prospered in his trade as tinsmith to the extent that he employed five or six young men, who, after the manner of apprentices of the time, lived in his home. In that year Mrs. Jackson was converted at a revival meeting conducted by James Evans, later famous as the inventor of the Cree alphabet. Her husband had been away on business at the time, but on his return he joined her at the altar. For forty years he continued in the way, "not slothful in business, fervent in spirit, serving the Lord." The Methodists were in the habit of noting and recording death-bed scenes, and the account of Edward Jackson's departure shall be given in Burwash's words:

At this time his friends were far from anticipating his speedy decease, but he was ready, and ere they were aware the hour had come. It was a beautiful Sabbath evening in July. The hour of worship was over, and the pastors with a few privileged friends had come to join in praise and prayer with the Lord's prisoner. After words of pleasant greeting, he himself led the way to the parlour, showed each one a seat, opened the piano, and asked Bro. Benson to lead in his favourite hymn, "The power of prayer." They then kneeled together and Bro. Hunter led in prayer. The aged saint was heard responding in fervent "Amens." Mr. Sanford, who was kneeling beside him, looked up, saw his face covered with a radiance of joy, and the next moment caught him in his arms, as the earthly tabernacle fell backwards, and the spirit was gone to the songs of the blest.[11]

It may be assumed that Burwash, who had lived at the Jackson home while stationed in Hamilton, had much to do with securing the bequest.

---

[11]*Canadian Methodist Magazine*, Feb., 1876. "The power of prayer" was one of the least familiar and most doctrinal of Charles Wesley's hymns. Was Jackson's favourite not rather the much-used gospel hymn,
"Sweet hour of prayer, sweet hour of prayer,
That calls me from a world of care"?

There was something about him—his piety, perhaps, and his simplicity of manner and strength of purpose—which inspired the confidence of devout men of wealth, as was later to be revealed, greatly to the advantage of the College.

By a curious coincidence, ostensibly for the purpose of sustaining or even expanding Methodism in Quebec, the Conference of 1872 was asked to sanction the establishment of a second centre of theological teaching. The Hon. James Ferrier had offered to endow a school in Montreal to the extent of $40,000 or $50,000. The announcement took the Conference by surprise, and it was proposed that a decision should be postponed for a year. Nelles, Ryerson, and Burwash took part in the debate, presumably supporting the postponement; but in the end the offer was accepted. A Board of five ministers and five laymen was appointed to take full financial responsibility, and that eloquent preacher, the Rev. George Douglas, was named Principal, not by the Board but on a motion in Conference, made, rather oddly, by Enoch Wood, Nelles' father-in-law. It would appear unfortunate that the two ventures could not have been united. At the farewell tea given him in Toronto in May, 1873, Punshon in the course of a laudatory reference to Victoria College made the rather cryptic remark that its "theological department had been only more rapidly developed by the Montreal movement."[12]

The transfer of Burwash to Theology meant a vacancy in Natural Science. On June 18, 1873, the Rev. B. F. Cocker, Professor of Mental and Moral Philosophy of the University of Michigan, wrote Nelles commending Eugene Haanel for the position in the highest terms. From this letter Nelles learned that Haanel was born near Berlin, had taken his Ph.D. at Breslau, had taught in small American colleges for some ten years, Latin and Greek in one, French and German in another, and finally Natural Sciences at Albion College, of which his wife was a graduate. He was then in Breslau, having returned to make a special study of physics and chemistry. He spoke English "with remarkable distinctness," Cocker stated, and was a fine teacher, able to inspire enthusiasm in his classes and interest in the general public. He had been converted during Cocker's pastorate at Ann Arbor and licensed as a local preacher. He was further described as capable of

[12]*C.G.*, May 28, 1873.

doing more hard work than anyone Cocker had ever known, a man of amazing technical genius and unbounded resources who had made a great deal of the apparatus at Albion with his own hands.[18] Later Nelles arranged through Cocker that Haanel should secure for Victoria from Europe what was described as "the best apparatus that is made in the world."[14] Support for Haanel's candidature was forthcoming from the Chancellor of Syracuse University and from the Board of Education of the Methodist Episcopal Church. The appointment was confirmed on November 20 at a salary of $1,500, and Eugene Haanel moved with his American wife and their three little girls to Cobourg.

His success was immediate. An agitation was soon started for better accommodation for a great teacher and his equipment. Two years later $12,000 was raised in Cobourg for the purpose, and by the Convocation of 1876 sufficient money was in sight to justify the laying of the corner stone of the new Faraday Hall. It stood a little removed from the College and to the east, a curious combination of limestone base and brick top, long pointed windows, steep gables, and a square tower in the centre rising to a cupola for the mounting of a telescope, the gift of friends in England. In an engraving which has been preserved, the Hall stands in the foreground dwarfing the old College to the eye, as indeed it did to the mind of many a student, an attitude by no means discouraged by the professor. The interior design had been of his making. Opposite the main entrance was a lofty lecture room, an amphitheatre in form, seating 122 students and built on special acoustic principles so that every word of the lecturer, as well as every phase of an experiment, could readily be followed by all. The blinds on the nine windows and the gas lights could be raised and lowered without delay from the lecturer's table by a lever and key. Under the tower a portion of the flooring could be removed by a special arrangement so that a massive ball of iron supported by a wire 75 feet long might form a pendulum to illustrate Foucault's experiment and prove the rotation of the earth. The mineralogy room was fitted with sixteen

---

[13]Cocker's enthusiastic commendation was confirmed at Victoria. Chancellor Bowles has described Haanel as the best lecturer he ever knew. Always clear and forcible, at times eloquent and dramatic, he compelled attention; one simply could not forget his words or his experiments.
[14]V.U.A., Cocker to Nelles, Aug. 3, 1873.

tables, each with test-tubes, blow-pipe, and an anvil—everything needed for the analysis of the specimens. The museum was a large, high room. Much of it was taken up with the cases containing the Harris geological collection. Two objects of especial interest were an Egyptian mummy, the gift of Lachlin Taylor, now traveller and lecturer, and the splendid meteorite discovered on the western plains by that intrepid missionary, the Rev. George Macdougall.[15] The former treasure, long an object of marvel and even of horror in the dark third hall of the present College, at length fell a prey to Professor Charles T. Currelly, a graduate of 1899 who became curator of the provincial museum; but the meteorite has resisted all attempts at removal, even that of the youth who, vainly rejoicing in his strength, merely left a scar in the floor.

Haanel's appointment served to raise the salary scale as well as the interest in science at Victoria. It had been necessary to offer him $1,500 in view of an offer made to him by Minnesota. The $800 which had been the original salaries of Reynar, Burwash, and Bain while bachelors, and which was not so absurdly inadequate when $120 could support a student comfortably for a year, had been increased by $200 in 1872. But the precedent of Haanel's case made it necessary to increase all the full professors' salaries to $1,500.

At the Convocation of 1872 Punshon was honoured with the LL.D. degree, and Nelles and Wilson as well. In fact after it became known that Punshon was returning to England in 1873, he received many honours and many indications of regret at his departure. It would appear that the new Premier of Ontario, the Hon. Oliver Mowat, made some move to retain his remarkable talents for Canada. A letter has been preserved from Punshon to John Macdonald of Toronto, dated New York, April 19, 1873. It speaks of a proposal from Mowat through Macdonald so "deeply interesting" that he had "rarely felt anything so flattering." He did not feel justified, however, in altering the course which seemed to be marked out for him. "It will, I think, occur to you on reflection that if there is no other reason, the relation in which I & our Church stand to Victoria College & the apparent disloyalty to its interests which my acceptance of such a position would entail would be fatal to the proposition. Victoria has had to struggle

[15]He was frozen to death in a blizzard. His son, the Rev. John Macdougall, also had a notable career as a missionary. One remembers him a conspicuous and central figure in the saddle at the first Calgary Stampede.

for life for many years, & has been harassed by foes without and foes within—& I could not honourably add to its embarrassment by the breadth of a hair." The question raised by this letter is perhaps insoluble, since Mowat had his correspondence destroyed. Was he preparing to retire McCaul in 1873 and appoint Punshon to the presidency of Toronto? Or was he engaging to secure his election as Vice-Chancellor, the position being vacant owing to the resignation of Crooks, possibly adding Wilson's chair in English, which would be free when he succeeded Ryerson in the Department of Education, as he was at this time hoping to do?[16] In any case loyalty to Victoria prevented acceptance.

The loosening of the purse strings of the friends of Victoria consequent upon the action of the Legislature in 1868 was seen in scholarships as well as in endowment. During the seventies a number of new prizes and scholarships appear, both for matriculation and in course. The Alumni Association was particularly active in pressing its members to assist the College in this way. For a time after graduation three of the years, '71, '72, '75, as groups contributed scholarships of $71, $72, and $75 respectively. But not being endowed these scholarships had all lapsed by the end of the decade. Individual graduates like James Mills and Dr. Hamilton Fisk Biggar of Cleveland were more constant. The former, writing as Principal of the Brantford Collegiate Institute on November 30, 1874, urged upon Nelles the view that scholarships were quite as necessary as endowment, and that without them Victoria could not compete with Toronto. Then in 1873 the sum of $300 in gold was received from the Rev. Edward Wilson of Metuchen, N.J., in "grateful remembrance of attention shown to the late Edward Wilson, student."[17] At first it was directed to a prize in astronomy, which was won in 1874 by William Renwick Riddell, later Mr. Justice Riddell of the Supreme Court of Ontario. The prize was attached to astronomy until the last Convocation in Cobourg in 1892, when it appears as the Edward Wilson Gold Medal in Classics; here it has stood (with slight aberrations) to this day.

In the year 1874 an amendment to the Charter was rendered necessary by a change in Methodist economy from an annual Conference

[16] See *E.R.*, II, 599–600.
[17] V.U.A., Senate, Minutes, May 27, 1873.

which adjourned for the College Annual Meeting to a General Conference meeting every four years and supported by several regional annual conferences. The Victoria University Act of 1874 transferred the authority hitherto residing in this annual meeting to the General Conference, and the members of the Board were now named every four years by this new body.

The reason for the selection of the text on the arch over the main entrance to the present building has sometimes been a subject of inquiry. The idea probably dates from 1874 as the result of the impression made on the mind of Burwash by the Baccalaureate Sermon of that year. Ryerson was the preacher and chose as his text, "The truth shall make you free," making it the basis of an analysis of the interdependence of church and state.

In December, 1874, the first "Bob" party was held in the College. Apparently no account of the affair has survived. Four years later, however, *Acta Victoriana*, founded in that year, speaks of the "Bob" as a well-established institution.[18] Music of a noisy variety relieved by Robert Beare's efforts on the flute, farce of the broadest type at the expense of the freshmen, rustic refreshments, and a Christmas purse to Robert ($26.50 in 1878) were probably constant features from the beginning. The first extant account informs us that "Prof." Robert "was elected to the chair of domestic economy in Victoria University, in 1871," so that he had been janitor three years before someone devised a benefit for him as a means at once of relieving and chastening the respective spirits of sophomores and freshmen. "And now, in conclusion, firstly," the account runs, "I must pay a passing tribute to the other professors of this noble institution: they are all men of sterling worth. They are passing through life, leaving behind them 'footprints on the sands of time'; but I venture to say that not one of them is leaving behind him larger footprints than Prof. Beare (He wears tens)." Certainly few of the professors during Robert's period of almost forty years of service left more lively memories than this stocky little man with his cropped and bristling black hair and beard, gradually grizzled with age, his sparkling wit, and his heart big enough for the whole College in all its parts, ubiquitous, obliging, and as efficient as a multiplicity of calls would permit. The undergraduates liked to

[18] *Acta*, Dec., 1878.

call upon him for a speech, and many happy remarks made on such occasions will remain in the memories of older graduates. This one occurs to me. It was about two o'clock in the morning after a conversazione at Toronto. We were seated at supper in Alumni Hall—the committee and representatives of sister institutions. Robert walked into the room, evidently with something to say. He informed us that he had learned that day from Dr. Potts (Secretary of Education and College Treasurer) that land north of Czar (Charles) Street was being purchased for a campus and ladies' residence. Up to that time the only playing field was in the corner to the northeast of the College where Burwash Hall now stands. A wag among the students, "Curly" Fowler ('02), shot this question at him: "Are they going to have a fence between?" Robert paused, looked solemnly at Fowler, and replied: "No, Mr. Fowler, they're not going to have a fence. They're going to put me there, with one eye on the field and one on the ladies' residence, and [ingratiatingly] when *you* come along, I'll have the eye towards the residence closed."

The next three years were uneventful. In 1875 the gold and silver medals were not awarded, for good and sufficient reasons, no doubt. George C. Workman was the Valedictorian. The following year two gold medals were awarded to candidates who were ranked equal, namely Arthur P. Coleman and James Smith. At this same Convocation the first degree of B.Sc. was conferred, on W. R. Riddell, two years after his graduation in Arts. The Calendar of 1873-4 had carried the curriculum for such a course, four years from matriculation, as "designed to meet the growing necessities of the country, and the growing preferences of our times." The course failed to attract any considerable number of surveyors or other technical scientists for whom it was mainly designed. In fact the total number of Science graduates between 1876 and 1892, when the last degree was conferred, was 21. Among these, however, were two who achieved great distinction— J. B. Tyrrell of 1889 and R. A. Daly of 1892. Curiously enough, the first woman graduate of Victoria was a B.Sc., Miss Nellie C. Greenwood, but she was deprived of the honour of sole priority by an *ad eundem* degree conferred at the same time on Julia F. Haanel, wife of the professor. This was in 1884. Three years later another woman, Miss A. Shenick, also earned the degree in course. But Haanel had no reason to be disappointed in his achievement. If the Science department fell short of expectations, the undergraduates in Arts were deeply impressed by his teaching, as the few who survive today agree in asserting.

In 1874 some of the ablest and most enthusiastic undergraduates formed themselves into a Science Association with limited membership. It was known as the V.P. Society,[19] and was assigned special rooms in the College for its library and meetings. In the end its exclusiveness and the practice of picking out a few promising men in the first and second years to fill up its quota of fifteen resulted in considerable friction among the student body. The feeling was such that a few years ago, when the late Professor A. E. Lang was delineating in a public lecture the Victoria of his day, he did not allow himself to speak of the V.P.; he was still sensitive to the hard feelings which attended his selection to membership in his first year.

In 1875 R. W. Wilson was advanced from Tutor to Adjunct Professor of Classics. Nevertheless he gravitated to law, and his place was taken by a cheerful young man from Syracuse University, Charles M. Moss, who, after suggesting certain changes in the curriculum to suit his preferences, wrote Nelles: "If my usual success does not suddenly desert me, I doubt not all will be pleasant and all pleased." He remained only a year, but, as an article in *Acta* written some thirty years later shows, retained happy memories of the College and of the society in the town. He was succeeded in 1879 by S. C. Smoke, a graduate of Toronto, who as Tutor and Adjunct Professor capably assisted Wilson in Classics until 1882 when he resigned to study law and his place was taken by no less a person and scholar than Andrew James Bell, also a graduate of Toronto. Apart from these changes in Classics the teaching staff of the College proper after 1873 remained unchanged for ten years. The staff of the Collegiate Institute changed frequently and was recruited mainly from recent graduates of the College. Among these were D. C. McHenry ('73); A. P. Coleman ('76), who for four years after graduation taught there, first Classics and then Classics and Science; B. E. McKenzie ('77), later M.D., founder of an orthopaedic hospital on Bloor St., Toronto, and father of two distinguished athletes

[19]The well-guarded mystery of the meaning of these letters may perhaps in this year of grace be published. They simply denote "Victoria Pyramids" and the society pin bore a pyramid.

of the University of Toronto; Edward Odlum ('79), father of General Victor Odlum; and W. S. Ellis (B.Sc. '80), long Principal of the Kingston Collegiate Institute. Miss A. Shenick appears as Preceptress, girls having finally been admitted.

Of student enterprises during the period two must be mentioned briefly and one other at greater length. In 1874 the Jackson Society, named after Edward and Lydia Jackson, was organized and for twenty years was conducted on lines similar to those of the Literary Association founded in 1857. Its membership included mainly men who were pursuing or expecting to pursue theological studies. It had a library and held its meetings at 7.30 on Friday evenings in Jackson Hall at the same time as the older society was meeting in Alumni Hall. The second new society was known as the Natural Science Association, as distinct from the Science Association (V.P.). It was organized in 1878 with R. N. Burns as its first president. It held its meetings on Saturday evenings in rooms assigned it by the College authorities, and was open to any student who was studying at least one scientific subject. It should be noted that the V.P. Society occupied a preferred position in being allotted time for an open meeting on the Monday of Convocation Week. On two of these occasions A. P. Coleman was the lecturer, and on the second, in 1880, took for his subject, "The Physical and Chemical Composition of the Sun." The lecture was illustrated by spectra thrown upon a screen by a battery of thirty cells. "The lecturer was of opinion that the spectra shown had never been exhibited in Canada before."[20]

The third venture of these years was the publication of *Acta Victoriana* in 1878.[21] The publication was as good as its name. From the first issue it undertook to record the "doings" of the College from the students' point of view, a duty faithfully performed until comparatively recent times, when the very laudable ambitions of budding "literati" have largely prevailed to subordinate fact to fantasy. In its "Salutatory," the new journal spoke of itself as the organ of the College societies and the Alumni Association. It did not claim to represent the Faculty or the Board, and at times made critical suggestions to both. "The reasons for our existence are," it stated, "a desire to make the

[20]*C.G.*, May 26, 1880.
[21]The files are complete with the exception of two numbers in the year 1879-80. Repeated efforts have thus far failed to fill the gap.

advantages of our College better known; to open a medium of communication between the Students and ex-Students; to furnish our friends with information upon education matters; to stimulate Students to literary effort; and to obtain an interchange of thought with Students of other Colleges."[22]

The venture was an immediate success. Even today volume I makes interesting reading, and one can well imagine how eagerly the numbers were awaited each month by the students. Its dimensions were eight by twelve inches, with the pages in three columns of solid reading matter; advertisements in those heroic days were kept in their place at front and back. Henry Hough (Valedictorian, '63) printed it in the *World* office at Cobourg. There was a Board of Management of twelve, the first chairman being Robert Whittington, who is described in the "Natural History of the Seniors" as "a worthy Scotchman of 39, but a good Canadian of 10 years standing. . . . Law will probably be his profession . . . wears mutton chops." The editor was Thomas W. Campbell, a man ready for his B.D. in May and ordination in June. During the year he was summoned from College to help the Rev. E. H. Dewart on the *Guardian*. There was an assistant editor in the person of A. P. Coleman, then Classical Master in the Collegiate Institute; also three sub-editors, each with his department. The business manager was a Junior, Clifford Sifton of Selkirk, Manitoba, who was gathering prizes and popularity in College as he was later to do in public life. The subscription was fifty cents a year, a sum in keeping with an annual cost for a year's tuition, board, and incidentals, now stated as not exceeding $150.

Apart from the considerable amount of College news and personalia and the frank discussion of larger college business and policies, three features would impress a reader of the *Acta* of today. Very little verse appears, usually one slight effort in each issue. The first issue carries as its first item a homely piece by "A Student" entitled "A Tale of Lost Friends"—the friends being a bright kindly clock, and a stove which had this fault, that "like some greater folk, he delighted to smoke." In the February issue Lyman C. Smith (Gold Medallist '77) essayed a more ambitious poem on "The Sculptor," very much after the style he still affected a half century later. The second feature is

[22]*Acta*, Oct., 1878, p. 4.

the slight reference to sports. The November issue complains that there is no proper field and advocates the preparing of one north of Faraday Hall. "Some play football and cricket on the race-course, and a few play alley." However, a football club has just been organized and already "there has been some capital play." In November matches were played with Port Hope and Peterborough. The following month a committee urged some action in the matter of a gymnasium. In April, with fair weather, alley was "all the rage." Alley, it should be said, was similar to the hand-ball of today, but was played with a heavy rubber ball about the size of a tennis ball. Nothing else is mentioned in the way of sport. Then again, the frequency of quotations from American exchanges is noteworthy. Apparently the contact with American colleges was much closer than it is today.

Certain other features of student life were developed during this period. A sort of cane, the private property of David Robson (Valedictorian '70), of such dimensions that it might almost have had its origin as a bedpost, was handed down on graduation to his friend of the third year, G. H. Watson, who was to be Valedictorian in 1871; whereupon this uncouth article assumed a fascial significance and was transferred each spring to a Junior selected by his class-mates for the honour. It was defined by *Acta* in 1885, when in the possession of R. P. Bowles, as a "token that the bearer was intellectually, morally, physically and erratically preeminent in virtue and otherwise, especially otherwise." By 1880, when it had rested in such hands as those of George F. Shepley, W. R. Riddell, C. A. Masten, and A. L. Sifton (brother Clifford in the same year had to be satisfied with the gold medal), it had become the custom to hand it over at some College function with speeches. On this occasion *Acta* sharply criticized the speeches of the donor and recipient as in the one case absurdly elaborate and in the other "gushy."

In 1879, after the final Literary Association entertainment, the graduating class was given a farewell supper by the Junior year, "initiating a custom which," said *Acta*, "we hope may long continue." It has continued these seventy odd years, in one form or another. Its donors have shifted from the Juniors to the student body at large, to the Faculty, to the Board of Regents, and now finally to the graduands with some help from the Board.

One institution which was not translated to Toronto had deep significance at Cobourg. Every Saturday evening from five to six a College prayer meeting was held. Less strictly devotional were the weekly meetings of the Jackson Society. In the December *Acta* of 1878 is to be found an excellent account of the second open meeting of that body, with H. T. Crossley (later famous as an evangelist) leading the singing and with a debate on the Class Meeting, that much controverted Methodist institution. It is not surprising then that, when an emissary from Princeton in 1880 introduced the Y.M.C.A., *Acta* should remark: "If that letter C. did not appear in the name of this society we would say that it was a piece of nonsense. There are more societies in connection with the College now than can be attended to."[23]

During the year 1878-9, R. B. Hare ('75) returned from Germany after four years abroad with a Ph.D. degree from Breslau. This was the first of several such degrees sought and won in Europe by Victoria men under Haanel's influence. Later Hare accepted a professorship in the Ontario Agricultural College under James Mills' presidency. *Acta* reports that two students were pursuing graduate studies in Science during 1878-9 at Victoria. It has sometimes been stated, inaccurately, that there was no postgraduate work at Cobourg. It is, however, true that able graduates were encouraged to continue their studies abroad.

At the second General Conference of 1878 two matters affecting the theological work came under consideration. It was decided to affiliate the Wesleyan Theological College of Montreal with Victoria University. The decision, however, does not appear to have had any practical effect. The question was also raised as to whether the Dean of the Faculty of Theology should not be a member of the Board, and a resolution to that effect was carried. When Anson Green died in 1879 and a vacancy was created in the Board, Burwash's name was proposed. A long and interesting discussion ensued in the Board itself, whose right it was to fill the vacancy. Nelles questioned the soundness of the constitutional principle involved in making professors of the University members of the Board[24] and in appointing one to the exclusion of the others. In this view he was supported by Ryerson. The proposal was defeated by a large majority, and Dr. John Potts was

[23]*Ibid.*, Nov., 1880.
[24]Twenty years earlier Nelles had taken the same ground in the case of Dr. Beatty.

chosen instead, not without some grumbling from *Acta* on behalf of the graduates, who were beginning to agitate for representation on the governing body.

After five years an amendment was sought to the Act, and in March, 1879, two significant changes were made in the constitution of the College. Again the Dean of Theology was involved, and the authority of Conference in the matter of theological teaching was asserted. The clause giving the Board power to appoint professors was amended by the addition of these words: "provided that the Dean of the Faculty of Theology shall be nominated by the said Board and appointed by the special committee of said Conference when said conference is not in session." This would appear to have been the first extension of the powers of Conference in college appointments beyond its indirect influence through naming the members of the Board. A second change effected by the Act of 1879 was the provision for representatives on the Senate from the graduates—four in Arts and one in each of Law, Medicine, and Theology.

After ten years of operation without support from the government, how did the College finances stand? *Acta* in its first issue publishes a summary of assets and liabilities, receipts and expenditures for 1877-8. The assets are put at $166,319.28, the liabilities at $21,699.47, and the debt during the year as increased by $346.47. The total expenses were $14,349.36—$10,675.00 was for salaries, $165.95 for repairs; nothing was charged against depreciation. The government grant of $5,000 up till 1868 was now more than offset by $6,134.50 from interest on the endowment fund, $2,509.84 from interest on the theological fund (the separation of the two is to be noted), and a grant of $2,000 from the Educational Society of the Methodist Church. The approximate estimates of the College for 1879-80 as published in the *Acta* of May, 1879, show a surplus of $207.00. But this had been accomplished only by chilling economy, by extraordinary demands on the devotion of the staff, and by the efforts of a college Agent who drummed the province with an importunity which the editors of *Acta* and doubtless many other friends of Victoria regarded as highly objectionable. It was not, however, entirely just to hint, as Goldwin Smith was rash enough to do, that in the case of Victoria and the other outlying colleges solvency was obtained only at the price of standards. The Arts degree at Victoria was a good degree. It could not be otherwise with men who had lived for four years in the presence of Nelles and Wilson, Burwash and Reynar, Bain and Haanel, and in a society so highly and usefully organized as was that of Victoria College in the seventies. But there was pertinence also in Smith's observation, the measure of which must await discussion in the next chapter.

VIII. THE FORGING OF FEDERATION
1873-1892

UNIVERSITY FEDERATION at Toronto has usually been represented as a product of the eighties—the child of this or that brain. Such a view is true to history only in a limited sense. It is a fact that the term "federation" as applied to the University came into use about the middle of that decade. It is true also that at a certain stage in negotiations someone got the idea that the proper division of labour as between the colleges and the University was on the basis of a rigid assignment of areas of instruction to each, and in doing so had hit on the device which distinguishes and has conserved federation at Toronto. It is, however, unjust to the efforts of earlier university statesmen to date the movement from 1880, 1881, or 1883, as has variously been done. For forty years men of vision and goodwill, Ryerson and Liddell, Leitch and Patton, Nelles and Snodgrass, with fickle assistance from successive governments, had been striving for a truly provincial university—something better than had yet been made of the Duke of Portland's munificent grant. And if it appeared in 1868 that utter failure had settled upon all their efforts, that was a superficial view. Only the financial rind had been pierced; the core of ideals remained unimpaired.

It was a resolution, to be sure, not a bill, which had been before Parliament in 1868; and if the actual effect was negative, Blake had sugar-coated his amendment by the assertion that the House was "prepared to give its best consideration to any scheme which [might] be laid before it for the improvement of higher education." But for fifteen years no Government rose to the occasion, neither that of Sandfield Macdonald, nor Blake's own brief administration, nor that of Mowat so long as Crooks was Minister of Education. Private citizens of public spirit were not so remiss. Among them was Goldwin Smith, late Regius

Professor of Modern History at Oxford, who after three years at Cornell had settled in Toronto, presently to marry the widow of William Henry Boulton and become the "sage of the Grange." He was far from satisfied with the university situation in Ontario, and doubtless had discussed it freely at Cobourg with Nelles during his visit in May, 1873, when he gave the Convocation address. Evidently Nelles had planned to give the question some study during his visit to England that summer. Smith sent him this note on the matter on June 23, 1873:

> I hope I may yet have the pleasure of seeing you. But in case I should not, I send you a letter to my great friend, Dr. Robertson of Oxford, the Professor of Physiology, who, if he is at Oxford when you visit it, may be of use to you in your inquiry and who will, I am sure, do anything in his power.
> I do not know what may be possible under existing circumstances; but my own preference would be not for local Colleges of any kind, but for the transfer of so much of the denominational institutions as is really of a University character to Toronto, where they might enjoy the full advantages of a great University, retaining their own religious character. Their heads might very well hold at the same time professorships of the University. The examination is but half the matter, particularly in the case of ordinary students. The great thing is residence & training in a great university. But my idea may be a dream.
> The University of Toronto is, I think, likely to enter on a course which will greatly increase its hold on the attachment of the people.
> I will not think of receiving any payment of expenses for what I assure you was to me an exceedingly pleasant visit.

The course of the University of Toronto referred to was that connected with the application of the graduates for representation, which resulted that year in their being given fifteen representatives on the Senate and the electing of the Chancellor. One of these graduates was William Mulock; and the position he took was that the University must "cease to plough its lonely furrow, must endeavor to establish friendly relations and co-operation with the various other great educational institutions of the Province."[1]

In the October, 1873, issue of the *Canadian Monthly*, under "Current Events," Smith returned to a discussion of university consolidation, begun, as he says, "some time ago." He speaks slightingly of the "so-called University of London," which, he says, was "called into exis-

[1]*The University Act* (an address at the annual banquet of the Ottawa Branch of the Alumni Association on March 21, 1924), p. 8.

tence solely by the obstinate retention of the Tests which excluded Nonconformists from Oxford and Cambridge"; also of two attempts at establishing universities at Durham and in Wales. In the United States he deplores the calamitous dispersion of resources and the equally calamitous prostitution of degrees, and refers to the situation in Ontario as a "similar disaster." Mere affiliation, he asserts, without migration would give something, but it would not give concentration of resources or the needed improvement of instruction. Nelles deprecated this implied criticism of standards in the outlying colleges, and Smith wrote a courteous and somewhat apologetic reply, while continuing to support his theory of consolidation.

The question was raised in the Legislature by Colonel A. T. H. Williams of Port Hope, who called for the appointment of a commission of inquiry into the subject. From another angle, that of the needs of research and instruction in science, the eminent engineer, Casimir S. Czowski, was also pressing for action. And George Munro Grant in his inaugural address as Principal of Queen's in 1877 thought it well to refer to a subject so much in the air. His familiarity with the historical attitude of Queen's may be doubted, but he put himself on record as believing "that Ontario should devote the whole endowment accruing from the lands set apart for university education to one good college, rather than fritter it away on several institutions."[2] (Not that anyone, at this stage, when the income of the provincial university had been so greatly reduced and the need of expansion was so evident, was asking for a division of the endowment.) And in the first issue of *Acta Victoriana* in 1878, the first serious article was one by D. C. McHenry, Principal of the Collegiate Institute, on the subject of university consolidation. At no time, then, in the seventies was the question dead or even dormant.

An envelope has been preserved with the Burwash papers with the notation in his own hand that it contained letters of 1880-1, not sent by advice of Dr. Nelles, which marked the beginning in his own mind of the federation scheme. When the correspondence came to the writer's hand only one letter remained within. It was dated January 28, 1881, addressed to the *Globe* and entitled "University Consolidation."

[2]W. Stewart Wallace, *A History of the University of Toronto* (Toronto, 1927), p. 118.

The letter has significance as indicating the attitude in 1881 of the man who was to play a large part in arriving at a solution and a still larger and more important part in giving it effect between the years 1890 and 1913. It is clear that at this time he had not in contemplation removal to Toronto or a division of the curriculum. Nor was he of a mind to make junior colleges of Victoria and Queen's. But the true solution was still hidden. One can only conjecture Nelles' reason for vetoing publication. He probably felt that it was hardly proper for such a statement to appear over the name of a professor—even if he were Dean of Theology—until the Board (and the President) had decided that it was time to speak, and to such effect. There could not have been anything in the argument with which he would not have agreed, except perhaps an implication of sympathy with the Liberal party.

In the University of Toronto, on the death of Chief Justice Moss an election to the vice-chancellorship became necessary. It was held on January 21, 1881, and the vote was William Mulock 11, Daniel Wilson 4, T. W. Taylor 3. At once Mulock proceeded to give effect to a policy of broadening out. On February 28 a large committee was set up to confer with the authorities of St. Michael's College on affiliation. On March 9 the committee reported, and affiliation was effected. The term appears to have implied two things: the inclusion of a representative of the College on the Senate, in this case Father Vincent; and the acceptance of certain modifications in the curriculum in favour of the College. It was agreed that in Medieval and Modern History, Mental and Moral Science, and Civil Polity no text-books should be prescribed, that the examiners in history should be instructed not "to be guided in determining the value of the answers by any special religious opinions or arguments therein introduced,"[3] and that the examiners in the other studies should judge the candidates "according to the accuracy of thought and expression." For four years St. Michael's stood alone in this affiliated relation. Then by a series of resolutions, Wycliffe College, the Baptist College (later McMaster), and Knox College successively were affiliated. Each of the three thus obtained representation on the Senate, where Principal Caven of Knox had already sat for some years as one of the nominees of the government.

[3]University of Toronto, Senate, Minutes, III, 410.

The curricular privileges accorded them differed from those originally given St. Michael's. By two statutes of the Senate, the last of January 14, 1885, six subjects, Biblical Greek, Biblical Literature, Apologetics, Ethics, Didactics, and Church History were permitted as options in the third and fourth years, and certificates from examiners in the several colleges were accepted in lieu of the regular Arts examinations in the subjects for which they were taken as options. St. Michael's also shared this concession.

Meanwhile, early in 1882 Mulock presented to the Senate his matured plan for expansion involving a wider curriculum, especially in the sciences, an increased staff, and additional funds from the government. In an address at Convocation in June, 1883, this policy was given to the public. Thus the question was brought squarely before the government and the people. Grant of Queen's was not slow to respond. Immediately and emphatically he took the position that the demands of Toronto could not be met by the government with special grants unless at the same time the right of the other universities to similar grants was recognized. The point was driven home in four addresses between October, 1883, and January, 1884. "More than one college is needed. . . . why, then, if public support is to be given, should it be limited to one?"[4] By resolution the Senate of Victoria University on December 20, 1883, also put itself on record as opposing additional grants to Toronto unless the historic claims of other colleges were equally considered. The Provost of Trinity College, the Rev. C. W. E. Body, placed his view, and presumably that of his Corporation, before the province in the *Mail* on December 14, 1883. He comments thus on the admission by Caven that an appeal to the graduates to come to the assistance of the University of Toronto had failed of the desired effect:

The Principal of Knox College somewhat naively continues:—"Whether any change in the constitution of the University would tend to open these springs of liberality is an important question, but hardly germane, perhaps, to the present discussion." Those who have already largely contributed to the support of higher education in the province, and would, if this proposal be carried, be compelled to pay over again to the University of Toronto, will probably think this "important question" most "germane to the discussion." The truth is, this question must be faced and

[4]D. D. Calvin, *Queen's University at Kingston, 1841–1941* (Kingston, 1941), p. 102.

satisfactorily answered before the Parliament of Ontario can be asked to vote for the supplies.

It is vain to contend that the additional endowment of the University by direct taxation is a foregone conclusion from past legislation. The proposal is an absolutely new one, and must be considered upon its own merits.

In the midst of the newspaper controversy produced by the new demands of the Toronto authorities, Mulock wrote a letter to the Hon. John Macdonald. They were political and personal friends, the former representing North York in the Commons, while Macdonald, previously a member of the Lower House, was now in the Senate. The letter discussed the need for some action which would bring the colleges together. Macdonald, who was a member of the Victoria University Board, sent the letter to Nelles, and he, having shown it to Burwash, thought the move of sufficient importance to merit a visit to Kingston and a discussion with Grant. There had already been intermittent correspondence between them on the subject, and Grant was doubtless more familiar with the situation than he had been at his inauguration. By February 2, 1881, he had arrived at a position where he could write Nelles, "While I have no faith in our locals hatching a scheme that you or I would accept, I do not wish to appear before the public as opposing Univ. Consolidation, for I believe a good scheme could be hatched, were our Educational authorities in Toronto wise, generous, & acquainted with the subject." This was the beginning of a series of unofficial conferences, the circle of which was extended to include Trinity and, by Mulock's wish, the four theological colleges as well. For it must be said that in later years, at all events, Mulock never appeared to see how wide was the gulf separating affiliation and true federation, as was indicated in his speeches to the Ottawa alumni in 1924, and again at Victoria University in 1943.[5] It is quite possible that he supposed that the outlying universities at length might have been resigned to settling for something like the status which had been granted under affiliation.

If Nelles was prepared to work with Grant, he was also trying to work with Wilson. He wrote to Wilson, presumably after receiving Macdonald's letter, and combined some comment on the agitation with the season's greetings. Wilson's reply on December 26, 1883, was

[5]E.R., II, 446 n.

friendly enough, but not such as to encourage his inclusion in the proposed planning. "But the young heads," he says, "are so much wiser than the old ones. I must be content to look on, and admire." Nevertheless on February 22, 1884, Nelles called on him in Toronto for a "long confidential discussion," at the conclusion of which Wilson wrote in his diary: "But I think I see my way to confederation on a just and sound basis, if the politicians, including our own Chancellor and Vice-Chancellor, don't sell us for their own party purposes. . . . Dropt a note to-day to the V.C. to let him know that I had a good inkling of what he has been about without telling all I knew."[6]

At the outset Nelles' position was very close to that of Grant. The latter having fully and repeatedly explained his attitude to his own constituency, went to the general public on January 16, 1884, through a letter to the *Globe*. He contended that the first duty of the Legislature, if it dealt with the question at all, was to consider the whole subject of the higher education of the province. "Surely," he added, "the question of how best to unite all who are really interested in our higher education that we may insure its richest and most harmonious development is one that may be discussed on its merits, and with sincere desire to do justly to the interests involved."

Two days later, the subject being in all minds, Nelles took occasion at a "memorial" to the late Dr. Richey to define his position. He noted that the denominational universities were quietly and successfully pursuing their own work without any intention of applying for legislative aid. But the reopening of the question by University College had altered the situation. He would say definitely, however, that Victoria would not be willing to accept aid in the form of an annual grant doled out by the government of the day. It was not this they had sought in 1860, but a faithful administration of the University Act of 1853. They were satisfied to stand on the principle of self-support if others were left to do the same. Then followed a sentence which went further than Grant probably would have gone at any time, reported as follows: "But though they were for maintaining several colleges with suitable freedom and diversity in their internal economy, they were not opposed to the union or federation of those colleges in one common university, or even to the centralization in one place of such colleges as may be

[6]H. H. Langton, *Sir Daniel Wilson* (Toronto, 1929), p. 122.

able to accept this feature." "Much must of course," he added, "depend on the details of the scheme, and this is a case in which the details may be important."[7]

In this spirit Nelles entered upon the series of private talks which led up to a conference called by the Hon. George W. Ross, Minister of Education, for July 24, 1884. From this date the question passed into the hands of the government, and the issue depended mainly on the degree of statesmanship possessed by the Hon. Oliver Mowat, the Premier, and his Minister of Education. On his accession to office in 1872 Mowat at once had evinced his interest in educational problems and his willingness to devote time to their study. Hence those Saturday afternoons spent with Ryerson at the Educational Office.[8] Ross was a man of energy and eloquence. He had been a teacher and inspector of schools, and entered upon his duties as Minister with a feeling that he had a mission. When asked to address Convocation in May, 1884, at Cobourg, in the course of a sparkling address, he professed himself a conservator of energy who believed that where it was possible by union of effort to lessen labour, there ought to be enough statesmanship in Ontario to find a way; and declared that if he "should prove a humble instrument in accomplishing the great task of the unification of our university system he would consider that a work had been done to which any true patriot might willingly devote his life."[9]

Three private conferences attended by representatives of the several colleges and the government were held in 1884. Between the second and third of these, that is between November 21 and December 20, two more restricted meetings were held. These, so we learn from Wilson's diary, were on December 5 and December 12. Those present were Nelles and Burwash, representing Victoria, and Mulock, Wilson, Loudon, and Caven from the Senate of the University of Toronto. Caven may have been regarded as holding a watching brief for the affiliated theological colleges as well. It may perhaps be concluded that this smaller group was convened when it was made apparent on November 21 that general agreement was impossible. Information as to what was discussed is confined to three bits of evidence. With the Nelles papers is preserved a draft of a letter to an undisclosed person in which the suggestion is made that two or three persons should sit

[7]*C.G.*, Jan. 23, 1884.   [8]*E.R.*, II, 602 ff.   [9]*Acta*, May, 1884, p. 11.

down together for a day and look closely into the Toronto curriculum. Then these two entries in Wilson's diary:

Dec. 5. . . . More and more convinced that the scheme is neither more nor less than a revival of the old attempt of the Methodists to lay their hands on the University endowment. There are other Jesuits besides those of Rome.

Dec. 12. Day of weary College affiliation conference. . . . Dined at the Club by invitation of the V.C. with the same gentry; and clipping, shearing, paring once more; got home to bed before one a.m. I wish it were possible to get a decent retiring allowance and be rid of political and clerical tricksters alike. But I must hold on, and hold them off. I did it before; why not now?

There can be little question that it was at this night session on December 12, 1884, that the formula was finally worked out. An earlier suggestion of a horizontal division of subjects, which would have assigned the colleges the minimum work for a degree and left honour courses to the University, was abandoned for a vertical division. The former arrangement would have given the college work an inferior status, which Wilson with his devotion to University College could never have accepted. To Nelles and Burwash the inferiority involved must likewise have appeared objectionable. The actual division, while based on the general distinction between the humanities and the sciences, was not entirely consistent. Although Ethics was made a college subject, Metaphysics was assigned to the University on the strength of Professor George Paxton Young's reputation, although he was then in his late sixties. Again, while Ancient History remained, appropriately enough, with the Ancient Languages in the care of the colleges, Medieval and Modern History were given to the University. Burwash used to say that this was on Wilson's insistence. In any case, at the time History had a very small place in the curriculum. And Italian and Spanish, also minor subjects at that time, were to be taught in the University in the interests of economy. Eight days after this conference, Ross, on behalf of the government, accepted this division of work as the fifteenth and sixteenth of the twenty-two points sent out to the colleges for their acceptance or rejection as a whole at meetings of their several governing bodies to be convened on January 9, 1885.

The meetings of the several governing bodies, considering the labour expended in conference, revealed considerable lack of unanimity. The

Senate of the University of Toronto accepted the proposal without amendment, and University College offered no separate opinion. Victoria and Trinity took a similar position, in general favourable but raising objections to certain features. The theological colleges were generally well disposed but did not favour any division of work which went much beyond the sort of arrangement they already enjoyed under affiliation. Queen's definitely declined acceptance. Burwash, who was closely involved in all the discussions, expresses the opinion that the failure to include financial considerations at an early stage had convinced Grant that the scheme was not for Queen's. But even very generous compensation would scarcely have drawn Queen's away from Kingston in 1885. Not only had new buildings recently been erected on valuable grounds, but the University was adding strength to strength. And Grant had an imperious mind which would never have been happy as second in Rome. Not that Kingston was in any sense an Alpine village. In many respects it was ideal as a site for a university. It stood midway between Montreal and Toronto, and was the gateway of the St. Lawrence whose Thousand Islands held at that time undisputed primacy among Canadian resorts. If the agricultural country immediately surrounding it could promise little in the way of financial support or of students, who could tell what expansion might come to adjacent towns or Kingston itself from the "National Policy" of Kingston's most famous citizen? At any rate Queen's declared for independence.

Opinion in the Victoria Board was by no means unanimous. Already opposition was developing in two directions. Some members were wedded to Cobourg, and others believed the solution was an independent status at Toronto or Hamilton. On this occasion an interim formula was found by Dr. Carman and accepted by a large majority. Carman after graduating in 1855 had been ordained in the Methodist Episcopal Church, of which he had become Bishop. He had been instrumental in establishing in 1857 the Belleville Seminary, afterwards elevated to degree-conferring rank as Albert College, and had become its principal. When union with the Methodist Episcopals was effected in 1884, and the presidency of Conference was divided between two General Superintendents, Carman became one of these. While small of stature, slight, and bespectacled, he had only to speak to reveal his native force. Sonorous eloquence, quick perception, and a fine acquaintance with constitutional procedure combined to make him pre-eminent as a presiding officer. His formula in this case, supervening on a motion and amendment, declared the present memorandum from the Minister of Education to be in harmony with principles long cherished by Victoria and indicated the Board's willingness on educational and patriotic grounds to join in confederation, provided that certain conditions were met. These included equitable compensation for losses incurred in removal, complete equality of all the colleges in the University, and a provision that any transfer of subjects from university to college or *vice versa* should be made only by a three-fourths majority vote in the Senate. With regard to this last *caveat*, Trinity, which made similar and carefully elaborated reservations, was prepared to accept a two-thirds majority.[10]

In view of the division of sentiment in the Board and the possibility that Victoria might be alone in acceptance it was decided to defer a final decision until the General Conference should have considered the matter at its quadrennial meeting in September, 1886. That meant a delay of almost two years. Nelles stated his personal position in a letter to Carman of April 10, 1885, inviting him to the Convocation exercises: "I suppose I must give some sort of address in view of the new official position you have all kindly assigned to me,[11] but if all are short, and we begin promptly, we can make room for a few ringing sentences from you. I hope God will give us all grace to avoid unseemly and pernicious antagonisms. My own views remain unchanged re Federation, *in view of all the circumstances*, but I agree with you that only our General Conference can judiciously (not to say judicially) give the final authoritative utterance on these questions now pending." By the parenthesis, Nelles, who could not resist play with words, is raising the question of the legal status of the Conference, which does not appear to have been analysed at this stage at least.

The Convocation of 1885 was a memorable one. Nelles presided as Chancellor for the first time. The union of all the Methodist bodies, which had reduced Albert College to a preparatory status, had neces-

[10] These reservations were given to the public in the *Mail* of Jan. 19, 1885.
[11] The title of Chancellor (in addition to President) conferred by the Act of 1884.

sitated a new Act. Victoria was named as the one university maintained by the Methodist Church in the province. The constitution of the Board of Regents (as it was now called) was altered. It was to consist of the two Superintendents, one of whom was to preside at its meetings; the Chancellor, who was also to be President of the University; the Vice-Chancellor, elected every two years by the graduates; twelve ministers and twelve laymen chosen by Conference; and seven elected graduates—thirty-five members in all. The new Chancellor at his first Convocation had to confer 104 degrees—20 B.A.'s (including one *ad eundem*), 9 M.A.'s, 4 B.D.'s (including one *ad eundem*), 3 LL.B.'s, 38 M.D.'s and C.M.'s (Toronto), 25 M.D.'s (Montreal), 4 D.D.'s, and one LL.D. (the Hon. Mr. Justice Rose, a B.A. of 1864).

The numbers were impressive, and the quality of the graduating class in Arts high. But the notable thing was Nelles' address. Acutely aware of the hardening of mind in opposition to federation in the case of many friends of the College, especially among the graduates, he attempted to raise their thoughts above lesser things to the great principles at stake. He was not blind to certain practical considerations which if disregarded might defeat the whole. This is made clear, but it is not stressed. In May, 1885, Nelles was prepared to trust the good faith of the government in matters of detail. The address fortunately is preserved in print; generally Nelles was too busy, or too modest, to see to this. But as possibly the finest product of his mature mind, and as necessary for a proper perspective, it must be reproduced here in part, however imperfectly that part may represent the force and symmetry of the whole.

You will, perhaps, expect me to offer today some remarks on the present state of higher education in the Province of Ontario, and especially in relation to our own University. I shall not attempt to argue, in all its bearings, what we are wont to call the University Question. . . . If I have the misfortune to differ from some good friends of our University, they will of course grant that this is not altogether my fault, seeing that they differ as much from me as I do from them. And if I seem to put a little strain upon sentiments and associations which our Alumni naturally cherish, they will remember that no one has more reason than I to feel the force of those associations, and that I would not be likely in any way to disturb them except from an honest regard for the educational interests of the country.

There is always some difficulty in discussing educational questions from the fact that, while few persons study them, every one seems to think that he knows all about them. I notice in our country to-day three or four currents of sentiment, each of which appears to me to set in in the wrong direction. First, there is the unhappy notion of those who disparage the advantages of higher learning, and who as a natural consequence are hostile, or at least apathetic, in regard to all appeals for the necessary funds, whether those appeals be made to the Legislature or to private individuals. There is, secondly, the opinion of some ill-informed people who imagine that a University can be adequately sustained upon twenty-five or thirty thousand dollars a year, and with such an endowment can successfully compete with neighboring Universities having a yearly income of five or six times that amount. Sometimes the difference in endowment is supposed to be made up by ecclesiastic influences—influences desirable enough when they secure to a seat of learning the resources requisite for efficiency, but not very desirable otherwise. Thirdly, there is the mistake of those who would give higher education an unduly practical turn, or what they erroneously consider to be practical, throwing out of doors, or at least far into the back-ground, the ancient languages and literature, with those higher philosophical inquiries, in which the ancients were the pioneers, and are still indispensable guides. And there is, lastly, the error of those who, either as a matter of preference or of expediency, would restrict the work of our national University to what are called secular studies, leaving all religious teaching and discipline to the pulpit and the Sunday-school.

I shall not now discuss these several views in detail. . . . I wish, however, to remark at the outset that the great matter with me is neither federation of colleges, nor removal of Victoria College from the town of Cobourg, but a satisfactory system of higher education for the Province of Ontario, and an honorable and effective relation to that system on the part of the Methodist Church. I desire, for my part, to rise, as far as possible, above both local and sectarian considerations, and to keep in view the great underlying principles which governed our fathers in establishing this seminary of learning, principles of a very broad and patriotic character and which are even more sacred and enduring than either Cobourg and Kingston limestone, or the inviting grounds of a Toronto park.

"At the revival of learning," as some one has said, "Greece arose from the grave with the New Testament in her hands." . . . It is one of the glories of Christianity that it can stand unabashed and unshaken in the presence of all forms of scholarly research, and make them tributary to its progress. . . . Every sect cannot have a genuine University, and the Legislature cannot recognize the claims of one sect over another. . . . We may, therefore, well begin to inquire, and the growing spirit of Christian union enables us to inquire with hopefulness, whether all the Churches of Ontario cannot combine in one national University, and with advantage to the common interests of science and religion. Those who distrust or oppose such a measure seem to me to raise imaginary obstacles, and also to fail in estimating the increasing extent of University work, and the consequent necessity of large endowments, such endowments as we can only secure in this Province by concentrating all our available resources. Such persons seem to forget that, if we keep our Universities poor, we shall have poor Universities in more senses than one. They also forget that in so far as any religious body stands aloof from the national system of education it not only deprives itself of advantages to which it is fairly entitled, but does what it can both to weaken and unchristianize that system. "Let us beware," says Mr. Gladstone, "of a Christianity of isolation."

The extension of University work arises chiefly from the progress of the physical sciences; but we have to remember that the newer sciences, or departments of science, have not rendered obsolete or useless the old academic studies, although they have deprived the latter of the monopoly which they once enjoyed. We have to provide for the ancient as well as the modern. Even the old classical and metaphysical departments are far from being stationary, but involve both new lines and new methods of research. I have no need to set up any special defence of classical studies as against modern science and literature. There is no proper opposition between the two forms of discipline, and no occasion for exalting the one at the expense of the other. . . . And when men tell us that it is better to study nature than literature, as the works of God are nobler than the works of man, we can but use the decisive argument which I once heard employed by Prof. Goldwin Smith, and say in reply, that man is also one of the works of God, and the highest one known to us; and that the study of man requires the study of his language and literature, and, among others, the language and literature of Greece. . . . We may, indeed, deny that Greece fully represents the varied wealth of modern learning, but we cannot deny that Greece gave the first great impulse out of which all modern culture has sprung, and beyond which, in some forms of excellence, no advancement has since been made. "Earth," says Emerson, "still wears the Parthenon as the best gem on her zone." . . .

More and more, and in all departments of learning, men are employing the historical method as an instrument of progress, running backward that they may the better leap forward. Not satisfied with the ordinary records of history, they are turning with growing interest to the obscure relics of pre-historic times, the ruins of ancient cities, and the customs and traditions of savage tribes, seeking everywhere to find the human footprints on the sands of time. . . . Back to Kant is the urgent cry lately set up among modern metaphysicians; back to Plato is a cry equally urgent; if indeed it has ever been possible to get wholly away from either the one or the other. . . . By a diligent study of these grand old masters, with their enduring "majesties of light," we are enabled to counterpoise a narrow materialistic empiricism, which, in an age like ours, inclines to a kind of usurpation in the kingdom of knowledge. The discoveries of natural science seem to reach the masses sooner, and more beneficially, than philosophic speculations; but, sooner or later, they both alike travel down into the hearts and homes of the people, interpenetrating each other for good, and sometimes, as in our day, contending in their encounter for the mastery, like the fresh waters and the salt, where a great river meets the rising tide of the sea. All honor to those teachers of physical science who are doing such wonderful things for the promotion of human comfort, and for what Bacon terms "the relief of man's estate"; but equal honor to those interpreters of the spiritual order, who reveal to us the eternal realities behind the shadows of time; who teach us to remember that man does not live by bread alone, and that Lazarus in his rags feeding upon crumbs may be nearer to God than Dives in his palace, though clothed in fine linen and faring sumptuously every day. But no regard for the old system of academic drill can blind our eyes to the fact that the educational problem and University work have undergone an immense transformation. The physical and so-called practical sciences have come to the front with multiplied claims and attractions that cannot be resisted, and should not be resisted. . . . Every University worthy of the name must not only furnish instruction in what is known of these sciences, but should, if possible, make provision for original investigations. And beyond all these, we must have such subjects as comparative philology and comparative religion, together with the study of what Macaulay calls the most splendid and the most durable of the many glories of England, our own magnificent English literature, now taking a new and well-deserved position in the curriculum of every University. . . .

The ever-enlarging proportions of the modern University call for funds and appliances commensurate with the variety and extent of the work to be done. It may be said that young men at college do not need to cover all this wide field of study, and are in fact not able to do so. This fact rather increases than lessens the difficulty, for it necessitates many special courses of study, and therefore an increased number of teachers, together with a greater variety of buildings, libraries, collections, and other appliances. We may hold different views as to the wisdom of so much specialization, and of making room for such a range of elective and optional work, but the necessity is forced upon us. We cannot prevent the growth of science and literature, even if we would; and as no student can master all subjects within an undergraduate—or even a post-graduate—curriculum, we are compelled to allow a division of labor. . . . And so we must elect and specialize, as the fashion now is, and try not to know everything, but some few things well. I can remember when a Canadian University could venture to issue its calendar with an announcement of a single professor for all the natural sciences, and with a laboratory something similar to an ordinary blacksmith shop, where the professor was his own assistant, and compelled to blow not only his own bellows, but his own trumpet as well. We can hardly be expected to go on in that style now. . . .

The obvious facts of the case, and even the very word University, seem to rebuke us for the appropriation of the name to anything else than a place where all sound means of discipline can be employed, and all forms of knowledge cultivated, with the best facilities of the age. Such a University we need for the Province of Ontario, and assuredly it cannot be said that we have such a University now. . . . Meantime the several Universities which we have are so related to each other, and have inherited such a stubborn old quarrel between opposing systems, that, instead of working as allies, they are rather playing a game of reciprocal obstruction and enfeeblement. The evil has reached a point where it must be met, and the most feasible mode of meeting it is by some plan of consolidation, such as would secure for the country a stronger and worthier University than is possible under the present order of things. Due regard should be paid, and I trust will be paid, by our Legislature to all existing interests, and to the reasonable plea of those who contend for variety, for competition, and for religious instruction, in the work of education. Nor should we forget the immense debt of gratitude due to those religious bodies which provided in earlier days, and which still provide, a liberal education for the youth of the country. But if, with proper consideration for these things, and without doing violence to the great principles on which Victoria College was founded, we can aid in building up a proper national University, and can even help to supply some elements in which we have felt the University of Toronto to be deficient, and can moreover give the Methodist people the full advantages of this improved constitution, then I maintain that no sectarian divisions, no undue regard for local interests, no sentimental attachment to an old order of things for which the occasion has largely passed away; none of these things should induce us to block the way to a great public good by opposing in the Legislature the improvement of a national institution which we profess to uphold, and which, in a new country like ours, will at the very best fall short of the true ideal.

Repeatedly during the past thirty years the authorities of Victoria University and of the Methodist Church have labored to bring about some form of University federation, but thus far without success. The present scheme has valuable features not embraced in any former plan, and seems to open the way, so far at least as Victoria is concerned, to a satisfactory settlement of this long-continued and injurious controversy. If I thought the scheme would be in any degree unfavorable to the great ends for which Victoria University was founded, then I for one would have nothing to do with the measure. But, as accepted by our Board of Regents on the ninth of January last, I find all reasonable security both for intellectual advantages and religious influences, with even greatly enlarged facilities for both the one and the other. . . .

I have not agreed, and I do not now agree, with those who think that the higher education of this country should be purely secular. I plead for a national University. But such a University for a Christian people should somehow employ, both in its lecture-rooms, and in the personal character of its professors, the highest and most effective of all spiritual forces known among men—the power of the Christian faith; otherwise, with all her cold intellectualism, she will stand, like Niobe of old, through her irreverence and despair, at last hardened into stone, and holding, not indeed the New Testament, but "an empty urn within her withered hands." . . . And now the federation of colleges affords an opportunity for the Churches to join hands in giving a more positive Christian character to our higher education, and apparently in the only way in which it can be fully done. Why should we let the opportunity pass? . . . I have tried to forecast the disastrous results to the Methodist Church which some of our friends prophesy from this scheme, and when I have summed them all up, and at the very worst, I can only find the following: First, improved intellectual advantages for all the youth of the country, including of course the youth of the Methodist Church; secondly, the same religious safeguards which we possess at present; thirdly, a wider range of religious influence; fourthly, increased facilities for the theological training of our ministers; and lastly, all of these with a smaller or at least a more productive outlay of money on the part of our Church than is possible under any other arrangement.

It will easily be conceived that I have not arrived at my present convictions without much anxious thought, nor without a sense of personal responsibility as well as of sacrifice of personal feeling. I had the honor of being one of the two students who first matriculated in Victoria University, in the year 1842, and I have had an official relation to the institution since 1850. My life's best energies have been put forth in her venerable halls, and I will bear no part in doing injury or dishonor to the institution. But I am a Canadian as well as a Methodist, and I am a lover of all sound learning; and finding, as I believe, all important interests likely to be promoted by this scheme of academic federation, I am inclined to give it my support. The final acceptance of the scheme on our part must, of course, lie with the General Conference of the Methodist Church; but if the conditions demanded by our Board of Regents be fairly complied with, I shall regard it as a calamity to the country should the measure finally fail of going into effect.[12]

Such was Nelles' attitude, so egregiously misrepresented by the biographers of Grant. "Dr. Nelles," they say, "was an ardent man, of quick, sanguine and perhaps hasty apprehension, of great enthusiasm, and apparently fond of canvassing and influencing others."[13] Only after much study had he finally been convinced that federation was best, if certain necessary conditions were met. Burwash assisted the cause by addressing the alumni in the hope of persuading them that federation was a necessity; he too emphasized the change which modern science had effected in the demands upon the universities, and made this startling claim, that "it was the impetus given by Faraday

[12]*Acta*, May, 1885, pp. 14–19. In the posthumous editing of Burwash's history this address appears (Appendix IV) as of May 13, 1855.
[13]W. L. Grant and F. Hamilton, *Principal Grant* (Toronto, 1904), p. 283.

Hall that moved the entire university work of Ontario off the old lines forever."[14]

The situation gradually deteriorated in following months. On January 27, 1886, Nelles laid the developments before Carman.

The fact is, Dr. Carman, that I see no hope now of a comprehensive scheme of Federation. . . . Now although the absence of Queen's & Trinity would not hurt but perhaps help Victoria, say in regard to attendance, etc., yet their absence from the *Senate* would work greatly to preponderance of the State College in all Senate action. Then again in the division among ourselves, you prefer independence, Dr. S.[utherland] & other strong men more than *prefer*, they will have nothing else. This want of harmony will be very detrimental in any great effort for endowment, buildings, etc. etc., and without a *great* effort no plan will set Victoria where she ought to be.

He is not disposed to blame the Government. He believes Ross and Mowat to be thoroughly sincere in the matter; but they cannot control Trinity or Queen's and, he fears, will give no promise of compensation for losses incident to removal. If as some warm federationists on the Board urge, the Conference should go ahead and hope that the Government will back them up, then the College would be mixed up inevitably with *party* politics. The Conservatives backed by Queen's and Trinity would oppose. Furthermore the measure requires money, and Mowat will want to be very sure of public support before he commits himself to expenditure. Then there is the opposition of Dr. Wilson to some of Victoria's conditions, notably that of the three-fourths vote in the Senate. At any rate, if it is to be Victoria alone, they would need to recast the whole measure. He is pressed in certain quarters to ignore the resolutions of the Board. "As an officer of the University," he says, "put in trust by the Church & the Board I am not disposed to do that, looking on it as a kind of disloyalty, or unwarrantable use of my official position. And I shall do no such thing for the sake of a one-sided and ill-defined measure such as Federation now has become." He ends with a prayer that the Father of lights may guide to a wise conclusion.

At the Board meeting in May, 1886, it was evident that there was a sharp and fairly even division of opinion in that body. Dewart was able to carry a resolution stating that in the judgment of the Board it

[14]Burwash, *History of Victoria College* (Toronto, 1927), p. 531.

was neither wise nor patriotic to reject the scheme because it was not in every particular all that they might desire, and recommending to the favourable consideration of the Conference the entry of Victoria into federation, provided a suitable site and the permanence of the University teaching were assured. But his resolution carried only by a vote of 10 to 9. In other words, Dewart was prepared to accept on faith whatever might be vouchsafed in the matter of equal status of the colleges and representation in the Senate. Nelles' letters to Carman and to J. J. Maclaren ('62) show how disturbed he was by the precipitancy and trustfulness of the editor of the *Guardian* who, to be sure, would not be called upon to administer the scheme. It was with not a little concern that he departed for England as Canadian representative to the British Conference late in the month and left the handling of affairs to Burwash. In a letter of May 27, he specifies seven points on which he is most anxious, and he urges Burwash to keep prominent the fact that more definite assurances from the government are necessary for success in the General Conference, and especially to contend for fixed university subjects, alterable only with the consent of every federating college.

At the Convocation of the University of Toronto on June 9, Chancellor Blake at length pronounced himself favourable to federation even without Queen's or Trinity. "It will be for all concerned," he stated, "to consider any modifications, if any are asked for, in a fair, liberal, yet prudent spirit. . . . No man can possibly, with honesty, accept this plan with destructive intent. . . . I shall heartily rejoice, if by the ultimate success of this plan, we may create both a formal and a substantial relation between the Provincial University and that great denomination, and thus add strength to the cause of higher education. . . ."[15] Blake's plea for fair consideration of modifications and his warning to those who might enter with "destructive intent" may have been due to what he knew or suspected of Wilson's attitude. This Wilson had confided to his diary of April 2, 1886: "Invited to the Ed^n. office to meet the Atty. Gen. and Min. of Ed^n. My concurrence wanted in a proposal to concede everything demanded on behalf of Victoria College. . . . Absolutely refused to concur in any such concessions. Have since written the Atty. Gen. offering to resign, if provided with

[15]*C.G.*, June 16, 1886.

a fair retiring allowance, and so clear the way for some better arrangement on the basis of a new Pres. acceptable to the Methodists." The resignation was not accepted, and it required a full twenty years to eliminate from the constitution of the University certain anomalies which at this time were included by the Government in order to placate the veteran champion of the claims of Toronto, who that year reached the age of seventy.

The increasing mistrust revealed in Nelles' letters through the spring and summer probably arose from some inkling he had as to Mowat's yielding to Wilson's demands. Indeed, in a letter to Maclaren he hinted that he had some grounds for believing that no concessions were to be expected from the Government. And as September and Conference time approached with no response from the Government on the points at issue, he reluctantly concluded that it was not safe for Victoria to surrender independence and degree-conferring powers on such terms as were offered. Burwash, as General Secretary of Education for the Church, had spent the summer trying to raise funds for endowment, and had been disappointed in the results. His judgment too was turning against the proposal. On August 24 Nelles wrote Carman: "Dr. Bh. seems now firm on independent line. So good a man & Dean of Theol. cannot backslide surely." Thus it was that men who had been accustomed to read his letters in support of federation were astonished on the morning of August 31 to read in the *Globe* a long communication signed by Burwash in which, after enumerating and weighing thirteen considerations, he concluded that the cause of religion and education would be best served by maintaining an independent position, at least for the present.

It is doubtful whether in his long and honourable career Burwash on any other occasion erred so greatly in diplomacy. If he hoped to move the Government to action on the points at issue, it was too late for that. No government was likely so directly to seek the favour of a religious assembly. And members of that body were certain to feel that he would have shown greater respect if he had waited a few days and spoken his mind from the floor of Conference rather than through the columns of the secular press. He was promptly reproved. In the same issue the *Globe*, after arguing that he had unduly magnified the difficulties in the way, continued:

The unanswerable arguments of Dr. Nelles, Dr. Burwash, Dr. Dewart and others have convinced the great bulk of the Methodist people that the Federation scheme presents a grand opportunity for the Methodist Church to connect itself more intimately and influentially with the University life of the country. Dr. Nelles and Dr. Burwash make a great mistake if they fancy that the people will fling away their convictions and wheel into line at a signal from any man. . . . Men of intelligence cannot be switched off and on so easily as Dr. B. seems to think.

Dewart in the *Guardian* made this sharp comment:

We are amused at the coolness with which Dr. Burwash appears to take it for granted that he has only to pronounce judgment against the movement, and the friends of College Federation will cheerfully stultify themselves by swallowing their principles, let the whole matter drop, and condemn what they have heretofore approved. . . . All parties will loyally accept the final decision of the General Conference, but not that of any inferior authority.[16]

Frequently in such errors of judgment men have been impelled to act by some petty irritation. Perhaps in this case the incentive was a piece of gossip. He has been particularly pained, Burwash says in the letter, "by the report which seems well founded that a deputation, including the heads of the theological colleges, waited on the Government to protest against our receiving a mere site for an arts college, and that hence the Government feel compelled to make the granting of such a site conditional upon their consent." There was, of course, nothing in the rumour, and it was promptly and indignantly denied. It is barely possible that it may have had some connection with another and not less malicious report that was going the rounds. This was to the effect that the building of University College, about which the theological colleges had clustered, was to be handed over to Victoria. The story was repeated to various persons by Wilson and finally appeared in print in the *University Monthly* of December, 1915. Wallace after careful inquiry was forced to the conclusion that the story "was a figment of Wilson's imagination,"[17] based on a jocular remark by Nelles on a visit to University College. Perhaps a more solid basis is to be found in a communication prepared for Ross by Nelles in 1884, in which he summarized his ideas of the requirements for federation under twelve heads, the fifth of which reads, "University College to have a separate building apart from the present University building, to

[16]*Ibid.*, Sept. 1, 1886.   [17]*History of the University of Toronto*, p. 127.

be under its own Board of Regents, to teach the same secular subjects as the denominational Colleges. . . ." The same point is made in a letter to Mulock, of which a draft is preserved, dated November 28, 1884: "to your fourth question, I would reply that the University work should be carried on in the present main building and the government should provide other suitable accommodation for U.C." One thing is certain. The inclusion of a mere rumour in Burwash's otherwise well-reasoned presentation of the case was not likely to lessen the tension of feeling aggravated by his publishing a letter at this particular time.

The issue which confronted Conference was briefly this: on the physical and financial side, whether the home of the College for a half century—and the claims of Cobourg—were to be scrapped for nothing more than a site in Queen's Park and the assurance of the Government that it would pass a measure which would provide free instruction in rather more than half the subjects of the curriculum, together with library, museum, and laboratory facilities, not necessarily without fees; on the educational side whether a unified, if somewhat restricted, course of studies conducted with intimate relations between staff and students together with a vigorous college life was to be exchanged for such advantages as might accrue from wider facilities in new fields of investigation, backed as they were by the resources of the state; and as affecting persons, whether a loyal and efficient staff would be asked to break up their homes and take their places as a minority group to work beside a state college whose head was known to be less than cordial to the experiment, amid theological colleges out of sympathy with the whole principle, and with no assurance that any provision would be made for those of their members who were teaching branches which were to be severed from college control. It was a difficult choice. Would so great faith be found in Israel?

The contest was joined on September 7, 1886, at the Metropolitan Church, Toronto, and the General Conference was locked for four days in a tremendous debate which was reported fully—largely *verbatim*—by the daily press and the *Guardian*. The protagonists were Doctors Dewart and Sutherland. Sutherland, who led off, spoke for an hour and three quarters. Dewart's speech must have been fully as long. On the whole his argument was more impressive, being less marred by the captious and the clever. He concluded amid "long continued applause" with the statement that the great central point was whether "they should shut out their young men from the advantages which the State has provided for them, whether they should tax their laity twice to pay for the same thing, whether they should rise above narrowness and sectionalism, and take their full share in moulding the character and life of the country in the chief educational centre."

Nelles and Burwash both spoke, the latter in a manner so judicial that few could have told how he was likely to vote. Nelles was hardly at his best; his sensitive soul had been deeply wounded by suggestions that he had shown the white feather, and this may have impaired an eloquence in any case scarcely forensic; but he made it plain that, however favourable he had been and still was to federation, he was not prepared to accept "such an unguarded, ill-secured scheme as the one before them."

The importance of the debate was shown by the presence of distinguished visitors. The Prime Minister, the Premier of the Province, the Minister of Education, the Chancellor and the Vice-Chancellor of the University of Toronto all were interested listeners at one or more of the sessions. When Sir John A. Macdonald was conducted to the platform by Dewart, he provoked much laughter by observing that he hoped they would not consider it a case of Saul among the prophets. In his brief remarks he spoke of his early connection with this "all-important question." Mowat and Ross were content to be spectators. Blake, however, made quite a speech, and said enough to show his concern for the success of any plan they would enter upon, and his sympathy "with the way Professor Burwash spoke of the responsibility to be laid on the shoulders of Dr. Nelles." His remarks were very warmly received. Mulock said that if anything was to come out of the scheme it must be "the outcome of mutual confidence."

The Hon. John Macdonald, who was a delegate, spoke the language of a business man, and may well have been responsible for turning votes. He created laughter and applause and murmurs of dissent by criticizing the financial policies of Victoria as "attempting to drive a wholesale business on the amount of capital that would be required for a small peanut concern." He effectively met the argument of the perils of a great city for students, and concluded by pledging $25,000 to the

JAMES RICHARDSON
(1791-1875)

ANSON GREEN
(1801-1879)

THOMAS WHITEHEAD
(1762-1846)

JOHN RYERSON
(1800-1878)

WILLIAM RYERSON
(1797-1872)

FIVE FOUNDERS

UPPER CANADA ACADEMY AND VICTORIA COLLEGE
(erected 1832-6)

MATTHEW RICHEY
Principal 1836-1840

EGERTON RYERSON
Principal 1840-1848
President 1850-1854

SAMUEL SOBIESKI NELLES
Principal 1850-1854
President 1854-1884
President and Chancellor
1884-1887

THE COLLEGE AT COBOURG, AND ITS HEADS

FARADAY HALL
(erected 1876-7)

| Eugene Emil Felix Richard Haanel (1841-1927) | Abraham Robert Bain (1838-1908) | Arthur Philemon Coleman (1852-1939) |

FARADAY HALL AND SCIENCE PROFESSORS

OLIVER SPRINGER
B.A. 1845, M.A. 1849

WILLIAM HENRY BROUSE
M.A. 1849

MOSES HENRY AIKINS
B.A. 1855

NELLIE CORA GREENWOOD
(Mrs. W. W. Andrews)
B.SC. 1884

AUGUSTA STOWE
(Mrs. Gullen)
M.D. 1883

MARGARET ELEANOR
THEODORA ADDISON
B.A. 1889

SIX EARLY GRADUATES

THE LIBRARY
Erected 1910. The first of the collegiate Gothic buildings in Credit Valley grey stone to be erected on the University of Toronto campus.

BURWASH HALL
(erected 1913)

CHESTER DANIEL MASSEY
(1850-1926)

RT. HON. VINCENT MASSEY, C.H.
(1887-   )

Opera enim illorum sequuntur illos

THE REUNION OF 1919

The group which gathered after the First World War for the great reunion of 1919. The following persons mentioned in the text may be identified: *centre*, Mr. Justice Maclaren (Vice-Chancellor); *to his left*, Dr. Bowles, Major MacDowell, v.c.; *behind him*, Dr. George Locke, Lt.-Col. Vincent Massey, Professor Lane. *Second to right of Dr. Maclaren*, Dr. J. W. Graham, *and behind him* Professor Greaves, Professor Michael, and Capt. G. M. Smith. *Front row to left*, Professors Robertson, Horning, and Potter (*end*), *and to right*, Professors Johnston and Macmillan (*second from end*). Leopold Macaulay stands behind Professor Robertson's right shoulder.

Andrew James Bell　　Lewis Emerson Horning
(1856–1932)　　　　(1858–1925)

John Charles Robertson　Augustus Edward Lang　Oscar Pelham Edgar
(1864–　　)　　　　　(1862–1945)　　　　(1871–1948)

FIVE SENIOR ARTS PROFESSORS OF 1913

WYMILWOOD, 1926–1952

GATE HOUSE FROM ST. MARY STREET

FRANCIS HUSTON WALLACE
Dean of Theology
1900–1921

ALFRED GANDIER
Principal of Union and
Emmanuel Colleges
1925–1932

JOHN FLETCHER
MCLAUGHLIN
Dean of Theology
1921–1928

RICHARD DAVIDSON
Principal of Emmanuel
College
1932–1943

FREDERICK WILLIAM
LANGFORD
Dean of Emmanuel College
1944–1945

DEANS AND PRINCIPALS OF THE THEOLOGICAL FACULTY
AND OF EMMANUEL COLLEGE

VICTORIA COLLEGE
(erected 1891–2)

EMMANUEL COLLEGE
(erected 1931–2)

NATHANAEL BURWASH RICHARD PINCH BOWLES EDWARD WILSON WALLACE
1887–1913 1913–1930 1930–1941

WALTER THEODORE ARTHUR BRUCE BARBOUR
BROWN MOORE
1941–1949 1950–

PRESIDENTS AT TORONTO

VICTORIA COLLEGE COUNCIL, 1952-1953

Principal H. Bennett (presiding), J. R. Grant (Secretary). *Reading clockwise round the table*: J. A. Surerus, H. G. Robertson, J. Macpherson, K. J. Joblin, D. P. de Montmollin, Miss L. Rièse, F. A. Hare, W. E. Staples, A. C. M. Ross, Miss M. V. Ray, Miss A. L. Cook, Miss J. Macpherson, C. V. McLean, J. D. Robins, R. K. Arnold, E. J. Pratt, K. MacLean, J. S. Wood, H. N. Frye, President A. B. B. Moore. *Standing left to right*: K. O. Kee, C. W. Leslie, D. O. Robson, J. A. Irving, Miss K. H. Coburn, G. W. Field, G. L. Keyes, C. C. Love, G. N. Laidlaw, W. H. Trethewey, D. J. Knight. *Absent*: Miss R. I. Jenking.

EMMANUEL COLLEGE COUNCIL, 1952-1953

Standing: Prof. George Johnston, Prof. F. A. Hare (Registrar), Prof. J. R. Guthrie, Prof. K. J. Joblin, Rev. A. Organ, Rev. C. E. J. Cragg, Prof. C. W. Leslie, Prof. G. A. McMullen, Rev. R. E. Spencer. *Sitting*: Rev. T. T. Faichney, Prof. C. V. McLean, President A. B. B. Moore, Principal A. D. Matheson (presiding), Prof. W. O. Fennell (Clerk), Prof. K. H. Cousland (Secretary), Miss M. V. Ray.

MULOCK CUP WINNING TEAM, 1923

The third in order of sixteen Mulock Cup winning teams. *Top*: R. B. Cowan (Manager), L. B. Pearson (Coach), Chancellor R. P. Bowles, W. J. Little (Hon. Pres. V.C.A.U.), "Parks" Whitebread (Trainer). *Bottom*: H. A. Hollinrake, H. M. Crosby, J. E. W. Sterling, J. E. Graham, F. S. Daly, L. P. Emerson, A. F. Hollinrake, W. S. Lane, R. H. Turnbull, G. M. Bastedo, Ralph S. Mills (Captain), W. L. Woods, R. F. Chisholm, J. H. Bales, W. M. Graham, A. S. H. Hill, A. B. Baker, K. P. Watson, E. Ferguson, F. E. Hudson, W. R. Brunt, H. A. Saywell, I. W. Mix.

THE JENNINGS CUP WINNING TEAM, 1938–1939

The twelfth in order of thirteen teams to win the Cup. *Top*: W. D. Johnston, J. F. Moeser, "Parks" Whitebread, Dr. A. A. Brant (Coach), Prof. H. E. Ford (Hon. Pres.), Rev. W. J. Little, J. A. Dean. *Middle*: W. O. Fennell, W. R. Wilson, E. S. Smith. *Bottom*: D. K. Matheson, F. J. A. Pollard, A. G. Holman, W. Hunnisett, F. S. Siberry, R. D. Sweet, G. D. Stone.

THE ARTS FACULTY CUP WINNING TEAM, 1945

The eighth in order of eight Victoria teams to win the Arts Faculty Cup. Men from eight countries of four continents played on this cosmopolitan team. *Back row*: Prof. C. B. Sissons (Coach), F. J. D. Hoeniger (Captain), L. Paszat, H. W. Rowlands, C. E. Elliott,* J. S. Adams. *Centre row*: N. M. Hassanali,* W. M. M. Aird, W. H. Plewman, E. C. Richards, J. E. Seunarine, E. S. Thompson.* *Front row*: S. L. Endicott, J. O. Walmsley, A. Hikichi (Manager), E. D. Roberts, J. A. Colvin, J. N. Reed, G. A. Cockburn. *Members of the Varsity First Team.

THE CAMPUS OF 1952

ANNESLEY HALL

THE WYMILWOOD OF 1952

College whether it should be in federation, which he preferred, or independent at Cobourg or Hamilton. When the votes had been counted at midnight on the fourth day of debate, it was found that Dewart's amendment authorizing the Board to proceed had carried by a vote of 138 to 113. The names were published, and it was seen that while the ministers had divided evenly, 66 to 66, the laymen had voted 72 to 47, and that the three professors who were delegates, Burwash, Bain, and Badgley, had all voted with Nelles in the negative.

The Government was as good as its word and proceeded to prepare a bill for the next session. Mowat himself gave much time and thought to its terms, and the excellence of the measure must be attributed largely to his deep interest, practical mind, and fine legal talent. The thing attempted was original and unique, and there were no guideposts to the future. It is surprising that the measure was as sound as it proved to be considering the fact that neither J. J. Maclaren, the solicitor for the Victoria Board of Regents, nor Wilson,[18] who was much consulted, was in sympathy with its principles. It is a long act of eighty-seven sections, several of them sub-divided, but clearly phrased and free from archaism and redundancy. Its provisions may be summarized so as to fall under four principles.

First, it introduced the federal principle. The idea which had created the Dominion of Canada twenty years before was applied to higher education in Ontario. The several denominational universities of the province were invited to co-operate with the state university to make a truly provincial university, each federated college surrendering a portion of its autonomy in so doing. That is to say, each held in abeyance its power to grant degrees other than those in Theology; each turned over to the state instruction in certain subjects, mainly the sciences, and retained instruction in certain other subjects, principally the languages; each surrendered to the University the control over discipline in the university area, retaining control over the life and conduct of the students on its own campus; and the control over examinations was also given to the University Senate, each of the denominational universities retaining such influence as was secured by the presence of its representatives on the Senate, and by the conduct of

[18]See Langton, *Sir Daniel Wilson*, pp. 131–51. Wilson's diary and his biographer's comment reveal how persistent was his attempt to embody terms which would defeat any federal principle, and how nicely he supposed he had succeeded.

examinations in certain religious knowledge options. Such was the federal pact.

Secondly, the Act embodied the principle that religion has a place in education that must be recognized and defined in any truly national system. The state aimed to enlist the moral and financial support of the several churches in the cause of higher education; the churches in return might avail themselves of the superior advantages afforded by the state for instruction in the newer and rapidly expanding fields of the physical and social sciences. Of the University and University College, it was written that there should be no religious tests for professors or students. Any religious instruction which a student of University College might secure was optional; optional also the acceptance of any provision for his soul that his college might suggest within its walls or in city churches. Lest the epithet of "godless," however, should continue to be levelled at its instruction, a section of the Act provided for such concern on the part of the authorities of the state college. What the federating universities might do in the matter was for them to decide. Fusion of the interests of church and state, then, was a vital principle of the Act of 1887, although more than a decade had to elapse before the Church of England and the Roman Catholics were ready to accept it for themselves.

Thirdly, the Act accepted the principle of state supervision in return for state support. The socialist idea which in the eighteen-forties had been applied to primary education, and in the sixties to secondary education, was now in the eighties extended to education at the university level. The government accepted financial responsibility for the state university, at length engaging public funds beyond the limit of the income from the endowment of 1797. But in so doing it required large concessions in the matter of control. The Lieutenant-Governor was named as visitor. The Lieutenant-Governor-in-Council, that is to say, the government, appointed the President and the professors and provided for their retirement. The Minister of Education was a member of the Senate, as well as nine others appointed by the government. Every statute of the Senate must be reported to the government within ten days of its passing, and was valid only when approved by the government. Within the University itself, under the suzerainty of the government, the Senate was the principal governing body, controlling

THE FORGING OF FEDERATION, 1873-1892

the degrees and the courses of study leading thereto, and adjudicating on petitions of students. More than that, the Senate under the Act of 1887 continued to manage many matters of business. There was no Board of Governors, just a Trustee Board whose powers were limited to the control of investments and of property. There were also two Councils, a University Council and a University College Council, with duties restricted to oversight of student societies and discipline. The Act said nothing of the internal organization of the federating universities; that was considered their own concern. The Chancellor, elected every three years by Convocation, that is, by the graduates, as President of the Senate and of Convocation for the conferring of degrees, enjoyed a position of dignity and power; likewise the Vice-Chancellor, elected every three years by the Senate and usually presiding at its meetings. The President occupied a somewhat anomalous position. Sir Daniel Wilson had insisted on the titles of President of the University and President of University College being held by the same person, and it was so enacted. But the dual position was to confer little real authority and proved far from satisfactory to the federating universities, or indeed to University College.

Fourthly, the Act embodied the principle of state responsibility for professional training. Education was included as one of the subjects of study in the university list, although it was many years before instruction was provided. But Medicine and Law, after an exile of twenty-five years, returned to Queen's Park. From that time Medicine has had a large place in university planning and finance. With Law it was different; the Law Society and Osgoode Hall had to be reckoned with. On the other hand, Upper Canada College, which since 1829 as an apanage of the University had extracted considerable nourishment from an indulgent *alma mater*, was cut off with its shilling—in the form of a $100,000 endowment. With excellent collegiate institutes across the province, the Legislature could not longer defend this special indulgence to Toronto.

Such was the Act in principle and in some detail. Rarely has an important piece of legislation been carried with such unanimity. The second reading was moved on April 13, 1887, by the Minister of Education, the Hon. G. W. Ross. The Leader of the Opposition, William Meredith, gave it his warm and cordial support. The only voice raised against it at this stage was that of Corelli C. Field, the member of the constituency in which Cobourg was situated, who feebly remarked that he was fulfilling a promise to his constituents. Later, in committee of the whole, some slight objection was raised to the section on Medicine, but it was allowed to stand without change. If Ross had smooth sailing for his measure, it was because the winds of heaven had exhausted their force. In other words, during a half century or more, and under our democratic system, the whole question had been so fully discussed in church and legislative assemblies that a common conscience had been reached.

It was provided that the Act could be brought into force at any time by Order-in-Council. That is to say, it awaited a signal from Victoria. That nod was three years in coming, and the consummation two years more. At the outset few could have anticipated any such delay. Many of those who had voted with the minority fell promptly into line. Nelles and Burwash set to work loyally with Potts, the successor of Burwash as secretary of the Conference Educational Committee, to give effect to the decision. A site was chosen at the northeast angle of the park. Earlier, Mulock had suggested a more central location, where Trinity now stands. The rental was a dollar a year, with a proviso that should Victoria at any time withdraw from federation, the property could be purchased at its value in 1890, which was to be determined by arbitration forthwith. Architect's plans were invited and secured, and Potts busied himself with the campaign for the $450,000 needed. On one Sunday in December, 1886, $110,350 was raised in Toronto churches. This sum, however, included $5,000 from Mulock and $600 from Blake. Even Sutherland, Maclaren, and William Kerr, now Vice-Chancellor, had concurred in these steps.

The first storm signal was raised during Convocation week, a month after the passing of the Act. The Alumni Association was the body responsible, and Henry Hough, its past president, the leader of the insurgents. After five hours of debate the members resolved by a large majority that no steps should be taken towards removal until the full $450,000 had been assured. The association, of course, had no legal standing, and its resolution had effect only in so far as it influenced the alumni representatives on the Board and Senate or as it discouraged subscriptions. The campaign was continued by Potts throughout the

d at the five annual con-
pposition to hasty action.
though his diary is inter-
not usually, of a Sunday
h meetings and lectures
ture at Trinity where he
y life and left little time
isposition and that after
r of September 28, 1887,
e "annexing to all sub-
ised" was good, and he
ovision in securing its
bscribers might indicate
ency, since this "would
eprecates, on the other
ne who pleads for cau-
days at Grimsby Park,
ks of the last day with
ave to gay, from lively
only vacation. By the
campaign, even under

his hand upon Nelles.
e died in the College
ars to a day from his
Four days earlier he

kness God has taken
I have so long borne.
unfavourable to tran-
future, to leave all in
signation. I am very
h he has granted me
fection,

College, p. 266, quotes
Guardian Dewart refers
d to have been Nelles'

188 A HISTORY OF VIC

to the tune of "On the old Ontar
known opponents of federation.

An *impasse* had been reached. T
the Act of 1884 to defeat the w
situation was further complicate
Cobourg of twenty-five acres of la
buildings, and $1,325 each year
H. A. Massey, whose heart was sti
his business from Newcastle to
quarter of the million dollars he
pendence at Cobourg. Dr. Potts
paign and was able to report t
received for the building fund a
building and endowment to dat
building had been presented. It
it would be safe to proceed wit
this effect was carried by the j
a vote of 23 to 14. When the B
injunction was served on the Ch
removal from Cobourg. The s
individuals who had contribut
Chancellor Kerr), and Kerr a
others as members of the Sena

Thus war was declared by
with the Cobourgians. The r
half, just when the Board wa
the conflict through the pu
creasing warmth of feeling, e
by Sutherland, which was r
From April to June, 1890, F
cause, since Dewart had clos
were thwarting the will of C
court made by the Board fa
1889, the injunction was
MacMahon heard the cas
August 9, 1890. After a c
and particularly of the fin

spring and summer in individual churches and at the five annual conferences, at all of which there were signs of opposition to hasty action. Nelles bore his full share in these appeals. Although his diary is intermittent, it is clear that he was frequently, if not usually, of a Sunday in some pulpit. This preaching, together with meetings and lectures at the College and abroad, including one lecture at Trinity where he was royally entertained, made for a very busy life and left little time for reading. Only once does he speak of indisposition and that after a severe bout of travel and speaking. In a letter of September 28, 1887, to Maclaren, he expresses the opinion that the "annexing to all subscriptions of a condition that $450,000 be raised" was good, and he notes that Queen's had made the same provision in securing its $250,000; but he frowns on a suggestion that subscribers might indicate which they preferred, federation or independency, since this "would undoubtedly be deceptive in its effect." He deprecates, on the other hand, Dewart's "terrorism" in branding any one who pleads for caution as disloyal. In mid-August he spent nine days at Grimsby Park, a sort of Methodist Chatauqua. Ormiston speaks of the last day with him there when their talk often turned "from grave to gay, from lively to severe." This would appear to have been his only vacation. By the opening of term in October the success of the campaign, even under Potts' capable management, was still uncertain.

In the midst of it all the angel of death laid his hand upon Nelles. After a brief illness, attended with little pain, he died in the College at Cobourg on October 17, 1887, sixty-four years to a day from his birth in a pious farm home at Mount Pleasant. Four days earlier he had dictated to his daughter a letter to Potts:

MY DEAR DR. POTTS,—During these hours of sickness God has taken away the burden of anxiety and apprehension which I have so long borne. My feelings have been very intense, and as such unfavourable to tranquillity of mind. I am now able, and shall be in the future, to leave all in the hands of God with entire trustfulness and resignation. I am very grateful to God for the light and consolation which he has granted me while lying on this bed of fever. With unabated affection,
I remain as ever. . . .[19]

[19]*C.G.*, Oct. 26, 1887. Burwash in his *History of Victoria College*, p. 266, quotes this same letter as addressed to Dewart, but twice in the *Guardian* Dewart refers to it and says that Potts showed it to him. This is supposed to have been Nelles' last letter.

While his general health had been impaired by the additional strain of the federation struggle, Nelles' death was "a sad surprise."[20] "The columns of the old portico," says *Acta*, "draped in deepest black, were suggestive of the sadness that filled all our hearts, and dimmed the eyes of many when his name was mentioned, or we recalled past memories." The funeral was described as "one of the largest ever seen in this Province."[21] It was, says Burwash, "a remarkable testimony . . . to the estimate in Church and State of his great life-work."[22] But it was more than this. For that day, as never before or since, the College was as a family in grief. From his residence in the College to the church, thence to the grave, its members followed his body afoot—the Faculty of Arts as bearers, the students, the alumni, the Senate (in that order); then the representatives of sister universities and clergy and citizens in general. And Reynar's address—it was Nelles' wish that Reynar should speak—in its understanding and grace added to the intimacy of the farewell. This tribute was preserved in full by *Acta*. Only a few sentences can be quoted here:

I said, a moment ago, that he was called to the Presidency of Victoria College. It is only by courtesy that it could be called a college at that time. . . . When the college was handed to him it was a wounded, suffering child; and he was to be father and mother, doctor and nurse. He sheltered and nourished and cherished her until she has become the bountiful mother,—the *Alma Mater*, whose sons are to be found in usefulness and honor throughout the wide Dominion, from sea to sea, and from the river to the ends of the earth. What wonder if, in all these years of care and watching, he developed a caution that to some unknowing observers may have seemed over-developed. . . . But he had conquests as well as conflicts. . . . Just at the same time came great perplexity of mind and pain of spirit. But he did not wear his heart upon his sleeve. His step was light and his words cheerful, and even playful, to the last. His power in the pulpit was, it is said, more marked than ever before. . . . His moods were as different as sunshine and shadow, and they sometimes followed one another with great rapidity. . . . He was preeminently a thoughtful man—from first to last a *student*. . . . His reading too was broad as well as deep. He used to say that the surest way to make a bad theologian was to give him a course of exclusively theological reading. . . . Something of the same humility of wisdom [as that of Socrates] graced the learning of our lamented Chancellor. In his intercourse with others he was marked by a surface sparkle of wit. They did not always discern the depths of thought and seriousness that lay beneath. . . . His sympathy was intense and constant with the sorrow and pain of others. This fact was always sure

[20]*C.G.*, Oct. 26, 1887.   [21]*Ibid.*   [22]*History of Victoria College*, p. 266.

to transpire in his prayers. . . . A few hours before his death, when he was already far down the dark valley, he sent back a message to the students as they were about to assemble for college prayers—"Give the boys my love and thank them for having been so thoughtful and so kind." . . . Amongst the requests he made in view of his departure was this one, that on his tomb should be inscribed nothing but these words, "Now we see through a glass darkly." To us there is here no treason against Christian theology. Others may think they have in their Divinity a clearer spirit of divination. Saint Paul had not. Our sainted friend and brother and father was of the school of Paul, and he is not ashamed to have it so marked where his body is to be laid to rest. . . . I pray you, as though our dead Chancellor did speak to you through me, I pray you to look away from him, to see what he saw through the glass darkly, and to have and hold his faith, his hope, his love.

Reynar closed by reading Cowper's hymn which Nelles had requested should be sung, ending,

> Then in a nobler, sweeter song,
> I'll sing thy power to save;
> When this poor lisping stammering tongue
> Lies silent in the grave.

Nelles' departure appears to have stayed progress with federation plans for a time. In November Burwash was chosen to succeed him by a unanimous vote of the Board. It was October, 1888, before a joint meeting of the Board of Regents and the advisory committee appointed by Conference decided that it was advisable to implement the legislation and authorized the Board to proceed with building under plans submitted by W. G. Storm. The strength of the opposition was shown by the vote, 22 to 15. The Senate was asked to concur in the Board's action. When the body met in Cobourg on November 13, 1887, a motion calling for concurrence was moved by Mills and the Rev. W. S. Griffin. A long amendment, in essence refusing to concur, was presented by Hough and Dr. C. M. Gould of Colborne. The Cobourg partisans found support among friends of independence in Hamilton and Toronto and were able to carry their amendment by a vote of 21 to 14. Of the members of the faculty, three abstained from voting, three voted with the majority, and two voted for concurrence. Burwash was in the chair, and his vote was not recorded. Interest in the meeting was intense. From *Acta* we learn how a group of students met the members at the door of the College and passed them through to the tune of "On the old Ontario strand," giving cheers for well-known opponents of federation.

An *impasse* had been reached. The Senate had used its powers under the Act of 1884 to defeat the will of the Board. At this stage the situation was further complicated by an offer from the Mayor of Cobourg of twenty-five acres of land, $25,000 for improvement of the buildings, and $1,325 each year for five years for maintenance. And H. A. Massey, whose heart was still in Cobourg, although he had moved his business from Newcastle to Toronto, offered to contribute one quarter of the million dollars he considered to be required for independence at Cobourg. Dr. Potts, however, proceeded with his campaign and was able to report that over $105,000 in cash had been received for the building fund and a total of $262,000 subscribed for building and endowment to date. A tender of $130,000 for the main building had been presented. It had previously been determined that it would be safe to proceed with $100,000 in hand, and a motion to this effect was carried by the joint Board and advisory committee by a vote of 23 to 14. When the Board assembled for action, however, an injunction was served on the Chairman by a sheriff's officer prohibiting removal from Cobourg. The signatories were the town council, three individuals who had contributed to Faraday Hall (one of them Vice-Chancellor Kerr), and Kerr and Hough on behalf of themselves and others as members of the Senate.

Thus war was declared by the forces of independence in alliance with the Cobourgians. The result was a further delay of a year and a half, just when the Board was ready to proceed. The recrudescence of the conflict through the public press and in pamphlets showed increasing warmth of feeling, especially in a personal attack on Burwash by Sutherland, which was replied to in a spirit afterwards regretted. From April to June, 1890, Hough even published a four-pager on the cause, since Dewart had closed the columns of the *Guardian* to all who were thwarting the will of Conference. Attempts at a settlement out of court made by the Board failed. By an interim judgment of September, 1889, the injunction was continued pending the trial. Mr. Justice MacMahon heard the case and finally handed down judgment on August 9, 1890. After a careful survey of the history of the College, and particularly of the financial obligations incurred at various stages from the original gift of land by George B. Spencer to the subscriptions secured by Potts, a verdict favourable to the Board was rendered. On one point the complainants were successful: the Board was found to have no right to suspend degree-conferring powers without the consent of the Senate. On the other and main point the plaintiffs failed: the College was not tied to Cobourg. Only in the matter of subscriptions to Faraday Hall and of the five acres of land, where definite promises of permanence had been made, was the College held liable for damages. But this had long been recognized and indeed had been provided for in 1886. The total damage was assessed at $19,580. The injunction against removal having been dissolved, all that remained was the persuading of the Senate.

In the meantime the way was made easier by the announcement of a bequest from William Gooderham who had died on September 12, 1889. He was one of the twelve children of that Gooderham who had migrated from England to found in 1832—as all the world knows— the firm of Gooderham and Worts. "He did not feel drawn to the special business in which the father had embarked," so his obituary reads, and went to Rochester, where he was converted. Returning to Canada, he gained wealth as a railway contractor, and for the last years of his life lived "in retirement from all but religious duties."[23] He died during a service at The Haven, one of his charitable interests. In his will the sum of $200,000, in addition to his subscription of $30,000, was left to Victoria on condition of its removal to Toronto. He had in contemplation a site of eleven acres on the brow of the escarpment west of where Casa Loma now stands, but did not seek to force that point. This bequest was a severe blow to the Cobourg party, and meant that acceding to their demands would cost the College over $500,000 as Potts was not slow to point out.

Release from the injunction came only a month before the Conference of 1890, and it was deemed wise to have the matter once more placed before that body. In doing so Carman prayed "that they be saved in its discussion from pride of opinion, zest of contention, and from struggles for personal or sectional triumph."[24] Through his action as chairman—arbitrary, some thought it was—he was able to

[23]*C.G.*, Sept. 18, 1889 (quoted from the *Faithful Witness*).
[24]*Ibid.*, Sept. 17, 1890.

keep discussion to a minimum. An amendment for independence was defeated and the motion by Douglas, seconded by Cox, to reaffirm the decision of 1886 was carried by a vote of 165 to 83. So settled was opinion that in four years federation had won over from independence less than thirty votes.

A sharper division occurred in the appointment of members to the Board of Regents. Here Burwash won an important victory. He had presented a slate favourable to federation, arguing that it was necessary that the Board should speak with one voice, especially in view of the complexion of the Senate with its strong alumni representation. Prompt and forcible objection was made by Maclaren. Potts even and the veteran Douglas, whose eloquence had greater appeal from the fact that he was now sightless and without feeling in hands or feet, would have had the nominations referred back. But Burwash persisted. As a theologian he knew something of the perseverance of saints; and he had suffered long from divided counsels, as had Nelles before him. His argument was that the actions of the Board and Senate were not subject to review by the General Conference. The Board's powers were executive and final and only by appointing men known to be in harmony with the mind of Conference could that mind be given effect. And he won his point.

On October 16 the Board met in Cobourg. The Senate had been called for the same day. By a resolution which stood in the names of Burwash and Dewart, the Board requested the Senate to relieve the University from the existing injunction. The Senate on resolution of Carman and Ryckman assented by a vote of 24 to 3 with some seven members abstaining. The statutory notice of this combined action was duly sent to the Provincial Secretary, and on November 12, 1890, the Act of 1887 federating Victoria University with the University of Toronto was proclaimed. By October, 1892, the solid structure, now the main building of Victoria University, was ready for use, and work could begin in Toronto. Let no man say that university federation in Ontario was lightly undertaken or easily achieved.

IX. "THE GOOD LIFE" AT COBOURG
1881-1892

THROUGH the fateful decade of the eighties the inner life of the College followed the general pattern set in the seventies. On the great question that was disturbing their elders, student opinion also was divided. One year an editor like G. W. Bruce might call for federation, deploring the straitened circumstances of the College which had "made thin soup of the bone of poverty until there is not a trace of marrow left."[1] Another year a local man like Mulholland as editor might permit Workman, then in Germany, to inflict on his readers each month for five months on end articles decrying the movement. Students of the period who survive today say that most of the undergraduates felt that removal to Toronto must come; such a demonstration as greeted the Senate in November, 1887, can always be arranged in times of excitement—and there were many ties with Cobourg.

The staff was strengthened in 1881 by the appointment of Andrew James Bell to assist Wilson in Classics. After graduating with distinction from Toronto in 1878, he had taught in St. Thomas, and was thus one of the first of a group of proven teachers with capacity for scholarship whose transfer from secondary school to college work during the next thirty or forty years was a source of strength to the universities. Stately and impressive as was his person in later years, a certain awkwardness and shyness of manner at this stage and his rather overwhelming scholarship created some dissatisfaction among the students at first. Whereupon Nelles called a few of the leaders in and told them that a man of great learning had come among them, the best-read man of his acquaintance, whose library put them all to shame. Thus incipient discontent was stayed; and the following year, on his marriage to

---

[1]*Acta*, Dec., 1884, p. 6.

"one of the prettiest and most popular young ladies of St. Thomas," he is described as a "tip-top fellow."[2] This indeed he fully demonstrated during his forty-odd years of distinguished and unsparing service to Victoria, and, as Professor of Comparative Philology, to the University of Toronto. After five years of teaching he requested leave of absence and spent three years at Breslau, winning his Doctorate with a dissertation in Latin on the genitive. His years in Germany served to turn in the direction of the language study there prevailing a mind which already embraced the world's best literature of many tongues. At an early stage in his career through etymological study he convinced himself that the Baptist ritual had scriptural support and he joined that body.

The following year another outstanding appointment was made. Arthur Philemon Coleman, who had maintained his connection with the College through teaching in the Collegiate department, returned from two years' study at Breslau with his Ph.D. and was appointed Professor of Natural History and Geology, thus relieving Haanel of some of his burden of work. At his inauguration Nelles made a notable speech. He compared the science of the day to Milton's half-formed lion still pawing to get free its hinder parts from the rude groundwork of hypothesis. He welcomed to the staff one who would unite "a profound knowledge of science with an equally profound spirit of religious reverence."[3] In answer to Haanel's friendly greeting Coleman said: ". . . from you I received the first strong inspiration toward what I have chosen as my life work."[4] Then he delivered his inaugural lecture on "The Geology and People of Norway," in the course of which he told of his first acquaintance with a glacier.[5] Perhaps no scientist of his day was better able to explain those high mysteries to a general audience; he combined a complete absence of affectation with an artistry in language the basis of which was simplicity.

In the same year the Rev. George Coulson Workman began his

[2]Ibid., Oct., 1882.   [3]Ibid., Jan., 1883, p. 8.   [4]Ibid.
[5]Oddly enough, the massif at the head waters of the North Saskatchewan, which bears the name of this world authority on ice, ancient and modern, reveals to the tourist no sign of a glacier. But on its north face, withdrawn from vulgar eyes, a splendid stream of ice flows from the peak some 2,500 feet into a glacial lake about a mile long. Coleman had passed close to the mountain in one of his early explorations, but had never climbed it. The writer had the honour of carrying Coleman's ice axe to the top in 1939; he had intended to revisit his mountain that summer but had died in February.

teaching as an assistant in Metaphysics and Theology. Like Coleman he never married, but this was one of the very few points of similarity. Keen scholar as he was, there remained with Workman to the end a fussiness and a desire to impress which much impaired his usefulness. A bigger man could have held and taught German-made ideas in theology without causing himself and others the troubles of later years. First impressions at the College were favourable. After two years *Acta* praised his taste in arranging the printed calendar and his adaptability as secretary of the Faculty. In 1884 he went to Germany, where he spent five years, mainly at Leipzig. On his return he was warmly welcomed. His work on Jeremiah was reviewed and praised by Burwash. A lecture on Messianic Prophecy, however, raised such a storm in the Board and was so strongly condemned by Dewart in the *Guardian*, that Burwash felt compelled to suggest his transfer from Theology to Arts. This Workman refused. He resigned, and his resignation was accepted, against Burwash's judgment, by a vote of 10 to 8 in the Board. After an interval of a year he was appointed to the staff at Montreal, where a similar incident presently occurred. Retaining membership in the Church, he supported himself thereafter by writing and supply preaching. On one occasion, about 1900, he unfolded his story, with some little complaining, before the undergraduates of the day at a meeting of the Literary Society. He was often seen about the College in later years, and he was buried from the Chapel.

In 1884 Workman's place was taken by the Rev. Eratus Irving Badgley, who transferred after the union from Albert to Victoria. He was a rather short man, slight of build, and conspicuous by reason of an immense moustache. His abilities as a teacher of philosophy were respectable, but in public addresses he was addicted, like many Methodist preachers, to telling jokes. He served the College faithfully in Cobourg and Toronto till his death in 1906.

During Bell's sojourn abroad Lewis Emerson Horning was brought in from the Peterborough Collegiate Institute to take his place. Horning had set a record by securing honours in four departments at graduation in 1884, although G. S. Deeks, afterwards equally successful as a teacher and as a railway contractor, stood equal with him for the gold medal. In appearance and character he showed his German ancestry. He was a large, square-set man, a prodigious worker, sure of himself and his opinions, of deep loyalty and sentiment. His cheerful optimism—so valuable an asset in a teacher—was indicated by a way he had in golf of keeping a "ringer" score, that is computing the sum of the lowest score he had made on individual holes at sundry times. He too repaired to Germany, in 1889, and returned two years later to become Professor of Germanic Languages and to play a large part in the future success of Victoria. He was a stimulating lecturer, broad in his scholarship and interests, open and friendly in disposition. One of the very few mistakes President Falconer made in the difficult position in which the First World War placed him was to pay undue attention to an attack made on Horning by an Orillia paper for some sympathetic reference to the German people made in an Extension lecture.

With the elevation of Burwash in 1887 the Rev. Francis Huston Wallace was appointed to the Faculty of Theology with the title of Professor of New Testament Exegesis and Literature. A son of the manse, he had attended University College and graduated with the gold medal in Classics. He became a Methodist, and on applying for admission to the ministry requested a period of study abroad. This unusual request was granted. It was while at Drew Seminary that he met his future wife, the daughter of Bishop Wilson and the sister of that Edward Wilson who brought to Victoria from Rutgers its song and its scarlet. Later Wallace sampled German scholarship. After some years in the itineracy including a term at Cobourg, he accepted a summons to College work from a charge at Peterborough. A careful and accomplished scholar, if hardly an inspiring lecturer, he had an honoured place in Victoria University as Professor and Dean of Theology for thirty-two years. Of all the professors' homes, none was more hospitable than his, and from it came three graduates of the College, all following a career in teaching and one becoming Chancellor of Victoria University. His Methodist convictions, once embraced, were held with great firmness, and he was the last of the professors to abandon the practice of kneeling at College prayers in the Chapel. Indeed the writer does not recall that he ever desisted.

For some time after the reorganization which introduced Wallace, no appointment to the deanship of Theology was made. Burwash evidently wished to keep his hand in this department, which now included Reynar, Badgley, and Workman, five in all. But the title of Dean was given to Reynar in Arts and to Haanel in Science.

In 1889 John Petch ('87) became Associate Professor of Romance Languages after a short period of study abroad. He too had served apprenticeship in the secondary schools of the province. His fields were French and Italian, and he served the College quietly and efficiently, though in failing health, until his death in 1897.

The Calendar of 1890 leaves a blank over the title *Dennis Moore Professor of Chemistry and Physics*. On Haanel's departure, of which more hereafter, Burwash had arranged to fill a position, which at best could only be temporary, by the appointment of his younger brother John. After graduation in 1863 John had gone to the Maritimes and been variously occupied in teaching at Mount Allison, in preaching, and in working as a geologist for the Province of New Brunswick. He was a big man, of great physical strength, rugged in character and in all matters forthright but kindly. His training may have been less than adequate for the particular work assigned him in Science at Cobourg— or indeed for the chair in Homiletics to which he was transferred in Toronto. But humbly and devoutly he followed what appeared to be the path of duty. When he died in Calgary in 1913, three years after his retirement, his body was brought to Toronto for burial from the College Chapel.

The last of the pre-Toronto appointments was that of the Rev. John Fletcher McLaughlin. In 1891 he and R. A. Daly (later Professor of Geology at Harvard) were appointed by the Board to assist John Burwash and Bain in Science and Mathematics. McLaughlin was a brilliant student. In his third year he won first class honours in two departments, Science and Philosophy. In his final year impaired health, his duties as editor of *Acta*, and difficulties later to be spoken of had restricted him to one honour course and the gold medal in Philosophy. Three years after graduation were spent in theology and in teaching at the Hamilton Ladies' College. On Workman's withdrawal he was transferred to the Old Testament chair, and spent two years of preparation at Oxford—not in Germany. His professorship was exercised with distinction and without doctrinal dispute through forty years, although his theology was as modern as that of Workman. His fine mind and complete consecration to his work enabled him not only to build up a vigorous department of Orientals in the College but profoundly to affect the life of the University and the Church. Like Bell in Classics, he did not consider it his part to spread his knowledge—and enhance his reputation—by publishing; he was content to sow the seed from day to day. He had no great talent as a preacher, but his Sunday afternoon Bible class, for years conducted in the old Library (now Alumni Hall) and mainly attended by Arts men, was a great institution. And he was not disposed to separate the sacred and the secular or sharply to divide arts and theology. His physical powers towards the end showed the strain of incessant work, although as an undergraduate he had excelled at football and in later years was said to be a first-rate man in the bush. When on his retirement he said farewell to his colleagues at a dinner in Annesley Hall, he introduced his remarks by recalling a striking incident. As he was sitting in his office at Emmanuel College thinking of what he might say, he became aware that the room was flooded with light. Awakened from his reverie he realized that it was just the reflection of the western sun from the windows of old Victoria. This he made the text of a beautiful and affecting speech.

The retirement of John Wilson in 1890 severed a connection with the College which dated back to 1847. He was given a small pension of $500. This was the first recognition by the Board of the claims of professors on retirement, unless certain arrangements as to Kingston's mortgage can be regarded as such. Nelles' widow also had received an allowance. For a short time Wilson gave what assistance he could to Bell. The College was never quite the same after "Old Trinity" left; in fact a distinguished graduate once remarked that it was worth the annual pilgrimage to Convocation just to see his face.

Haanel did not wait for the blow to fall at federation. He accepted a professorship at Syracuse University in 1889. No attempt appears to have been made by Toronto to secure the services of this remarkable man. In fact it may well be that the failure of the University to open its arms to Haanel and Bain and to offer a man like Coleman something better than a position in an affiliated institution may have had something to do with Nelles' mistrust of the whole scheme.[6] It should be said, however, that the way to a decent proposal to Haanel from Toronto was not rendered easier by an observation introduced (rather surprisingly) by Nelles towards the end of his speech at the Conference

---

[6]When Trinity College entered federation, provision for three members of its staff, mentioned by name, was stipulated in the agreement.

of 1886 to the effect that Haanel greatly preferred independence at Cobourg, even at a much smaller salary. After some ten years at Syracuse Haanel accepted the important position of Superintendent of Mines at Ottawa, where he was responsible for certain valuable developments in the process of smelting.

To turn from staff to students, the eighties saw the entry of women into the life of Victoria. In the fall of 1880, as has been noted, Miss Nellie C. Greenwood, a Cobourg girl of American birth, proceeded to enrol in the Science department. "Of course," says *Acta*, "such a rare sight as a lady attending College excited at first great amazement, but as she came and went to and from her classes in a quiet, unobtrusive, and lady-like manner, our surprise gradually passed away, and we grew to respect her more and more."[7] Although the youngest member of her class, she competed on equal terms with the men even "in the Mathematical line, in which ladies are generally deficient." When she took a B.Sc. in 1884, she became the first woman to graduate in course.[8] In 1887 she married the Rev. W. W. Andrews ('86), and still survives, clear of memory and quite active. Two years later, in 1886, Miss K. K. I. Willoughby of Whitby received her B.A. degree to become the first woman graduate in Arts. In 1887 Miss M. E. Donly graduated with the silver medal in Metaphysics, the gold medal going to C. W. Brown, father of Professor George W. Brown ('15). Thereafter for the next few years women appear at Convocation in ones and twos. It was 1887 before, on petition to the Senate, they were granted a room to themselves in the College. During 1889-90 they formed the Ladies' Literary Society. A Missionary Society was also formed in the same year which met on Saturday evenings, every other week, alternating with the Literary Society. The first joint society of men and women students was the Missionary Society. The date of union was 1891. Already Japan had been occupied, and China was being opened to Canadian Methodist missionaries. In 1891 Miss M. F. Libby shared the gold medal in Moderns with W. J. Sykes, while Miss Mary E. Highet won the silver medal. Miss Highet continued her studies at

[7]*Acta*, April, 1884, p. 11..
[8]Miss Augusta Stowe had in 1883 received her M.D. and C.M. from Victoria University, thus becoming the first woman doctor in Canada; but in Medicine Victoria merely conferred degrees without giving any instruction.

Cornell, where in 1895 she won her Ph.D., "perhaps the first Canadian young woman to secure the doctor's degree."[9]

Evidently the first women students of Victoria took their work seriously. From the beginning, however, they showed an interest in the "Bob." In December, 1881, *Acta* informs its readers that "One of the most interesting parts of the programme was the cutting of a beautiful pyramid cake presented to the 'Bob' by the young ladies attending the Collegiate lectures. It contained a ring, a five cent piece and a button. A Soph. got the ring, a Junior the five cent piece, and a 'Freshie' swallowed the button." Five years later they had caught the spirit of the "Bob" more nicely. *Acta* devotes an amusing column to a lady students' meeting. All seven were present and Miss Donly was called to the chair. It appears that it had become the custom for the ladies to provide each freshman with a cookie at the "Bob." The question at issue now was whether a raisin should be inserted in each cookie. The arguments *pro* and *con* are solemnly presented. Miss M. E. T. Addison was the main opponent of the raisin, her speech beginning, "I think, ladies, this is a matter in which we should move very cautiously."[10] Such was Miss Addison's bow to the Victoria public.

In the fall of 1886 revival services in the town conducted by Crossley and Hunter served to postpone the "Bob," and an attempt was made to cancel it. But it was presented in January. "All honor," exclaimed *Acta,* "to the faithful few, who upheld the class's trust. . . ."[11] As early as 1884 we read of members of the faculty being "bobbed," and then in 1887 during "a bold attempt at mimicry of our church and college fathers" a session of the General Conference was portrayed. A serious effort was made at this time (and for thirty years more at least) to study the voices and mannerisms of the various professors. The account continues: "During the discussion on the memorials, the cursory remarks, humorous and pointed, delivered with a decided rising inflection, might almost have deceived our esteemed President himself. And

---

[9] *Acta*, Oct., 1895, p. 8. At the end of a long period of teaching in Elmira College in New York State, she retired to Barrie, Ontario. For several years she offered a prize in German in Victoria College and also contributed annually to a loan fund maintained by the College for students in need. When she died in 1943 it was discovered that Victoria was to receive under her will half the estate (the other half going to Elmira College) for the establishment of scholarships to stand in the name of her mother, Elizabeth Ann Highet. The bequest amounted to $17,595.58, sufficient to endow two matriculation scholarships of $300 and $150.
[10] *Acta*, Jan., 1887, p. 17.
[11] *Ibid.*, Feb., 1887, p. 3.

"THE GOOD LIFE" AT COBOURG, 1881-1892   199

yet it was only Drope behind the necessary beard. Dr. Dewart was logical and impressive, Dr. Burns vigorously bowed and shook his coat, Dr. Douglas spoke with his own measured tread and peculiar intonation, Dr. Burwash knew all about the subject from the initiatory to the final, and Dr. Badgley clinched his argument with a powerful and unanswerable syllogism."[12] When it was all over and each freshman had been properly chastened, someone remarked, and *Acta* repeated it, that the "Bob" was as good as a revival meeting for the freshman class. Chancellor Nelles' death in October, 1887, caused the "Bob" to be dropped for that year, but when it was proposed to continue the period of mourning into May and eliminate the conversazione, *Acta* objected and that function was held. The students, however, did not forget to make up a purse for Robert, the acknowledgment of which with thanks was made the first item in the May *Acta*. The following year in spite of "wars and rumors of war to be made against the dear old institution," the "over-governed Sophomores"[13] revived the performance. Afterwards the accustomed procession through the town, beginning at 2 A.M. and delayed only by William Kerr's regular barrel of apples, finally wound up for early morning breakfast at Robert's. Here the "cub" (Bear it was then spelled, not Beare, and so pronounced), who had timed his entry into the world for the previous Convocation day, was brought in and received the name George Henry Russell after three recent and prominent graduates, G. W. Kerby, Henry Langford, and J. R. L. Starr. In December, 1889, *Acta* was compelled to deplore the action of a majority of the Sophomores in not proceeding with the "Bob," but the following year it returned in spite of the rumour "that Messrs. Dewart, Potts & Co. had arrived with men, trucks and elephants and were about to remove the College to Queen's Park."[14]

The plethora of societies in Victoria was such that, as has been noted, *Acta* objected to the introduction of the Young Men's Christian Association. However, the Y.M.C.A. became firmly established and, until it was supplanted by the Students' Christian Movement in 1921, shared with the Missionary Society the direction of the religious life of the College so far as this was subject to student control.[15] In accord-

[12]*Ibid.*, Jan., 1887, p. 17.   [13]*Ibid.*, Dec., 1888, p. 18.
[14]*Ibid.*, Dec., 1890, p. 18.
[15]In 1881 Burwash became national President of the Y.M.C.A.

ance with its constitution it entered into social activities, offering an evening reception each year and clearing a space 160 feet by 80 feet for flooding a rink. In 1890 both John R. Mott and a representative of the Students' Volunteer Missionary Movement visited the College.

Politics had little place in the College. Discussions of a political nature were from the first barred from the Literary Association and, of course, from the Jackson Society. But on November 30, 1886, politics invaded the College in a virulent form. Sir John A. Macdonald was to visit Cobourg, and a complimentary address of welcome from the students was proposed. A meeting was called for 2.15, and *Acta* says that every student was in Alumni Hall.[16] Hardly had the resolution been presented, when C. W. Kerr, who is described as "the irrepressible and ardent leader of the Reform party,"[17] leaped to the platform. His rapid-fire speech was cheered incessantly. Then E. B. Ryckman "scrambled upon the platform, struck a defiant attitude, and posed as an independent, but was so convinced by his own logic that ere he sat down he espoused the cause of the G.O.M." By this time "the last faint spark of piety had taken wings . . . and wild and unthinking enthusiasm had rushed in." Kono, a Japanese student, alone maintained his equanimity. The details which follow come from the lips of two participants, the Rev. Dr. A. J. Irwin and the Rev. W. B. Tucker. When the meeting was asked to divide for the vote, physical force was used to pull men from one side to the other, and one man voted minus a sleeve. So says Tucker. Irwin reports that the vote was so close that the decision depended upon himself and another who were supposed to be Conservatives, but they had been convinced that the resolution was being sought for party advantage and by shifting to the other side they gave the negative a majority. At this stage Nelles appeared on the scene, coming downstairs from his apartment; everything quieted down and further trouble was avoided. Kerr telegraphed the news to the *Globe*; but if he prevailed in this contest he never had the success that attended Ryckman in political battles of the future.

One College institution continued to cause friction. The V.P. Society with its narrow membership was not of the genius of Victoria. Its aims and standards were high. It had the active support of Haanel and Coleman. Its publications, the *Kosmos* and the *Journal,* were excellent

[16]For an account of the meeting see *Acta*, Dec., 1886.   [17]*Ibid.*, p. 18.

in material and format. But its exclusiveness created opposition, of which the main ingredient was probably jealousy, increased no doubt by the official recognition given the V.P. in the assigning of certain rooms for meetings and a library. Nelles had been compelled to lay the students' protests before the Board, and on his death Burwash inherited the problem. The Board decided that, all things considered, it was better that the V.P. Society should be disbanded. Burwash thought it well to lay the verdict before the students at a general meeting, but in doing so he spoke of the society as having included some of the best students in the university.

In reporting the meeting the Local editor, Henry Langford, observed: "We think it was hardly necessary to give it an advertisement before a students' meeting at the expense of the other societies, and to point out how much superior its members were, in his estimation, to the 'mob' outside the pale of their benign and holy influence."[18] Under the same department in the March issue a note appeared sharply criticizing the quality of the series of lectures given by visiting lecturers under the auspices of the Theological Union; also a brief article which contended that Mineralogy was not a proper subject to be made compulsory for Pass men in the third year and described a requirement of 100 per cent for the examination on that subject as smacking somewhat of absurdity.

As a result J. F. McLaughlin, the editor-in-chief, and Langford were called before the Faculty and a resolution read in which they were required to apologize on pain of suspension. They asked to be permitted to make some defence. This request was refused, and they then declined to make an apology, which at best would be insincere. The Chancellor again called a public meeting and announced that the editors had been suspended for a year. Presently in conversation with two students he indicated a willingness to re-open the question. They arranged for a joint meeting of the Literary and Jackson societies, who were responsible for appointing the staff of *Acta*. These bodies expressed regret and agreed to a formula according to which complaints of this sort would be referred to the authorities rather than exposed to the public through *Acta*. Thus, without the required apologies, McLaughlin and Langford were permitted to write their examina-

[18]*Ibid.*, Dec., 1887.

tions. And Victoria was spared any such upheaval as those which resulted on two occasions, in 1895 and in 1905, from similar attacks by the *Varsity* against the administration of the University of Toronto. In later years McLaughlin never spoke of the matter, and met any hint at the incident with one of his quiet smiles; so that there was much incredulity as to the report of the suspension from the College of one in reference to whom Chancellor Bowles remarked on a certain occasion, "we have one Christian on the staff, anyway." But McLaughlin probably felt that he must support his Local editor, especially in view of the conduct of the Faculty, which must have appeared arbitrary. For after all he had his origin in Cartwright Township and was a brand plucked from the North of Ireland.

The Langfords, Arthur, Henry, and Fred, were among the leading athletes of the decade; all of them, and they alone, accomplished the feat of kicking the football over the College. Association football remained the principal competitive sport, and in the mid-eighties the best teams of the province, Galt, Berlin, and Varsity were met on fairly even terms. Perhaps the most notable game of the decade was one played against Varsity. When Vic. scored the first goal, *Acta* reports, "the ladies waved their handkerchiefs. . . . Drs. Haanel and Coleman in their ecstasy unitedly lifted the meteor. . . . Professor Horning's 'basso-profundo' was heard far above the ordinary cheer."[19] But Wattie Thompson, the Varsity centre, whose skill in dribbling amazed English competitors during a Varsity tour overseas, would not be denied and accounted for two goals, the final result being 2-1. On this Victoria team were J. R. L. Starr in goal and A. J. Irwin at right forward. They both played the game for the College later on the Board of Regents, the former as its chairman for several years, and the latter giving especially valuable service during the Jackson controversy. Inter-class football was played during several years, and now and then the schedule was carried to a conclusion. In 1881 an attempt was made to transfer to rugby, but the effort does not appear to have been sustained beyond one year. Lacrosse and baseball and cricket made sporadic and brief appearances. Hockey emerged only in the last year at Cobourg. Alley, of course, continued, and here contests were waged between the years and even between boarding houses. A side of four was easier to organize than one of eleven, and generally the authorities were able to

[19]*Ibid.*, Nov., 1886, p. 16.

keep the alley-board in repair; the levelling and maintaining of a playing field was another matter. Indeed until the "barn," the ramshackle building with a checkered history behind the College, was burned one night in 1885,[20] and the $600 insurance was available for that purpose, there was no playing field at the College, and town facilities were used. In several years an athletic meet was held, with standing broad jump and standing hop, step and jump, kicking the football, and throwing the cricket ball added to the present list of events, and javelin, discus and hurdles absent. A definite plan for a gymnasium was a federation casualty, and indeed all sports showed a decline towards the end.

As the Cobourg era drew to its close, *Acta* thought it well to publish photographs and biographies of Nelles and Burwash and the twelve professors of the College. In this number is Workman, whose resignation in January *Acta* had made the occasion of implied criticism of the Board and open criticism of Dewart. Coleman also is included; he was coming down from Toronto to lecture, and even after the removal to Toronto was retained on the faculty in an honorary capacity.

Examinations were held in the first two weeks in May, and so prompt were professors and registrars of that day that by the following Saturday the results were posted. Meanwhile the week's festivities,[21] the last in Cobourg, had begun: on Thursday evening a reception given by the faculty in the College; on Friday evening the Senior Dinner at the Arlington, with its ten toasts and thirty-one speeches, E. C. S. Huycke (B.A. '83, LL.B. '87), who was that year giving certain lectures in the College, presiding, and the oratory being continued till 1.30 with comic songs and rollicking choruses interspersed; on Sunday morning the annual sermon of the Theological Union in the Division Street Church, preached by Dr. S. P. Rose, and there also in the evening the Baccalaureate sermon by Dr. Alexander Sutherland, followed by the Chancellor's address to the graduates; on Monday a breakfast to the Seniors by Dr. and Mrs. Reynar, in the afternoon the annual lecture to the Theological Union by the Rev. W. S. Blackstock on "A Study in Soteriology" (in other words, says *Acta*, "the lecturer's theme was atonement"), and in the evening the closing meeting of

---

[20]The name of the undergraduate responsible for the fell deed has been whispered to the writer. He went into law. The morning after the fire a cartoon appeared in the College showing Nelles and Badgley playing at cards and kicking over the light.

[21]See *Acta*, May, 1892.

the Literary Association with recitations and songs and a dangerously political subject for debate; on Tuesday a morning meeting of the Senate to award degrees and honours and lay plans for the opening in Toronto, afternoon meetings of the Modern Language Club and the Missionary Society, and the annual evening meeting of the Alumni Association, with John Burwash the retiring President, Coleman the President-elect, and Professor C. C. James, late of the Agricultural College and now Deputy Minister of Agriculture and as good a friend as Victoria ever had, as Secretary; finally on Wednesday the Convocation in Victoria Hall in the afternoon, and a brilliant conversazione in the evening at the Arlington where a few "guests" remained behind, *Acta* reports, "to offend the opinions or prejudices, if you will, of their hosts, by having a dance."

But before this last conferring of degrees at Cobourg, an unscheduled event must be noted. About 3 A.M. on Tuesday morning the skeleton was removed from the biological laboratory by two students, carried across the roof of the College and tethered to the tower by a rope around the neck, where it remained until dislodged by the wind in the morning and dismembered by the fall to the lawn. One of the perpetrators of this venture in symbolism was no less a person that George H. Locke ('93), who on the previous Friday evening had received the Senior Stick from Arthur Allin ('92). Student sentiment manifested itself during the afternoon in a somewhat less sombre form when from the gallery they relieved Convocation proceedings by singing to the "Meerschaum Pipe" air, "Oh, who will spark my Cobourg girl, when I am far away?" The Valedictory address having been given by C. B. Keenleyside, who won the George A. Cox medal in Natural Science, the Chancellor conferred these last degrees (by special dispensation[22] to all but the seven recipients in Theology): B.A., 23; B.Sc., 5 (all former graduates in Arts); B.D., 5; M.A., 6; M.D. and C.M., 32, *ad eundem*, 7; C.M., 1; M.D., 2 (from Montreal); LL.D., 2; D.D., 2; LL.D. (hon.) 7. The list of LL.D.'s included the Hon. G. W. Ross and Burwash himself, together with three of the strongest opponents of federation. Thus did the Senate in exercising for the last time rights it had enjoyed for fifty-one years seek to heal old wounds before it embarked upon a new era in Toronto.

[22]The federation act of 1887 had now been proclaimed.

X. PIONEERING AGAIN
1892-1913

DURING the long delay resulting from divided counsels the original plans for building had undergone considerable change. Burwash after inspecting American colleges had reported in favour of a group of buildings: a main building flanked by a residence and a library, with a separate chapel also envisaged. At the outset he had found difficulty in securing support for his group idea, and when the way to proceed had been opened it had been decided to erect a single structure, solid but rather elaborate in ornamentation and design according to the style in fashion at the time. By the afternoon of June 15, 1891, all was ready for the laying of the corner stone. For the dignitaries a platform had been erected, resting upon and extending beyond the main foundations, and around the stand a throng gathered estimated at about 3,000. Six immense Union Jacks floated over the pile, whose lineaments were revealed by an artist's sketch on an easel. "Old Sol outdid himself," says the *Empire*, "in his anxiety to make the occasion bright and cheerful."[1] In other words, it was a very hot summer day. Rumour has it that the situation of the spectators was far from comfortable, while that of those on the platform for whom escape was more difficult was almost intolerable. Yet the speeches were prolonged to almost three hours. Several of them were notable, and three outstanding, those of the Minister of Education and of the two Chancellors. Such importance did the press attach to the occasion that the *Globe* reported several of the speeches *verbatim* and the whole to the extent of some 10,000 words.[2] It was an age where men were inured to, and even delighted in, sustained eloquence, and when editors had

[1]*Empire*, June 16, 1891.
[2]*Globe*, June 16, 1891. Quotations from these speeches given below are taken from this issue.

faith that their readers could be instructed through the artistry of words rather than the medium of a camera.

The stone was laid by Mrs. George A. Cox, wife of the able and devoted Treasurer of the College. In it was deposited, in addition to the usual current documents, an historical sketch (not entirely free from inaccuracies) which Burwash read before giving his address. It is interesting to compare his address with that of Blake. Both dealt with the long train of events which had led up to that day, Burwash emphasizing the stern struggle against exclusiveness and privilege, and Blake the fight to preserve one great centre of learning. On two points they were in complete agreement. The first was in relation to the place of religion in education. Burwash put it this way, "A greater mistake the Church could not make than to abandon all these fields of university work to the purely secular interest"; and Blake, "it was most important to the true advance of this land that the churches should not stand aside and leave the secular institution, with all the difficulties involved, in isolation." The other matter of agreement was an interest in the wide diffusion of university training. Burwash believed that the day was "not far distant when the Public School, instead of being the ultimatum of the masses, will be but their starting point." He was convinced that a man would be a better farmer or mechanic, as well as a better lawyer or clergyman, for college training. "I never followed the plough or swung the scythe with greater zest," he said, "than after I had won my B.A. degree. . . . My vision of the future for Canadian sons is, that the great majority of the leading young minds of the day will begin the work of life with an education which will represent literary refinement, scientific accuracy, and philosophic breadth of thought." And Blake, who through his munificent scholarships tenable in any arts college has made this ideal possible for hundreds of students, averred: "I have said in the halls over yonder, and I repeat it here, I want to see our University a poor man's university, to see its doors open as wide as possible. I want to see it possible for the prudent and frugal poor man, if his son has such natural talents as to render him fit, to send him to these doors, and to have him sent out from them the peer of the highest and the proudest by descent who may be found in the land." He went further than this—and in a company graced by the presence of two Knights: "For though we have now very few—and I wish they were less—though we have now very few stars, knighthoods and orders of nobility, we shall not in the future be without a nobility, we shall not be without an aristocracy; we shall have not a hereditary aristocracy but an aristocracy of learning and talent, of integrity and virtue." Of the federation agreement itself, he was free to admit that while it did not in every aspect meet his views of the best, while it was not a very "symmetrical, reasonable or defensible scheme in all its details," it did represent mutual consideration and an advance on anything hitherto attained, and he was content. A like spirit in the future would carry them still further. He was pleased, however, that provision had been made on a fair basis for the transfer of the site to Victoria, if ever she should wish to resume degree-conferring powers merely suspended. He was convinced that the gain would be so great that she would wish to stay, but freedom of action was best.

The warmth of the congratulations of the Hon. Geo. W. Ross left no doubt as to where his inclinations had lain from the beginning. In a particularly arresting passage he declared: "Let me say as a Canadian, though not a Methodist, that this university is not the property of the great Methodist Church. We allow them to lay this foundation stone . . . but we, the people of Canada, in every department of educational activity, claim to have a share, not simply in the honors of to-day, but we claim to have a very decided share in the results of this day's celebration." Which, of course, was precisely the attitude of the founders. He concluded pertinently with the stanza,

> Ring out the old, ring in the new,
> The larger heart, the kindlier hand;
> Ring out the darkness of the land,
> Ring in the Christ that is to be.

Sir Daniel Wilson's brief words of welcome showed that he had not entirely caught the spirit of Tennyson's salute to the New Year; he must hark back to evil assaults on the endowment. Several other speeches followed.

At this juncture the chairman in a humorous manner informed the assemblage that, although Sir Alexander Campbell, Lieutenant-Governor of Ontario, had gone, they still had with them the little king of Ontario, and he had great pleasure in calling upon the Hon. Oliver Mowat. Thus introduced, the Premier of Ontario stepped forward amid the cheers of the hundreds who still bore the heat with the utmost fortitude. Mr. Mowat was compassionate, and with just a shadow of a smile said he endorsed everything that had been said so eloquently now for some hours. (Laughter). There was not one of all the speakers more pleased to see federation accomplished than he was. "I am not one of you Methodists," continued the Premier, "but"—"We'll take you in" cheerily said Dr. Potts. "If I were not a Presbyterian, I would like to be a Methodist," retorted Mr. Mowat, "but I could not leave the greater for the less good." In conclusion he said that at the present time when Christianity was assailed from so many different standpoints he was glad, in the interest of the country and of the common Christianity, that federation had been accomplished, and felt sanguine that great good would result."

The formal opening took place on the afternoon of October 25, 1892.[3] The capacity of the Chapel was quite unequal to the occasion. At the outset Zeus thundered on the left. When Carman, as Chairman, called on the Rev. George Bishop to read the Scripture lesson, there was a pause. No Bible was available. The Chairman explained the situation, adding in a humorous tone, "It's a strange Methodist College without a Bible on the platform. The first thing we will need here will be a protracted meeting." Then a patriotic address was read to Sir George Kirkpatrick, the new Lieutenant-Governor, who replied in an eloquent and appropriate speech, which concluded with a tribute to Victoria's first principal: "Such a man was Egerton Ryerson—(prolonged applause)—and I do not think that any body of Methodists could be assembled together on such an occasion as this without remembering with gratitude that great man and all he did for this college and this Province." The Hon. Richard Harcourt, representing the Government, Mulock and the new President, James Loudon, representing the University, Goldwin Smith, Principal Mills, and Principal Sheraton of Wycliffe College were the speakers, and all were well received. But the highest pitch of enthusiasm was created when Potts read the letter from H. A. Massey containing a check for $40,000 to endow a new chair, and when the donor was called forward and told of his brief periods of study at Cobourg fifty years before. The enthusiasm was maintained when Burwash was called upon and received a beautifully illuminated address from the undergraduates. The proceedings were continued in the evening with brief addresses and music, the whole being concluded by the *Hallelujah Chorus* sung by Dr. Torrington's choir.

Two other events marked the college warming, a dinner of the

[3]*C.G.*, Nov. 2, 1892, provides an account of the opening.

Alumni Association and a joint open meeting of the Literary and Jackson societies. The dinner was held in the main hall, which for the next twenty years continued to be used for the annual Senior Dinner. On this occasion tables were laid for 175 graduates and Senior students. A. P. Coleman, as President of the Alumni Association, was in the chair. Grant had come up from Queen's for the dinner. He emphasized the closeness of the ties between Queen's and Victoria, and then uttered these prophetic words: "Another bond between Victoria and Queen's was that of closeness of belief. He could say without hesitation that no two Churches came so near each other in religious belief as the Presbyterian and Methodist. He sometimes thought that it was almost a crime that they should continue to live apart. . . ."

For staff and students the transfer to a new, well-heated, and well-appointed building must have been heartening. There was room aplenty for the 226 students in Arts and Theology of 1892-3. Burwash had spoken of 300 as an ideal number for a college, but actually had built to give fair accommodation to twice that number. In sixty years the allotment of space has been significantly altered. At that time all four corners of the first floor were occupied by lecture rooms. The Chancellor's office was that now occupied by the Registrar, and next it was his class-room. The Dean of Arts' and the Registrar's lecture rooms were in the southwest and the northeast corners respectively, with their offices adjacent. Indeed at first each professor had a private office and a lecture room which stood in his name, the two usually connected by a door. Opposite the main entrance was the library, with shelves towards the door and tables within the bay of the great windows. There was no west entrance. The room at the west end of the hall was at first designated as a "parlour" for the men students, but very shortly became a reading room with newspapers and periodicals, after loud complaints arose against the damp and cold southeast corner of the basement originally assigned for that purpose. Three rooms on the second floor were set apart for other purposes than teaching: the Chapel, very much as it is today except for the paintings and busts; the ladies' parlour in the southeast corner; and the business office of the College, narrowly confined to what is now Room 21, with Dr. Potts' office separated from that of his assistant by a glass partition. For many years Miss Mary Wilson occupied that position, received fees, and kept the books, her efficiency, kindness, and keen interest in all that concerned the College, its staff, and students nicely fitting into the intimate and friendly society of the place. The only other secretarial assistant was Miss Bertha Toye, who did her best to keep the Chancellor's correspondence in order, but was always ready as time permitted to help the staff with typing. The third floor contained classrooms and offices again, and here most of the theological lectures were given; but the northeast room was called Alumni Hall and the northwest room Jackson Hall. The former was fitted out by the students and alumni with curtains and furniture, including three imposing chairs on a dais at the north end. Here each Saturday evening the meetings of the "Lit." were held under parliamentary rules. The Y.M.C.A. claimed Jackson Hall and held weekly afternoon meetings there, and daily meetings during a week of prayer in the fall term. The long and rather dark hall of the third floor contained the museum material. This was arranged around the walls in locked cabinets. The meteorite and the mummy sarcophagus, secure in their weight, were exposed on the floor.

The grounds were bounded on the north by Charles (then Czar) Street which at its western end was merely a sandy and little-used road. Even within this restricted area the southwest corner was occupied by the Drynan residence. Thus there was no proper space for a playing field. However, goal posts were set up facing east and west to the northeast of the college—"playing in a fence corner," *Acta* called it. Even alley had been forgotten in the press of building. The October *Acta* in 1892 carried in the "locals" this item: "A face we miss—the face of the Alley Board." In surroundings so utterly strange, one relic served to recall Cobourg days. The old sun-dial had been brought up and set in the walk midway between the front gate and the portico.

College life was seriously disrupted. *Acta*, though less ably edited in this first year than usual, bears abundant evidence of this. Had funds permitted the residences of Burwash's original plans, it might have been different. But scattered in boarding houses through the city, with no facilities for games, and little social commingling with other student bodies whose welcome was scarcely even formal, the students found this first year rather desolate. "We were waifs to begin with," is the way the Rev. Dr. A. P. Addison, who was entering his second year, puts it.

If the "Bob" was thought of, heart was wanting to give it effect. How could they sing the "Bob" song in a strange land? The city churches, however, sought to make the students feel at home, having organized what was known as a "Social Union" for that purpose. One result of extra-curricular inertia, no doubt, was closer application to studies, if for no better reason than to demonstrate how little substance there was in the boasted superiority of Toronto honour standards. And the fourth year succeeded in doing so pretty conclusively. For the last two years in Cobourg, to be sure, the curriculum had been altered and additions made to honour work with a view to easing the transition. When the fourth year results were announced in 1893, it was found that of the 23 candidates, 20 received honours (4 in first class, but one with a "star,"[4] and 10 in second class), one who attempted honours was given a pass degree, and of the 2 students in the Pass Course one got a clear degree and the other had two stars. In any year this would count as a very creditable record. The second and third year results were also satisfactory, particularly the former. It was clear that on the whole the previous training of students at Cobourg had not placed them at a disadvantage. And it is significant that so few of them were enrolled in the Pass Course.

In that first year in Toronto, Arthur Leopold Langford ('84) joined the staff as Lecturer. In his undergraduate days he had specialized in Classics and football. The disrespect which he and his younger brothers, Henry and Fred, showed to the height of the College has already been mentioned. Four members of this family, whose father was a Methodist minister of distinguished appearance and talents, graduated from Victoria, the youngest becoming the wife of Newton Wesley Rowell. Arthur Langford had prepared himself for his work at Victoria by secondary school teaching at Brantford and Winnipeg, and by a period of study in Germany without, however, proceeding to a degree. Tall and dark, his fine presence and personal qualities gave him an honoured place in the College, especially in later years when he became first Registrar and then, for the last year of his life, Dean of Arts. He died at the age of sixty-one. Each year his memory is—or should be—freshly recalled, when the Athletic Stick, which he instituted in 1898,

[4]The term euphemistically applied in Toronto to failure in a Pass subject, which might be atoned for at a Supplemental examination in September.

passes from the hands of the man in the final year whose contribution to athletics is voted the most outstanding in his year and whose scholastic record has been untarnished by a star, to a successor of the following year similarly credited.

By the autumn of 1893 the student body had sensibly recovered from the shock of removal. The alley-board had risen in a retired spot about where the receiving desk of the Library now stands. Acutely aware of the disfavour into which he, and to a degree the Chancellor, had fallen through lack of playing facilities, Potts as Bursar, in his ignorance of such matters, actually made an outlay of $800 to build the more easterly of the two tennis courts north of the main building. Without regard to the porous nature of the soil, the ground was excavated to a quite unnecessary depth of two feet and replaced by crushed stone covered with cinders. This court probably has had the longest life of any in the city. A year or two later the undergraduates smiled at Potts after they had built two more courts for $150 end to end west of the alley-board between Czar Street and the Drynan property. The Chancellor's apparent failure to realize the important place of athletics in college life is not a little surprising. He himself was powerfully built, and his "grass-cutters" in cricket were held in memory. Furthermore his four surviving sons (four other children, one a little girl, had died from diphtheria in 1891) were all respectable athletes; and Lockie, the second son, was famous as a scrimmage man in Varsity rugby. A desperately hard worker himself, Burwash must have been a little jealous of any interest which served to distract the students from serious study. Urged on by criticism in *Acta*, the College authorities presently sought to secure from the University additional land beyond Czar Street. All efforts, however, for several years proved ineffectual.

The organization of the Athletic Union in December, 1894, gave added impetus to sport. A hockey cushion was maintained where North and Middle Houses now stand, and an extension to the west for skating and social intercourse was presently added. Inter-class contests in alley, hockey, and even association football in "the fence corner" were carried on each year; also a tennis tournament with College championship, handicap, and open events, in the last of which some of the best players from the city competed. The draw and the results as published in *Acta* find no parallel today. Meanwhile Victoria College men were gradually being included in University teams. During the first winter in Toronto Alan Shepard and Harry Field played with the Varsity seven in hockey, and in the same spring Shepard and R. A. A. Shore were two of the nine members chosen by ballot for the Athletic Directorate. The University gymnasium, occupying the more westerly part of the land where Hart House now stands, was completed in 1894. A fair number of Victoria students paid the four-dollar fee; and if they did not take advantage of the classes in gymnastics, boxing, and fencing under "Prof." Williams, at least they used the track and apparatus to keep themselves in physical trim throughout the year.

One reform effected in College organizations during the second year in Toronto was the combining of the Jackson and Literary societies to form the Union Literary Society. The division had never been a healthy one, nor in the character of Victoria, being based on a cleavage between arts and theology. Thereafter, for a quarter of a century the "Lit." not only gave the men students through its weekly meetings an opportunity to develop a talent for public speaking and to familiarize themselves with parliamentary procedure, but also, except for a brief period, managed all matters of student business (including the publishing of *Acta*) which did not fall within the province of the Athletic Union or the Y.M.C.A. and Missionary Society. The undergraduates of Victoria of that date had only themselves to blame if they left college unfitted to take their place in public life. Of course membership was voluntary in the "Lit."—as in all other organizations—on the payment of a small annual fee. This policy had one advantage over the present compulsory fees collected by the College office: where the undergraduates were free to contribute or not to contribute, both they and the officers of the organizations were likely to see that value was received.

In the summer of 1894 a notable addition to the staff was made. John Charles Robertson resigned from the principalship of the Toronto Junction High School to become Lecturer in Greek. "J. C.," as he is still familiarly known, had graduated from University College in 1883 with the gold medal in Classics. Thereafter as Fellow in Classics in University College, in graduate studies for a year at Johns Hopkins under Gildersleeve, and as Classical Master at Brampton and Owen Sound, as well as at the Junction, he had gained a reputation as a foremost classical scholar and author. He appears to have had more faith in Victoria than another graduate of University College, the son of a Primitive Methodist minister withal, is reputed to have expressed. About this time conversation was had with W. S. Milner, presumably about the same position, and he predicted that Victoria would never turn out a first class honour graduate in Classics—a prediction which in later years as Professor of Ancient History in University College his own verdict as examiner repeatedly contributed to refute. For twenty-seven years Bell and Robertson worked together, side by side, to build up a secure reputation for sound scholarship and excellent teaching in Classics at Victoria College. There was some significance in the fact that two students in Classics at University College destined for the Presbyterian ministry, one entering the fourth year and one the third year, transferred to Victoria in the fall of 1894. After some years, having advanced from lecturer to professor, and his work now well in hand, Robertson became deeply involved in college and university committee work. For twelve years he was Dean of Arts at Victoria, and in the University Council of the Faculty of Arts he became one of the two or three most influential members. Indeed it was remarked that only two men knew the University Calendar in all its complicated detail, James Brebner, the Registrar, and J. C. Robertson. Tall and spare, inclined to be reserved and severe in appearance, to the freshmen he was rather forbidding, and he used his red ink pen on Greek prose exercises with telling effect. But this feeling of aloofness gradually receded as men advanced to his magnificent course in the *Republic* of Plato in the third and fourth years, and as he became known in his own hospitable home. In fact while his wit was caustic at times, fun was never far to seek, and he became known as one of the best after-dinner speakers in the University. At the time of his retirement according to rule in 1932, the classes in Honour Greek were the largest in the history of Victoria. After a few years, when his younger brother (later Chief Justice) became judge of the Supreme Court of Ontario, he drily observed that his brother was elevated to the bench at the very age at which he was put on the shelf.

In student activities 1894 was distinguished as the year of two "Bobs." The Sophomores were not disposed to accept as a permanent substitute the oyster supper offered in the fall of 1892; but the forces favouring Victoria's traditional method of initiating freshmen did not gain sufficient momentum to burst the official dyke till after the Christmas vacation. It was January 23, 1894, before what was known as the "Columbus Bob" was staged with G. W. Bruce ('85) as Chairman. The institution once restored, again in November the largest Freshman class up to that time was duly chastened, and J. W. St. John ('81), M.P.P., was in the chair to lend prestige to the operation. This class, furthermore, included B. A. Cohoe, the winner of the Prince of Wales scholarship, the highest award at matriculation. For twenty years the "Bob" went on its merry way without interruption. There were, of course, excesses and reforms in cycle, and rumblings now and then of a positive veto. The very next year, for example, the Women's Literary Society wrote a letter to the Faculty protesting the "bobbing" of women. The ladies not only had their way, but also provided the "Bob" of 1895 with a most amusing Faculty scene in which that august body pondered their missive.

It was in 1894 that a beginning was made of valuable scholarships in course at Victoria. Bell, always generous to a fault, offered an annual scholarship of $60 in Honour Classics of the third year. The following month Horning, with the assistance of some friends, created an identical scholarship in Modern Languages. The sum was sufficient at the time to cover a quarter of the expense of a year at Toronto. Then followed scholarships presented by A. E. Ames in Honour Moderns of the first year ($60) and the Rev. E. A. Chown in third year Honour Ethics ($50), and, two years later, the J. C. Robertson scholarship in Honour Classics of the first year ($50).

The student body at Victoria managed to keep clear of the upheaval in University circles in 1895. Burwash, knowing that the budding politicians of the newly formed Political Science Association were mainly responsible for the trouble, summoned the Victoria College students in this honour department and counselled abstention, and his advice was heeded. But University College during the winter and spring was a lively society. The net result was the dismissal of one member of the staff, William Dale, who was thereby translated from the life of an excellent professor of Latin to that of an equally excellent farmer near St. Mary's; the suspension of the editor of the *Varsity*, James A. Tucker, who thereupon took his degree at Leland Stanford;

a first taste of notoriety for two other students involved, Lord Greenwood and Mackenzie King; and a growing realization that James Loudon, while his action had been correct enough in this instance, was wanting in certain valuable qualities of patience and tact. Although the Victoria students took no part in the general strike called, it would not be surprising if many of them found the fireworks between W. R. Riddell, counsel for the students, and S. H. Blake, University counsel, before the commission presided over by T. W. Taylor, Chief Justice of Manitoba, more attractive than the current lectures.

The "Bob" of 1898 very nearly ceased to be, at the will of an outraged Freshman class. It happened this way. Three of their most prominent members had been served with summonses for disturbing the peace in the vicinity of the College during one of the nocturnal processions of the class when they were practising their "Bob" songs. Although apprehensive that it might be a hoax, the year decided that they would obey the law, and proceeded to the court in strength, taking with them a lawyer whom they had hired to protest their innocence. They sat through the snappy proceedings of Colonel Denison's famous tribunal and saw the long list of drunks and others duly admonished, but their names were never called. To their lawyer's inquiry, the bench blandly replied that their case was not on his list. Having paid their lawyer, they returned to the College in a furious mood, and for some days it was touch and go whether the "Bob" would proceed without the Freshmen present, if such a thing were possible. Only when spokesmen for the "Bob" committee in a tumultuous Freshman meeting had asseverated (what was near enough to the truth) that the committee was not responsible for the events of that unhappy morning, did they consent to reverse a previous decision and attend. As a matter of fact, the brains of the conspiracy was a rather mature student with noticeably thinning hair, destined for the ministry, and long since gone to his reward, the last man in the year who would have been suspected of such deviltry, while the policeman who extracted from the authorities the uniform and summonses was a burly private member of the class now practising law in Toronto. How the Colonel was won over was never disclosed.

The financial situation was tolerably sound during these early years in Toronto. Senator Cox, as Treasurer, saw to that. The building itself had cost $222,000, and was opened free of debt. The subscriptions had slightly exceeded $500,000 from 5,109 subscribers, but some $100,000 of this was never collected. The failure to collect all can hardly be wondered at. The early nineties saw dreadfully hard times in Canada. Senator John Macdonald's executors, for instance, requested and were granted a deduction of $5,000 from his donation of $25,000. A municipality like Toronto Junction went into bankruptcy. Even in 1897 a rural school-teacher was considered lucky if he had a salary of $300, and a barrel of Northern Spy apples might be bought for fifty cents. It was only with altered fiscal and immigration policies that the picture changed. The Canadian Pacific Railway was encouraged to load its returning vessels with profitable ballast in the form of European immigrants to swarm over the western plains. The credit, or blame, for this policy can justly be assigned to the Hon. Clifford Sifton ('80), Minister of the Interior.[5]

In spite of rigorous economy the annual deficit from 1893 to 1899 averaged over $9,000. This was partially offset by the $25,000 which in 1897 the government paid for the old building at Cobourg. It was the interest of the Massey family that placed the College on its feet. When Hart A. Massey died in 1896 he not only left $200,000 to Victoria, $50,000 of which was designated for a residence for women students, but he bequeathed in his three surviving children[6] a deep concern which served largely to create the Victoria University we know today. In an article in *Acta*, "*In Memoriam, Beati mortui qui in Domino moriuntur . . . opera enim illorum sequuntur illos*," Reynar estimated his benefactions to good causes at $2,000,000. Three sentences in this informative and graceful tribute would appear to indicate that the strenuous political campaign of that year on the merits of the National Policy had invaded Reynar's ivory tower.

Our young country has already produced a score of men or more who, judged by their successes, have been his equals in financial genius. But when the names of some other Canadian millionaires will be forgotten or despised, the name of Massey will be one of the few names held in honor

[5]It may be remarked that in later life Sifton appears to have taken very little interest in the College, and towards the end of his life none whatever. But in 1895 there was a Sifton meeting in Massey Hall at which Burwash took the chair and was mildly reproved for so doing by Potts, and in 1898 he was chairman of the Senior Dinner.

[6]A younger son had died while studying at the Massachusetts Institute of Technology.

for the noble way in which his millions were spent. . . . It is further worthy of note that since about four fifths of the students in our Canadian Colleges are the sons and daughters of farmers, Mr. Massey has really made a wise and generous return to the farming community of the profits of the business to which they have contributed.[7]

Financial relations with the University became a matter of public dispute in 1897. Five letters in all passed between Burwash and B. E. (later Sir Edmund) Walker between May 8, 1897, and April 29, 1898. These were later printed to form a pamphlet of twenty-eight pages. Briefly the situation was this. The University trustees, of whom Walker was one, were not balancing their budget, and on appealing to the government for assistance had been promised $7,000 provided they would raise an equal amount by fees. Since the federated colleges received the tuition fees of their own students, the only way in which Victoria College students could contribute was through other levies such as had already been imposed for examinations and the maintenance of the library. It was now proposed to increase these special fees. In the course of a cogent argument Burwash admits that he was inclined at first "for the sake of friendly co-operation to yield to the extent proposed," but the strong opposition of his Senate led him to investigate the subject further. This study convinced him that Victoria would not be justified in accepting the proposal, since an additional fee was not required to cover the cost of examinations, and the fee already charged quite met the cost of such use of the university library as Victoria College students were able to make. The true cause of the annual deficits, he proceeds to show by statistics, was over-expenditure on University College with a corresponding neglect of the University departments. "What we do object to," he contends, "is such a policy as robs the University Faculty of its reasonable claim, and then, in the face of both Act and agreement, seeks to impose fees for maintenance on our students."[8] The whole passage at arms, and particularly the section where Walker quotes President Loudon, indicates that after five years there was still an element in the University which failed to regard the federation agreement as just or Victoria College as an equal partner. In such an atmosphere it is not surprising that the College should request and secure from the government in 1898 legislation which extended for a further six years separate representation of its

[7]*Acta*, March, 1896.
[8]V.U.A., Burwash-Walker letters (pamphlet), letter of May 9, 1898.

graduate body on the University Senate, which was still the principal governing body of the University. At the expiration of this extension, the entry of Trinity into federation on the same basis of separate representation had settled the principle, and in the general reform of the Act in 1906 the provision for a common election of alumni representation on the Senate appears not to have been considered.

If Loudon and Burwash clashed on this subject, on another financial matter they took common ground. The occasion was an agitation on the part of Queen's looking to the establishment of a School of Forestry at Kingston. In 1893 Queen's had received a grant of $6,000 toward a new School of Mining and Agriculture established in 1892. Agriculture was very soon dropped, but the School of Mining continued, and in the first ten years of its existence received from the government $162,000 in grants. With the prospect of a Forestry School in addition, the authorities of the University of Toronto thought it high time to raise the whole question of grants to institutions under private control while the crying needs of the provincial university were still unsatisfied. And Burwash came to Loudon's aid with an argument in the *University Monthly* of May, 1903, not entirely in accord either with the historic position of Victoria or with a fraternal spirit to Queen's. Loudon's presentation of the case had appeared in the April issue.

The growing importance of Modern Languages coincident with a relative decline in Classical studies was shown in two appointments to the Victoria staff. In 1897 Augustus Edward Lang and Oscar Pelham Edgar were appointed Lecturers, the former in German and English, the latter in French. It would be difficult to find two university men differing more widely in background and in personal qualities; yet until Lang's retirement in 1932 they worked together comfortably in the same or allied departments, each in his own way making a distinct contribution to the success and prestige of the College. Lang was by nine years the older. He had been born of German parents in a comfortable farm home set in the rich soil of the upper Ottawa. After graduating in 1889 from Victoria, where he became deeply interested in science as well as in literature, he taught continuously in the Napanee High School until invited to return as Lecturer to the College. He had thus no special preparation for university teaching other than that which is afforded by a keen and cultivated mind, a fondness for books, and a widening acquaintance with men and affairs. Above the average in height, exceedingly broad shouldered, he strode through life firm of step, intense in his likes and dislikes, in private conversation and especially as host the most interesting and charming of men. One likes to think of him in the home of his later years amid the flowers and trees planted and tended by his own hands on the heights above the Scarborough bluffs with a magnificent prospect across land and water. He would have preferred a chair in English; but when Edgar succeeded Reynar, he accepted a professorship in German and, together with his friend, C. C. James, assisted in the building up of several collections of English authors, and especially of Canadiana in the new Birge-Carnegie Library, of which he had charge from 1907 to 1924. His interest in books, as well as his capacity for business, found scope during his later years in the vice-presidency of a publishing firm. He died at Scarborough Heights in 1945, and was buried from the College Chapel after a fitting tribute from President Brown.

Edgar was aristocratic in appearance, and, if such a thing may be said in Canada, in parentage. His father, Sir James Edgar, had been Speaker of the House of Commons, and his mother was a Ridout. He had been educated at Upper Canada College, University College, and Johns Hopkins, where he took his Ph.D. in English. After teaching at Upper Canada College for two years he accepted the position in French left vacant by the death of Petch but transferred to English on Reynar's retirement. He was tall, slender, and graceful, and his fine features gained further distinction from a mass of dark hair and a heavy moustache. In his first year at College he would come over from the Edgar home on Bloor Street, afterwards purchased by the College for the Chancellor's residence, with his terrier on leash and tie the dog to a leg of the desk as he taught the Freshman class French. "Pelham," as the select circle of his friends knew him, soon became a foremost literary critic, whose judgment was widely respected by publishers. He was thus the means of assisting several young Canadians on the road to distinguished authorship.[9] Two of his own books, *Henry James* and *The Art of the Novel*, have become standard works. As a lecturer he had a devoted following, and as a reader of lyric poetry was unrivalled.

[9] E.g., Pratt, Robins, Knister, Pickthall, Bush, Frye, and Pacey. E. K. Brown, when a professor at University College, readily assented to the request of a group of Victoria students who wished to "audit" his lectures, with the comment that he welcomed the chance to reciprocate a privilege he had enjoyed when Pelham Edgar was lecturing at Victoria and he was an undergraduate at University College.

His "Bobbing" was always a feature of the faculty scene. He was frequently represented with one leg wrapped about the heavy oak lectern from which he liked to read his lectures. This piece of furniture was to achieve fame. Edgar at times lectured in what was known as Dr. Bell's room (24), and he would have the lectern moved into the room for the occasion. Bell, who liked—and required—space on the platform, as frequently instructed the janitor to remove it, and became increasingly incensed when he found it back and in his way. This happened once too often. Striding into the room from his office, he found the detested bauble again on the platform. He walked over to the southeast window, threw it open, called one of the students to help him, and together they heaved the lectern from the second storey to the lawn below.[10] During the winter before his death in 1949 Edgar returned to the College to give a course of lectures on the modern novel, greatly to the satisfaction of the Honour students and the High Table at Burwash Hall.

Thus at the end of the nineties Victoria University was manned by an all-Canadian permanent staff of thirteen, assisted at times by sessional appointments. Of the thirteen, eight were its own graduates, four were graduates of University College, and one of Albert College. Most of these had pursued graduate studies in Germany, England, or France, only three in American graduate schools. It was a well-balanced and strong staff, particularly in Arts. Several of its members were active in the Ontario Educational Association, and favourably known to the secondary school teachers of the province. Thus, although the increase in Arts enrolment generally owing to economic conditions was not rapid during this decade, that at Victoria was well maintained and by 1900-1 had reached 295. In Theology the output of students was unequal to the pulpit demands of the province and of the rapidly expanding Canadian West; yet at the end of the decade, the Forward Movement for Missions invaded the College to attract some of its finest minds to work in China and Japan. Occasionally men who had taken their Arts work in Manitoba (at that time the only university of the Canadian West) came to Victoria for Theology, one of these (in 1898) being J. S. Woodsworth.

It was 1900 before Burwash felt constrained to relinquish a respon-

[10]This lectern and its inseparable patron share immortality in one of the stained-glass windows of the Faculty Union dining hall in Hart House.

sibility he had held since 1873 and recommend the appointment of Wallace as Dean of Theology. It was not his manner to commit to others what it appeared he might do himself. And while democratic in his bearing and a Liberal in politics, he had never accepted Solomon's repeated admonition that in the multitude of counsellors there is safety. Professor J. C. Robertson in a letter written in response to a request for his impressions of these early years under federation notes this characteristic.

... That what I have to write should consist so largely of negatives and explanations of negatives, is itself, perhaps, a significant and sufficient impression of what the working of Federation meant to me and, I think, most of us on the Victoria staff....

To begin with, when I joined the Faculty in 1894, I had been for some years engaged chiefly in secondary school teaching, and the years of my tutorial fellowship in University College lay many years behind me. This meant that my chief task for several years was to fit myself for my new work, and my horizon was pretty well bounded by the walls of my classroom.

In the second place, no member—certainly no junior member—of the Victoria staff had anything to do with the working of the Federation scheme (beyond doing our own tasks as well as we could). That applies not only to the larger aspects of Federation as a matter of University statesmanship but also to the details of the fixing of the curriculum of study, the holding of examinations and the determination of standards and so forth. These belonged to the University Senate, and apart from Dr. Burwash and his two chief lieutenants and consultants, Bain and Reynar, the rest of us had nothing to do with that august body and often knew very little of what went on there. There was nothing even remotely corresponding to the Council of the Faculty of Arts, so far as the members of the staff of the Arts Colleges were concerned. And there were no Departmental meetings as there are today, with any power to make recommendations or to decide any question relating to the work prescribed by the Curriculum drawn up by the University Senate....

My part, therefore, in helping to make Federation work was pretty much confined to what I did in the class-room and in preparing my lectures. In the department of Classics our relations with our colleagues were more amicable than was the case in some of the other departments. Fletcher, who came in 1896, greatly admired Dr. Bell and saw a good deal of him, as I did of Milner. Hutton, who had known me ever since he came to Toronto in 1880, was friendly enough, but always, of course, in a detached, Olympian way. He took no part or interest in the interchange of lectures which grew up after 1895 and later proved of great value and importance. This interchange was begun under the authority of Loudon and Burwash, but grew and developed by consultations between members of the staff in Latin in University College and the Victoria Classical staff. . . .

The prospect of the University of Trinity College joining the federal system was warmly welcomed by Victoria. During the nineties Trinity had observed federation from a distance of five miles and had concluded that Victoria's action in accepting the Act of 1887 on faith had not been so ill advised as then appeared. In 1900 the Rev. T. C. Street Macklem, who had just been appointed Provost, spoke at the Charter Day exercises at Victoria and took occasion to express the hope that the day was not far distant when Trinity would become a great college in a great university. Certain impediments had first to be dealt with, and three of these were removed, at least partially, by the University Act of 1901. In this Act a step was taken towards the ultimate separation of the University and University College by provision for the appointment of a Principal and College Council for University College. Secondly, the principle of separate representation in the Senate of graduates of the federated colleges was now definitely accepted. It was further enacted that representation of any university subsequently coming into federation should be "in the proportion of one representative for every one hundred graduates in Arts." Thus proportional representation was conceded, a basis on which Victoria at the beginning had been allotted five graduate members as compared with twelve for University College.[11] The third point was the promise of a site in or near Queen's Park free of ground rent, and until buildings should be erected, provision for the duplication of university lectures at the old Trinity College.

The status of Trinity was never elaborated in a separate act. Statutory provision is limited to the Federation Act of 1887, the brief relevant sections of the University Act of 1901, and one short section in the Amending Act of 1904. The meat of the matter, however, is in an agreement concluded on August 25, 1903, proclaimed by the Lieutenant-Governor of Ontario on November 18, and published in the Ontario *Gazette* of November 28. This agreement was given the force

[11]By action of the University Senate in 1952 this principle was reaffirmed, and in accordance with it University College received 7 members, Victoria 6, St. Michael's 3, Trinity 3.

of law by sections 43(5)-47 in the Act of 1901. Of the items of this agreement, several had particular interest for Victoria. Provision was made for a common Calendar to be published by the University; for a separate registrar for University College; for the purchase, in event of withdrawal from federation, at a price to be fixed by arbitration of any buildings which Trinity might erect on its new site; and for the distribution of theological options evenly "over the four years of the Pass Course and as far as possible over each year of the several Honour Courses." Thus Trinity was able to make Religious Knowledge a compulsory subject for all undergraduates, a right which Victoria had never sought, or indeed desired; and when the site was settled in 1910 with ample grounds for a main building, men's and women's residences, and a spacious campus, provided free of cost, the second denominational college to enter federation could reflect that something had been gained by waiting and permitting Victoria to make the plunge. It is interesting also to note that should federation miscarry and either college wish to leave Queen's Park—a remote contingency— Victoria would be required to pay for its site at the value of 1890 and make what disposal it could of its buildings, while Trinity would merely abandon a site for which it had paid nothing and could claim a fair price from the University for its buildings. All of which shows that Sir Robert Falconer did not miss the mark when he smilingly referred to Provost Macklem as "conserver of the rights and extender of the privileges" of Trinity.

The provision of residence accommodation for men had been projected by Burwash in 1890, but the women students won by ten years. As early as 1896 the will of Hart A. Massey had made $50,000 available for women's residences, but the hesitation of the University of Toronto trustees to set free the required land had retarded the project. The general reason given was that it was needed for university purposes, one such purpose mentioned being a group of residences for members of the faculty. In the meantime the ladies were active. As early as 1895 Miss M. E. T. Addison and Mrs. Burwash had correspondence on the subject. An auxiliary was formed named the Barbara Heck Memorial Association, after the mother of Canadian Methodism. This was in 1897, and in the following year the Alumnae Association was formed with Miss Addison as President. When finally arrangements were made late in 1901 for the purchase of land north of Czar Street, 290 by 608 feet for $50,000, the western face of this property was assigned to the residence for women. In April, 1902, the corner stone was laid by Chester D. Massey, acting for his mother, and by October of the following year a home for some sixty students was available, the furnishing and equipment being provided through the efforts of the women's association. There was a little flurry about the name. At first it was proposed to honour Barbara Heck, but in the end the mother of the Wesleys was preferred. Euphony rather than a resurgence of colonialism was no doubt mainly responsible for the change. Or perhaps it had come to be known that neighbours of those sturdy pioneers on the upper St. Lawrence were never quite sure whether Barbara's surname was Heck or Hick.

Miss Addison was asked to give up her position as teacher of Modern Languages at the Lindsay Collegiate Institute and become the Dean of Annesley Hall. A happier choice could hardly have been made. Herself reared in a devout and cultivated home—her father, Peter Addison, was a Methodist minister whose solid preaching in old age could fill the Collier Street Church at Barrie during the summer vacation of the pastor—she combined a firmness of purpose and deeply religious attitude towards her work with a wealth of sympathy and understanding for young people. The result was a certain flexibility and a greater readiness to adapt herself to changing conditions than some others thought desirable, with rather important consequences to the College ten years later.

Events were now converging on 1906, a focal date in the history of the University of Toronto. After a third of a century of power—or four years more, if the term of J. S. Macdonald be included—the sands of the Liberal party were running low. In a spirited election, in which more important matters than the *Minnie M.* and a certain piano-box had their place, the Ross Government was defeated and James Pliny Whitney became Premier. Whitney, who had represented Dundas County since 1888, had consistently advocated more generous treatment of the University of Toronto. One of his first acts was to name a Royal Commission of seven outstanding citizens to report upon "a scheme for the management and government of the University of Toronto in the room and stead of the one under which the said University is now managed and governed."[12] Those named were J. W. Flavelle (Chairman), Goldwin Smith, W. R. Meredith, B. E. Walker, H. J. Cody, D. Bruce Macdonald, and A. H. U. Colquhoun (Secretary). Whitney had made no attempt to give representation to various interests; the personnel was chosen solely on merit. Their report of 348 pages, dated at the Grange, April 4, 1906, will rank as one of the ablest pronouncements ever issued on university education. The general argument and the draft bill based on it extend to 99 pages. The rest consists of information secured from other North American universities, statements made by the various colleges on the campus and by private individuals and organizations, and several of the earlier University Acts.

The legislation of 1906 was based squarely on this report. To discuss its nature in general or in detail is not our part. A good summary under nine heads appears on page xx of the Report, and the whole has been sufficiently praised elsewhere, perhaps at times unduly, with implied disparagement of the at least equally great achievement of 1887. It will be sufficient to indicate certain features of the legislation which affected the federated colleges. The most important perhaps was the creation of a Council of the Faculty of Arts. This provided a forum for the discussion of Arts work, and through such discussion and the work of its several committees it made for a sounder basis for decision on matters of educational policy than had been possible in the Senate. In the Council, in addition to the staff in University subjects, all members of the teaching staffs of the colleges above the rank of lecturer were voting members; even lecturers on the permanent staff were made assessors. It became a thoroughly democratic body, in which officials had influence only in proportion to the weight of their opinions. The Commissioners described it as the most important of the Councils, and as such stipulated that the President, not the Dean, as in the councils of the other faculties, should be its chairman. The fact that Arts has continued to occupy a central and paramount place in the University of Toronto, in contrast with some other state institutions, must be attributed largely to the constitution of its Council.

In their paragraph on the college system the Commissioners remarked:

[12]*Report of the Royal Commission on the University of Toronto* (1906), p. iv.

Through federation we have developed a form of organization that is unique. The State provides a complete system of education in Arts in the University of Toronto and University College. The subjects taught in University College are taught also in the denominational Colleges of Victoria and Trinity. All the students who take lectures in the University subjects must be enrolled in one of these three Colleges. We believe that the University has thus, by apparent chance, hit upon a system which, if properly and loyally worked, provides a combination of strong personal influence on students with the broad outlook and widened sympathies that come from membership in a great University.[13]

The solution, of course, was less by chance than the Commissioners supposed. It may be noted that both the Senate of Victoria University in its observations and Burwash in a long private memorandum had recommended the organization of the Council of the Faculty of Arts with much the same duties as were actually assigned it. The Senate, however, would have had the Council elect its own officers.

Another change deeply affecting the colleges was the large power now entrusted to the Board of Governors, and to the President, one of its twenty members. The transfer of direct authority over all but the purely academic interests of the University (which remained with the Senate) from the government to the Governors was a reform of far-reaching importance. At the time it was thought, by ear-marking a certain portion of the succession duties for its support, to make the University financially independent of the government of the day. The Minister of Education was dropped from the Senate, whose statutes, or so many of them as dealt with matters over which the authority of the Senate was not final, were now referred to the Board and not as formerly to the government. Appointments also were transferred to the Board, but with a proviso which gave to the office of President an authority it had hitherto lacked, namely, that no appointment to, promotion in, or removal from the teaching staff of the University or of University College could take place except upon the recommendation of the President.

In connection with appointments, Burwash in his memorandum had urged the introduction of what he calls "cabinet government."[14] He would have revived the University Caput of Baldwin's bill to be composed of the President, deans of faculties, and heads of colleges, seven in all, and would have erected this body into a sort of cabinet, which

[13]*Ibid.*, pp. xlvii–xlviii.   [14]*Ibid.*, p. 104.

inter alia would have advised the "appointing bodies" in the case of new appointments. He had expressed the opinion that such a system was preferable to "a strong, personal headship, an autocracy, if you please." As a matter of fact, on the recommendation of the Commission, the Caput was actually revived, and constituted as he proposed, but its powers were mainly disciplinary and had no reference to appointments.

With regard to the demand for the separation of the University and University College in such a way as to give equality of status to the Arts colleges—a point on which Trinity had laid particular stress—the Commission responded with a qualified negative. As this was "a matter deemed of moment" by the federated colleges, however, it recommended that University College be separately officered with a Principal and a Registrar of its own, but added with some emphasis, "The time has now come, we think, when the policy of maintaining a complete system of higher education by the State with one purse and one governing board, should be regarded as definitely settled."[15] The "continuance in good faith" of the division of subjects between college and university was recommended, and no transfer of subjects was to be made without the full assent of the federated colleges. All this was written into the Act. On the physical separation of the University and University College Principal Maurice Hutton in his memorandum offered this sage observation: "There is no necessity to legislate in a hurry, for a grievance which time is curing. . . . This local separation is growing. The Main Building will go, by a natural process, to University College, as residuary legatee, in a few years. It is only necessary to wait a little longer."[16] After almost fifty years the physical separation is still imperfect. The mathematicians continue to hold the tower in the old building, and the philosophers have consorted with Spanish and Italian to retain a foothold in the West Wing.

The framing of a new constitution was attended by the appointment of a new President. Loudon's incumbency, never quite comfortable, had become increasingly beset with difficulties. Even the Alumni Association, organized in 1900 on his initiative, failed to furnish needed support to his administration. It did succeed by means of two large deputations which invaded the Parliament Buildings in 1901 and 1904

[15]*Ibid.*, p. xxix.   [16]*Ibid.*, p. 97.

in extracting additional financial support, mainly for buildings; and it collected money to erect Convocation Hall. But its over-energetic secretary, Professor J. C. (afterwards Sir John) McLennan involved the President in serious trouble through a charge of favouritism in connection with the awarding of the 1851 Exhibition scholarship. Again, as ten years previously, the matter was ventilated in *Varsity*. A committee of the Senate which was appointed to investigate found irregularity but exonerated the President. However, by this time it had become evident that Loudon could no longer conciliate opposition or confirm public confidence in himself and the University. On the engagement that he should receive his full salary for life, he resigned in 1906 and declined to continue till his successor should be appointed. Thus Principal Hutton was asked to fill the gap. For a year he performed the duties of the presidency with dignity and grace, so that *Acta* was not alone in regretting that he was not a candidate for the office. The choice fell on a young Presbyterian minister, Robert Alexander Falconer, a native of Nova Scotia educated in London, Edinburgh, and Germany. At the time of his appointment he was the Principal of Pine Hill, a theological college under the Presbyterian Church, at Halifax. In 1905 he had received an LL.D. from St. Francis Xavier at Antigonish, an honour indicative of the liberal views and policies he was to bring with him to Toronto.

In their brief to the Royal Commission the authorities of St. Michael's College had stated that "notwithstanding the federation of St. Michael's College for a quarter of a century, the University of Toronto has not succeeded in gaining the confidence of the Catholic population of Ontario."[17] But in 1910, having found in Falconer the qualities which had attracted St. Francis Xavier, it abandoned the quasi-federation of 1887 for the same relation as that of Victoria and Trinity, except that in the case of Honour Philosophy it was permitted a separate curriculum and examination. Since then the Arts colleges may be said to have stood four-square against a prevailing tendency to materialism in university education.

To Victoria the coming of President Falconer was as a cleansing wind. What remained in the University of mistrust in federation was soon blown away or appeared only as wisps of cloud. Old disputes, old

[17]*Ibid.*, p. 121.

attachments had no force to distract his mind from the business in hand. He could appreciate the place of religion in education and the value of enlisting the support of the churches. When after twenty-five years he gave over the presidency to Dr. Cody, the feeling of Victoria was expressed in an address presented to him at the Senior Dinner of 1932, a few sentences of which may be quoted.

But what is uppermost in the thoughts of Victoria at this time is not the amazing growth during your Presidency, nor even the ability and the statesmanship which you have shown in guiding the policy of the University and in coping with its problems. That which comes first and chiefly to our minds to-night is what your régime has meant to our own Victoria College.

Colleges have long memories; and on the occasion of your retirement, Victoria's memory turns naturally to the decade or more before you came to Toronto. It was a time when the success of Federation was still to be determined; when, during the difficult period of adjustment to new conditions, there were many possibilities of misunderstanding and friction; and when, moreover, perfect harmony and concord were not always and everywhere found to reign in the University family into which Victoria had lately come....

From the very beginning of your Presidency all danger of faction and friction disappeared, and nothing in your administration has so completely united all voices in the University in praise and commendation as the universal feeling that in our President we have had a man who is impartial, fair-minded, and approachable, genuinely and deeply concerned for the welfare of every part and of every member of the University.[18]

It will have been noted that most professors of Victoria have continued in the College, if not to retirement, at least to advancing years. Two Victoria men appointed in this decade were exceptions. Austin Perley Misener had graduated in Oriental Languages in 1900. Pursuing his studies with ardour he secured his M.A. in 1901, his B.D. in 1904 and, after a year's study at Leipzig, his Ph.D. from Toronto in 1909. Although ordained in 1902, he did not take a circuit but came directly into the College and was ably assisting McLaughlin as Lecturer and Associate Professor. Indeed, in his day Orientals attracted students as never before or since. But he drove himself too hard. In addition to close application to study and teaching duties, in which he would not spare himself, he developed a men's Bible class at Sherbourne Street Methodist Church which made a wide appeal. His health broke under the strain and after a long and distressing illness

[18]*Victoria College Bulletin*, 1932-3, p. 43.

he died in 1912. Misener's death was a serious loss to Oriental Studies and to the College.

The second man to be cut off was George John Blewett. At graduation in 1897 he stood first in Philosophy and won the Governor-General's Gold Medal. Graduate study was pursued at Harvard under the George Paxton Young Memorial Fellowship, in Germany, and at Oxford under Caird. Blewett also felt that his place was not in the pulpit and in 1901 accepted a position in Wesley College, Winnipeg. On Badgley's death he was called to Victoria, with duties divided between Arts and Theology. While bathing during a vacation at Go Home Bay in 1912 he died of a heart attack. He had already established for himself a wide reputation as a fine scholar and brilliant lecturer and author. He left two works, both in the area where philosophy meets religion, *The Study of Nature and the Vision of God*, and *The Christian View of the World*. His wife, also a graduate of Victoria, was Miss Clara M. Woodsworth, silver medallist in Classics in 1901, daughter of the Rev. Richard Woodsworth and granddaughter of the Toronto contractor, Richard Woodsworth, who for many years was a member of the Victoria Board. Their daughter, now assistant to the Registrar, has by her thoughtfulness and unobtrusive efficiency made for herself a large place in the College.

In 1907 Charles Earl Auger was appointed Lecturer in English and Victor de Beaumont Lecturer in French. Auger had graduated in Modern Languages from Victoria in 1902. He had been prominent in student activities, in his second year being chairman of the "Bob" committee (and "Bobbing" the Chancellor), and in his fourth year editor of *Acta*. The five years after graduation he had spent in teaching in the United States and in graduate work at Chicago. His contribution to Victoria College must rank very high, as is indicated by the fact that its most valuable matriculation scholarship was given his name. Yet he left no scholarly publication, and as a public lecturer his delivery was hesitating and unimpressive; it was in the class-room and particularly in personal interviews with students that his fine qualities as a man and as a teacher were revealed. An intolerable burden of essays was piled on him during his earlier years on the staff,[19]

[19]"The fifth recommendation of the Chancellor read as follows: That Prof. Auger deliver four lectures [i.e. a week] and review 1600 essays. Moved and seconded that recommendation be adopted. Carried." V.U.A., Board of Regents, Minutes, Jan. 14, 1910.

which he bore with sufficient cheerfulness as in a good cause. The esteem in which he was held increased with the years, and when he succeeded Langford as Registrar, a happier appointment could not have been made. His wisdom in counsel and unaffected courtesy and kindness contributed not a little to establish the reputation of the College as a friendly place in which to live. His death in 1935 at the age of fifty-seven was a grievous loss.

Victor de Beaumont was born in the United States, graduated from Columbia in 1901, and spent the next three years in graduate work there and abroad. He was called from Williams College in 1907 to Victoria College where his teaching span, including three years after formal retirement, extended to forty-five years. His carefully prepared lectures were at times enlivened by bursts of eloquence. He was an effective speaker on the rare occasions when he took part in University debates; in the College he was quite active when library matters or questions of general policy were under discussion. On succeeding Ford as head of the French department, he was most punctilious in the exercise of his duties. With his final leaving in 1952, the gravel drive of the College will be less picturesque. The eye will miss his little car of ancient vintage which, trim and precise as was its owner, was wont to stand like a western bronco, tail to wind.

In the following year Norman Wentworth DeWitt was appointed to the staff in Classics with the title of Professor of Latin and Ancient History. At matriculation from Hamilton Collegiate Institute he won the Prince of Wales Scholarship, but he missed "Bobbing" and somewhat marred his course by continuing at the Collegiate for his first year's work. In his fourth year he presided in the Literary Society with dignity and poise, and won the Edward Wilson Gold Medal in Classics. The nine years after graduation in 1899 were spent in teaching in four colleges in the United States, in graduate work at Chicago where he won his Ph.D. with a thesis on "The Dido Episode," and in Europe on a fellowship offered by the Archaeological Institute of America. Returning to Victoria he at once became a popular lecturer, much in demand for public addresses by reason of his wide acquaintance with literature and his brilliancy of wit. His tall and distinguished appearance exhibited a saturnine touch which soon vanished when he began to speak. After 1913, as Professor of Latin Literature he shared the work in Latin with Dr. Bell. It should be said that in 1908 Dr. Bell was honoured by a University appointment as Professor of Comparative Philology, which he held concurrently with his professorship at Victoria. DeWitt kept in touch with classical scholarship in America perhaps more closely than anyone else in Toronto. From 1923 to 1928 he was Dean of Arts in Victoria. After his retirement he was elected President of the American Philological Association, the first Canadian professor to have that honour.

The session of 1909-10 saw two members added to the teaching staff, George Jackson and the writer, the former as Professor of English Bible, and the latter as Lecturer in Classics. Jackson's relations with the College were continued through four years, the writer after forty years of teaching (twenty-eight of them as Nelles Professor of Ancient History) persists as an Emeritus.

The appointment of Professor Jackson was attended by a contest which threatened to split the Methodist Church in twain. And in the struggle Victoria University—its President, its Faculty of Theology and its Board—played a part which deserved and won recognition in the world of religious thought. To understand the whole matter it is necessary to go back to 1905. At that time Jackson was ministering to a Methodist charge in Edinburgh. Here after seventeen years he had built a mission into one of the largest congregations of the city. He already enjoyed a reputation as a leading preacher in British Methodism, and had published many of his sermons. His method was direct and evangelical, free from any straining after effect by flights of oratory or sensationalism. He impressed the writer in an evening service in 1901 as a humble and devout Christian. Strangely enough, his text still holds in memory, "a double-minded man, unstable in all his ways." He visited Canada in 1902, where his sermons, delivered from Montreal to Vancouver, made him many friends. The result was an invitation in 1905 from the Board of Regents of Victoria University to accept a chair in Homiletics. The years at Edinburgh had told on a constitution never robust, and he was tempted to accept, but replied that he was called to preach.

The appointment of Dr. Bowles (of whom much more hereafter) to the chair of Homiletics left a vacancy in Sherbourne Street Methodist Church in Toronto. Jackson was then asked to accept the pastorate for the remaining three years of Dr. Bowles' term. For financial, and probably sentimental reasons as well, he did not wish to sever his connection with the parent Conference; and the requirements of the constitution were met by the appointment of the Rev. George Brown, an older minister, as Superintendent of Sherbourne Street with Jackson as Assistant. The arrangement was accepted at the time by the General Superintendent, Dr. Carman, and by the President of the Toronto Conference. Thus a fruitful pastorate was begun in a congregation which included several of the most influential and wealthy laymen of Methodism. In its third year the invitation to the College was renewed. On this occasion a new chair was to be created, that of English Bible, the name being intended, perhaps, to imply that the occupant need not have specialized in Hebrew or Greek. After negotiation, mainly concerned with ways and means of reconciling the princely salary of Sherbourne Street with the "poor dying rate" of college professors, Jackson agreed to accept. Meanwhile during the winter months he had continued his preaching to large and attentive congregations. In addition he prepared a series of lectures on biblical problems which he delivered to a men's club at the church and proposed to offer in a series at the University of Ohio in March. Up to this time no public criticism of his views had emerged. The Pulpit Supply Committee of Sherbourne Street could state: "His pulpit ministrations have been a benediction in our families, and, we believe, his residence in Canada has been of great benefit not alone to the Methodism of this city, but throughout the Dominion wherever he has been heard."[20]

But now came a fateful decision. He accepted an invitation by the Y.M.C.A. to give them one of these addresses, dealing with the early chapters of Genesis, already delivered without repercussions at his men's club. A brief account appearing in the morning papers was taken up by the evening press, and was followed by some few letters. The matter might have rested there without serious results. But the General Superintendent, Dr. Carman, would not have it so. Under pressure from certain ministers and two members at least of the Board of Regents, of which he himself was Chairman, without having seen the text of the address or communicating with Jackson, Carman prepared a

[20]*Globe*, Feb. 27, 1909. *Memorandum re Theological Teaching* (Toronto, 1910), p. 9.

letter for the Toronto *Globe* condemning Jackson on grounds personal as well as doctrinal. Recently Dr. Bowles has characterized this letter as one "which, it is hoped, will be buried in the Archives of the *Globe* office."[21] It shall not be exhumed here. But it cannot be overlooked. Beneath the rhetoric and riot of metaphor characteristic of Carman, at all events in his later years, the burden of complaint was that Jackson "as a minister from Britain," "hired as an assistant," "not responsible to any body in particular,"[22] had abused the rights of hospitality by disseminating false doctrine. The one sentence quoted from the address is distorted. In Carman's letter it appears as "a correct theory of the origin of the universe, the origin of the human race, and the origin of sin, is no part of the Christian faith"; in the manuscript it reads, "A precise theory of the origin of the universe and of man and of sin is surely no essential part of the Christian faith." The quarrel broke at the time of the Kinrade murder and was given equal prominence as front-page news. It appeared that a fire had been lit which Noah's deluge could hardly have quenched.

After forty years an attempt to assess the motives of the two men is perhaps justified. Jackson was essentially a gentle man, by no means aggressive or polemical. If he erred in judgment in presenting his views to such a body of men as would come to hear him at the Y.M.C.A., it was because of a settled conviction that the Word of God was for the many, not merely the few. As an Anglican cleric remarked after listening to Jackson speak before the Rural Deanery, "He is doing for theology what Huxley did for science."[23] Firm in his own faith, he would have others equally firm. And he could not turn away from any problem offered by Holy Writ. Carman also was sincere, but he was a man of seventy-seven, too old to change the simpler faith of his youth. Indeed, he was much less of a theologian than an administrator; as a presiding officer he had few equals. It is difficult, however, to avoid the conclusion that he was to a degree the victim of an inherited antipathy. Carman was born in 1833; the Canadian Methodist Episcopal Church in 1835. The dispute resulting in the secession of the Episcopals, of whom Carman was the last bishop, arose largely from

[21]Annie Jackson, *George Jackson: A Commemorative Volume* (London, 1949), p. 32.
[22]*Globe*, Feb. 26, 1909.   [23]*Toronto Daily Star*, March 1, 1909.

their feeling that the Wesleyans were more colonial than Canadian in their attitude. The intrusion of the British Wesleyans and the deference involved in the acceptance by the Canadian Conference of an annual president from the "home" Conference must frequently have been a subject of comment at the table of his father, Philip Carman, a stout Reformer and fervent Episcopal Methodist. Here, he may have felt, was another intrusion, coupled with the circumventing of church discipline by a wealthy congregation.

The literalists from among the Methodists rallied to Carman's support, and letters from Presbyterians, Anglicans, and Baptists of like views added words of encouragement. Carman's second letter to the *Globe* was only slightly less harsh than the first. A crisis for Victoria University had arrived. The liberal spirit in which theological studies had been carried on, emblazoned on the College arch in the words, "The truth shall make you free," could not survive this open attack by the Chairman of the Board with the support of several clerical members. At this stage, Newton Wesley Rowell appeared as mediator. At the age of forty-two he had become a leader of the Ontario bar. While not palliating Carman's offence both against Christian charity and against the prerogative of a Conference president, he seized upon every opportunity for a settlement before the College and Church should suffer irreparable harm. In letters and conversations he worked with Carman and other members of the Board. With the approval of the Board he wrote Jackson regarding his interpretation of the terms "common sense" and "myth" which had raised difficulties in the minds of some, and received from him a reply which cleared up these points, on which, as Rowell had told him, those familiar with his preaching needed no assurance. This explanation by Jackson was published in the Toronto press on March 22, 1909. On that day a meeting was called in the President's office, where a statement drafted by Bowles but presented by Reynar, which set forth the position of the members of the Faculty of Theology on the controverted matters of doctrine, was approved by all. There were eight of them—Burwash, Wallace, Reynar, John Burwash, McLaughlin, Bowles, Blewett, and Misener; and Jackson, who would not become one of them till July, was also present to add his approval. This statement, signed by Burwash and Wallace, was laid before a Board meeting the following day. After considerable discussion it was finally accepted and authorized for publication in the *Christian Guardian*. The minute records that the meeting closed in good Methodist fashion—is there any other communion which turns so readily to a hymn on such occasions?—with the singing of "Blest be the tie that binds."

But could it continue to bind? In April, when Jackson delivered the Merrick lectures in Ohio, a few strands were snapped. He had submitted his manuscript to the President of the Ohio Wesleyan College to make sure that his ideas would be acceptable. The President judged them innocent of offence. Not so certain American literalists, who in correspondence stirred up kindred minds in the Board of Regents. These accused Jackson of violating the truce. Carman was urged to cancel his appointment to the University even at this stage. Burwash and the Board of Regents, however, held firm, and Jackson took his place on the Faculty as Professor of English Bible. The pulpit is not an ideal preparation for the desk, but Jackson was a good teacher, and won and held the respect of his colleagues and his classes. But the defenders of the faith, as they saw it, were not appeased. A preliminary skirmish was staged at the annual Conference at Toronto in June, 1910. It was unpleasant enough, but had no bearing on the case, except to reveal what was pending in August at the General Conference at Victoria, B.C.

There the forces met, first in the large Educational Committee, and finally on the floor of Conference. The struggle in the committee was grim and prolonged. Men feared that there was no escaping a calamitous split in the Church. But after a session of heated debate a solution appeared to the fertile mind of the Rev. A. J. Irwin. The Conference was not the place to settle nice questions of doctrine. That must be evident to thoughtful members. The Jackson case was a matter for judicial decision. Why not then apply in the realm of high theological problems when doctrinal offences were charged the same principle which had long been employed in dealing with charges at other levels? Why not invoke the practice of trial by one's peers? So Irwin argued, and the legal acumen of the committee succeeded in devising a periphrasis for peers, to wit, "ministers of good repute for their knowledge of questions of doctrine." It was thereupon decided to recommend to the Conference machinery by which any five members or ministers of the Methodist Church as complainants against a professor could apply for and secure the setting up of a tribunal of five ministers of piety and learning. The whole arrangement was set down with precision in the report of the committee to the Conference.

The final debate took place on August 27, 1910. When adoption of the report of the committee was moved, the Rev. Dr. S. Cleaver and F. W. Winter of Toronto as mover and seconder proposed an amendment which recited four phrases or sentences from Jackson's printed words as deserving censure. Carman, who in his presidential address at the opening of Conference had pointedly referred to Jackson and Sherbourne Street in terms of censure, as a good presiding officer was compelled to rule the motion out of order as not a proper amendment to the report. The report of the Educational Committee including the clause as to procedure was then presented and accepted, whereupon Cleaver was permitted to introduce his resolution. Immediately Dr. A. D. Watson of Toronto and the Rev. J. W. Sparling of Winnipeg were ready with an amendment which declared that Conference had "provided adequately for cases such as are referred to in the resolution" and added a note of "faithful adherence to the Word of God which liveth and abideth forever."[24]

Cleaver and Winter were given time to enlarge on their resolution, and it was decided that after Burwash and Rowell had replied supporting the amendment, a vote should immediately be taken. Two better champions of freedom in the pursuit of truth could not have appeared. Both were devout men. Burwash, though past his prime, was still of vigorous mind and had behind him a long record of high service to church and state. His prominence as a theologian had been shown by the fact that in 1905 in the early stages of the Church Union movement he had been appointed convener of the Methodist section of the Committee on Doctrine to confer with similar representatives of the Presbyterian and Congregational bodies, and had been named chairman of the composite committee. Rowell had a legal mind rarely equalled, perhaps never excelled, in Canada. His contribution as a statesman was still to come, but on the altar of the church here on this day perhaps his richest gift was laid.

Burwash spoke "in a calm and earnest way that made a deep im-

[24]*C.G.*, Sept. 14, 1910, p. 9.

pression upon Conference."[25] He averred that every member of his Theological Faculty held the essential doctrines as firmly as the mover of the resolution. Single sentences quoted out of their context should never avail to condemn a man. As for doctrine, on many points Wesley was far from dogmatic. The account fails to tell us whether in support of this view he had recourse to a quotation from Wesley which the editor of the *Globe*, Dr. J. A. Macdonald, had used in a strong editorial in support of Jackson: "The Methodists alone do not insist on your holding this or that opinion; but they think and let you think."[26]

Rowell declared that while theology was not his field, he had read both sides carefully and exhaustively. This he exhibited by citing on the points at issue the opinion of leading theologians from John Knox forward. He concluded a convincing argument with the appeal: "Brethren, let us go forth as men to preach that God is able and willing to save men from their sins, and let us cease this haggling about non-essentials."[27]

Cleaver made a halting reply in a sentence or two, and the amendment was put and carried by a vote of 125 to 84. No one was found to institute proceedings against George Jackson, and he continued to teach at Victoria and lecture in Canada and abroad. In 1912 he gave the Fernley Lecture in England and he was also elected to the Legal Hundred, thus joining the *élite* of British Methodism. Whether encouraged by these manifestations of respect "at home," or worried by occasional rumblings in Canada and the knowledge that the personal rift had never been completely joined, he decided to accept a chair at Didsbury.

Since 1910 no group has ever tried seriously to interfere with theological teaching at Victoria University; yet McLaughlin, in Old Testament, and other members of the Faculty have not hesitated to spread before students the same problems which Jackson essayed to explain to the many. It may be that their language has been more happily chosen than was Jackson's in that Y.M.C.A. address, or that his ideas have now more general approval, or merely that men are less deeply concerned about matters of doctrine than they once were. But in the main the fact that Victoria has been spared the upheavals that have shaken other religious foundations may be attributed to the wisdom

[25]*Ibid.*   [26]*Globe*, Feb. 27, 1909.   [27]*C.G.*, Sept. 14, 1910, p. 10.

and firmness displayed by Burwash, the Faculty, and the Board in dealing with the Jackson controversy, and more especially to the strong blow that was struck for academic freedom in the realm of theology at the General Conference of 1910.

In March, 1910, Robert Beare died. He was given a funeral by the College befitting his thirty-nine years of faithful service and his unique place in the life of the College. And in the Library building, over the entrance to the stacks, the beautiful clock, its face designed by the distinguished architects of the building, so long as it tells the hours for successive generations of students will stand as a permanent memorial. It bears the legend: *"In memoriam Roberti ex dono xv virum viriditati delendae annis MCMXI-XII."*[28]

The new Library was completed in September, 1910. It had been built through the joint liberality of Andrew Carnegie and of Cyrus A. Birge of Hamilton, with a long list of others of lesser means assisting. In architecture it broke new ground at the University, and set the pattern for several later buildings on the campus. The material chosen was grey Credit Valley stone and the style collegiate Gothic. Its interior arrangement and fittings were the product of careful planning by the Senate and oversight by the librarian, Professor A. E. Lang. The transfer from the crowded quarters of the main building was a great event in the history of Victoria. There, under the somewhat casual direction of R. H. Johnston, and later under Professor McLaughlin with Miss Rose Barker as assistant, the needs of students and staff could be met only imperfectly. In the new building every necessary facility was provided. The students had three spacious reading rooms, the faculty suitable quarters in what became the George Locke room, and there were several small rooms assigned to research. Miss Barker was reported to have known the place of every book even in the new stacks, and was jealous of sharing her knowledge even with the card catalogue. The duties of cataloguing for some years were in the hands of Miss Marjorie L. C. Pickthall, whose too short association with the College is gratefully remembered. Indifferent health took her back to England during the First World War, and when she returned to Canada it was to the Pacific Coast.

[28]I.e., these two "Bob" committees had contributed, or surrendered, the usual souvenirs (such as canes) for the purpose.

Meanwhile trouble was brewing in the management of the Women's Residence. The difficulty was partly constitutional, partly personal. The Barbara Heck Memorial Association had been continued as the Women's Residence and Educational Association. This body had contributed $5,000 towards the purchase of the ground on which Annesley Hall was to stand. It had also assumed financial responsibilities in connection with the furnishing of the Hall itself and, after the securing of the Drynan property in 1905, with the renovation of this building, which was known commonly as "the annex" and officially as South Hall. The Association itself under the presidency of Mrs. Burwash was directed by a Committee of Management consisting of eighteen, several of whom in themselves or through their husbands represented considerable wealth. The members were self-nominated, six retiring each year, but their appointment was by the Board of Regents. Furthermore, the constitution given the Committee by the Board had expressly stated, "in all matters relating to the government of the students, the final appeal and decision shall remain with the Chancellor and Senate of the University."[29]

One other body was involved. In 1906, in response to a general demand among students for self-government, the Annesley Student Government Association was formed with a small executive committee whose chairman was known as the Head of the House. The student association in conjunction with Dean Addison elaborated the following rules of conduct:

1. After dinner no student may leave the Hall without the permission of the Dean, and those who ask leave of absence must give in writing the address of the place to which they wish to go, and must report themselves to the Dean, and in her absence to the Director of the Household, on their return, not later than 10.30 o'clock.

2. Students of the first and second years may not accept invitations to social entertainments which will keep them out later than 10.30 o'clock, except those given in connection with their own College or on Friday evening, when they may not be out later than 12.30 o'clock.

3. Students of the third and fourth years may be permitted to go out on other evenings than Friday, and, if in groups of three or more, may have the use of a latch key.

4. Students in Annesley Hall may not attend public evening entertainments other than those of their own college, unless accompanied by a

[29]*Documents for the Use of the Commission on Annesley Hall* (1912), p. 5.

chaperone approved by the Dean or by an escort formally approved by their parents or guardians.

5. Students may receive gentlemen callers only on Friday evenings from 7 to 10, and on Sundays after church until 10 o'clock. In case of out-of-town friends, exception will be made by permission of the Dean.

6. First and second year students may not go to evening church with gentlemen except members of their immediate family, and no student may go out walking or driving in the evening with gentlemen.[30]

Such were the official bodies concerned and such the rules. The personal factor centred about Mrs. Ema (this was her spelling) Scott-Raff. She had come to Toronto from Owen Sound, with talents which won for her the patronage of Mrs. Timothy Eaton and an appointment to the headship of the Margaret Eaton School of Expression on North Street (later included in Bay Street) near Bloor. Then in 1900 she had replaced a Mrs. Cutter, after a year's very satisfactory service by that lady, as instructor in physical training for the young women of Victoria. A move made to extend this work was met by a decision of the Board of Regents on May 22, 1903, to the effect "that the Board place on record its opinion that no further study than Physical Culture be authorized in connection with the Women's Residence."[31] However, two years later, Miss Addison was shocked (as her diary reveals) to find that Mrs. Scott-Raff had been assigned by the Committee of Management definite duties in Annesley Hall with a small stipend. And as time went on it was evident that Mrs. Scott-Raff's particular contribution, which many regarded as superficial, had made a strong appeal to Mrs. Burwash and to the Chancellor. The proceedings of the Board of the date of 1910 bear the following minute: "The sixth recommendation of the Chancellor read as follows: That to give more time in individual work in Elocution $1500 be set apart for that department and arrangements if possible made with the Margaret Eaton School. Moved and seconded that recommendation No. 6 be referred to the Faculty Committee for report." It thus became apparent that the Chancellor's thought had been to give Mrs. Scott-Raff a larger place in the College, either in Annesley Hall or in teaching theological students how to preach, while the Board and the Senate had no desire to do either one or the other.

The trouble came to a head in January of 1911. On the 30th the

[30]*Ibid.*, p. 9.   [31]*Ibid.*, p. 26.

Chancellor wrote Miss Addison of his dissatisfaction with the discipline of Annesley Hall, and his intention to lay the matter before the Senate three days later. This was his charge:

> I am told that many students have the habit of sitting up and visiting in their rooms until 12 o'clock at night, that students are allowed the privilege of going out on visits every night in the week, and that students have gone to dances without a chaperone and to dances probably the character and conduct of which we know nothing, and have come in as late as 2 o'clock in the morning. These are matters which, if mooted abroad, would destroy the value of our residence for young women in the eyes of our Methodist people, and, apart altogether from public opinion, they are things which should not be allowed in a well regulated college.

For more than a year the situation was under review. A committee of the Senate, consisting of Reynar, Robertson, and Edgar, gave careful study to the rules and their enforcement. In the end it appeared that student government had commended itself not only to the undergraduates and to Miss Addison but to a majority of the Committee of Management, who forwarded to the Senate an expression of "renewed confidence in Miss Addison and in the general working of student government."[32] The Alumnae Association also forwarded to the Senate "its unanimous approval of the principle of Student Government."[33] The fact emerged that in the sixteen weeks of the fall term six students had attended dances, four of these being students in science courses, who by reason of their laboratory work were cut off from any of the student activities available to those taking literary courses.

A new draft of rules, only slightly modified from those above quoted, was drawn up by the committee and presented to the Senate. A motion was made that the Chancellor be authorized to sign this agreement. An amendment that the rules regarding dancing, theatres, and chaperonage be referred back to the committee for careful reconsideration was moved by Dr. Bell and seconded by the Chancellor, who had left the chair for the discussion. The amendment was lost, and the motion carried, together with a subsequent motion of confidence in Miss Addison and the suggestion that all officers of the Hall should be under her direction. An appeal by a minority of the Committee of Management, which included its chairman, for a stiffening of the rules was made to the Board. On April 30, 1912, on motion of J. R. L. Starr and N. W.

[32]*Ibid.*, p. 18.   [33]*Ibid.*, p. 19.

Rowell the Board referred the whole question to a committee of seven of its own members, who together with the Senate's committee and a group of seven members of the Women's Committee were to form a joint commission to report to the Board.

Later in the same meeting a motion by the Rev. Dr. Rose and Dr. Reeve "that the Chancellor's request for a year's rest be granted with salary" was carried. Arrangements were made that he should accept an invitation to tour the Methodist missions of Japan, after a visit with relatives in the Canadian West. From Calgary, he forwarded his resignation as President and Chancellor. Both the Chancellor and Mrs. Burwash were unwilling to sign the agreement with the women students approved by the Senate, and the required signatures had to await the appointment of their successors. Thus ended a great presidency. The manner of its ending invites the reflection as to how much better it would have been had the resignation attended his victory for freedom of thought in 1910 rather than his defeat on the lesser issue of freedom of manners two years later. The question is also raised, when it is noted that in 1912 Burwash was in his seventy-third year, whether the time does not come in the area of university administration, perhaps rather earlier than in that of teaching, when even the firmest powers are likely to falter under the weight of multifarious and perplexing detail.

XI. THE DIVIDE
1913

IT is well to pause at the year 1913 for a closer examination of the state of the realm. In many respects that year was a landmark in the history of Victoria. It witnessed the end of the Burwash régime of twenty-seven years, and the entry of a new president and several new professors. During these years Victoria had gone far towards attaining its ideal. Financial stability had been achieved. The student body was of such numbers as to form a polity where "the good life" might be realized. Arts and Theology worked comfortably together in a just relation to church and state. In the University, as in the country, our place had been firmly established. Principal Hutton's words at the great luncheon given to Dr. Burwash in the new hall which bears his name were not the idle compliments which so often mar such occasions:

Dr. Burwash proposed and has continued to work our confederation in a spirit of friendship, justice and Christianity; and Christianity after all, I apprehend, is the only asset in the political future of the universities or the world—and therefore it is that our system which might have broken down in a dozen places, which might have exploded into sky rockets of agitation and newspaper controversy, with crises in the University once a week and crises in the evening papers every evening, has, on the contrary, worked smoothly and softly and tamely, with nothing in it for the journalists and the scaremongers and the mischief-makers; so that to-day we most of us never recognize our blessings fully and shall never know except in a vague, unconscious way, how much we owe to the honesty and generosity and statesmanship—and these things are statesmanship in their results if not in their precise motives—the statesmanship, generosity and honesty of the first President of Victoria College under confederation, Dr. Burwash, our "Nathanael without guile."[1]

A university president, like a premier, is to be judged largely by the type of men he contrives to have about him. By this criterion also,

[1]*University Monthly*, Nov., 1913, p. 19.

Burwash proved a statesman. His staff was able, industrious, and efficient. And it was thoroughly Canadian. Of the faculty of 1913, one had served with Nelles, five, including the president-elect, had been trained under his mild and beneficent system and had carried down the rich heritage of Cobourg days, four contributed University College traditions, and others the combined influences of federation. Only three members of the staff of 1912 had been born outside Canada. A college thus distinctly Canadian attracted students in considerable numbers from the Western provinces, of which at the time Manitoba alone had a university offering a course leading to a degree in Arts; also from Newfoundland, where the Methodists had anticipated entry into federation by seventy-five years and in 1874 embraced a strong cause in that colony under the jurisdiction of the General Conference.

The changes effected in college life by the event of August 4, 1914, can hardly be appreciated by a later generation. Since 1866 the students of Victoria had scarcely thought of war, except as something alien and repugnant to the advancing standards of the civilization they knew. Victor Odlum, to be sure, had rushed off to the Boer War, been wounded at Paardeberg, and on his return had been carried about Alumni Hall by four stalwart members at a Saturday evening meeting of "The Lit.," while all sang "The Soldiers of the Queen." At a later stage in that war, A. J. Brace had also enlisted. This business, however, affected the College only remotely, and some even, whose minds travelled so far, may have agreed with Lloyd George that it was a ghastly mistake. But 1914 was different. In many ways Victoria has never recovered from it. In a pregnant sentence at the farewell dinner given him by the faculty, Sir Robert Falconer observed that after the war he was never able to get on the same footing with the student body as before. Perhaps its tragedies and a certain disillusionment had left their mark on himself; certainly the student body had changed. War, as the earliest of the great historians has remarked, is a βίαιος διδάσκαλος, a rough teacher. Hence we may pause and look at the College in the days just before its brand was burned on our society.

During the twenty-one years in Toronto financial support had come to the College such as had never been vouchsafed to Nelles at Cobourg. The days of small things were over. The financial statement of April 30, 1913, shows assets just under $1,400,000, but they do not include

Burwash Hall, which was almost completed and was included next year at a value of $450,000. The income for the year was $78,544.20. Of this amount, $17,773.50 came from students' fees, $6,147.77 from the Educational Society of the Methodist Church, and $1,870 from rentals. Apart from a sum of $4,760 contributed by generous friends to keep the salaries of professors within speaking distance of University of Toronto salaries and those of city ministers, the remainder accrued from endowments, the principal of which now stood at $729,000. Of this sum, $200,000 was general and stood under the Hart A. Massey estate; $85,000 was assigned to three chairs bearing the names of Ryerson, Nelles, and "the President." For the rest, the policy had been adopted of commemorating the generosity of benefactors by allocating their names to certain chairs of their own or of the Board's choice. If the income was insufficient for the whole salary, it was supplemented from the general endowment. These chairs were the John Macdonald in Latin endowed at $20,000, the William Gooderham in English ($40,000), the Eliza Gooderham in French ($35,000), the George A. Cox in New Testament ($50,000), the Margaret Hopkins Cox in Homiletics ($50,000), the J. W. Flavelle in Orientals ($25,000), the Hart A. Massey in English Bible ($60,000), the Eliza Phelps Massey in Orientals ($60,000), and the W. E. H. Massey in Greek ($66,000). The Ryerson fund was assigned to the chair in Ethics and the Nelles to that in Ancient History. While the increased income had hardly kept pace with expansion and there was likely to be a deficit of two or three thousand dollars a year, as Mr. Justice Riddell remarked at the inauguration of the new President, "no college worth its salt ever had or ever will have enough money."[2] However, by 1913 the finances of the College were at length on a sound footing.

The number of students had nearly doubled in the preceding ten years. In 1903-4 it had stood at 342 in Arts and Theology; in 1913-14 it was 622. If those undergraduates who were not in attendance, being in their first year at affiliated institutions—Albert College, or Columbian College, New Westminster, or the Ontario Ladies' College at Whitby—be deducted, the enrolment still approached 600, a number which could comfortably be handled in the existing buildings. In 1913-14 the women students numbered 140; and Annesley and South

[2]*Acta*, Nov., 1913, p. 68.

Halls provided ample accommodation, although only some 20 per cent of the students of this period had their homes in Toronto. Of the Arts students, 29 were from British Columbia, 13 from Saskatchewan, 10 from Alberta, and 7 from Newfoundland. The university class lists afford an explanation of the increase in numbers. The examination results show that in all departments, both those in which college subjects predominated and those in which the subjects were mainly taught in the University, a reputation for sound scholarship was being securely established. Some 70 per cent of the students were enrolled in honour courses, but many men of ability and ambition had chosen to graduate in the General Course. This had replaced the old Pass Course in 1895, with the entire approval, and indeed largely at the instance of the Victoria staff. It was less specialized than the honour courses, and required only four years from pass matriculation. Hence one might shorten one's course by a year as compared with the time required for Classics, Mathematics, Moderns, and the several sciences, for which senior matriculation was required. Certain honour courses, however, like Political Science and Philosophy, could be entered in the second year by students who had attained high standing at senior matriculation or in the first year of the General Course. Of the 94 students who received their Bachelor's degree in June, 1913, 68 were in Honours and 26 in the General Course; in June, 1914, 53 graduated in Honours and again 26 in the General Course.

It may be instructive to notice the standing and subsequent record of certain students in attendance during the year 1913. Among the graduates of that year Victoria College stood first, second, and third in the University in Moderns (Teutonics); first and second in Philosophy (Blewett's last graduating class); first, second, and third in Orientals; first in English and History (Moderns option); first in Commerce and Finance; first in Geology and Mineralogy. In Moderns, the names were Miss V. E. Whitney (Mrs. E. J. Pratt), Miss L. I. Douglas (Mrs. J. D. Robins), and Miss R. E. Spence (Mrs. Ernst Arndt of South Africa); in Philosophy, (Professor) John Line and (the Rev. Dr.) A. Lloyd Smith; in Orientals, (the Rev. Dr.) W. J. Mumford, (the Rev.) William Coutts (a Presbyterian minister), and (the Rev.) W. E. W. Hutty (retired from the ministry and in business at Fort Nelson); in English and History, (Professor) J. D. Robins;

in Commerce and Finance, (the Rev.) W. J. Little (late Bursar of Victoria University) ; and in Geology and Mineralogy, A. C. Hazen (Principal of the Port Rowan High School). In Classics, L. C. Cox, who had headed the course in the first three years, was compelled to take an *aegrotat* degree; W. F. Huycke (now a barrister at Peterborough) stood first in second class honours and also carried English and History. Another able man who, following a major interest, elected to take second class—it would be interesting to compare the subsequent careers of first and second class men—was G. L. Haggen. Rhodes Scholar for British Columbia, and winner of the Cobden Prize in his first year at Oxford after the war, he returned to take his B.C.L., and became a barrister so learned in the law that he has been examiner at Oxford, Cambridge, London, and Leeds, where he has resided for many years active in good works.

Turning to the year which graduated in 1914, Victoria College students stood first, second, and third in the University in Orientals; first in Biological and Physical Sciences; first in Household Science, first in Political Science, and first in Biology. In Orientals the names were E. D. Beynon (an Episcopal minister in the United States, deceased), C. B. Wood (Registrar of the University of British Columbia), and (Professor) W. E. Staples; in "B. and P.," N. Found (a physician in Toronto); in Household Science, Miss M. V. Manning (Mrs. Charles V. Scott); in Biology, W. Morley Smith (now a Queen's Counsel and member of the Board of Regents) and H. B. Sifton (Professor of Botany in the University of Toronto). In Moderns, after the sweep of the previous year Victoria had to be content with seconds, while in Classics, H. G. Robertson and J. W. Taylor stood second and third in first class honours. The former was to succeed his father as Professor of Greek; the latter, after taking his Ph.D. in Chicago and teaching for a time, entered a publishing firm in the United States.

What of the religious life in a college which after all was a religious foundation, albeit of the broadest type? To quote again words of Mr. Justice Riddell at the graduates' welcome to President Bowles, "Roman Catholic, Anglican, Presbyterian—all were as welcome and were as well received in her classrooms as was the Methodist; and this continued even after other religious bodies had instituted colleges of their own, and it continues to this day. In Victoria, none was the son of the bondwoman who should not be heir with the son of the freewoman, but all were brethren; if her first graduate was a Methodist, her second was a Presbyterian."[3] No compulsion was laid on any student. All were free to embrace or avoid the religious exercises and studies of the College. The regular chapel service from Monday to Friday for twenty minutes each morning from 9.50 to 10.10, the weekly meetings of the Y.M.C.A. on Wednesday afternoons from 5 to 6, similar weekly meetings of the Y.W.C.A., special groups such as the Missionary Society and the Student Volunteers for the foreign field, occasional service in the Chapel on Sunday morning—these religious exercises were open to all. But there was always a proportion of the students who held aloof, or who found that their science laboratories or the demands of athletics interfered. Nevertheless, the free commingling in the halls and on the campus with fellow-students who had dedicated their lives to the Christian ministry—and many of the strongest students were finding their way into Theology—could not fail of effect. For several years it had been the custom with men who were looking to the foreign fields to spend much of their summer in touring the province or at summer camps in the interests of missions. In 1913-14 there were ten members in this "Volunteer Band." Not content with their summer work, during the spring term they visited churches in seven of the larger cities of the province, delivering 177 addresses. The College itself was supporting a missionary in China, Homer G. Brown ('06), who had joined a group of Victoria University graduates on the China Mission, by 1910 numbering twenty.

It is doubtful, however, whether religion had as large a place in the life of the College as it had had ten years earlier. Industrial expansion and the increasing proportion of students from urban occupations had touched the spiritual life of the College. It was the recognition of this, perhaps, which suggested an editorial in *Acta Victoriana* of April, 1913, on "Victoria and Puritanism," in part as follows:

> Victoria is the daughter of the Wesleyan Revival and the grandchild of the Puritan movement. It is a lineage of which she may well be proud. So long as men remember the Grand Remonstrance and Milton and Bunyan in Bedford jail, so long as men honour the memory of the Pilgrim Fathers, so long as their blood is stirred by the story of the stern and sublime struggles of the psalm-singing Covenanters, so long will men revere

[3]*Ibid.*, p. 66.

Puritanism! Wherever a Fiji Islander reads his Bible in his own language, wherever a free African blesses unconsciously the name of Wilberforce, or a reformed convict bears unwitting testimony to Howard and Miss Fry, there will the Wesleyan Revival be honored; for these things, outside of and more than the Methodist Church, are its great monuments! Let Victoria pause long before she forswears her ancestry. Is there any fear of that? Perhaps not, yet the spirit of this exuberant age is Cavalier rather than Puritan. The cry is for complete self-expression, too often taken to imply absence of self-restraint. . . . It is this recognition of the necessity of restraint that has made Puritanism stand for so much of solid achievement. It is self-limitation to-day for the sake of higher and broader self-expression to-morrow. It is a self-restraint that has forged iron purpose and strength of character to will and do the hard and noble. What of iron there is in British blood to-day it owes in large measure to Puritanism. Any man, therefore, who will be a strong man must be puritan, and so long as we honor strength, so long must we honor Puritanism. Its greatest claim, however, to be cherished in our college is for the sake of the high moral tone of which it is the source. . . . Let Victoria cherish her bias towards Puritanism, not in blind acceptance of it as traditional, but in clear recognition of it as the tendency most fruitful in character and power.[4]

Among the College societies, the Union Literary Society still held primacy, although its position had been challenged. In 1903 Edward Wilson Wallace, later to be President of Victoria University, was largely responsible for launching the Students' Alma Mater Society of Victoria College. It was argued that the time and attention of the "Lit." were being diverted to business that might better be assigned to another society. However, any intention of poaching was disavowed: "The new society will usurp no functions; it will undertake only such duties as are voluntarily placed in its hands."[5] The hope was expressed that college spirit would be fostered in the general meetings of the society to be held twice a year. Wallace was chosen the first president, and the managing of the business of the conversazione was taken over at once by the new organization. But it soon became apparent that the student body was not prepared to confer any great authority on this group, certainly not to concede to it a position similar to that held by the society of the same name at Queen's. Thus, after a tenuous existence of four years, the Alma Mater Society ceased. A more useful and durable offshoot of the "Lit." appeared in 1911 under the name of

[4]The editor-in-chief of this year was J. D. Robins.
[5]*Acta*, March, 1903, p. 406.

the Collegians' Debating Club. It was organized by students of the first and second years in Arts and C.T. men, that is, those who were taking their theology under the direction of the Conference but not proceeding to an Arts degree. The president was regularly a second year man. Its object was the cultivation of debating power and skill in public speaking. Meetings were held each Thursday at 4 P.M.

Never in the history of the College was there so keen an interest in debating. Inter-year, inter-faculty, and inter-university debates were conducted among the men under the direction of the "Lit." and similar contests among women students by the Women's Literary Society. In the inter-faculty contests for men, a much-coveted shield was the trophy. McMaster University and Osgoode Hall were included with the Arts and theological colleges among the contestants, and the final debate, which Victoria won in 1911-12 and again in 1913-14, produced an audience of respectable size. The same thing was true of the women's debates, and here again in 1913-14 Victoria was the winner in inter-faculty competition. But it was in the Saturday evening meetings of the Literary Society itself that the men students of Victoria continued to receive the greater part of their training in public speaking, in parliamentary procedure, and to a degree in matters of business. Under the last were included the publication of *Acta*, the control of the "Bob" and the conversazione, the maintenance of the common rooms and the lockers in the basement, the provision of certain magazines and periodicals, the appointment of representatives to outside functions and the payment of their expenses, the naming of debaters to represent the College, and the nominating of a manager for the Book Bureau, which conducted a considerable business in the sale and exchange of books. The comfortable and appropriately furnished quarters of the "Lit." on the third floor, now Room 39, had been excellently suited to the purpose while the College remained small. Something was lost when the place of meeting was changed in 1911 to a larger Alumni Hall on the main floor, formerly the library.

Acta Victoriana was conducted with much the same format and policy as had obtained for twenty years. The nine numbers each ran to about fifty octavo pages of text and illustrations, with advertisements still excluded from the body of the text and confined to the opening and closing pages. The December number was slightly larger and was printed on paper of finer quality; but no attempt was made to rival the elaborate Christmas numbers of the previous decade, when Canadians prominent in literature and public life were approached for articles and so successfully that in one year several contributions had to be held over for the January number. In 1902-3, under the editorship of R. G. Dingman, later editor of the *Financial Post*, the Christmas number had reached 138 pages of text and illustrations; but in 1904-5, with H. H. Cragg as editor, it attained 182 pages. In each case the advertising is to be added. In 1913 the editorial staff consisted of ten, three of whom were women. There was a business manager who had two assistants, and Pelham Edgar and C. C. James appear as an advisory board. About two-thirds of each number was assigned to general or scientific articles, poetry and short stories, and was thus literary in character. A considerable proportion of these articles were written by undergraduates. The other third consisted of editorials and news of the College and its graduates, with a generous coverage of sports. Group pictures were freely interspersed. Locals, that is amusing sayings and doings in the College, might run to three or four pages.

Curiously enough, the Victoria man who has attained great eminence in poetry, as an undergraduate never used *Acta* as a field for practice. E. J. Pratt graduated in 1911 in Arts with the silver medal in Philosophy and in 1913 in Theology as gold medallist. His first serious contribution in verse to *Acta*, entitled, "The Wind of the West," was in October, 1914, and his second in December of that year, beginning, "Tell me thy secret, O sea," a prayer not unanswered through the years. However, A. L. Burt of 1910, at that time in Oxford as a Rhodes Scholar, and now a Tyrrell medallist of the Royal Society of Canada in History, scorned not the sonnet but contributed no fewer than three during the year. Like Pratt, Mary Lowrey (Ross), who graduated in 1912 in English and History, forbore during her college course to reveal in *Acta* her remarkable literary gifts. Again, Arthur R. Ford ('03), who as editor of the *London Free Press* has received the highest honours in the gift of his fellow-journalists and is Chancellor of the University of Western Ontario as well, abstained from *Acta* during his course at Toronto. Nevertheless the College magazine afforded a considerable number of students an opportunity to gain experience which prepared them for authorship or the fourth estate. It is an interesting fact which may have significance, that two of the authors whose works were recently selected by a committee for UNESCO in compiling a list of one hundred outstanding books produced in Canada, were former editors of *Acta*—Professor J. D. Robins (*The Incomplete Anglers*) and Professor H. N. Frye (*Fearful Symmetry: A Study of William Blake*).

The vitality of the student body at this period appeared in an ambitious and "long talked of" project by the Glee Club. During the session of 1913-14 a tour of Great Britain was successfully planned and accomplished. With E. R. Bowles as conductor, the Club had appeared on the stage at Massey Hall in 1913 and had given a concert the following year in Burwash Hall. In the summer of 1913 two of their number were in England making arrangements through an organization known as the Federated Brotherhoods of Great Britain. The business arrangements were in the hands of J. W. Moyer ('14), whose capable management presaged his later success in law and business at Calgary. The group of eighteen sailed from Montreal on June 2 on the *Royal George*. On their arrival at Bristol they were received by the Lord Mayor and Council, and there their first concert was given. They had the temerity to visit Wales, the home of choral singing, first. Everywhere they were enthusiastically welcomed. At Abertillery they were met at the station by the Mayor and aldermen, and the large pavilion in which they sang could not contain the crowds. At Llandwhern they were the guests of D. A. Thomas, the coal baron. They spent five days in London with as many appearances, the last being at the Connaught Rooms at a reception and dinner given to the overseas ambassadors and representatives of the Empire. After a trip north they returned to the metropolis, where they filled another engagement and were given a reception by the Lord Mayor at the Mansion House. The next day they returned to Bristol. Here they sang again, and after a luncheon and formal reception by the Lord Mayor and a motor trip which took them as far as Bath were returned directly to the ship. They landed in Montreal just ten days before war was declared. This and much more is recorded in a delightful article in *Acta* of October, 1914, by "J.H.F." who must be Hubert Fenton, a cheery member of the Hamilton Conference. His second trip overseas was on a very different mission. In shaking hands with the writer before leaving, he remarked that he had signed up in the suicide squad, but that it was all right. He died in action in France in 1916.

While music flourished at Victoria, a dramatic club had not yet been formed. The fact that joint societies for men and women were still the exception may in part account for the late development of what is now a popular activity. In fact, the only extra-curricular enterprises common to men and women were *Acta*, the Classics and Modern Languages clubs and, of course, the class parties, one or two of which were held by each class during the year. Dancing was still of the future. The Annesley Hall Commission of 1912 was able to report:

At a meeting of the first, second and third year students of the Annesley Student Government Association, the following resolution was adopted:

Whereas in the general opinion of this student body it is considered detrimental to highest scholastic achievement and moral well-being that students should attend public dances during their undergraduate years,

Therefore be it resolved that we, the members of A.S.G.A., place on record our disapproval of such attendance.[6]

The rink, however, had come to be a great social institution. A large area of the campus was flooded, and the skaters had a fine sweep around a hockey cushion in the centre. Any afternoon when the weather permitted a considerable portion of the student body took to skates after lectures. And Saturday afternoon saw the ice thronged. Then and in the evenings, especially when a band was permitted, public patronage of a select character was invited. Thus the Athletic Union, which managed the rink, was able to set aside profits reaching as much as $3,000 a year from the revenue of the rink and the hockey cushions. This money was used to liquidate the old debt on the Athletic Building, and subsequently to repay a loan of $8,000 from the Board of Regents for the gymnasium completed in 1913 at a cost of $13,000.

By the year 1913 sports, which form so essential a part of healthy academic life, were flourishing at Victoria in all departments. The officers elected each spring by those who chose to become members of the men's and women's athletic societies arranged a busy programme of games. A fee was charged to cover all sports. It was small as well as voluntary, and it was customary for the player to provide his own tackle. For the men the fall commenced with a field day in connection with the Charter Day celebration. This was held on the playing field.

[6]*Documents for the Use of the Commission on Annesley Hall* (1912), p. 22.

Some of the best men were likely to compete in the Varsity games held a little later or in the intercollegiate contest. In rugby, soccer, hockey, and basketball the University of Toronto had already gone far in the development of intra-mural contests, which today are the cynosure and envy of universities across the line—a development conceded to be largely the result of the federal system at Toronto. But in Victoria keen inter-faculty competition had already been responsible for a decline in inter-year contests. Inter-year rugby was attempted, but was too costly in equipment and injuries and never became established. In soccer it proved too difficult to secure a free campus for inter-year games, since each afternoon a squad preparing for inter-faculty competition was certain to be occupying the field, sometimes two such squads, one at either end. The fact was that the new campus had already become too small for a college of some four hundred men. In hockey, however, it was easier to carry the inter-year schedule to a conclusion. Tennis and alley still flourished, spring and fall. Basketball had recently become a popular sport during the winter months. Water polo, boxing, wrestling, and fencing also had their appeal.

The numbers at Victoria were now sufficiently large to make winning teams a possibility. Each year one at least of the four leading trophies was pretty sure to rest in the cabinet in Alumni Hall. In 1909-10 it was the Mulock Cup in rugby football and the Jennings Cup in hockey. The rugby team captained from quarter-back by Jack Birnie had beaten Dents 19-0 in the semi-finals, and in the finals the score against Junior S.P.S. was 18 to 16. On November 20 this same team had journeyed to London and in slush defeated Western 20-0. The soccer team also won against Western on the same day, 1-0. In 1911-12 the Jennings Cup was again won, after a terrific game at the Ravina rink against Dents which went to forty minutes of overtime. The score was four all at full time. But finally Thane McDowell carried the puck the length of the ice and scored. He was captain of the team and played the position immediately in front of goal, then called "point." G. L. Rodd repeated a minute or so later to make the game safe. It must be remembered that in those days no substitution was allowed, and forty minutes over the hour tested the amount of iron in a man's frame. The goal-keeper was an extremely youthful-looking lad named George W. Brown. In soccer the cup donated by members of the Arts

Faculty, and first competed for in 1896, came to Victoria in the fall of 1913. In the finals, after two tie games with Knox, a third contest saw the score 2-0 against Victoria when Morley Smith ('14) kicked a ball over his head past a surprised Knox goal-keeper. This started the team on the way to a 3-2 victory. The cup was retained the following autumn by an eleven with many of the same players. In 1914 a basketball trophy known as the Sifton Cup also came to Senior Vic., that is, a team of men of the two upper years. Until 1922 there was no cup for tennis, but twice in the previous ten years the University champion had been a Victoria College man, R. G. Dingman in 1903, and W. B. Wiegand in 1911. And in 1913 two Victoria men of the class of 1915, Harold Bennett and George Brown, had surprised themselves by winning the University doubles. All five of these tennis champions, it may be noted, were first class honour men; it was still possible and not uncommon for a man to excel in games and also in studies. In hand-ball—a name which had displaced the time-honoured "alley"— the only competitors on the University campus were St. Michael's and Victoria. In 1912 Victoria was the winner, and in 1913 St. Michael's. Lacrosse never became a regular inter-faculty game, but for some years it had been the practice to send a University team on a tour of the United States after the May examinations. In any case, being a summer game, like cricket and baseball, it could hardly have become a major college sport.

The Glee Club adventure was described as a mark of the vitality of the student body in the period immediately preceding the First World War. The word "vitality" fails to do complete justice to another student enterprise of the time. In the December *Acta* of 1913 L. W. Moffit celebrates what he designates as "the movement which culminated in student control in Victoria."[7] He links it with the urge which Canada as "the true daughter of the motherland" felt towards self-government. He admits that in Victoria the "restraining hand of authority" had been "less heavily felt than in most colleges," but says that for many years the students had "longed to see student control established on the old Ontario Strand." Finally, in the spring of 1912, the "Lit." established a committee, the names of whose members he thinks ought to go down in history. They are H. J. Goodyear, J. D.

[7] *Acta*, Dec., 1913, p. 147.

Robins, and H. C. Jeffries of 1913, and J. W. Moyer and W. Morley Smith of 1914. The committee drafted a constitution, but after conferences with a committee of the Faculty were persuaded to abandon their constitution in favour of an agreement between the Faculty and the men students. It should be noted that the negotiations were carried on in the absence of the President and with his resignation already tendered, that the women were not included, and that the similar agreement with the Annesley Student Government Association still awaited the signature of the President. Moffit reports that the arrangement was submitted to a mass meeting in March, 1913, where "the result of the vote was an overwhelming majority in favour of adopting the agreement."[8] The minutes of a Faculty meeting give the actual figures: out of a total of 395 male students, 220 voted for and 66 against the agreement.

It is not necessary here to reproduce the document, important as it seemed at the time to the student body. The preamble reads,

Whereas the men students of Victoria College have expressed the desire to have a larger measure of responsibility and control in connection with their student life, the Faculty of Victoria College (with the consent and approval of the President and Senate of the College) hereby agrees to entrust to the men students of Victoria College, as represented by the Victoria Student Council, the management within the limits hereinafter defined of all matters concerning the conduct and activities of the said students that are not strictly academic.[9]

The limits to be sure were of considerable area. All academic matters were definitely, under provincial law, in the control of the Senate, and all matters of business and property ultimately in that of the Board of Regents. Discipline within the buildings was subject to the rulings of the University Caput in the case of University buildings and the Board of Regents in Victoria buildings. Furthermore, the new organization had no *locus standi* in the men's residences about to be opened. Its province, then, was restricted to minor matters of discipline, the conduct of meetings, and such business affairs as the Literary Society and Athletic Association might surrender to its jurisdiction. And even in this narrow field its function was consultative rather than executive. The ten men who formed the Council provided a useful medium of approach to the student body by the Faculty in connection with any

---

[8] *Ibid.*, p. 149.   [9] *Ibid.*

matters of dispute affecting the life of the College, but nothing more than this. And the new President, doubtless realizing all this, signed the agreement, in spite of the fact that a member of his Board upon whose counsel he frequently relied had written him: "I think the agreement *infra dig* on the part of the Senate. You may loan the Students' Council your authority, but should not enter into an agreement with them. A commercial analogy is the way a man's banker gives him a line of credit...." The Students' Council of 1913-14, however, was a group of able and solid men who probably did their fellows and the College good service, although in a much narrower field than they first envisaged.

Another event which gave distinction to the year—in this instance of a profound and permanent character—was the opening of the men's residence. It was the wish of Chester Daniel Massey, the donor, that the name should be Burwash Hall. The donor's portrait, with that of Burwash, hangs over the high table together with the royal standard of Queen Victoria which was flying over Osborne House in the Isle of Wight at the time of the Queen's death. "We could wish for nothing fairer or nothing more commodious or well-appointed than has been given us in the four houses of residence and the dining hall," said President Bowles in his message to the students.[10] Again Victoria had pioneered; there was nothing comparable to Burwash Hall in any Canadian university. The three men's residences of the University of Toronto, built largely through the generosity of E. C. Whitney, the brother of Sir James, were not so handsome or well appointed, and they lacked a dining hall. The College was also fortunate in having C. Vincent Massey, fresh from two years at Balliol College, Oxford, as Dean of Residence. He held a post as Lecturer in Modern History in the University. Massey, while a graduate of University College, now identified himself closely with the interests of Victoria. With the assistance of dons for each of the four houses, the selection of which was left by the Board to the President and himself, he endeavoured to transfer to Burwash Hall something of the Oxford atmosphere. It would be too much to say that all of the 116 men for whom rooms were provided were able to appreciate fully the formalities and refinements (such as the Latin grace at dinner) which were introduced. A

[10]*Ibid.*, Oct., 1913, p. 3.

definite ethos would have been a matter of many years, and after one session the war intervened.

A certain danger to College unity which might arise through the residences was noted by *Acta*: "While the opportunities there afforded for close friendship with congenial souls should be used to the full, it must never be forgotten that, whether living in residence or out, we are all students of the self-same College, whose privileges and whose honours must be equally available to all."[11] The editor's prescience detected what proved to be an unfortunate tendency to separation of residence men from the main body of students. A tight corporate life in residence in a college town like Oxford, compulsory on all students for part of their course at least, is one thing. A very different situation existed at Toronto, where two-thirds of the students either had homes in the city or preferred and were free to live in boarding houses. Great as has been the value of residence life to the College, it could not be expected that it would have the unifying and pervasive influence of the older halls on which it was modelled.

One other feature of this *annus mirabilis* remains to be described. It brought to Victoria a new president, one full professor, two associate professors, and two lecturers. Richard Pinch Bowles has not been a stranger to these pages. The talents which had made him conspicuous as a student had soon carried him to the first pulpits of Methodism in Canada—St. James at Montreal, Grace Church in Winnipeg, and the Metropolitan and Sherbourne Street churches of Toronto. In 1905 he had been appointed Professor of Homiletics at Victoria. The manner of his selection to succeed Burwash as President in 1913 was novel. The Board of Regents determined to entrust the recommendation of a successor to a committee consisting of the first seven members to receive a majority vote of those present. Four were chosen on the first ballot, one on the second, and two on the third. When the committee reported the name of Bowles, and the acceptance of the report was moved, an amendment was introduced and carried that additional nominations should be permitted. Thereupon three other names were presented. The first two men, being in attendance, withdrew their names, and absence only, one suspects, prevented the third from doing likewise.

[11]*Ibid.*, p. 35.

A curious error has crept into the record. In an article in the *Victoria College Bulletin*, Dean Wallace wrote: "He [Bowles] is of that sturdy Palatinate German stock from which so many eminent Canadians have sprung."[12] If ever there was an Irishman, Richard Pinch Bowles was one—in features, in temperament, at times even in accent. The only Palatinate corruption of the pure Irish was through one of his grandmothers; his paternal ancestors came straight from Tipperary to their farm in the shadow of the Caledon Hills. In another sentence, Wallace was happier:

A Canadian by birth, training, life and sympathies, he knows the spirit and ways of Canadian students; a Victoria man, he is intimately familiar with the history, traditions and ideals of the College over which he is called to preside; well and widely known as pastor and preacher, he commands the respect and confidence of the Church; as a professor for eight years, he has secured the affectionate esteem of all his colleagues and the high regard of the student body; as a man of a genial, generous spirit and catholic sympathies, he will readily adapt himself to his numerous relationships and duties in connection with the University of Toronto; as an admirable public speaker, he will ably represent his College before the general public.

All these qualities Chancellor Bowles demonstrated during his seventeen years of office. The prediction of his Dean of Theology was fully realized. He directed the policies of the College through the dislocation of the First World War and through the equally difficult period of reconstruction after the war; and towards the end of his term he threaded the arduous path into Church Union, involving as it did the welcoming of an alien tradition with regard to Arts work. There may have been errors in judgment, but they were not many; and he himself, with the humility which attends true greatness, would have been the first to admit them. There was genuine regret in the University of Toronto, as in Victoria itself, when at the age of sixty-five he laid down the reins, held firmly if with apparent lightness. In one of the most eloquent and moving addresses ever made in the College, at the farewell dinner given him by his colleagues at Annesley Hall, he gaily described these years of travail as a mere interlude between farm and farm.

Six appointments to the teaching staff in one year was a number

[12]*Victoria College Bulletin*, 1913-14, p. 57.

without precedent. The new Professor of Ethics who was asked, with the assistance of a lecturer, to fill the vacancy caused by Blewett's death was Wilmot Burkmar Lane. His Bachelor's and Master's degrees were secured at Toronto from University College in 1893 and 1894. For a year he had studied Theology at Victoria, but had not proceeded to a degree or to ordination. He gained his Doctor's degree at Wisconsin. His earlier interest in graduate work was in Psychology, which no doubt was valuable to him for his teaching in the Faculty of Theology, where he had the title of Professor of Ethics and Didactics. He came to Victoria from Randolph-Macon Woman's College at Lynchburg, Virginia. During the summer he lived in Prince Edward County, where he had acquired considerable farming and business interests and where he found pleasure in engines and fast motor launches. Rather short but wiry of frame, he kept himself fit during the winter by walking back and forth to the College from his home five miles distant. His public speech was characterized by amazing rapidity and fecundity in words. During his years in Toronto he published two volumes of verse. In 1939 he retired to his country estate.

The second appointment in Philosophy—with the rank of Lecturer—was that of Walter Theodore Brown, later to become Principal of Victoria College and still later President of Victoria University. He had graduated in 1907 with the gold medal in Philosophy and, like Lane, had taken some Theology without proceeding to a degree. After earning his Ph.D. at Harvard, he had accepted a post at Bowdoin College in Maine, whence he was recalled to his *alma mater*. He was a man of powerful physique and strong personality and became an impressive public speaker. He had been brought up at Lakefield, where his father was a famous builder of canoes. Walter liked to recount the thrill it gave him on one occasion to see on the Isis a craft fashioned in his father's shop. As in the Langford family, four of the Browns graduated from the College. Brown soon established himself as an outstanding teacher. In 1928 he accepted an invitation from Yale to set up a new department there, but in 1932, after Victoria and Emmanuel became separate colleges, returned as Principal of the former.

In 1913 for the first time direct importations from Great Britain were essayed by the Board of Regents, which in the absence of a president had to take full responsibility for appointments. The Rev. John

Hugh Michael was brought from an English pastorate to become Associate Professor of New Testament Exegesis. He was Welsh by birth and training. Tall and of imposing appearance, deliberate of speech, with a fine voice, clear in enunciation, and evangelical in his message, his pulpit ministrations were much in demand. In the class-room his emphasis on jot and tittle proved tedious to some of the young brethren who preferred to take the Kingdom by banalities. But his teaching, as well as his occasional articles in the learned journals and his published work on Philippians, had in it the quality of true scholarship. Before his term was reached, ill health necessitated his retirement in 1943.

The second importation was unmistakably an Englishman and one of the most versatile men and scholars ever to come to Toronto. He was Samuel Henry Hooke, graduate of London and Oxford in Arts and Divinity. He was of medium height, broad shouldered and loosely knit, gnomish in features as at times in behaviour. While named Associate Professor of Oriental Languages and Literature and learned in that field, his little work on the *Life of Jesus* marked him as both a sound New Testament scholar and a master of English prose. Then, shortly after coming to Toronto, being invited to assist in Modern History, he found himself giving instruction in Canadian constitutional history. Largely responsible for the founding of a University monthly called the *Rebel*, he was likely to appear in its pages in any guise. When the Students' Christian Movement displaced the Young Men's and Young Women's Christian Associations, he was responsible at times for giving its meetings a surprising twist. But that was not all. He was addicted to games and unusually proficient in several of these. He was one of the best chess players in Toronto. At one perplexing stage in his career he received a tempting offer to become a professional in golf. He was an excellent doubles player in tennis, and the challenge match between himself and a colleague and the undergraduate champions of the College was quite an event each autumn for several years. Although in his late thirties when he came to Toronto, he took up figure skating with avidity and on any fine day in winter was likely to be seen gyrating on the rink. Much to his own regret and that of many others, after ten years in Victoria he returned to the University of London, where he is still employed in scholarly publication.

At the same time Carleton W. Stanley became Lecturer in English.

His undergraduate course at Victoria, interrupted by the necessity of financing himself, was completed in 1911. He graduated with the Governor-General's Medal, first in first class honours in Classics among a remarkable group of scholars. C. N. Cochrane stood second and F. H. Underhill third. In English and History, Classics option (all three carried both courses), the order of standing was reversed. Victoria, by the way, had three others in first class honours in Classics in this year, one in second and two in third, the largest class to graduate in this course in the history of the College. C. D. Massey became interested in Stanley and assisted in financing his two years at Oxford[13] on the undertaking that he should return to Victoria. The contract was kept and maintained for two years of teaching in the department of English. Students who worked with him in seminars and groups found him a profound thinker and an inspiring teacher, but class-room lecturing was not so much to his taste. He left university work for a successful spell in business. Then he returned to teaching, this time in Classics, at McGill, where he became assistant to the Principal. Later he became President of Dalhousie, but retired in 1945.

Such at closer range was Victoria University in activities and personalities at the end of an era.

[13]Stanley and Underhill secured firsts in "Greats," and Cochrane a high second.

XII. A STRAIGHT FURROW
1913-1930

PRESIDENT Bowles assumed office on August 1, 1913. The interval of a year before the German assault on Belgium was sufficient to reveal something of his qualities. A true son of the soil, he was not inclined to move with precipitancy; nature must be waited for, and all things advanced in season. The Board of Regents was not called together until the next annual meeting in May, 1914. The Faculty committee of the Board met twice and the Finance committee three times; that sufficed for business. The Senate met five times, with a complete absence of controversy on academic questions. Twelve meetings of the Faculty—an unusually large number for one year—dealt with the necessities of the students. In pursuance of a policy of "screening" freshmen which was at the time taking form, three men were sent home at the end of the first term. And in the movement towards student government, the women of the College were permitted to establish a Women's Council, thus compelling the men to change the name of their organization from the Students' Council to the Men's Council. The signatures to the charter of the Annesley Student Government Association, withheld by Chancellor and Mrs. Burwash, were promptly affixed.

Meanwhile Dr. Bowles was working quietly towards a revision of the Act. On February 24, 1914, he wrote to the Rev. J. S. Ross: "What I am particularly anxious to get is a compact, unified Board, every member of which I could keep in touch with and every member of which would take a real interest in the workings of the Board. In my experience nothing so much makes for inefficiency in Boards of Trustees as to have a margin of indefinite uninterested members hanging around it." Already the Senate had approached the question from a different angle. At a Senate meeting on April 8, 1910, on motion of

Lang and Bell, the question of reorganization of the governing bodies had been referred to a committee of that body, which included two Board members.[1] Some difficulty had arisen in convening the committee. At length, however, it met and reported progress, but apparently a final report was precluded by the serious difficulties of the Annesley Hall situation. Lang's plan, it would appear, was to prepare a memorandum for the Board of Regents and the General Conference recommending such an alteration of the governing structure as would bring Victoria within the scope of the Carnegie pension scheme, the benefits of which were denied to colleges definitely under church control. Now a committee of the Board took up the question. After two meetings the committee on August 11, 1914, produced a printed report of some two thousand words, which formed the basis of the Act of 1915.

This interesting document quite transcends the terms of reference. Referring to the concern of the Senate four years earlier, it goes on to note the profound effect of federation on the governing system of the College, how "the Senate was shorn of a large part of its dignity and power,"[2] how the two main bodies of the College, the Board of Regents and the Senate, were thus in danger of drifting entirely apart, and how the loyalty of the staff was "constantly under strain." But if the Faculty had "lost in prestige and influence under the new conditions of federation," it had gained materially by its influence in the Council of the Faculty of Arts, where members of the Victoria staff had "taken their full share in shaping the policy of the University." Here, the report concedes, "the interests of the Board and of the Faculty might possibly not always be seen to lie in the same direction," although it was imperative "that these two bodies should work together in close, harmonious relationship." From these premises the committee proceeds to recommend a Board of twenty-eight members, so constituted as to satisfy the claims of the graduates without weakening those of the Church, while at the same time opening the way to the acceptance of the College by the Trustees of the Carnegie Foundation.

The report was adopted by the Board and passed on to the General Conference, which met in September at Ottawa. It would appear that no serious opposition to the proposals developed in Conference. The

[1] All members of the Board were at that time also members of the Senate.
[2] V.U.A., Board of Regents, Minutes, Sept. 8, 1914.

Guardian complained that the daily press gave only meagre reports of proceedings, preferring war news and the baseball series, but itself made no attempt to follow the discussions day by day according to its traditional policy. Hence no detailed record remains of the manner in which the Church accepted proposals of considerable importance affecting its relations to its oldest and leading college.

The changes sponsored by the Board, with the blessing of the Conference, were drafted and submitted to the Legislature. The result was "An Act to consolidate and amend the Acts respecting Victoria University," appearing in the Statutes of 1915 as Chapter 91—five pages, clear and concise as might be expected in a document which had passed under the new President's hand. The Board was reduced in size from thirty-five to twenty-eight members. But while in the Act of 1884 twenty-six members were named by the Conference, of whom two *ex officio* were the General Superintendents, now only twelve were named by Conference, to include the General Superintendents (still two in number, although Carman was now Emeritus) and the Secretary of Education. In 1884 it had been specified that of the elected members half should be ministers and half laymen; now nothing was said on this point. The number of members elected by the graduates in 1884 had been seven, in 1915 in a smaller board it became eight. The remaining eight members were to be chosen by the twelve Conference members and the eight graduate members. By this new and ingenious provision of co-option any want of balance in personnel might be adjusted. It was recognized, of course, that the Conference members constituted a three-fifths majority of those choosing the remaining eight members.

One other change—entirely novel—was effected in the Act. It was provided that all professors appointed to the Faculty of Theology must receive not only a majority vote of the Board but also a majority of votes of those members of the Board appointed by the General Conference. And since it was enacted that the Chairman should be a General Superintendent, it is evident that pains were taken, in spite of the reduced proportion of Conference nominees, to see that the influence of the Church was duly maintained. One further feature of the Act was the failure to arrive at any clear definition as to how the powers of the Senate could be extended, a subject on which much had been said by the committee. Apart from its responsibility for theological degrees, the Senate's authority was embraced within a nebulous phrase, "all matters strictly pertaining to the work of education," regardless of the fact that many such matters were determined in the Arts Council and the Senate of the University of Toronto. Nor was the Faculty accorded any standing or indeed mention in the Act. For thirteen years more it was to continue—Arts and Theological professors together—to hold meetings and pass resolutions with no validity in law. Under the Act of 1915 it was for the Board to determine "the studies, lectures and exercises of the students, and all matters respecting the same"—presumably in so far as these matters were not "strictly pertaining to the work of education." No mention was made of discipline or of the students' councils.

Not content with taking steps to reduce the size of the Board, the new President was responsible for a further simplification. At the annual meeting of the Board in May, 1914, it was resolved that an executive committee of eleven members should be appointed "with all the powers hitherto given to or held by the Finance, Faculty and Building and Grounds Committees." To this the President, three other ministers, and seven laymen were named. Five members constituted a quorum, although usually eight or nine members were present at the monthly meetings. For several years most of the business of the Board was transacted by this inner group, the Board in general simply receiving reports and confirming the decisions of the executive.

In addition to effecting these constitutional changes, Dr. Bowles at once came to grips with problems of finance. A surplus of $2,128.58 in 1911-12 had turned to a deficit of $3,303.20 in 1912-13, which was to reach a low point of $17,962.34 in 1915-16. But by 1914 it was quite apparent that some extraordinary source of revenue must be found. The business recession of 1913 had reduced revenues on certain investments. For instance, the $50,000 promised by Cyrus A. Birge for the Library in the end yielded only some $30,000 owing to the decline in Canada Steel. When the war broke out in 1914 credit was restricted by the banks and many business ventures crashed. An enrolment of 622 in 1913-14 was to fall to 369 in 1918-19, with serious loss of fees. Then the changes in the staff in 1913 had added to the expenditures, as well as to the retiring allowances, for which at this time no special fund had been set aside. The residences caused no difficulty, being self-supporting, though with no reserves for depreciation. To meet the situation it was decided to appeal to the churches of three Ontario conferences—Toronto, Hamilton, and London—for increased givings to the Educational Society, with the understanding that the increase should come to Victoria University. The Rev. A. Lloyd Smith was in charge of this campaign for two years and subsequently the Rev. W. B. Caswell, as Bursar, until 1920. For several years the pulpits of these three conferences were opened on one Sunday each year, in connection with this appeal, to representatives of the College, including the Chancellor and members of the faculty, clerical and lay. Later the amount coming to Victoria was set at 35 per cent of the total collections for the Educational Society from these conferences. The additional funds thus secured were never less than $10,000 a year.

Further, an effort was made, ultimately successful, to increase the endowment by $500,000. Wealthy members of the Church were approached by Dr. Bowles himself, often accompanied by a business friend or associate of the person solicited. The subscriptions were to be paid within five years and to carry interest from the date of subscription. On these terms, by March 26, 1918, subscriptions of $50,000 had been received from Sir J. W. Flavelle, H. H. Fudger, E. R. Wood, H. C. Cox, and Sir John Eaton; $25,000 from C. D. Massey and $75,000 from the Massey Estate; $20,000 from W. A. Kemp; $10,000 from A. E. Ames and G. H. Wood—$390,000 in all. The campaign for endowment in the churches of Toronto yielded another $59,929; Hamilton was responsible for $18,317, Brantford for $5,038, and a town like Barrie for $3,315. By January 28, 1919, the goal of $500,000 had been reached and passed by $11,124. At one stage of this most carefully planned and executed venture, some embarrassment was caused by the public announcement that Victoria University had been made the residuary legatee of the estate of Mrs. Lillian Massey Treble, who had died in November, 1915. Chancellor Burwash had been her confidant for many years, and it had been through him that she had made known to the University her purpose to donate the Household Science building. Now on her death less than a quarter of her estate was reserved for relatives and friends, and all the rest was bequeathed to religious and charitable objects. As the Senate stated in its resolution of November 5, 1915 (written by Burwash): "Her chosen world was not the world of gay and fashionable life, but in high ideals of thought and active work, and it touched the lowly and the most degraded as well as the highest and the best." At first it was supposed that the residue would bring about $450,000 to the College; but as most of it stood in shares of Massey Harris stock and as these after marked vicissitudes in the end greatly increased in value, the Board eventually realized more than three times that amount from the bequest.

All appointments to the staff during these years were in the nature of replacements. With the retirement of Burwash and Reynar (who had long served the Faculty of Theology in Church History) and the elevation of Bowles to the presidency, it was necessary to make an appointment in Church History and Homiletics. After much correspondence the choice fell on the Rev. Alfred John Johnston. He had taken honours in Philosophy at Victoria with the class of 1901, but a neglected condition in Greek had stood between him and a degree until 1907. Two recollections of his college course stand out in memory, his impressive reading of *Andrea del Sarto* in the "Lit." (of which he became President), and his turning a series of cartwheels down the field after a victory in soccer. He was an active member of the little group of kindred souls of 1901 who called themselves the Eta Pi society, because when they met for discussion or foolery they performed just that ritual. He was brought to the College in 1914 from a charge in London with a reputation as an excellent preacher. Entering as associate he became a full professor in 1919 and retired in 1937. In 1914 also, John Daniel Robins ('13), after attending the College of Education, was appointed Instructor in German. He took the place of Francis Owen, who had assisted in that department since his graduation in 1907. A peculiar combination Owen was, of poet and pedestrian. In the former capacity he frequently appeared quite creditably in *Acta*; in the latter he had been known to walk 65 miles in a day and 150 miles in three days. Having some personal reasons for disliking the Germans, he had enlisted in August, 1914, as a private in the famous "Princess Pats." He fought through several of the toughest engagements of the war, was wounded, mentioned in despatches, and won his commission on the field. On his discharge he joined the staff of the

University of Alberta, where he still serves as Professor of German. Robins remained in German for some years and then transferring to English rose through the various grades to become the distinguished head of the largest department at Victoria.

Another replacement became necessary in 1915 on the resignation of Francis Haffkina Snow. He was a Ph.D. of Harvard and had been appointed Associate Professor of French in 1912. He was a fresh-complexioned, rotund little man with a dark, pointed beard. An accomplished musician, for several years in later life he was organist in Phillips Brooks' old church in Boston. His main asset was a gift for languages (he was said to have a speaking acquaintance with fourteen), and his main liabilities, a peppery temper and "Madame Snow." He left Toronto in a whirlwind of debts. For a year the College pieced out with temporary assistance while a full professor for the department was diligently sought. Finally the choice fell on Harry Egerton Ford, the son of a prominent physician and Methodist layman of Norwood, Ontario. He graduated in 1895, and thus had spent his first year at Cobourg. For several years he had been on the staff of Washington and Jefferson College, but was quite ready to return to Canada and his *alma mater*. An accomplished French scholar, particularly on the language side, of quick perception and generous disposition, and a good administrator, he fitted admirably into the life of the College and the University during his period of teaching, which terminated in 1940.

When the Great War broke upon an astounded Canada, its full impact was only gradually felt at Victoria. Immediate enlistment from the universities was not encouraged by the government. As a matter of fact the first contingent to leave Toronto was largely made up of men out of work, many of them heroic fellows who saw in the generous separation allowance offered by the government a ready means of supporting their families. College men were urged to prepare themselves as officers. Thus more than two hundred undergraduates of Victoria enrolled in the Officers' Training Corps. They formed two companies under the command of Captains C. V. Massey and G. M. Smith, both lecturers in Modern History, the former the Dean, and the latter a don, of Burwash Hall. As the academic year drew to its close there were enlistments for overseas service, but not many. The following year it was different. Forty per cent of the men who registered in October had enlisted by the following spring, and by midsummer three undergraduates had already fallen in battle.

Neither professors nor officers said to any man, "You ought to go." The men were quieter and more thoughtful than usual. They talked over the matter of enlistment among themselves. It was not because they were out of a job or because there was nothing better showing up in their line that so many of them came so bravely to the great decision. They were all of them ambitious. Before every one of them was opening a gateway to a life of usefulness. But one by one, or in groups of twos and threes, they came back from the recruiting depot, and the word flashed around, "Bob's going." Nobody need ask *where*. There was only one *where*. In a few days a carter would come for a trunk. Its loading was superintended by a young man in a suit of fresh-looking khaki.[3]

During the session 1917-18, the number of men enrolled in Arts was 81, about a third of what it had been in 1914. So complete had been the response to the nation's call, that the College was to afford exemplary support to those who had argued against the need of conscription. When conscription came after a shattering political contest in 1917, it found just one eligible man in Victoria. By the summer of 1918, Burwash Hall was entirely under military control and much of the College grounds under canvas. In all, 530 members of the College (undergraduates, graduates, and members of the staff) served with the forces. It was the custom to fly the College flag at half mast as intelligence was received of each fatality, and for the Chancellor to make an announcement at prayers. During the last months of the war, in breaking the German lines and pushing back the tide of battle no fewer than 15 Victoria men fell. The total during the war was 67. In the tower of the main building where the flag was kept, the caretaker, James Lyon, a native of Glasgow who succeeded Robert Beare in 1910, inscribed these words, neatly printed high on the north wall: "This tattered piece of Bunting registered Victoria's Griefs during the Great War, for 4 years it never flew at top mast."[4] The first to fall was

[3]*Victoria College Bulletin*, 1917-18, p. 5.
[4]From Bermuda James sent a letter to the writer dated January 2, 1951: ". . . Re your enquiry about flag. . . . I have always had a feeling that I had exceeded myself in doing what I did, and was hoping that the incident would fade out, but when it was done I was labouring under a feeling of emotion. It was the day that the Armistice was declared and every one was so happy about it and Mr. Caswell who was then Bursar ordered me to get a new flag instead of that old thing which gave me a strange feeling & in that mood I did as I felt, knowing I had climbed those stairs to the Tower over sixty times to unfurl our sorrow for another one of our sons and to me it was always one of our outstanding men and I used to know them so well, & I felt at least it might have also registered our joy. . . . JAMES."

Ross Malcolm Taylor, a Prince of Wales scholar who headed his course until he enlisted in his third year. War was relentless in the case of the Taylor family. The three sons of Wilson Taylor, a mathematical master at Chatham and St. Catharines Collegiate Institutes, were among several scholarship students he had prepared for university. All three had come to Victoria. Ross was the youngest. The second son, Fred, was killed in the last push in August, 1918. The third son, John, survived, but lost his only son in the Second World War.

In the history of Victoria there have been few occasions so memorable as the service in the Chapel on the morning of October 17, 1919. The survivors had been gathered in for a reunion, the events of which extended over two days. On the second morning all assembled, present and former students, for a simple and intimate service. Dean Robertson read the Scripture, Dean Wallace offered a prayer of thanksgiving and dedication, and the Chancellor spoke briefly, in part as follows:

Memory is very active to-day. The great events of four years of war on the most stupendous scale crowd the canvas. We see the swift onset of the mightiest army that ever had trodden the earth, its sweep westward beyond its own borders, death and destruction, terror and anguish going before and following after—the turning back of these hosts at the Marne—then the siege of great armies on far-flung battle lines such as the most war-mad imagination had never dared conceive, the lifting of the siege here and there in colossal battles which made insignificant the greatest battles of history—the appalling roll-call of the dead and wounded—and flaming against the blackness of it all, deeds of bravery and heroism, and nations stirred and thrilled with sublime passions. Above the tumult of it all we hear the great voices of Justice and Liberty and Humanity calling men and nations to their service, even unto death. To-day these gigantic events form the background for our more intimate and familiar memories. Particularly do we see the bright faces of the men who once had their places in these halls and classrooms, but who will not return. We hear their voices as they hail one another and their shoutings on the campus. And some of you have vivid memories of these men as you saw them last in Flanders or France, in Italy or Egypt or Mesopotamia or India. In the light of such memories we think to-day of these our immortal dead. . . .

Men and women of the College, students and teachers, we are entering this year upon a great heritage of fine example and inspiring memory. Being dead these speak—speak to us in stirring tones and with persuasive power. . . .

Let me make more definite and concrete my meaning. Some of these fallen comrades (you will recall them) were leaders on the campus. There they played the game with skill and prowess and with a clean and chivalrous spirit, fair and generous alike in defeat and victory. To lose self-mastery in speech or in action, to take unfair advantage, to show a grudging or envious or boastful spirit, I ask you, would it not be to violate the sacred memory of some of these men who so well represented you on the athletic field? True to them keep always on the campus the ideals of clean speech and clean sport.

Some of these were our scholars. They won honours for themselves and their college, in the exacting, if less spectacular, competitions of the Examination Hall. Some of them had won the highest prize in the gift of the University. If ever these standards fall, and we as a college are content with second rate, mediocre scholarship, we shall have forgotten these men who forsook their brilliant university careers, gave up their scholar's ambition to fight and die for honour and freedom.

And some of these men were known as leaders in the religious life of the college. Of some of them you were accustomed to say, "If there is a Christian among us he is one." There was about them the indescribable touch, the grace and charm, the authority of the spirit of Christ. Such men were the salt of your common life, and the memory of them will abide a spiritual inspiration—a benediction upon the college for years to come. Cold, calculating rationalism, cynical indifference to religious feeling and conviction would pour contempt upon these sacred memories....

It is told of one soldier that to his friend, whom he rescued and for whom he gave his own life, his message was, "You must live for both of us." He wished for his friend life so complete and so rich that it would be as the life of two. May it not be that there is no cause in our land which shall be the poorer, and no ideals which shall suffer because, and inasmuch as, you, upon whom come these memories, shall have lived your lives richer and nobler by that much the more. Let us put away depression and unbelief. These men, your fallen comrades, did help to vindicate and establish Justice and Honour; they did this on this scandalized and disgraced earth; they did this amid the weaknesses of the flesh. In the New Land and morning to which they have gone not less but greater will be the tasks assigned them—and so

> At noon day in the bustle of men's work-time,
>   Greet the Unseen with a cheer!
> Bid him forward! breast and back as either should be,
> "Strive and thrive," cry "Speed—fight on—fare ever,
>   There as here!"[5]

The service concluded with the roll-call of the sixty-seven names, followed by the solemn notes of the last post from the hall.

During the two days a series of events was carried through including football matches between students and old boys, the Charter Day Convocation, a great luncheon at Burwash Hall, *Twelfth Night* performed by the women students, a reception at Annesley Hall, and last of all an old-time "Bob."

[5]*Acta Victoriana War Supplement* (1919), pp. 5–7.

All these ceremonies, though conforming fully with tradition, produced results quite unlike those of any similar event in the annals of the College, and quite surpassing all plans and expectations of those concerned in the preparation.

No one had ever before heard a graduate of Conference Theology allude facetiously to his experiences as officer in charge of one of His Majesty's minesweepers in the Adriatic, or another graduate include among the horrors of war a sense of embarrassment in having to appear for the first time as chaplain of a Highland battalion with knees of an unseasonable whiteness. But the climax was reached when a popular graduate, who had been a capable student and essayist, who had won almost every military decoration, including the Victoria Cross, and who could have conversed on the subject of football by the hour, became quite tongue-tied when asked to speak of his military experiences. No one wished it otherwise, and least of all the returned men themselves. They had gone away quietly without fanfaronade. They had not desired a noisy welcome, and their whole demeanour expressed that character of modesty and dignity which is consistent with true chivalry and substantial worth.[6]

The names of the fallen were recorded on a brass tablet on the east wall of the porch of the College. In December, *Acta* produced a beautiful memorial volume of 120 pages, in two parts. The first part contains an account of the memorial service, twin sonnets "*In Memoriam*" by E. J. Pratt, photographs of the fallen, with details of their lives, their military service, and the manner of their death, 4 pages assigned to the decorations won (with citations), a page to Victoria women in war work, 34 pages of names and records of members of the College in the services and photographs of 480 of them. The second part consists of a number of timely articles, sketches, and news items, together with illustrations, one of which, that of a group at the reunion, is so clear that even yet a key could be prepared.

Of the many honours which came to Victoria men in the war, one must be mentioned. Thane W. MacDowell ('14) had been an outstanding athlete in hockey and rugby, and as a student in the General Course well above the average in ability and application. Modest and retiring he always was, and so he remained. In November, 1916, as Captain of B Company of the 38th Battalion, he won the D.S.O. by advancing within range of German machine guns, south of the Ancre, which had been holding up the advance, and after severe hand-to-hand fighting captured three officers and fifty of the enemy crews. Some six

[6]C. E. Auger in the *Victoria College Bulletin*, 1920-1, pp. 36–7.

months later (the date and place are not given in the citation), now Major in the same battalion, he won the Victoria Cross,

For most conspicuous bravery and indomitable resolution in face of heavy machine-gun and shell-fire. By his initiative and courage this officer, with the assistance of two runners, was enabled, in the face of great difficulties, to capture two machine guns, besides two officers and seventy-five men. Although wounded in the hand, he continued for five days to hold the position gained, in spite of heavy shell-fire, until eventually relieved by his battalion. By his bravery and prompt action he undoubtedly succeeded in rounding up a very strong enemy machine-gun post.[7]

Another memorial to the fallen was projected but never executed. It was to take the form of a chapel at the corner of Queen's Park and Avenue Road. A sketch drawn by Henry Sproatt appears as the frontispiece of the *Acta War Supplement*. To many members of the College the University of Toronto memorial, the Soldiers' Tower adjoining Hart House, may well have seemed sufficient. Indeed the chairman of the Tower building fund was Mr. Justice Masten, who had carried the Senior Stick at Cobourg in 1878-9.

Two losses incurred by Victoria University at home during the war years must be recorded. Charles Canniff James died suddenly at St. Catharines in 1916 at the age of fifty-seven. After graduating from Cobourg in 1883 with the gold medal in Science and teaching in the Cobourg Collegiate Institute for three years, he was named successively Professor of Chemistry at the Ontario Agricultural College in 1886, Deputy Minister of Agriculture for Ontario in 1891, and Dominion Commissioner of Agriculture in 1912. When the war broke out he became largely responsible for the campaign for increased production of food, and his untimely death two years later was a great national loss. His intimate knowledge of certain phases of Canadian history was frequently subject to call by *Acta*. He gave a fine collection of Canadian poetry to the College during his lifetime, and his Tennysoniana was bequeathed to Victoria; both have been placed in the Library in a room which bears his name. A further bequest was the interest in the College of his son, Wilfrid Crossen James ('16), Chairman of the Board of Regents from 1942 to 1951, and since then Bursar and Secretary of the Board.

Then, on March 30, 1918, at the age of seventy-eight, death came to Nathanael Burwash peacefully and suddenly. His history is closely

[7]*Acta Victoriana War Supplement*, p. 26.

interwoven with that of Victoria, the progress of which he was to record during his years of retirement. On January 18, 1917, he had inaugurated the Burwash lectureship, which former students and other friends had raised $5,000 to endow. His subject was "The Men of the Early Days of Victoria." When he was compelled to desist before the end of the lecture, Mr. Justice Britton mounted the platform to move a vote of thanks and recalled how sixty-five years before he had shared a room in the old College with the chubby-faced boy who, full of years and honours, had just taken his seat. In his later years Burwash had turned to the field of Canadian history, in two areas of which, the church and education, he had knowledge perhaps unequalled in Canada. His first serious literary adventure in this field was his life of Egerton Ryerson in the "Makers of Canada" series. In the *Proceedings* of the Royal Society of Canada, of which he had been elected a Fellow, other contributions may be found. From the days of the Fenian raids, he maintained an interest in the Canadian militia and was an honorary colonel of one of the city regiments. He lies buried in the little cemetery at Baltimore near Cobourg, and within sight of the home of his childhood.

The spacious residence at the north-east angle of Queen's Park was about this time added to the group of College buildings, though not at the time by purchase, and was for some years known as the Dean's House. It became the home of Vincent Massey, who had recently married Alice, daughter of Sir George Parkin, the trustee of the Rhodes Scholarship fund. G. M. Smith, who had returned from the war with the Military Cross, became Acting Dean in general charge of Burwash Hall and the residences. For some years Mr. and Mrs. Massey continued to take a large part in College affairs, especially those concerning the men's and women's residences. Eventually their main university interest was centred on Hart House, built by the Massey Foundation and opened for student use in the fall of 1919.

Two appointments made to the staff in 1919 indicated a new trend in theological training. The institutional, as distinct from the strictly evangelical, church was on the march. John Walker Macmillan was appointed Professor of Sociology and Frederick William Langford, Associate Professor of Religious Pedagogy. Both these men were ordained ministers of some years' standing. Macmillan was a Presbyterian who had been teaching in Manitoba College and at the same time acting as Chairman of the provincial Minimum Wage Commission. He was a very tall man of sober mien and firm tread, impressive alike on the platform, at a conference table, and with the pen. His views on social and economic subjects were balanced and conservative. He was quite ready to shake the dust of Winnipeg from his feet; since the general strike of that year which had split the city into two hostile camps, with the labour sympathizers, to judge from subsequent elections, numerically in the majority, it was not a pleasant place in which to profess sociology. On coming to Toronto he was appointed Chairman of the Ontario Minimum Wage Board. His teaching programme was never heavy. When he died in 1932 the chair was not filled. In 1923 by resolution of the Board he was included in the Faculty of Arts as well as in that of Theology; but no attempt appears to have been made to transfer Sociology from the University to the college list in the University of Toronto curriculum, although it was one of those borderline subjects the addition of which to the curriculum was beginning to disturb the balance in teaching load.

"Fred" Langford was an alumnus of Victoria in Arts ('05) and Theology ('06). As an undergraduate he had been active in the religious life of the College and after ordination and a successful pastorate had specialized in Sunday School work, taking the degree of Master of Religious Education at Boston. For a time after his appointment he retained an association with the Sunday School department of the Church with a certain saving of salary to the College. A clear and incisive speaker and a capable teacher and administrator, he won for himself an increasingly large place in the theological faculty. On the retirement of Principal Davidson in 1943 he became Chairman of the Council of Emmanuel College, and in the following year under the new Act he was the first Dean. He retired in 1945.

Another and earlier appointment in Theology showed the same bent to the practical. William Hubert Greaves had been brought from Queen's as Associate Professor of Public Speaking in 1912. His training had been received at Boston. He was a hearty and robust man, who soon gained a fine reputation both in the College and in the city Y.M.C.A., where he conducted classes. Furthermore, as a public lecturer he was most entertaining. It was something of a trial to teach in a room near or under Jackson Hall, where he conducted his classes, and the type of oratory he inculcated was vastly different from that of Nelles or Bowles, refined by "the pale cast of thought." But his success and public appeal were such that in 1929 he received and accepted the professorship of Public Speaking at Yale. He had never assumed Canadian citizenship.

Several junior appointments, all of graduates of the College, were made to the Arts Faculty in 1919 and 1920 to meet the increasing enrolment. In 1919 Miss Mary C. Rowell, who had studied in Europe, and Alexander Lacey, who had held an American fellowship for a year, were appointed Lecturers in French. No better person than Miss Rowell could have been chosen to break the crust of prejudice against the appointment of a woman to the staff. Already a graduate of twenty years, quiet, dignified, large in sympathy, feminine but not a feminist, she played a useful and unobtrusive part in the College until her retirement in 1935. Lacey was a Newfoundland man and never so eloquent as when he was elaborating on the wrongs of the colony and how to meet them. He wrote well but all too little. His health was never rugged, but he lived to see four of his children graduate from the College. Hartley Grant Robertson in 1920 joined his father in the department of Classics. His graduate studies with Bonner at Chicago were interrupted by the war, but after hostilities he spent two terms at Oxford and returned to Chicago to complete work for the Ph.D. He collaborated with his father in writing an excellent little work *The Story of Greece and Rome*, after some twenty years still much in use as a text-book in England and Canada. He now occupies the chair of Greek. In 1920 Edwin John Pratt, after sojourning awhile with the psychologists across the Park, returned home. Son of a Newfoundland parsonage, once he reached Toronto he was content to stay; all four of his degrees were won there. Similarly in his teaching; finally committed to English, he put behind him the philosophy and theology (he once undertook even to teach Hebrew) and psychology—or made them grist to his mill. And a busy and fruitful mill it has been. During these years also three young graduates who have since attained eminence received temporary appointments as instructors or teaching fellows: W. G. Hardy, Instructor in Ancient History, now head of the department of Classics in Alberta; J. D. N. Bush, Fellow in English (but a Classics man) now a Professor of English at Harvard; and

T. R. S. Broughton, Fellow in Latin, now Professor of Latin, Bryn Mawr.

Burwash Hall was becoming the scene not only of several regular College functions, such as the "Bob" and the Faculty Dinner to the graduating class, but also occasionally of meetings of public significance. One such was a great *Bonne Entente* luncheon early in 1917. The College thus identified itself with a national movement aimed at healing the wound caused by a piece of school legislation on the part of the Ontario government known as Regulation Seventeen, which was regarded as an attempt to proscribe the use of the French language in Ontario. The *Bonne Entente* movement failed of its immediate purpose, as subsequent federal elections were to show, but it was something for Victoria to give it support. Some five years later, however, when the Hon. E. C. Drury, Premier of Ontario, wrote the President to ask that one of the professors should be allowed to stand for election in a French county to plead the cause, a request backed by a deputation of three prominent and responsible citizens who promised that the seat should be his probably by acclamation, the President demurred, and with the entire approval of the professor concerned. There was no lack of appreciation of the generosity of such an offer to a Methodist who spoke only English, simply because at one time he had published a work in the interests of elementary justice and national unity. The negative was solidly based on the ground that a professor could not do justice to his work and at the same time hold a seat in the House.

Life in the men's residences was not permitted to come within the view, not to say control, of the Senate or Faculty. This remained true even after the Act of 1928 had given the Faculty a legal status. From the outset discipline was in the hands of the President and the Dean, with such assistance as the dons and the student committees of the houses might afford. There were, of course, plenty of problems of discipline, particularly in the first years after the war, when the habits of former soldiers at times failed to conform to the standards of a Methodist college. With the women's residences it was somewhat different. The Board, as has been noted, had delegated certain authority in this area to the Senate. In the early twenties two critical situations developed among the women students, one of which caused quite a stir.

The earlier arose over a sharp difference of opinion in the Committee of Management. The resignation through illness of Miss M. H. Skinner ('99), who had been in charge of the Women's Union for two years, and the fact that Miss Rowell had found it impossible to combine supervision of a Bloor Street residence with her teaching duties had opened the way for a complete reorganization of arrangements for women students. It was decided to appoint Miss Addison Dean of Women with oversight of both the Union and the residences. She was not to live in residence, but five young women were to act as dons, one in each unit of residence. This arrangement would appear to have been connected in origin with criticism in the Committee of Management, on the part of one influential member at least, that the traditional policy of Annesley Hall as "a home from home" with an older woman *in loco parentis* was antiquated, and that life should be as free as possible, with less emphasis on creature comforts and more on intellectual quickening. Indeed the suggestion was that rules were now too restrictive which ten years earlier had been pronounced too lax. The students, however, rallied to the support of Miss Addison and petitioned for her continued residence in the Hall; the majority of the Committee of Management agreed in thinking that under her direction the life of the residence had really not failed to emphasize the cultural; while the College constituency generally was inclined to feel that Annesley Hall's primary function was just that of a home and that the professors could be trusted to take care of intellectual needs.

In all this discussion and agitation it was apparent that the future of co-education in Victoria was brought into question. There was not a little concern when it was noted that the upsurge in enrolment of men after the war had halted and that of women had increased to a point where it appeared likely that they would predominate. A proposal was introduced but not forced to an issue in the Faculty that enrolment be denied to first year women with junior matriculation if they came from schools where senior matriculation might be secured. A disorderly incident between the first and second years when a photograph of the first year was being taken, in which the women were involved, evoked from the Chancellor an emphatic letter ending with these words: "May I also call the attention of the Class to the very palpable fact that many things which might be overlooked in a women's college or a men's college are entirely out of place in a co-educational institution such as Victoria is at present?" In fact the question was vaguely canvassed whether the wisest solution for the future might not be separate colleges for women after the fashion of Oxford and Cambridge and as widely adopted in the Eastern States. On October 21, 1929, Walter T. Brown, writing to the Chancellor from Yale made the following reference to the situation at Brown University: "You may be interested in knowing that they have separate colleges for men and women with a common faculty such as you have sometimes proposed for Victoria. The women's college has a campus of its own about four short blocks from the men's college, and the courses are taught separately except in the case of science where they have common laboratories. The women's college was founded over thirty years ago and according to the lady students whom I met the arrangement is highly satisfactory."

Into the midst of a society in some uncertainty as to the future of co-education, the problem of sororities was projected in 1923. A group of women students approached the Chancellor with a request to form a new sorority. He informed them that the matter must be referred to the Senate. In 1907 consent had been given by Chancellor Burwash personally to the formation of a sorority in the College. In 1911 this group was formally constituted a chapter of Kappa Kappa Gamma. An arrangement was made that in the University of Toronto this sorority should be confined to Victoria, and that students of the College should not be "rushed" by other sororities. In 1915 some agitation arose among the Victoria College women against the sorority, and the matter was laid before the Senate, which had previously been entrusted by the Board with the delicate question of student government in Annesley. The Senate after considerable discussion finally adopted the report of a committee which recommended "in the presence of the unparalleled world calamity" that "the Senate leave the matter to the good sense and loyalty of the students themselves."[8] When the agitation was revived in 1923 Kappa Kappa Gamma had become firmly established with a membership of thirty-three. The claim of a new group desiring a sorority, somewhat forcefully presented as one against monopoly, again called forth a protest from representatives of the women students against sororities in general for Victoria. Again a committee of the Senate was appointed to report. It consisted of six members,

[8]V.U.A., Senate, Minutes, Nov. 5, 1915, p. 198.

two from the Faculty, and four who were members of the Board, including the two women members of the Board elected by the graduates. The committee conferred separately with each of the interested groups and with the President and entered into some correspondence on the general question. Its report was ready by the spring of 1924, but it was decided to leave the final decision to the autumn. Then, after much discussion in two very full meetings, the report signed by five of the six members (the sixth would have transferred jurisdiction to the Board) was adopted with a slight amendment. The first and principal clause stood. It read as follows: "That the Senate declare it to be its judgment that it is essential to the harmony and well-being of this College that no Sorority exist within its students." From the second clause a request that the President report to the Senate what action he deemed it advisable to make was deleted and the clause as amended and accepted read: "That with this expression of its judgment the Senate leave the President to take the initiative in such further steps as he may deem advisable."[9]

The result was in every way creditable to the good sense of the women students, which the Senate had been prepared to trust in 1915. The new application was withdrawn, and the existing sorority agreed not to solicit or accept new members. In conformity with this action other sororities in the University have taken the same stand with regard to Victoria women. And since that time any woman who wishes to enjoy such advantages as sororities may confer simply does not enrol at Victoria. But that situation is the result of action by the women themselves, and not of dictation by the College authorities. The Senate, of course, had no legislative or executive authority in the matter; and in referring the petition to the Senate rather than to the Board for advice, the President had created a precedent with wide implications.[10]

In the spring of 1925 the women of Victoria received a rare gift. Mrs. E. R. Wood deeded her lovely home, Wymilwood, to the Board of Regents as a social centre, and her friend, Lady Flavelle, who lived in the spacious house adjoining it, donated $60,000 to remodel and furnish it. By January 12, 1926, it was ready for occupation. On the ground

[9]*Ibid.*, Oct. 17, 1924.
[10]The men students have never had an exclusively Victoria College chapter. A very few, then as now, have connected themselves with fraternities, and these have been largely men living in the city.

floor were four reception rooms, one large enough to seat over fifty persons, an office, a small dining room, a capacious kitchen. The second and third floors provided rooms which served to add to the residence accommodation. The building was set in beautifully kept lawns and gardens. Miss Dorothy Kilpatrick, a daughter of Professor Thomas Kilpatrick of Knox College, and at the time on furlough from missionary work in India, was placed in charge as head of the Students' Union, and made a charming hostess, establishing traditions in keeping with the exquisite surroundings. These traditions were maintained by Miss Muriel Manning during the twenty years of her headship. Thenceforth while Wymilwood appears on the books among the assets at $100,000, its influence on the tastes and manners of undergraduate men and women during a quarter-century can hardly be appraised. And with the replacing of P. Brangyn, the steward of Burwash Hall, on January 1, 1925, by Miss Dorothy Falconbridge, a woman as kind as she was capable, the students of the late twenties were to be congratulated on the provision for their aesthetic and physical comforts.

The year 1925 saw the consummation of Church Union. The Methodists, the greater part of the Presbyterians, and the Congregationalists, after many years of deliberation and planning, had voted to form one body to be known as the United Church of Canada. Victoria University had long been looking forward to the event. Already for some years considerable sharing of work had taken place between the Faculty of Theology at Victoria and the staff of Knox College, all of whom had taken their stand for Union. But as the time for decision on a permanent policy drew near, the traditional divergence of views on the relation of Arts to Theology became all too apparent. Perhaps it may best be presented in President Bowles' own words, as he describes a conference of the combined theological faculties in a letter of February 19, 1925, to Professor A. L. Phelps ('13), of Wesley College, Winnipeg, who was disturbed about the situation there:

At the same time I made it clear to the friends in Knox that if Knox did not come in I believed the policy of the new Church would be to bring the present Knox Faculty and students over to Victoria and continue in a new Theological building in the very closest relations possible with the Arts College the work practically as it is now going on in Victoria. . . . A form of government which would unite the two as the property of one Church exercising its teaching functions in two directions was imperative.

This statement brought out a difference of opinion especially between Principal Gandier and myself. While Principal Gandier believed that there should be a very close relation between the new Theology, which it was hoped would be done in Knox, and the Arts in Victoria, he did not see the need for the organized unity. Moreover, he strongly defined the policy of the Presbyterian Church as maintaining a close relationship with the State College, and he took the ground that the Church would require a different form of Charter for the two Colleges. . . . I undertook to expound as I see it the Presbyterian ideal of Higher Education, namely, the close relationship of the Theological institution to the University. I said that I thought there was much to be said in favour of it; but coming down to the facts of the case in Toronto, I maintained that Knox College was counting for less and less in the life of the University as the years went by, whereas I believed that Victoria was counting for more and more. . . .

It seemed to me that Principal Gandier's idea was not practicable, and that if the Theological College was the property of the same Church as also owned and cared for the Arts College, the two must come near together with a necessary loosening of the direct connection now existing between Knox and University College. At this point Professor Kilpatrick spoke in favor of the ideals which I was upholding. He drew upon his experience in Manitoba College, and he pointed out that a Theological College gains immensely in prestige and influence if it is also doing Arts work. . . . In other words, he practically put himself on record as in favor of what seems to be more a Methodist policy at present than a Presbyterian one.

I think our friends in Knox College appreciate our situation. They realize that to take the Theology that is now being done in Victoria over to Knox College is a sacrifice on the part of Victoria of very great significance. I pointed out that for myself, so far as I was concerned, it meant a Victoria College bereft of half its power and glory. . . .

Fourteen months later it was decided by the Ontario Legislature that the Knox College building should go to the non-concurrents. Gandier still hoped to retain the charter and the endowment. He had conceded the necessity of one Board, one President, and one Senate, but still was seeking a means of retaining a certain autonomy. On April 13, 1926, he wrote Bowles:

Let the two Colleges together constitute a University to be known as the University of Victoria and Knox Colleges, which will confer all degrees, while Knox will give its own diplomas and retain its own name, corporate seal and place in the University Federation. . . .

With one Board and one Senate for the University, Knox College, instead of being organized under a Board and Senate as at present, might be organized under its own Principal and Faculty or Council, which, without the name of a Senate, might have some functions both of a Board and Senate. . . .

Severe as was the blow to Gandier when the building was lost, the final decision that the charter and two-thirds of the endowment should go with the building was a greater grief. Even Strachan's loss of King's College in 1849 had been less cruel. Strachan had erected his college through funds secured from the public purse; Gandier had begged the $500,000 needed for building Knox practically single-handed. "He went all over Western Ontario, through cities and towns and villages, and along the country roads, day after day, week after week, year in and year out, gathering subscriptions of two, five, ten, or twenty-five dollars at a time, sometimes a $100, rarely as much as $500—always cheerful, confident, tireless."[11] In the end despite such labours this was all he was able to bring in his hand: endowment to the extent of $145,000; the principal's residence and the use (with an annual payment for upkeep) of the college library. All the teaching staff, it is true, had accepted Union, but Kilpatrick's health had failed and MacNeil had gone to Chicago. There remained Gandier himself, Richard Davidson, John Dow, and Hugh Matheson, the librarian. Arrangements had already been made to bring over from Scotland another scholar of distinction, John Baillie, who began work in 1927, as did Kenneth Harrington Cousland, a Canadian trained in Oxford who with the rank of Lecturer took MacNeil's work in Church History. McLaughlin in all grace and humility exchanged the title of Dean of Theology, to which he had succeeded in 1920, for that of Registrar.

The loss of the charter meant the loss of the name. For a time the former Knox staff carried on work under the name of "Union College," and in conjunction with the Victoria Theological staff. In the meantime a long and diligent search, with one abortive decision, was made for a new name. "The Faculty of Theology of Victoria University" would not serve, and "Caven" and "Westminster" were not pressed, as being too Presbyterian in flavour. The choice narrowed down to "St. John's" and "New," and each had strong supporters. Finally, the name "Emmanuel," "God with us," was suggested, voted upon, and

[11]Richard Davidson, *In Memoriam, Alfred Gandier, 1861-1932* (Toronto, 1934), p. 6.

accepted, this at a meeting in the Victoria College Chapel. Whereupon, Dr. J. R. P. Sclater, pleased with a name reminiscent of Cambridge, pointed to the light streaming through the Wesley window with its text, "The best of all is God with us," and everyone was content.[12]

Nowhere was the generous attitude of Victoria to its new citizens more signally shown than in the matter of retiring arrangements. Before Church Union and when the financial situation at length warranted it, the long contemplated pension scheme was brought into effect, present members of the staff on a non-contributory, and future members on a contributory, basis. The distinction was made on the ground that those who had borne the burden and heat of the day on salaries admittedly inadequate merited a consideration not accorded to those who were entering service with better returns in prospect. The maximum retiring allowance for the former group was $1,800, widows receiving half that amount with a certain deduction, however, in proportion as they might be younger than their husbands. In the case of Methodist ministers on the staff who were on the Superannuation Fund of the Church an equitable deduction was made from the payments by Victoria University in consideration of their annual receipts from the fund. Now the new members of the staff from Knox—coming in, so to speak, at the eleventh hour—were given the same consideration, or even more, since for them there was no superannuation fund. And Kilpatrick, already retired and almost spent, was granted an annuity, continued in part to his widow. Thus warmly was the hand of welcome extended.

One feature of the retirement scheme must be noted in passing. In its first report the committee of the Board had recommended automatic superannuation at the age of sixty-five, the Board, however, reserving

[12]The prolonged contest evoked this bit of verse from an irreverent Arts man:
"O happy day, that fixed my choice
  On thee, Emmanuel, at last.
Well may this glowing heart rejoice
  And all its raptures loud broadcast.
"Now rest, my long-divided heart,
  Fixed on this name unanimous;
Caven, Saint John, and New, depart;
  Emmanuel abides with us.
" 'Tis done, the great transaction's done;
  The name's euphonious, orthodox;
The meaning's best of all, bar none,—
  The Lord's with us, and not with Knox."

the right by special action taken annually to continue a professor in active service for five years longer—precisely the system in the University of Toronto. In a subsequent report this reservation was omitted but an amendment was accepted, as just to those who would not be prepared for such sudden action, that no one should be superannuated within three years. The President himself retired promptly at the age limit, but his successor, feeling that during his first year in office he would be better served by age than by youth—that is, age in the persons of Lang, McLaughlin, and Robertson—had their period of service extended one year beyond the three.

The changes resulting from Church Union were embodied in "An Act respecting Victoria University and Union Theological College," assented to on April 3, 1928. The principal new features concerned the constitution of the Board of Regents and the setting up of councils for the two colleges with definite powers and duties. Gone with the wind were the principles on which the Board of 1915 had been constructed. The number of members was increased from twenty-eight to forty-two, almost double that of the Board of Governors of the University of Toronto. Twenty-two were to be appointed by the General Council, the new term for General Conference; five by the graduates in Arts, Medicine, Science, and Law of Victoria University, who had named six under the old Act; five by the alumni of Emmanuel College, the term being extended to include all ministers of the United Church who had spent a year studying theology at Victoria or Knox; and there were to be seven co-opted members rather than the eight of the earlier and smaller Board. The influence of the Church in the Board of Regents, if increased in regard to representation, was reduced, or in any case altered, in another respect. The Chairman was now elected by the Board. Formerly the General Superintendent had been *ex-officio* Chairman. His successor under Church Union, known as the Moderator, held office for two years only, and even if at the time of his elevation he might have considerable acquaintance with Victoria University affairs, it was not well to permit biennial changes in headship of a body responsible for long-term business policies. Under the powers of the Board, one new and important provision was included.

No appointment to the permanent teaching staff of either college shall be made until the Chancellor and the Principal of such college shall have consulted with the teaching staff of the department concerned in the case of Victoria College, and with the council of the college, in the case of Emmanuel College and until the result of such consultation has been reported to the Board. The appointment of the principal and professors of Emmanuel College shall be subject to confirmation by the General Council of the United Church of Canada or by a duly authorized board or committee of the General Council.

The provision in the Act of 1928 for a Council of Emmanuel College consisting of the teaching staff (which constituted a permanent executive), six members elected every two years by the General Council, and six by the alumni introduced a new principle. These outside members were all ministers and all alumni representatives on the Board or on the Senate. Their inclusion in the group which the President was bound to consult before recommending to the Board any appointment in Theology, together with their voice in preparing curricula and arranging for examining candidates, matters over which the Senate had final control, was what remained of Gandier's original idea of a separate board and senate. It carried the impairment of the absolute authority of the Board in the matter of appointments a step further than had the provision admitted in 1915.

The provision for a Council of Victoria College gave a definite status to the Arts faculty. The principal duties assigned were to exercise direction, guidance, and oversight of the work and life of the College, to deal with all applications and memorials by students or others in which College action was required, to conduct College examinations, to appoint its representatives on the University Senate, and to report directly to the Board any matter affecting the College which to it might seem meet. This last duty has seldom been exercised, and never except through the President. Both the President and the Principal were to be members of Council, the latter presiding. The Council was promptly organized, elected a secretary to hold office for two years, drew up by-laws, and formed standing committees. From that time it has held regular meetings on a stated day each month, and kept a proper record of all proceedings. Even President Bowles, who was allergic to such meetings and who presided as Acting Principal during the remainder of his term, ruefully testified to its usefulness, and indeed he had admitted the necessity of its being given a legal status.

An event of 1926 of some significance must be recorded. At the Board meeting of February 2, dancing was officially sanctioned. The word, so abhorrent to all Methodist traditions, does not appear in the minutes. Nor was the matter ever referred to the Faculty or the Senate. The Board took full responsibility, thus deviously: it sanctioned the formation of a Social Caput, a committee consisting of the President, four other administrative officers, and four representatives of the undergraduates with authority "to permit (and supervise) all social functions of the Arts students of Victoria College."[13] The primary purpose of this body was, of course, recognized as being to bring dancing under official regulation. There were two dissenting votes among the sixteen members of the Board in attendance. Advantage was promptly taken of the provision, and dances began to be held in the College buildings. Church Union may have contributed to, but was not responsible for, the departure. Gradually the attitude of Methodists had been changing. In explaining the action to a brother minister who had protested, Dr. Bowles said that 80 per cent of the young women who came to Victoria were already accustomed to dancing and that it was necessary that student recreation be brought within the College, rather than driven outside. The only formal objection came by way of petition from a group of theological students. But time played the whirligig. Presently such anomalies as tea dances, and dances after abbreviated "hikes," were introduced. Thus students who lacked a taste for modern dancing, together with those who objected to it on principle, found themselves looking on the social life of the College from without; Terpsichore, by nature an imperious wench, for a time held undisputed sway within.

In weightier matters of University policy an important incident occurred in 1926. The University Act of 1906 had sought above all else to free the University from political control. Even in finances it had been hoped that the allocation of succession duties for its support might obviate the dangers incidental to dependence on an annual grant. But both the death and the avails of men of wealth proved too uncertain as regular support and the system of annual estimates and grants was continued. For twenty years, however, there had been no serious intrusion on the part of the government in matters of cur-

[13]V.U.A., Board of Regents, Minutes, Feb. 2, 1926, p. 277.

riculum. Then early in 1926 the Hon. G. Howard Ferguson, Premier and Minister of Education, informed President Falconer that he had reached the conclusion that the first year work of the University should be transferred to the secondary schools. The President was asked to take the question up with the various colleges and request their co-operation. This was done. Dr. Bowles referred the point to the Senate. After two discussions the opinion of that body proved to be singularly unanimous, and the Chancellor was asked to gather "the sense of the meeting," Quaker fashion, and forward it. Thereupon Dr. Bowles drew up a concise and cogent argument in general opposition to the proposal, submitted it to the four members of his Arts staff whom he considered most conversant with the subject to make sure that nothing had been overlooked, and with some slight revision sent it forward to President Falconer as the judgment of the Senate of Victoria University.

While stating at the outset that for over eighty years the course in Victoria College had been a four years' course and that the proposed change might seriously diminish the influence of the College upon its students, the Senate nevertheless had endeavoured to consider the matter in the light of the educational welfare of the province at large. From this point of view, it wholly condemned the proposal so far as it related to the honour courses, on grounds of "cost, efficiency, and the new stimulus which University life would give the student."[14] With respect to the Pass Course, which it believed "would be better designated the General Course," the Senate was less emphatic. It recognized that the present conditions were "not entirely satisfactory," but felt that the remedy suggested could only postpone their correction to "what might be called the second, but would really be the first, year of the University course." It admitted that a certain percentage of those now entering would be "better advised to remain another year at home." Many, however, had very sound reasons for coming to college. Not a few did so well in their first year Pass that they were "gladly admitted to some of the most important honour courses of the second year." After describing three classes of students to whom the proposed change would be a hardship, the Senate expressed the opinion that "the present age at which the students are entering the Uni-

[14] V.U.A., Senate, Minutes, March 25, 1926.

versity" was "higher than was necessary"; a too rigid system was retarding the natural pace of promising students. Further the writing of matriculation on "the instalment plan" was deprecated. The whole argument ends with a significant warning. "The Senate did not take into consideration any rights or claims which Victoria University may have under the Federation Act, or any rights possessed under her present Charter. This, however, is of course submitted without any prejudice to the rights."

This incident serves to illustrate the way in which the more independent situation of the federated colleges has proven a safeguard to the integrity of the University. The outcome was that the four years of Honours were retained and the first year of the Pass Course transferred to the schools. The effect of the change was from an educational point of view not seriously detrimental, but it did make for many annoying administrative difficulties, and of course it disrupted the year organizations of the colleges.

In 1926 an attempt was made by the alumni to institute a new college "function." The first Founders' Dinner was held in Burwash Hall on March 24, the anniversary of Ryerson's birth. The first three presidents of the College were celebrated in speeches, Ryerson by the writer, Nelles by Judge Huycke, and Burwash by the President. The writer had already begun the work on the Ryerson papers which was to constitute a parergon through so many years. To be sure, the choice was a *pis aller*. Dr. Bowles had written Professor G. M. Wrong asking him to interest Lester Bowles Pearson, then on the History staff, in this bit of research, but Pearson evidently was attracted to other fields, including the campus on which he coached the rugby team to win the Mulock Cup in 1923. At the Founders' Dinner of 1927 the speakers were A. P. Coleman, Mr. Justice Riddell, and Mr. Justice Masten. The third Founders' Dinner was addressed by W. S. Herrington ('83) of Napanee, barrister, historian, and Fellow of the Royal Society of Canada. The practice was not continued; it may be inferred that interest in the history of the College was unequal to the burden of sustaining two annual functions, and it was decided to concentrate on Charter Day, October 12.

Two other dinners provided by the Board serve to indicate the vitality of College life during the late twenties. On April 18, 1928, a dinner was tendered by the College to the members of six winning teams. During that session the men had won the three major interfaculty cups in rugby, soccer, and hockey, and the women the major events in basketball, baseball, and hockey. And on January 21, 1929, similar honour was paid to the fifty-two winners of scholarships during the previous year. The speaker on this occasion was the Rt. Hon. Arthur Meighen, who fascinated the company which filled Burwash Hall yet could hear him perfectly without strain on his part or theirs.

Changes in the staff were not numerous during this period. On the administrative side, in 1921 the Rev. Frank Louis Barber ('03), who had also won his Ph.D. in Psychology at Toronto, was appointed Bursar. Later he succeeded Lang, on the latter's retirement in 1924, in the librarianship. This busy, rather over-prompt, and infinitely obliging little man added greatly to the pleasantness of the high table, the volley-ball court, and life in general at Victoria during twenty-four years. And his humour lived after him; in the case of a bequest of $30,000 to establish a fellowship, he willed that the money should go to the Salvation Army unless the terms of the bequest should be implemented with exactitude. Also in 1921, the Rev. William Jackson Little ('13) was appointed Accountant. His energy, efficiency, and financial wizardry in time brought him a spate of onerous duties. For many years he directed the affairs of the Alumni Association. When sudden death came to him in Kincardine he was carrying the three offices of Bursar, Superintendent of Grounds and Buildings, and Secretary of the Board of Regents.

In appointments to the teaching staff the custom was continued of selecting recent graduates as fellows or instructors, and, if they gave promise, of encouraging them to pursue further studies abroad with a view to taking a place on the permanent staff. In the mid and late twenties one full professor and one associate were added to the Victoria College staff. In 1928 John Line ('13) was brought from Pine Hill to succeed W. T. Brown in Philosophy when the latter left to become chairman of the new department of Religion at Yale. Line was born in England, seasoned in Newfoundland and under Peter Bryce in Earlscourt, and leavened in Arts and Theology at Victoria. In the following year Eric A. Havelock, a Cambridge man with a first in the classical tripos and distinction in ancient philosophy, who had spent two years at Acadia, was added to the staff in Greek. After seventeen years of distinguished teaching and distinctive political predilections, he accepted a position at Harvard with larger salary and opportunity for scholarly publication. Graduates of the College still on the staff who began service during this period are: John Alvin Surerus ('15), born of German pioneer stock in Huron County but thoroughly Canadian in outlook and interests, who, after service overseas, a mastership at Appleby Boys' School, and graduate study in Chicago, was appointed Lecturer in German in 1925, a department of which he is now the head; Miss Alta Lind Cook ('13), who had spent considerable time in France and was brought into the French department from Malvern Collegiate Institute; Miss R. I. Jenking ('25), as Fellow in Classics; Miss K. H. Coburn ('28) in English; and Miss Laure Rièse ('33), a native of Switzerland, in French. Two men trained in continental Europe were added to the staff in Modern Languages: Robert Karl Arnold, a Ph.D. of Prague, who became Lecturer in German in 1929, and Henri Lasserre, a Swiss lawyer in middle age whose passion was the co-operative movement, in 1926.

Meanwhile finances again became a problem. Current expenses had mounted ominously from duplication in the theological staff; and with Knox lost in the Union, new buildings for Theology in keeping with the Library and Burwash Hall were considered necessary. Furthermore the women were demanding consideration, their residential accommodation being quite inadequate. And the chapel long in contemplation was still wanting. These objects were combined in a great appeal to the Church and the graduates. All were urged to give to the general campaign or to one of the special objects. Together the President and the Principal of Emmanuel College laid siege to the churches, and a well-organized campaign office brought pressure on the alumni. The objective was $1,200,000, the proceeds $737,081 with an additional $97,925 secured in 1937 as a "centenary fund." Since the cost of Emmanuel itself was approximately $400,000 and that of its four units of residence an additional $300,000, little was available for the needs of the women and nothing for the chapel. Several factors contributed to the indifferent success of this campaign. Just when the committee was ready to go to work, the appeal was postponed for several months at the request of the Church authorities in the interests of a special appeal for the Missionary and Maintenance Fund. Thus the crash of the markets in December, 1929, caught the campaign in mid-course. But apart from these untoward circumstances, it must be admitted that Union had not yet effected complete unity of spirit or of aims in education; if there were former Presbyterians who were less than enthusiastic about a university predominantly Arts in character, there were former Methodists who gravely doubted the wisdom of the segregation of theological instruction and life involved in the two splendid buildings planned.

In the meantime it became known that the President, having reached the age of sixty-five, was about to retire, and that the Board had found a successor in the person of Edward Wilson Wallace ('04), son of the former Dean of Theology. Since graduating in Arts and Theology, he had been engaged in missionary and educational work in China, and in 1923 had become General Secretary of the China Christian Educational Association. On his first furlough he had married Miss Rose Cullen ('03), a sister of Dr. Cullen of Johns Hopkins, but she had died in China, leaving one son. Early in 1929 he married Miss Velma Hamill ('07) in New York. Her health was pronounced unequal to life in China, which in any case had become almost impossible for foreign missionaries as a place of residence and work. Wallace had gained an excellent reputation as an administrator in China and had spent one of his furloughs in taking an M.A. in Education at Columbia.

President Bowles had never been entirely happy in administration. Hence in part his success, since he realized that in all proper collegiate societies administration is at best ancillary. On one occasion, in 1924, he had confided to H. H. Fudger, with whom of the business men of his Board he found most in common, "The more I write theology and read books, the bigger grudge I develop toward executive and administrative duties of the kind which necessarily fall upon the President of this institution." The last financial campaign he had found intolerably burdensome; also the constant effort required to apply brakes to expenditures under the new arrangement. The final blow came after his announced retirement—although he may have felt it imminent. The United Church cut its grant to a sum below that previously granted by the Methodists to Victoria or the Presbyterians to Knox. Writing to

Dr. J. W. Graham, Secretary of Education, on December 4, 1929, he pointed out that this action practically meant that endowment funds hitherto possessed by Victoria would be diverted to other colleges of the United Church. He describes it as "a rank injustice to Principal Gandier and his staff."

Certain letters written on the announcement of Dr. Bowles' retirement indicate not only the widespread regret but also the closeness of the relations maintained with the Canadian West during its years of settlement and expansion. Wallace Sterling ('27), now President of Leland Stanford, then coach of the rugby team of the University of Alberta and reading history under A. L. Burt, writes: "I can't explain the feeling—but every now and then I do feel—proud and loyal—that if Vic has a Great Task to carry on, we *are* carrying on." From the reply this must be quoted: "I am sure you never think of me as President without recalling the morning I flew off the handle in the office here and gave you and—I forget the other fellow's name—a calling down. Such pleasant functions are now coming to an end." Professor Clyo Jackson ('05), also from Edmonton, wrote: "You will have little conception of the sense of loss that has come over me, almost loneliness. You made articulate for me the hopes I cherished of the ministry." To which in his reply Dr. Bowles said: "I recall the days to which you refer in Victoria. I think they were the most joyful days of my ministry. Never did I enjoy anything like those first lectures in Homiletics. I remember your sermon, read in the class, yet." George A. Cruise ('05), a K.C. of Saskatoon, had stated his profound regret, to which Dr. Bowles replied:

To be reminded again of your interest in Victoria is a real pleasure. It seems to me that nothing could be more natural and reasonable than my retirement now that I have reached the age of sixty-five years and there is available someone whom the Board unanimously considered the right person for the office. In addition I may say that for some years owing to much illness in my family[15] and Mrs. Bowles' finding it impossible to live in the city, the work has been very difficult and, indeed, has not been done as it should be. Personally of course I feel as fit as ever, and am looking forward with a good deal of zest to my retirement from official cares if not from actual work.

[15]His only surviving daughter (a second little girl had died at the age of eleven) had contracted tuberculosis shortly after her marriage to the Rev. J. E. Griffith ('15). After fighting the disease for eight years, she had died at the farm in June, 1928.

The dinner given by his colleagues at Annesley Hall has been noted earlier. To the more formal gathering in the Great Hall at Hart House he described his remarks at that time as a very fine speech because he had not thought of a word he would say when he went there. But now at Hart House, having listened to the praises of Fudger, Coleman, Robertson, and Sir Robert, and having had a couple of weeks' warning, he felt that he was "doomed to talk about something more objective. . . ."[16] No one who heard both speeches would, I think, fail to prefer the former. Two serious notes, however, in the Hart House speech stand out amidst much play about rules and committees and the absurdity of a profit and loss entry in the books of a college. These were an emphasis on Freedom—spontaneity in studies as opposed to the dissemination of knowledge—and on Religion in a University.

The following morning he bade a simple farewell to faculty and students in the usual Chapel service. That same evening, in an inauguration ceremony at Convocation Hall, Dr. Wallace was publicly declared Chancellor and President in his stead. Dr. Bowles retired to his cottage on the wooded shores of Lake Scugog near the childhood home of his wife. On rare occasions only has he emerged from seclusion, to assist at a centenary celebration, to show his respect at a funeral, to give a paper on an obscure point of Pauline teaching, or, as recently as 1949, to introduce the speaker at the autumn Convocation. Then by the pith and humour of his brief remarks he held the undergraduates in astonished attention—here was a type of speaking quite beyond their experience.

He could lay aside his office in good conscience. In all his chaff about business and system, there was a Socratic touch. As an executive officer he was careful, shrewd, and clear-sighted. The records of the period are full and accessible. The mine of goodwill in the Church constituency and in the general public, bequeathed by Burwash, he had richly developed. In these seventeen years the assets of Victoria had more than trebled, having grown from $1,399,226.85 in 1913 to $4,713,493.66 in 1930. The endowment now appeared ample. The enrolment had increased from 549 in Arts and 225 in Theology, a net of 622, to 944 in Arts and 147 in Theology, a net of 1,045. The professoriate was of good report in the University, the Church, and the

[16]*University of Toronto Monthly*, Feb., 1930.

country. There were, it is true, some clouds appearing over the horizon. The reduction in support by the Educational Society of the Church was one. The growth in numbers was another. The question had been raised in the Senate but never fully met, as to whether it was not becoming increasingly difficult to maintain the recognized advantages of the small college and the traditional spirit of Victoria. But these clouds were hardly bigger than a man's hand. Richard Pinch Bowles could indeed lay aside office in good conscience.

XIII. THE SECOND CENTURY
1930-1952

THE last twenty years are surveyed with some hesitation. The events are too close to be seen in true perspective and the actors too familiar to require, or indeed admit of, the personal delineation of earlier chapters.[1] After the attendance had reached a peak of 1,270 in 1932-3, and receded to 1,038 in 1939-40, the Second World War brought the number of students below 900, two-thirds of them women. But a just and far-sighted public policy in respect of veterans once more filled the class-rooms and carried the enrolment far beyond satiety. A plant designed in 1890 for 300, and even with additional buildings taxed to accommodate 900, found itself in the year 1946-7 under the necessity of providing its share of instruction for 2,564 students in Arts and 101 in Theology. Since that time the flood has receded, except in Theology, until in 1951-2 there were 1,214 full-time students in Arts and 106 in Theology.

Within two decades two presidents have taken and relinquished office, both through ill health. From the faculty the last link with Cobourg days has disappeared. Cordial relations within the University of Toronto have never been seriously interrupted. Indeed, federation is now so closely knit that it has become a question whether in the end it will be possible to retain that particularity which is the essence and strength of a federal system and which in political associations time has tended to weaken or dissolve. But this is one of the problems which in 1950 were entrusted to the new President, the Rev. Dr. Arthur Bruce Barbour Moore, to be solved with the assistance of Board and Senate and Councils under the new constitution of 1951. An even century after a vastly different burden was laid on the shoulders of another young man—Nelles was not yet thirty while Dr. Moore was

[1]Throughout a distinction has been made in this regard between those still in service and those retired or deceased.

in his early forties—he has been chosen the seventh President of Victoria. He was born in the Maritimes, trained at McGill, the United Theological College, Montreal, and Oxford, has had preaching, teaching, and administrative experience in central Canada, the United States, and the Canadian West. In his church background he represents the least numerous and least ecclesiastical in church government of the three bodies forming the United Church. In his studies his main interest has been in the field of history.

The installation of Edward Wilson Wallace, as was noted, took place in Convocation Hall on January 31, 1930. He was a stately and impressive figure in his new gown, rich in gold and scarlet. And his address did not disappoint the many friends of former days on the dais and in the audience. After twenty-three years in China as missionary and educational administrator, he was returning to direct his own college. One face was missed on the platform. His father, Dean Francis H. Wallace, lay at home, nearing the end of a long and painful illness. Dean Wallace's father, it was recalled, had been one of the first three graduates of Knox College.

In the first year of Wallace's presidency one important resolution was adopted by the Victoria College Council. The resolution suggested

such amendments to the provisions as to retirement as will make it possible for the college to benefit from the experience and erudition of professors between the ages of sixty-five and seventy, thus bringing the practice of Victoria College into line with that of University College and reducing the disparity of opportunity as between the profession of learning and other learned professions where men are free to continue their life work past the age of sixty-five.[2]

The subject was at length brought before the executive committee of the Board by Principal Brown on February 28, 1933, where "after long discussion" it was referred to a "special committee with instructions that a fresh inquiry be made into the whole matter." There it languished for four years more, when the committee reported in favour of a policy which on the recommendation of the President and the Principal of the college concerned may extend the term of service to the age of sixty-seven. In certain cases partial service has been requested and given beyond that time. Indeed a policy is taking shape of retaining such service up to the age of seventy.

[2]V.U.A., Victoria College Council, Minutes, Nov. 18, 1930.

Although the building campaign had been halted with less than two-thirds of the desired funds in certain prospect, this fact was not allowed to delay the undertakings regarded as most essential. The corner stone of Emmanuel College was laid by Sir James Woods, chairman of the building committee, on April 19, 1930. The official entrance took place on February 28, 1931, when the Hon. N. W. Rowell, Chairman of the Board, receiving the key from Henry Sproatt, the architect, opened the doors and invited professors and students to enter. This was the official entrance; the official opening was celebrated with due ceremony on September 22, 1931. On April 4, 1930, a meeting of the Board with sixteen members in attendance had determined to proceed with the building of a residence for Emmanuel students in five contiguous houses at a cost of $250,000. At the next meeting of the Board on May 28, a letter was read from Miss Addison recommending that a similar sum be expended on a women's residence of five units. And on September 12 the Board considered and rejected a proposal to reduce the number of Emmanuel houses to three, in order to make some provision for the women. The Women's Committee had to be content with $50,000 for renovating residences already purchased along Bloor Street. Faced with an accumulated deficit on current account amounting to $56,754.46 and its commitments for the Emmanuel residences, the Board at its annual meeting in 1931 resolved to mortgage its property and raise $200,000. Built as they were during years of depression, both the main building and the residences of Emmanuel, although splendidly designed and appointed, were kept within the appropriations. The latter largely consisted of double suites, with separate bedrooms and a common study. Since the number of Theological students was never sufficient to fill them, it was always possible to satisfy the superior tastes of a group of Arts students. In 1946 two houses were permanently transferred to Arts use. The five had been named in order from north to south, Ryerson, Nelles, Caven, Gandier, and Bowles; now Ryerson and Nelles took their places with North and Middle and Gate and South houses in the Arts list.

The women, meanwhile, occupied rooms in Annesley Hall, Wymilwood, and, for a time, in the former Deaconess Home at St. Clair and Avenue Road. Gradually, however, additional houses were acquired on Bloor Street sufficient to meet the demand, and these smaller units have been found to offer certain advantages as compared with the larger halls. The business of the residences and the Women's Union under Miss Muriel Manning was a model of efficiency, and every year with only one exception returned a surplus. In 1946, the last year before Miss Manning's resignation, there was an accumulated surplus of $25,646; this in spite of the fact that adequate provision was made for renovation. Miss Mary Van Allen ('26) was promoted from the position of Dietitian to succeed Miss Manning as Warden.

Miss Addison after twenty-eight years as Dean, first of residence and then of the women students in general, resigned in the fall of 1930, her resignation to take effect at the end of the session. During the spring she received many tokens of esteem and affection, among them the creation of a fund, now standing at $17,000 and allocated to the endowment of a graduate scholarship awarded to a woman every second year for study outside Canada. Some time elapsed before the Board ventured to name a successor. For three years Dr. Norma Ford, then Associate Professor in the Department of Biology, gave such time as she could find to the duties. Finally, in 1934, Miss Jessie Macpherson, a graduate of University College in Philosophy (English or History), who had taken postgraduate work in Psychology, was chosen for the position. In addition to other qualifications of talent and personality, she brought to her new position some years of experience in Y.W.C.A. work.

From the first Wallace was inclined to stress the historical background of Victoria. In 1931 an incident occurred which gave a new impetus to the study of our origins. E. C. Guillet ('22), an enterprising writer and teacher of history and a native of Cobourg, had secured through the caretaker of an old house in that town certain early records of the College. The find had been placed temporarily for safe-keeping in the provincial archives, and the College was made acquainted with the fact through Dr. A. H. U. Colquhoun, the Deputy Minister of Education. It now appeared that the house in question was the former home of Dr. John Beatty and the property of his daughter, Mrs. C. E. Ryerson. Whereupon, one raw winter day, Dr. E. S. Ryerson, son of the owner, together with the Chancellor, Dr. Barber, and the writer, drove to Cobourg and brought to the city in two suitcases the remaining documents, several of them already damaged by weather. After Guillet had made the material he had secured the basis of a series of copyrighted articles in the Toronto *Mail*, the whole body of material was finally assembled and placed in the Archives of Victoria University. A letter from Mrs. Ryerson, dated February 4, 1931, and preserved in the Board minutes, records her pleasure in presenting the documents to Victoria. Dr. E. S. Ryerson, whose good offices were fully at our command in the matter, was a grandson of Egerton Ryerson and of Dr. John Beatty, and the great-grandson of the Rev. John Beatty, first treasurer of Upper Canada Academy. Hence the presence in the collection of early account books as well as six subscription books. These latter, together with a seventh book, long a cherished possession of the College, afford a fairly complete record of the names and places of residence of some two thousand subscribers to the founding of Victoria. Taken in all the documents throw much light on the early history of the College, on the economic conditions at the time, and on the distribution of population.

This revival of interest in our early history was a prelude to the pilgrimage of 1932. On June 7, in perfect weather, 217 graduates and friends of the College journeyed to Cobourg to celebrate the centenary of the laying of the corner stone of the old building. Sir William Mulock, Chief Justice of the Province of Ontario and Chancellor of the University of Toronto, accompanied the pilgrims and paid a warm tribute to two friends of former years, Nelles and Burwash. The *Victoria College Bulletin* of 1932-3 records,

... the day was essentially one of tribute to the great teachers who had made the College and the University. . . . This was the note struck by Dr. George C. Workman, '75, in the first speech, neat and precise, at the luncheon, and it was the note of the eloquent periods of Justice Riddell, '75, in the closing address at Trinity Church.

The names of Nelles, Burwash, Bain, Reynar, Wilson and Haanel, their distinctive qualities as scholars and teachers and men, were recalled in affectionate and discriminating terms by all the speakers. For the moment even donors and benefactors and the lost corner-stone were forgotten, and Victoria was represented as the work of great and devoted professors.

Appropriately the guests of honour of the day were five former professors of Victoria, whose work reached back to the Cobourg days: Dr. A. J. Bell, Professor A. P. Coleman, Dr. George C. Workman, Judge E. C. S. Huycke, Dr. J. F. McLaughlin.

Chancellor Emeritus Dr. R. P. Bowles, in his speech at Trinity Church, caught the very spirit of the Victoria of Cobourg in a noble tribute to Dr. Nelles and the atmosphere of freedom and culture he created and maintained.

Wreaths were placed on the graves of former members of the College, including that of Robert Beare, in the Cobourg and Baltimore cemeteries.

The year 1932 equalled 1913 in the number and importance of changes in Victoria. Four outstanding personages left the stage, Gandier, Lang, McLaughlin, and Robertson. The members of the staff who attended the dinner at Annesley Hall and listened to their words of farewell could not fail to recognize how difficult it would be to fill the void. Actually Principal Gandier died in harness. Though firm and vigorous in speech at the dinner and never more impressive than in his sermon to his last graduating class at Convocation, death came to him on June 13, 1932, at the age of seventy. June 30 would have been the date of his formal retirement. McLaughlin survived only a year. He died on July 5, 1933, in his seventieth year. On December 26 Andrew James Bell died at the age of seventy-six. He had been in complete retirement from teaching for several years, but his home was close to the College, where his presence was still felt. He had lived long enough to enjoy the description by one of his brilliant pupils, Professor Douglas Bush of Harvard, which appeared in the *Canadian Forum* for September, 1929, commencing as follows:

On an afternoon a decade ago a rather unusual spectacle might have been observed on lower Yonge Street. Two figures emerged from Britnell's old bookshop and strode northward. I say "strode," but the word applies to only one of the two, a tall and more than substantial man of about sixty, with a full, ruddy face and bright blue eyes, who progressed with long and stately steps, *verus incessu patuit deus*. He carried his massive head a little on one side, and a small soft hat rode buoyantly on the waves of his white hair. His sober topcoat, restrained by only one button, floated behind him in the breeze; and while one hand rested in the small of his back the other rhythmically brandished a furled umbrella in the manner of Mr. Stokowski. Beside him a shorter and slighter young man of twenty kept more or less in step, by means of a stride alternated with a brief trot. The latter was saying nothing, having no breath anyhow, but he was listening ecstatically, for, from the heights above him, rolled a continuous stream of thunderous music. The older man, whose imagination was far away, and whose waving umbrella caused an occasional astonished pedestrian to leap off the curb, was chanting Kipling with royal gusto. On they went, the St. Bernard and the terrier, through Queen's Park, up to Avenue Road, and the glorious recital—from Kipling to Heine, Lucretius to Gautier—never ceased until the pair reached the old scholar's home.

That home had become a familiar place to the young man, a Zion where one could be happily at ease, and he knew how to thread his way dexterously over floors almost covered with tall piles of books which frequently tottered, but by a miracle never fell. The two settled down in the study—there was still room to sit, for two—and talk began.

Bell was buried from the College Chapel after a fitting tribute from DeWitt. As six of his former students bore the bier, the ringing verses of Browning's "Grammarian's Funeral" might well have been chanted.

Several new appointments were thus rendered necessary. Already in 1931 the Rev. John Macleod of Kilcreggan, Scotland, had been appointed to the chair of Systematic Theology. At length also the vacancy in Public Speaking was filled by the appointment of the Rev. George Adams McMullen ('16), who after war service had assumed charge of extension courses organized by Greaves. William Ewart Staples ('14), a Ph.D. of Chicago, after war service and archaeological training in the East was appointed Lecturer in Orientals. The death of the Rev. William Arthur Potter ('00), of this department, occurred under particularly sad circumstances. Potter had been brought into the College in a temporary position in 1912 after the death of Misener. An excellent teacher of Hebrew, and an incisive speaker, especially valuable in financial appeals, he had gradually established himself in the College. He was advanced to the rank of Associate in 1919 and full Professor in 1925. During the session of 1930-1 he was given leave of absence for study in the East, with a special grant from the travelling scholarships set up by C. T. Currelly for this purpose. After visiting Palestine and Egypt he was pursuing his studies at Edinburgh when he became ill and died on March 2, 1931.

In Classics, in addition to Robertson's retirement, Miss R. V. Kendrick, who was on the permanent staff as a lecturer, had resigned, being about to be married to Donald Oakley Robson ('28). The effort to secure Harold Bennett ('15), which some years earlier had been unsuccessful, was renewed, and he was induced to return to his *alma mater* from the University of Wisconsin as Professor of Latin, albeit at some financial sacrifice. In the years when Toronto was still attracting Western students, he had come to Victoria from Calgary with experience in business behind him. Enrolling in the Pass Course with Political Science in view, during his first year he had become attracted to the classics and began the study of Greek, which he continued through the summer. In view of his excellent record in the first year of the Pass Course the department of Classics permitted him to enter Honour Classics of the second year. This very unusual proceeding was justified in his record; he graduated first in first class honours. After war service and graduate study at Chicago, he had taught for some years at Lebanon Valley College in Pennsylvania. On Auger's death in 1935 he was appointed Registrar, and in 1944 became Dean of Victoria College. When President Brown's health failed in 1949, and before the appointment of the new president, he ably filled the two offices of Acting President and Dean until the autumn of 1951, when under the changed nomenclature of the new Act he became Principal of Victoria College.

Frederick Archibald Hare ('30) became a Fellow in French on graduation and Lecturer in 1933. Now an Associate Professor, in 1952 he has been named Registrar of Victoria University, for which position his interest in people and affairs fits him admirably. A second lecturer in the German department, T. C. Shore, a Queen's graduate, was brought in from Pickering College in 1932, but shortly after returning from military service he resigned for a post with the United Nations. In 1932 also a second notable addition was made to the staff in Classics. Moffat St. Andrew Woodside came to Victoria from University College, exchanging positions with B. R. English, mainly to work in Ancient History. He was a son of the manse, McCaul medallist at University College, and Rhodes Scholar at Corpus Christi. He succeeded Bennett as Registrar in 1944, and the writer as Nelles Professor of Ancient History in 1947. After twenty years of service, in 1952 he has been nominated by the President and appointed by the Board of Governors to the deanship of the Faculty of Arts in the University of Toronto, an honour the more signal since he is the first professor from any one of the four colleges to be elevated to that position.

During the latter part of the thirties there were several additions to the permanent staff. William Hilliard Trethewey ('23), a graduate in French, Greek, and Latin, with a doctorate from Chicago, and some years of teaching at Mount Allison, entered the French department as Assistant Professor. In 1937 the Rev. Arnot Stanley Orton, a former pupil of Davidson's, was brought from St. Andrew's College, Saskatoon, as Professor of Homiletics and Associate Professor of Old

Testament Literature and Exegesis. He was a sound scholar and most agreeable companion, but developed heart trouble in his early fifties and died in 1947. The Rev. Charles Whitney Leslie ('30), who had been the last president of the Students' Parliament and otherwise prominent as an undergraduate, left a pastorate to become a Lecturer in Ethics.

At this same period three new members were added to the staff in English. Joseph Fisher, B.A. and B.Litt. of Oxford, came from the University of Alberta as Assistant Professor. Two years later Kenneth MacLean, a Harvard Ph.D., was brought from Yale, where he had been for five years an Instructor in English, as Assistant Professor. Herman Northrop Frye ('33), a graduate in Theology as well as Arts, with an Oxford degree added, entered as Lecturer. Miss K. H. Coburn ('28), who had also a degree from Oxford, where she had already begun her important study of the Coleridge notebooks, joined the permanent staff as Lecturer. On July 1, 1952, Fisher succeeded Robins in the chairmanship of the department. During the summer he underwent an operation but survived only a few weeks. His death on October 4, at the age of forty-five, was deeply regretted. To the College it meant the loss of an inspiring teacher, a scholar whose erudition gave promise of rich fruitage, and a man of foresight and courage in University councils.

In 1932, after four years, the triumviral arrangement contemplated in the Act of 1928 came into operation. The theory behind the three administrative officers was that on the academic side it was well to have in each college an administrative head, while the president would exercise general oversight with special emphasis on finance and relations with the Church and the public. Both Bowles, until his retirement, and Wallace, for two years, had held the principalship of Victoria College as well as the presidency and chancellorship of Victoria University. In 1932 Walter T. Brown returned from Yale to become Principal of Victoria College. And Richard Davidson succeeded Gandier. Davidson was a Canadian, born on an Ontario farm near Ayr, who had graduated from University College in 1899 and taken his Ph.D. also at Toronto. He had come over to Emmanuel with the Knox staff. As an Orientals scholar excellently equipped, in the precise use of language (which was at its best in the introduction of candidates for the D.D.) without a superior, in religious exercises inclined to formality, in private relations warm and friendly, he filled the office of Principal of Emmanuel College with distinction and entire devotion until his retirement in 1943.

Wallace was not disposed to leave College participation in the Faculty of Arts of the University of Toronto mainly to his staff, as had his predecessor. From the first he took an active part in committee work. He was largely responsible for setting up the new General Course in 1932. He would have preferred, as would most of the Victoria College staff, to have replaced the three years' Pass Course by a four-year general course, but it was impossible to carry this in Council. In practice the new arrangement created many difficulties in administration; and it disappointed the expectations of its sponsors, in that comparatively few Pass Course students were able to resist the attraction of an earlier degree, and the General Course was largely peopled by less successful candidates for honours who were permitted to transfer to it under certain conditions. But while it was a nuisance to the Registrar's office and the departmental heads or committees, during the seventeen years of its existence it afforded some seven hundred students a good four years' course and a better degree than otherwise they could have had.

A second Council of Arts debate in which Wallace took a prominent part was in connection with the protest from certain honour courses against the time allotted to Religious Knowledge as a result of the concessions made to Trinity College at its entry into federation. The situation thus created was that all students in honour courses had been required to take one hour of Religious Knowledge in the first year, two hours in the second year, and three hours in each of the third and fourth years, or else to substitute some other subject presumably of equal weight for it. This had led to various subterfuges, since the honour courses with their tendency to become increasingly specialized were jealous of yielding up so much of their precious time. Victoria College had offered courses in Religious Knowledge in all the years, but freely permitted optional subjects. University College offered a form of Religious Knowledge known as Oriental Literature and also permitted options. The rub was with Trinity College, where Religious Knowledge was compulsory. Eventually a compromise was worked out under which the time allotted to Religious Knowledge was reduced to one hour in each year, and one hour options were offered in several subjects on the principle that students in honour courses consisting mainly of University subjects were required to choose a college subject as their option, and *vice versa*. Thus a student in Honour Classics might find himself dabbling in Anthropology or one in Chemistry diverted to Greek History, and not infrequently with much relish.

At the outset Wallace was inclined to lean rather heavily on the Victoria College Council. For a time he used the chairmen of its standing committees as an advisory body, and at his request three members of Council were named to a residence committee—a distinct (and temporary) departure in policy. The Council gave preliminary consideration to ways and means of limiting attendance, and the question was carried to the Senate and Board. At one stage the Chancellor produced a scheme for limitation, but it was riddled with exceptions and would have been too difficult to administer. The only point on which there was fairly general agreement was that women with only pass matriculation who came from Toronto and other centres where honour matriculation was available might well be excluded; their entry with pass standing only, it was felt, was probably suggested by the abundant social life of the College.

In 1931 the Council instituted a custom which has continued to the present of asking its members to deliver a series of four public lectures in the spring term. For a few years they were delivered in Wymilwood following tea, but presently were transferred to Alumni Hall as having sufficient appeal without the tea. In recent years one of the lectures has been given by a visiting professor.

The Chancellor had never been a man of rugged constitution. Now early in 1933 he was stricken with cancer. He was absent for a year, the latter part of which was spent in Jamaica, but never after returning to duty was he in vigorous health. Even before his illness the Board had become deeply concerned about the financial situation. With the increase of the staff from thirty-three to forty-three, a surplus of $24,324 in 1928 became a deficit of $30,140 in 1931. This was pared down to $19,483 in 1932, the salaries of the staff being cut by 5 per cent. The spectre of these deficits was never far from the thoughts of Principal Brown when he was named Acting President.

The pilgrimage of 1932 had been planned merely as a prelude to celebrating the centenary of the granting of the Royal Charter in 1836. As early as 1934 a committee under the chairmanship of W. C. James, who had been co-opted to the Board in 1930, were at work on the programme. The issue was a series of events in every respect worthy of the occasion. The functions of the Centenary proper were carried over three days, Friday, Saturday, and Sunday, October 9, 10, and 11, but the celebration was extended in four historical lectures given later in the year under the Burwash Memorial Lectureship by four distinguished graduates. The whole was given permanence in a publication, *On the Old Ontario Strand*, which contained an account of the various functions with their several addresses, including the Burwash Lectures. The first volume of *Egerton Ryerson: His Life and Letters*, by the writer, published the following spring with a foreword by Chancellor Wallace, was also announced as a feature of the celebrations.

The events began with a reception on Friday evening. The *Mail* reported it as "a grand party" in every way.

From all parts of the province, from distant points all over America, and from all walks of life, men who wore mutton chop whiskers when they were "under-grads" and women who remembered when co-education was a new and alarming institution, returned to their Alma Mater.... It proved to the satisfaction of the most talkative a revival of the art of conversation, for although the ballroom of Burwash was jammed with dancers, visiting was the big feature of the night, and all through the other buildings where drama and music were presented and historical exhibits were on display people overflowed in all nooks and crannies to visit.

His Excellency Lord Tweedsmuir received with Chancellor and Mrs. Wallace. Being a man of letters he found himself much at home in all three of the functions in which he took part. He was particularly interested in certain of the historical documents on display in the Emmanuel Chapel and in the valuable Erasmiana from Dr. Bell's library. The undergraduates of the Dramatic Society gave two performances of a one-act play *Turnpikes in Arcady* in the lecture hall of Emmanuel, while the Music Club also repeated their offering, selections from *Iolanthe*, in the Victoria College Chapel. This on Friday evening.

On Saturday there were three events, a luncheon in Burwash Hall for all graduates up to and including the year 1892, a joint convocation of the University of Toronto and Victoria University in Convocation

Hall, and a great dinner at the Royal York Hotel. The luncheon, presided over by Mr. Justice Riddell, was an intimate and delightfully informal affair, and no record has been preserved of the speeches—or conversation—during which much history no doubt was spilled. The convocation (or rather the two convocations) in the afternoon reflected in a striking manner the spirit of federation. At the first Sir William Mulock, as Chancellor of the University, presided. Dr. H. J. Cody, who had succeeded to the presidency in 1932, addressed the Chancellor explaining the significance of the occasion. Then Principal Brown presented four candidates for the LL.D. Three of these were graduates of Victoria—J. R. L. Starr ('87), Chairman of the Board of Regents; A. M. Scott ('96), retired superintendent of the secondary schools of Calgary; and the Rt. Rev. C. W. Flint ('00) formerly Chancellor of Syracuse University and now Bishop of the Methodist Episcopal Church, North. The fourth, W. E. Rundle, had recently resigned from the treasurership of Victoria University after twenty-two years of service. Bishop Flint replied briefly for the four recipients. He predicted that in educational consolidations due to take place in the United States, the pattern of the University of Toronto would be followed more and more closely. After the words "*convocatio dimissa est*," the second convocation, that of Victoria University, was established, with Chancellor Wallace presiding. His speech of welcome in recounting the origin and development of Victoria University included this observation: "This gathering is a remarkable, I believe a unique, demonstration of the unity of spirit and of purpose which can animate churches and creeds and societies within the framework of a state, a unity which is perhaps the greater because it consists in a common purpose rather than in mere uniformity of name or of action."[3] Thereupon Principal Davidson presented for the degree of Doctor of Divinity five persons, Lord Tweedsmuir himself, the Rt. Rev. Peter Bryce, and the Rt. Rev. Malcolm A. Cameron, moderators respectively of the United and the Presbyterian churches, Provost F. H. Cosgrave of Trinity College, and Chancellor H. P. Whidden of McMaster University. For these five His Excellency made a brief and sparkling reply. "There is another feature in Canadian life," he remarked, "which I heartily applaud—I do not know any country where the Church and

[3]*On the Old Ontario Strand* (Toronto, 1936), p. 23.

the World, or shall we say the better side of the world, work together more harmoniously. The proof is that today Victoria University has conferred a Doctorate in Divinity upon a layman. Well, I am certain I am the first Governor-General ever to be a Doctor of Divinity."[4]

More than eleven hundred guests, graduates and friends of Victoria, attended the dinner on Saturday evening. The Hon. N. W. Rowell, Chief Justice of Ontario, who had relinquished the chairmanship of the Board for the less onerous duties of Vice-Chancellor, presided. He read letters of felicitation from His Majesty, King Edward VIII, from the General Council of the United Church, and from the Hon. Vincent Massey, Canadian High Commissioner in London, who spoke of the happy recollections of his years spent as a member of the staff of the College. The Chief Justice emphasized the importance of the Church and the University going hand in hand to assist young men and women with "the great and serious problems that are perplexing the people of every land," so that they "may find, not a cheap solution which catches the crowds and carries them away on an impulse of the moment, but a sound solution which will stand the test of time, based on reason, on conscience, on a clear conception of national duty and of the relation of the material to the spiritual."[5] The one toast of the evening—other than that to the King—was to Victoria University. It was proposed by His Excellency and responded to by Dr. George H. Locke ('93). Both speeches were excellent and brief, both serious but sufficiently relieved by flashes of wit. Locke brought together Strachan's exclusiveness in education and the former John Buchan's most popular novel in a reference to the thirty-nine steps necessary for salvation and education, a sally which convulsed His Excellency. His speech was set in history, that of Lord Tweedsmuir in philosophy, the latter concluding with a passage richly Scottish in its thought.

There is a prayer used in my own Church of Scotland before the opening of Parliament which runs something like this: "Bless O Lord the two Houses of Parliament now assembled and overrule their deliberations for the people's good." Overrule, mark you, not guide or direct, the assumption being that they are almost certain to be wrong. I would take these words as a parable, for they might well be our attitude towards life and that law and government without which life cannot be lived. We dare not

[4]*Ibid.*, p. 26. One other layman has been honoured by Victoria with a Doctorate of Divinity, F. C. Stephenson, M.D., for his service to Christian missions.
[5]*On the Old Ontario Strand*, p. 32.

over-value authority, since we know that it is our own creation; but we dare not under-value it, because we realize its supreme practical need. So we obey it, and we pray for it.[6]

The centenary sermon was preached on Sunday morning in the Metropolitan Church by Dr. Jesse H. Arnup ('08) from the text, "Wherefore seeing we also are compassed about with so great a cloud of witnesses, let us run the race that is set before us." It was an impressive service—although more formal than the founders would have approved—and the powerful sermon recalled vividly to the great audience the vision and faith of the cloud of witnesses who had watched over the birth and growth of Victoria.

The four lectures later in the year were all historical in character, and had essential unity. They were: "The Founding of Victoria College" by Professor George Brown of the Department of History, University of Toronto; "Victoria and a Century of Education" by Principal W. T. Brown; "Victoria and a Century of Theological and Religious Life" by the Rev. Dr. A. Lloyd Smith; and "The Spirit of Victoria" by Dr. Bowles.

The centenary itself was a great success. Not so its sequel. A financial campaign by which the Board had planned to raise a Centenary Fund of a million dollars was not launched till 1937. In fact it did not get properly under way until Dr. E. W. Stapleford ('05), who as Principal had made a financial success of Regina College, was brought in to take charge of it. He was added to the list of administrative officers with the title Assistant to the President, "to direct the general and continuing cultivation of our constituency over a period of years."[7] By June 30, 1939, the Board could report $92,805 subscribed and $70,488 paid. In the same autumn at the annual meeting the deficit for the year reached a high water mark of $39,387.47, and the friends of the College began to wonder how long the dykes would hold. Presently Stapleford was called to Ottawa and war work. The net total, with expenses deducted, accruing from the campaign was $83,489.68.

But the College was not without friends who were ready to contribute to a cause which made a more potent appeal. As tuition fees had been gradually increased through the years from $40 in 1924 to

[6]*Ibid.*, p. 41.
[7]V.U.A., Board of Regents, Minutes, March 24, 1938.

$75, then $100, then $115, then $125, and now in 1939 to $150, and incidental fees had advanced so that they were never less than $40, a subtle change had taken place in the University. At Victoria College the proportion of students from the farms had dropped below 10 per cent while that from Toronto and suburbs had come to exceed 50 per cent. The fact was that an Arts course was tending to become a privilege determined less by intellectual fitness than by economic and residence considerations. Realizing this the alumni and other friends of higher education were turning their thoughts to making it possible for less privileged students to enter upon and continue an Arts course. For instance, in 1938 the secretary of the Alumni Fund could report the sum of $2,150 offered that year by several groups of graduates for matriculation scholarships. J. E. Atkinson of the *Toronto Star* contributed $5,000 a year for several years for bursaries, but would not permit the fact to be made public. Hardly a Board meeting was held without announcement that some gift or bequest had been received for scholarship or bursary purposes. The Board itself determined to set aside a portion of the increased fees for bursaries. In 1940 $2,653 was distributed among deserving students according to need; in 1949 the sum of $6,480, among ninety recipients. Then in 1943 the Dominion and provincial governments came to the rescue with a generous plan, which in 1945 was further elaborated as follows: if he can establish need an out-of-town student with an average of at least 66 per cent in eight Grade XIII papers may receive a subvention of $400 on entrance, and a city student $200. After the first year the subvention remains available to students of at least second class standing and varies in amount according to established need. Thus in 1950-1, nineteen students entered Victoria with $400 and two with $200, and in the upper years the number in receipt of Dominion-provincial scholarships was fifty-three, the subvention varying from $75 to $350. In matriculation scholarships offered by the College itself, as distinct from bursaries (the term scholarship, strictly speaking, is applied to an award based on standing in competitive examinations), it has been determined to limit the number and amount to ensure a fair competition with other colleges. The number of matriculation scholarships to which free tuition is added is twenty-four. Thus between scholarships and bursaries a considerable proportion of the student body each year receive assistance without which it would be impossible for them to pursue their studies.

Victoria was not alone in its financial troubles. The Governors of the University, failing in their request for sufficient government assistance, pressed for an increase of the incidental fees which were paid by the students of the federated colleges to the University, the tuition fees, of course, being retained by the colleges. The colleges accepted an increase of $5 in the Library fee, but balked at a proposed registration fee of $25 as endangering the framework of federation. Finally a compromise was reached under which during the four years from 1939-40 to 1943-4 tuition fees to the amount of $45,138 were remitted by Victoria to the University of Toronto. In the meantime discussions were to be resumed on the question of co-operation in teaching between University College and the federated colleges and on the transfer of certain subjects of the curriculum from University to college instruction. By 1944 the situation had changed. The Government was of a different complexion, and the Governors of a different mind. Thus an expedient dangerous to federation was dropped, in spite of the fact that no progress had been made with either of the two policies mentioned as calculated to give relief to the University chest.

The Second World War neither surprised nor disturbed the College community so profoundly as had the first.

Then in 1939 we had to take up once again the torch that had not shown the way to peace in 1918. The sons of those who marched in '14-'18 did not do less than their fathers, but there was a deeper questioning, I think, of the situation which made this second sacrifice necessary, as there was a deeper sense of privilege and obligation in those who came back to college for the second post-war period. The trumpets that sent us off 35 years ago had not blown in '39 and the easy sense of fulfilment and triumph of 1918 was not, and we should give thanks for this, repeated in '45.[8]

It was March, 1940, before any mention was made of the war by *Acta*, either editorially or in a news item. Then it reported that two members of the College and of the C.O.T.C. had decided to serve their country and were taking an artillery course at Kingston; it bade them Godspeed "with the sincerest respect." It would be a mistake, however, to suppose that the whole College was so nonchalant as *Acta*. That journal

[8]From the inaugural address of the Hon. L. B. Pearson as Chancellor, as published in *Victoria Reports*, vol. II, no. 1, p. 8. This little publication of thirty-two pages was first issued in 1951, three numbers to appear in each year.

had eventually reached the point where it regarded itself as under no obligation to report the *acta* or "doings" of the College. The editor of 1935-6 had put its policy this way: "It will aim less to mirror slavishly the life of the College and to stimulate College spirit than to gather the undergraduate intellectual and artistic life of the College into a focus." Thus the editor of 1939-40 could quite overlook the enlistment of Professor Joseph Fisher immediately on the outbreak of war, and relegate the recurring illness and leave of absence of Chancellor Wallace to a footnote accompanied by a pen-and-ink sketch. Of course a more definite manpower policy on the part of the government from the outbreak of war, culminating in conscription, created a different situation in the universities from the voluntary enlistment of 1914; men who remained at their studies felt they did so by right. But the students of the College, including editors of *Acta,* did their duty. Over 1,400 members of the College, including graduates, were in the forces. Seventy-six did not return. The first Victoria man to give his life was Pilot Officer Robert L. Edwards ('35), on August 28, 1940. The enlistment of College men in the Air Force during this war was heavy; also the casualties. One of these was Edward Wilson Wallace ('38), the only son of the Chancellor and a young man of great promise.

A recurrence of the disease made it necessary for the Chancellor to ask for leave of absence in 1939. In February, 1941, he resigned and on June 20 found release from suffering. He was a man of fine intellectual qualities and social graces. Ill health, however, did not afford him time to translate an extended experience in China into Canadian terms adapted to the demands made upon the executive head of a university within a university. Principal Brown was now asked once more by the Board to assume permanent responsibility, and thus became the sixth Canadian and the first layman to be President of Victoria during the even hundred years since it had acquired university powers.

In the autumn of 1942, at the height of the war, the Board of Governors of the University of Toronto decided to bar Japanese and German students from the University. At a subsequent meeting on November 12, this action was modified. Japanese students who were Canadian citizens were allowed to enrol, but on a tie vote the decision as to German students was confirmed. An issue vital to federation had been raised. Time was an important element, in view of the predicament of the students. The Senate met the following evening. At the conclusion of the meeting, on the opportunity offered by the regular question, "Any further business?" the writer rose and gave notice of motion for an inquiry into the regulations governing admission into the several faculties of the University. "At the next regular meeting?" the Chairman asked. "At the next regular meeting, or at a special meeting," was the reply. By ten o'clock the following morning the four additional signatures for a special meeting had been secured from Principal Malcolm Wallace of University College, Dean S. Beatty of the Faculty of Arts, Dean W. P. M. Kennedy of the Faculty of Law, and Professor H. A. Innis. Such was the interest in the question that the meeting of November 23, 1942, proved to be the largest in the history of the Senate, ninety-four members being present. The young men who were to be excluded had come to Canada under these conditions. At the outbreak of the war the British authorities had taken all enemy nationals into custody without regard for political views. Those of military age were shipped overseas and placed in internment camps. Among these were a good many German nationals who had been studying at schools or colleges in England, where they had been sent to escape racial discrimination or Nazi indoctrination. After these had languished for some two years behind barbed wire, the Canadian government with the concurrence of the British authorities sought Canadian sponsors and homes for them. Several who had been pursuing their studies in camp were sponsored by university people. Among these was a young man named F. D. Hoeniger. He was released in February, 1942, with the writer as sponsor. On February 21 he had been informed by the Registrar of the University of Toronto that his certificate would admit him to the first year in Arts. In order to meet the requirements for Honour English, for three months he concentrated on Latin, which he had never studied, and secured two firsts in the subject at the departmental examinations. Now in November, having begun his studies at Victoria College, he received a second letter from the Registrar which stated that the Governors had refused him registration, and his certificates were returned. On advice he continued his studies, as did some others, but several dropped out or left for other Canadian universities.

Now the writer was fully convinced that in instructing the Registrar to write this letter, the Governors had contravened the spirit and the letter of the University Act, and he believed that in any case their action violated sound policy for a great university. At the crowded meeting the President, Dr. Cody—it was known that he was not happy about the Board's action—was requested by resolution to make a complete statement concerning the proceedings which had led to the withholding of admission. This he did, at some length. Thereupon the main motion was presented as follows:

(a) That it is the considered view of the Senate of the University of Toronto that students duly enrolled in the Arts colleges may not be refused admission to instruction in any subjects, college or university, except where they are deemed by the Senate not to have satisfied the admission requirements laid down by the Senate;

(b) That students are enrolled in the faculties or schools, etc. other than the Faculty of Arts subject to the statutes of the Senate.

The debate—if such it can be called, since there was virtually no opposition—by reference to the Act and the history of the University clearly established the authority of the Senate in the matter of admissions. Although Trinity College had no students involved, Provost Cosgrave and Dr. C. S. MacInnes, an eminent barrister and member of the Corporation, urged the indisputable rights possessed by the Arts colleges under the federation agreement; the college could register any student who had met the matriculation requirements set by the Senate and at the end of the year could present him to the University for examination. The resolution was adopted, "no member dissenting." A second resolution sanctioned the registration of the refugees. These resolutions were forwarded to the Board. At the next meeting of the Senate a letter was read from that body which stated that, since the military authorities were prepared to admit the refugees to military training, the Board had no objection to their enrolment. This was its form of apology for intrusion. The record of the students was excellent. One striking fact must be mentioned: four years later the two students who stood first and second at graduation in Honour English were German nationals, members of this group. In addition one of them had been editor of his college paper and had captained the soccer team which had won the inter-faculty cup.

In 1943 Principal Davidson, having reached the age of sixty-seven, was retired. Although vigorous at the time—the Board was divided as to applying the rule in his case—he survived retirement less than a year. It was decided to revert to the title "Dean" for the head of Victoria College and to employ the same title in Emmanuel. The new Act of 1944, indeed, was mainly concerned with titles. Other changes were of minor consequence. The office of Chancellor after sixty years was separated from that of President, and the President became Vice-Chancellor. This division increased the number of the Board from forty-three to forty-four. The Chancellor was to be chosen by the Board and not by the alumni as in the old Victoria before 1884, the date at which the office of Chancellor was combined with that of President. Identical powers were given each Dean: "He shall be Chairman of the Council of . . . College and shall advise the President on all matters concerned with the life and work of the College. He shall assist the President by performing in the College such administrative duties as may be assigned to him by the Board." The internee business was reflected in the section dealing with the duties of the Victoria College Council; the Council was empowered to determine what students possessing the academic qualifications prescribed from time to time by the Senate of the University of Toronto should be admitted. Major General A. C. Spencer, prominent in business and church circles in London and a graduate of the Faculty of Applied Science with a distinguished war record, was named Chancellor. As such he not only presided at Convocation, but took an active part in the Board of Regents.

Rehabilitation policies for ex-service men from the early stages of the war had been a concern to the University. When the time came the number taking advantage of the Arts course as distinct from the professional courses was heartening: 1,306 veteran matriculants—apart from those who had interrupted their courses for war service—elected to enrol at Victoria College alone. The vitality and appeal of Arts work at Toronto was thus exhibited. In the generous provision offered by the federal government the emphasis was placed on occupational training; and one emissary, a Western educational administrator, in consultation with a committee of the Senate of the University of Toronto, showed obvious surprise when it was suggested to him that some of the veterans might prefer just to be educated. Within the University a select committee actually reported in favour of segregating the returned men somewhere near the city, only to learn that the judgment of the Senate was that their education should be conducted amid the amenities of college and campus life.

Every effort was made to provide the best instruction and services possible for this group of older and in general serious-minded students. Nevertheless there was much overcrowding in class-rooms and in extra-academic activities, and the period from 1945 to 1950 was one of great strain on the teaching and administrative staffs. The veterans themselves assisted not only in a lively response to the attempts to meet their needs but also in the contribution of their fees and the grants from the Department of Veterans Affairs. Thus in time the accumulated deficits of the previous decade were melted away. As Dean Bennett neatly put it in his annual report for 1950 as Acting President, this was "a difficult but prosperous period in which the teaching staff of Victoria College has made a notable contribution both to post-war reconstruction and to the financial position of Victoria University."

In 1944, largely at the instance of President Brown, Emmanuel embarked on an enterprise in theological co-operation. The governing bodies of the four theological colleges or faculties, Emmanuel, Knox, Trinity, and Wycliffe, combined to institute the Toronto Graduate School of Theological Studies. A Committee of Direction was set up consisting of one member from each of the faculties. Emmanuel was represented by Professor John Line. The school was not incorporated and did not confer degrees, although it was responsible for suggesting a new degree, Master of Theology. The course also leads to the degrees of Bachelor of Divinity and Doctor of Theology. The School offers courses one day a week for the convenience of part-time students.

On the retirement of Davidson, Langford, who had been named Chairman of the Council for a year, became Dean of Emmanuel College. After a year he retired, and the Rev. Alexander Dawson Matheson, a Queen's man, was brought from a successful pastorate of twenty-two years at Quebec City to become Dean and to be inducted into the Margaret Cox chair of Homiletics. The Rev. Kingsley John Joblin ('32) was introduced from the pastorate in 1946, and is now Associate Professor of English Bible. The Rev. William Oscar Fennell ('39), equally distinguished as an undergraduate in Philosophy and in athletics, was also appointed in 1946, and is now Assistant Professor of Systematic Theology. In 1949 the Rev. Charles Victor McLean, a graduate of Toronto in 1909 and a Ph.D. of Columbia, succeeded Orton in Old Testament. In the same year the Rev. James Rattray Guthrie brought from Edinburgh to the department of Christian Education (for some time untenanted) a rich Scottish accent and tradition. Dow retired in 1952 and returned to his native heath, but his roots are deep in Canada. He was succeeded by the Rev. George Johnston, a Scot trained in Glasgow and Cambridge and for several years in the New Testament department in the Hartford Theological Seminary. Line also retired in 1952, but will continue part-time teaching. His chair passed to Leslie, who was formally transferred to the Emmanuel staff, although he will continue to teach certain courses in Arts. Cousland is thus the senior member of the regular Emmanuel staff in point of service. In addition to his professorship of Church History, he continues to give leadership in many activities including athletics and the cultivation of church music. The position of secretary of the Theological Conference which he held for many years has been assumed by Joblin.

The Victoria College staff was considerably changed during the 1940's. In Classics, the retirement of DeWitt and the writer, and the departure of Havelock for Harvard and S. H. Gould ('29), who had attained the rank of Assistant Professor, for Purdue and a post in Mathematics was met by further co-operation with Trinity (in 1948 University College gave notice of the cessation of all interchange) and by the appointment of three Toronto men: in 1947, Donald Oakley Robson ('28), Wilson gold medallist in Classics, who had taken his Ph.D. at Toronto and for some years had been on the staff of the University of Western Ontario; in 1947 also, Gordon Lincoln Keyes ('41), who secured his Ph.D. at Princeton as holder of the coveted Proctor Fellowship; and in 1950, John Ratcliffe Grant, McCaul medallist at University College in 1936, with a doctorate from Harvard. The two latter had teaching experience in the United States and hold the rank of Assistant Professor, while Robson is Associate Professor. In 1949 de Beaumont's partial retirement brought John Sinclair Wood with degrees from London and Paris to the permanent staff in French as Associate Professor. In the same year George Norman Laidlaw, who holds degrees from Mount Allison, Oxford, and Columbia, joined the staff in French with the rank of Assistant Professor. Wood is now Professor and Laidlaw Associate. The same department has now two assistant professors, Daniel Philippe de Montmollin and Alan Charles Moffat Ross. The former, first appointed in 1946, holds a Doctor's degree from Neuchâtel won by a distinguished work on Aristotle. Ross graduated from McMaster, rose to the rank of Major in the Army, and in 1952 comes to university teaching from the secondary schools, thus reviving an earlier practice. In German, George Wallis Field ('35), after some years of teaching in Japan and service throughout the war in India, returned to secure his Ph.D. at Toronto and to become a member of the permanent staff in 1948. He is now an Assistant Professor. In English, two permanent appointments have been made: Miss R. I. Jenking ('25), who had won her spurs as a sessional lecturer and Shakespearian scholar; and Christopher Charles Love of Cambridge University and a Ph.D. of Toronto, who after teaching some years at Bishop's College School spent the war in the Navy and in the end was in command of a corvette. Both Miss Jenking and Love, now Assistant Professors of English, took undergraduate degrees in Classics. Love is also Senior Tutor in the men's residences. Miss Coburn has been advanced to the rank of Associate Professor, as has Miss Rièse in French. In 1944 John Allen Irving ('26), a Doctor of Princeton, was brought from the University of British Columbia with the title of Professor of Ethics and Social Philosophy. The Dean of Women, Miss Jessie Macpherson, now a Ph.D. of Toronto, also lectures in the department with the rank of Associate Professor. In Orientals, Staples is now Professor, with the Rev. John Macpherson, a McGill and United College man from Montreal with some years' service in the pastorate, as Assistant Professor. In the Library the plan had been to succeed Barber by R. G. Riddell. A graduate of Manitoba and Oxford, he had for some years been Senior Tutor in the men's residences, while at the same time Lecturer in the History department. He determined, however, to join the group of Toronto men in the Department of External Affairs, and while ably representing Canada at the United Nations died sudenly in 1951. Robins was asked to assume the post of Librarian, which he contrived to fill while a busy teacher and administrative head of the department of English. Miss

Margaret V. Ray ('22) had been Associate Librarian since 1935, and on Robins' formal retirement in 1952 she became Librarian. Her duties include supervision of the valuable archives of Victoria University. The Rev. J. S. Lawson, a Ph.D. of Toronto, is Assistant Librarian and Library Tutor in Emmanuel College. The staff thus remains predominantly a home product, although recent appointments, including that of the new President, indicate that the Board is not averse from going afield for a pinch of leaven.

For faculty and students alike the post-war situation presented grave problems. How could adequate instruction be provided for more than two thousand students, and how could those less tangible advantages of college life be retained and made accessible? Traffic jams in the halls, on the stairways, even on the routes across the park—snow-paths in winter and wading pools with the spring thaw! Hopelessly inadequate playing fields, and the floors and swimming pool of Hart House equally so! However, discussion and good fellowship were free as air, and books were obtainable, with patience, at the libraries, even if Mark Hopkins and his log had joined Nineveh and Tyre. So the University survived, and the colleges, and students were measurably thankful for what they got. How seriously the traditional life of the College has suffered, time will tell. The "Bob," our most typical institution, seemed a total casualty. At least those who were unfortunate enough to witness the performance in Massey Hall in 1946 would have so declared. But in 1949 it recaptured something of its original character as a Freshman-Sophomore initiation, and certain vaudeville features were sloughed off to be assumed by a new entertainment called "The Scarlet and Gold." The weekly meetings of the Men's and Women's Literary societies have long disappeared. In their place is a monthly meeting of the Students' Parliament for debate, attended by both men and women. Facility and poise in public speaking, however, have noticeably declined among undergraduates. An interesting attempt to arrest the trend is being made by holding contests in impromptu speaking once a week at noon. The Music and Dramatic clubs are still lively and efficient organizations, while necessarily reaching a smaller percentage of the student body than formerly. This is also true of the two societies for religious fellowship, the Student Christian Movement and the Varsity Christian Fellowship. Both are co-educational; they differ merely in doctrinal approach. Emmanuel students who are graduates of Victoria frequently continue their undergraduate association with one or the other society. In addition they have their own Theological Society, which holds weekly meetings for discussion. Each of the political parties has an organization in the University, and Victoria men take an active part. Occasionally formal Hart House debates are held in which a distinguished guest speaker participates, but they attract only a small fraction of the undergraduates.

The trend in athletics is definitely towards centralization. The very efficient intra-mural office in Hart House has largely taken over control of college contests. Inter-year matches have quite disappeared from the Victoria campus; improvised rough and ready games between the houses of residence alone survive. The single hockey cushion, which for many years had been all that was left of the once popular rink, was not even erected in 1952.[9] The aim of the Athletic Directorate of the University of Toronto is twofold: the development of highly skilled athletes to compete with other universities (to fill stadium, arena, and coffers), and the arranging of intra-mural contests between some twenty colleges or faculties in as many sports. The purpose is to encourage general participation, and in the major games, with the exception of rugby football,[10] each of the larger units is likely to have several teams entered.

Nevertheless athletic facilities in Toronto fall far short of those available in Oxford and Cambridge, where the tradition persists that the early afternoon in all seasons should be given over to recreation. A penalty must be paid for setting a great university in the centre of a great city, and the crowded curriculum, which has now pushed classes far into the afternoon, also interferes seriously with participation in games.

In intra-mural competition Emmanuel with its small numbers does creditably, particularly in soccer and hockey, and Victoria has won rather more than her share of honours. Statistics show that between 1930 and 1950, the number of years when the trophy rested with Victoria was in rugby 9, soccer 5, hockey 6, basketball 3, track 4,

[9]This coincided with the illness and retirement of Parker Whitebread, for forty years the capable ice-maker and groundsman.
[10]The determining factor in rugby is the expense of equipment for the large "squads" required under the present practice of substitution.

water polo 5, indoor track 6, lacrosse 2, harrier 1. The record of the current year, 1951-2, is so remarkable that it must be noted. In rugby Victoria contributed 8 men to the champion Varsity team, and 3 to the intermediate, including the captain; in senior basketball 3; in senior hockey 3; in several other sports a good representation, including the outstanding long-distance runner. Then in intra-mural competition Victoria won in rugby with an unprecedented final score of 25-0; in hockey, with scores in the two final games of 11-0 and 12-3; in senior golf; in senior and junior harrier (this is the special interest of Professor Laidlaw). In tennis and junior golf, Victoria was in the finals, and in track won a good share of the events.

In December, 1948, President Brown suffered a cerebral haemorrhage. His recovery though excellent was not sufficient to permit him to resume work, and his resignation was accepted as of June 30, 1949. Like Burwash he was a man of great physical strength and mental vigour. Determined and self-reliant, he could not spare himself. Anxiety over the deficit which had confronted him when he assumed office, the emotional strain of the war years,[11] and the heavy responsibilities of the post-war influx of students had noticeably begun to tell on him even before the break came. He was worried also by the unexpected discontent aroused by the Act of 1944, which he had sponsored. The Act was designed to draw the two colleges, Victoria and Emmanuel, closer together. But the change in name from Principal to Dean was resented by certain theological alumni. They interpreted the change as calculated to lessen the dignity and influence of the head of Emmanuel. Others, however, felt that the name was less important than a clear definition of the powers of the three chief offices, and discussions to that end were already under way when the President was stricken.

He had the satisfaction, at least, of knowing that finances had been restored to a healthy condition; this in spite of the fact that the financial campaign of 1947-8, with every detail of which he had identified himself with his accustomed energy, had proven a grave disappointment. The objective was $2,000,000; the collections $563,461 up to 1952. But the buoyant income from veterans' grants and fees, the sacrifices of the staff in salaries and teaching load, and prudent investments made on the advice of E. W. Bickle, who had been named Treasurer by the

[11] He made it a point to visit every bereaved home.

Board in 1941, had combined to wipe out the accumulated deficits and to present a moderate surplus on operating expenses. The result was that Bennett in the interval of his acting presidency, extending to nearly two years, was able to give effect to certain projects already in hand. One of these was the settlement of claims for rental of University lands occupied by Victoria University buildings, including the President's house, Emmanuel College, Wymilwood, and the women's residences on Bloor Street. As the leases had matured, the University of Toronto Comptroller was demanding higher rentals for their renewal. The whole business, which had for many years been a matter of dispute, was cleaned up in one transaction. At the heavy cost of Wymilwood, the site of which the University was anxious to recover for use, all the land involved was secured either on perpetual lease at a dollar a year or on freehold tenure. Four hundred and eighty feet of valuable frontage on Bloor Street thus became the property of Victoria, subject only to the restriction that it must be used for educational purposes.

A special committee of the Board under the chairmanship of H. E. Langford ('25) was thus able to report a general plan for the future Victoria. Certain units of this plan are nearing completion at the time of writing. A new Students' Union, for both men and women, adjacent to Annesley Hall and facing Charles Street, will be ready when college opens in the fall of 1952. The playing field, with fresh turf and a north and south axis, together with a new field-house at the eastern extremity of the old field, equipped with lockers and showers, will at length furnish something like adequate facilities for athletics, when taken in conjunction with what is provided by the University of Toronto. A complete gymnasium fronting on Charles Street, for use by both men and women, is to be added when funds are available.

Realizing also that buildings and grounds do not make a university, the Board at length addressed itself to the matter of salaries. It was resolved to adopt the University of Toronto schedule and in one or two years to raise the remuneration of lecturers and the three grades of professors to the University level. Corresponding adjustments were made in retiring allowances.

Three other matters affecting church relations which had been discussed for some time were also concluded during the year following Brown's retirement. The joint responsibility of the Boards of Victoria and Knox for the maintenance of the Knox College library was terminated. In an amicable agreement Knox got the books, and Victoria the archives, with mutual freedom of access accorded ministers and students of each denomination. Provision was now made for a new honorary degree which might be conferred on laymen for outstanding service to the United Church or its colleges. After some discussion in the Senate, it was determined to call the degree Doctor of Sacred Letters (D.Litt.S.). Two such degrees have already been awarded, one in 1951 to Gershom W. Mason, who piloted the Church Union Act through Parliament and became treasurer of the Law Society, and the second in 1952 to Major General A. C. Spencer on his retirement from the chancellorship. The third matter concerned the United Church Training School. For some years the school had been making increasing demands on the teaching staff of Emmanuel College in training its young women. It was now decided that the amount paid for these services should be increased from $2,000 to $6,000. This brought the total sum accruing directly and indirectly from the United Church to Victoria University to $23,000.

The last major event to be chronicled was one of the most notable in the century and a quarter of the history of Victoria. On February 4, 1952, the Honourable Lester Bowles Pearson ('19) was welcomed as Chancellor. A grandson and son of the parsonage, as an undergraduate he had taken an active part in the varied life of the College. For a time he was a member of the staff in Modern History, but finding the making of history more to his taste than its teaching, he entered Parliament by way of the civil service. Honours everywhere accorded him as Secretary of State for External Affairs left him unscathed; he was still "Mike" to scores of those present at the luncheon in Burwash Hall, the installation at Convocation Hall, and the crush of the reception in the main building. The general opinion among the 1,500 present in Convocation Hall was that they had never heard a better series of speeches. The recently elected Chairman of the Board of Regents, Leopold Macaulay ('11), Q.C., a former minister of the Crown in Ontario and now Chairman of the Central Council of the Canadian Red Cross Society, presided. After the Vice-Chairman of the Board, the Very Rev. George C. Pidgeon, delivered the installation prayer, and the Chancellor had been duly clad in scarlet and gold, and the

Gate House[12] contingent strategically located in the top gallery had showered the platform, Dr. Pearson delivered an eloquent and intimate address. He was followed by the new Principal of Queen's, Dr. W. A. Mackintosh, who brought greetings from the universities of Canada in a fraternal message as bright as it was cordial. President Moore in brief and happy words of welcome voiced the feelings of the members of Victoria University.

After sixty years of operation it is now possible to pronounce the federation experiment definitely a success; and much of the vigour which Arts work continues to exhibit in the University of Toronto—much of the reputation also which it holds on this continent—can justly be attributed to the fact that it enjoys the combined support of church and state. The mutual respect and friendship established under Sir Robert Falconer have continued with scarcely a ripple. President Cody brought to his work much learning in the Classics and beyond, long familiarity with the University, a knowledge of church colleges developed during his teaching at Wycliffe, and an interest in people which supported an amazing memory for names and faces. He and his wife frequently graced academic and social affairs at Victoria, and Mrs. Cody liked to recall her descent from Moses Blackstock, the pioneer Methodist preacher. President Sidney Smith, of Methodist background and an elder in Bloor Street United Church, from the first has shown that he appreciates this contribution which the denominational arts colleges have made in Toronto. At the inauguration of Dr. Moore on November 15, 1950, speaking in Convocation Hall as President of the University, he used these words: "The principle of the federation of church-supported colleges with a state-supported college and state-supported faculties and schools, is of the very genius of the University of Toronto. While the whole is greater than any of its parts, the strength of every part determines the welfare and progress of the whole. Victoria's strength is our strength. . . . In congratulating Victoria, we, in a mood of enlightened self-interest, felicitate ourselves."

The division of subjects between the University of Toronto and the Arts colleges, established in the Act of 1887 and restated in each en-

[12]Pearson's house, when an undergraduate in residence.

suing University Act, has been scrupulously maintained. In the teaching of the college subjects, there has been some co-operation among St. Michael's, Trinity, and Victoria. University College also has occasionally entered into a temporary and informal arrangement for exchange of lectures in cases of illness or leave of absence or when it was desired to take advantage of special scholarship in a particular field. No addition has been made to the list of subjects assigned to the colleges at federation. Several subjects, however, have been added to the University list, especially from among what are known as the social sciences, and many of the original subjects have been sub-divided and greatly expanded. During recent years, moreover, there has been a marked tendency among students to neglect the humanities in favour of subjects which are regarded as more practical and which have a more obvious vocational value. The result has been a decrease in the ratio of college to University teaching and in that intellectual intercourse between professors and students, which is the final justification of the college system. Even the ancillary advantages of residence life have less effect than they once had owing to the increased proportion of students from the city and suburbs. Thus, of recent years it has become evident that the college curriculum must be expanded to meet the changed conditions. The University Act offers no impediment to such change, if general agreement on details can be reached. The adjustment would mean additional cost to the colleges, but seems essential to the continuing success of federation. Discussions already taking place in a committee composed of representatives from the University and the colleges on the general theme of the future of the humanities in Toronto may present suggestions pointing to a solution.

Graduate studies also present a problem. Victoria is primarily interested in the integrity of the Bachelor's degree, and would resist any tendency to depreciate the standards in the interests of graduate work. On the other hand, even in Cobourg days postgraduate instruction was offered by Haanel and Coleman,[13] and since graduate work was instituted in Toronto professors of Victoria, in response to requests from students of their own or other colleges, have borne their part merely as work superimposed on their regular schedule of teaching. It was

[13]Clifford Sifton, for example, remained after graduation for further study in Science.

felt that, apart from other considerations, graduate work in those fields assigned to the colleges under federation could not be surrendered without loss of prestige. Indeed, under the able administration of Dean Innis, the School of Graduate Studies has made it very clear that the participation of college men is welcomed, and that much of the strength of the School as a centre of advanced study and research lies in the fact that it has available in the four colleges of the campus a numerous group of scholars with special and varied fields of knowledge to whom it may turn. In Victoria College an effort is now being made to reduce the amount of undergraduate teaching for those members of the staff who are giving graduate courses or supervising the research of students working for their doctorate. This again imposes a financial burden not contemplated in the federation agreement. A special committee appointed by President Smith is at present studying ways and means by which the colleges may "speak with a united voice at the graduate level."[14]

If the strength of a federation is the strength of its parts, what has the future in store for Victoria University? For the Arts college, with attendance apparently likely to stabilize at about a thousand, to retain an ethos which justifies a separate existence will demand statesmanship of a high order in the several governing bodies. The task, once recognized, is difficult but not impossible. Emmanuel College has a different problem. In a compact intra-mural student body hovering about the hundred mark, the intimate sharing of experience which makes college life vital is readily attainable. The real difficulty will be to avoid developing a cloistered life apart from a world inclined to materialism, vast areas of which are now closed to any direct missionary effort. But as the two colleges work side by side they will continue to represent that fusion of the sacred and the secular which is the tradition of the founders and the spirit of the evangel.

[14]Circular letter of Dec. 6, 1951.

APPENDIX

THESE DIED IN THE WAR
(1914-1918)

Coleman B. Adams
J. Reginald Adams
Frederick S. Albright
Elton Culbert Allin
Wilbur Fawcett Annis
Frederick E. Banbury
Joseph Alburn Bassett
William J. Beattie
Lawrence S. Beatty
Ewart A. Blatchford
Harold S. Brewster
George William Bruce
James Gordon Burns
Warren K. Campbell
Allen C. M. Cleghorn
Carleton M. Clement
William H. Clipperton
Gordon Willson Crow
Melville Allen D. Davis
C. John Dickinson
Douglas Dickson
Hubert S. Dowson
George W. Dundas
Norman Oliver Dynes
Hubert J. Fenton
George R. S. Fleming
Hedley J. Goodyear
Thomas S. Gordon
William Robert Green
Orville Dwight Haist
Douglas K. Hamilton
William Neil Hanna
Ivan Dwight Hayes
Alfred Hall Henry
Asa Milton Horner
George E. C. Howard
Lincoln G. Hutton
F. Arthur Huycke

James Stewart Hyde
James Harvey Jackson
Eric F. Johnston
Reginald H. M. Jolliffe
A. Caton Jourdan
Nelson Clarke Kenny
Lily Denton Keys
Sidney James Luck
John G. Lumsden
Aubrey M. Marshall
Thomas Allan McComb
Aubrey T. McFadden
Reuben De L. Millyard
Charles W. D. Mooney
James Henry Oldham
Balfour M. Palmer
George L. R. Parrish
Charles F. Patterson
Roy Irvine Poast
Laurence H. Rehder
William P. Richings
Frederick G. Scott
Colin Simpson
Harry Roy Smith
T. Vincent Sparling
John H. A. Stoneman
William A. D. Sutterby
Alfred L. Taylor
Ross Malcolm Taylor
John William Tribble
Hugh Jarman Watson
James Symington Wear
Edward Alfred Webb
George Roy Weber
W. Kenneth White
William A. Wilcox
Douglas A. Wright

THESE DIED IN THE WAR
(1939-1945)

James Davidson Allan
Wilmer James Armstrong
Frank Arthur Arnston
Ivor Benjamin Baldwin
Frederick Grant Banting
Raymond Paul Becker
Frederic Judson Bell
Howard Bruce Boddy
George Gordon Bradshaw
Kenneth Stickney Brenton
George Alfred Chapman
Norman Aage Christopherson
Curtis McLam Cole
Hubert Vincent Coulter
Donald Alexander Court
Lawrence Ellwood Cryderman
Frederick St. Leger Daly
George Walker Davidson
Donald Keith Dawson
George Clingan Denton
Robert Lesley Edwards
Forbes Bell Fisher
Thomas Francis Ray Fisher
William Campbell Gordon
Edwin Roy Gray
Donald Francis Fulton Hall
William Lionel Halperin
William Ray Hart
Wilbert Arley Healey
James Armstrong Hertz
John McLeod Hogg
Donald George Innes
Harvey Edgar Jones
Stewart William Jones
Harry Leslie Kay
Harold Leon Kemp
John Roberts Kenmure
Hubert Lloyd Kerr
Angus Lloyd Kippen
Peter Childs Lailey

John Edward Leach
Roy Walker Lent
Duncan Cameron Mackenzie
Ian Pearson Maclaren
Rodolfo Mendizabal
Frank Wilfred Moffit
Carl Hamilton Morrow
Elmer John Mutton
Kenneth Alexander Bernard
   McArthur
Hugh Percival McKee
William Donald Nelson McKessock
Irvin Robert McNay
James Rogerson McNeily
Thomas Westcott Nixon
Melvin Robert Oliver
Henry Beresford Perrin
Irwin James Reed
Byron Ball Reid
Robert Burns Ridley
Donald Hamilton Robb
Mervyn Esmond Llewellyn Scovell
William James Aubrey Shapter
Richard Stanley David Slade
George Kenneth Alfred Smallwood
Edward Walter Smith
William Robert Smith
Robert John Stingle
Clarence Franklin Thompson
Douglas Stewart Tickner
William Thomas Tranmer
Alfred Robert Clark Walker
Edward Wilson Wallace
Allan Ward
James Owrey William Weldon
William Ward White
Keith Doane Wilson
Elmer Stanley Winn
Harold Redfern Wright
Harold James Young

INDEX

Acta Victoriana, 49n, 50, 255; first issue, 152–4; on Puritanism, 250; in 1913, 252–4; sees danger from Burwash Hall, 260; war supplement, 275; and Second World War, 315–16
Addison, Rev. A. P., 210–11
Addison, Miss M. E. T., 198, 224, 241, 242, 243, 281, 301; the graduate scholarship, 302
Addison, Rev. Peter, 225
Aikins, James C., 32, 140
Aikins, Dr. Moses Henry, 101
Aikins, Dr. W. T., 98, 142
Albert College, 139, 167–8, 193, 247
Alder, Rev. R., 24
Allin, Arthur, 204
Allison, Rev. C. R., 21
Alumnae Association, 224, 243
Alumni Association, 184, 204, 209, 293
American Philological Association, 233
Ames, A. E., 215, 259
Andrews, Rev. W. W., 197
Annesley Hall, 225, 241, 255, 258, 301; A.S.G.A. rules, 241–2; "a home from home," 281
Armstrong, James R., 8, 83
Arndt, Mrs. Ernst, 248
Arnold, R. K., 294
Arnup, Rev. Jesse, 313
Athletics, 50, 154, 202–3, 210, 258; athletic stick, 211; Athletic Union organized, 212–13; in 1913, 255–7; six winning teams in 1928, 293; trend towards centralization, 324–5
Atkinson, J. E., 314
Auger, C. E., 231 and n., 232
Aylesworth, Rev. I. B., 123

BADGLEY, Rev. E. I., 181, 193, 194, 199, 203n.
Bagot, Sir Charles, 48
Baillie, Rev. John, 286
Bain, A. R., 125, 128, 130, 147, 157, 181, 196, 303; his versatility, 131
Baldwin, H., 26
Baldwin, Robert, 10, 50f., 53–7, 59, 62, 64, 66, 68, 74, 77, 81f., 85, 91, 227
Bangs, Rev. Nathan, 48
Barber, Rev. F. L., 293, 302
Barclay, Rev. J., 133
Barker, Miss Rose, 240
"Barn", The, 98, 203 and n.
Barnes, Miss, 47
Barrett, Dr. Michael, 98
Barron, F. W., 71
Bath Academy, 23
Beach, D., 59
Beare, Robert (*see also* "Bob"), 149–50, 199, 240 and n., 272
Beatty, James H., 88
Beatty, Rev. John, 7, 8, 17, 303
Beatty, Dr. John, 69, 73, 81, 83, 90, 99, 100f., 103, 114, 119, 155n., 302f.
Beatty, Miss Mary, 48n.
Beatty, S. (Dean), 317
Beatty, W., 133
Beaubien, Dr., 125
Beaven, Rev. James, 51, 81
Bell, A. J., 128, 151, 191, 195f., 214f., 221f., 233, 243, 266, 304–5, 310; sketch by Bush, 279–80
Belton, Rev. Samuel, 61
Bennett, H. (Principal), 257, 305–6, 320; as acting President, 326–7
Benson, Rev. Manly, 144

335

Berryman, Dr. C. B., 102
Beynon, Rev. E. D., 249
Bickle, E. W., 325
Bidwell, Barnabas, 23
Biggar, Dr. H. F., 148
Birge, C. A., 240, 268
Birnie, J. F. P., 256
Bishop, Rev. George, 208
Blackstock, Rev. Moses, 328
Blackstock, Rev. W. S., 203
Blake, Edward, 122f., 135, 158, 180, 184; his formula, 136; at length supports federation, 176; at laying of corner stone, 206
Blake, S. H., 216
Blewett, Rev. G. J., 231, 236, 248
Board of Education, Upper Canada, 4
"Bob," The, 149–50, 198–9, 211, 214–15, 216, 221, 231, 252, 274, 280, 323
Body, Rev. C. W. E. (Provost), 162
Bond Head, Sir Francis, 20
Bonne Entente, 280
Book Bureau, 252
Boulter, Miss E., 47
Boulter, Miss Maria, 34
Boulton, W. H., 159
Bowles, E. R., 254
Bowles, Rev. R. P. (Chancellor), 146n., 154, 202, 233–5, 249, 279, 292, 295, 297, 303, 307, 313; manner of election as President, 260; sketch of, 261; works for revision of Act, 265–8; and executive committee of Board, 268; his first financial campaign, 268–70; his address at reunion of 1919, 273–4; and co-education, 281–2; on relation of Arts and Theology, 284–5; and dancing, 290; resists pressure from government, 291; second financial campaign, 294–5; his qualities, 297
Brace, Rev. A. J., 246
Brangwyn, P., 284
Brebner, James, 214
Brethour, H. W., 143
British North America Act, 132, 139
British Wesleyan Conference (*see also* London Missionary Committee), 10, 28, 36, 53, 77

Britton, Byron M., 101, 124, 279
Broughall, Rev. A. J., 80
Brouse, William H., 32, 49, 59, 82
Brown, Rev. C. W., 197
Brown, E. K., 220n.
Brown, George (the *Globe*), 110, 118
Brown, G. W., 197, 256f., 313
Brown, Rev. Homer G., 250
Brown, Peter, 56, 72
Brown, W. T. (President), 220, 262, 293, 306f., 309, 311, 313, 320; on co-education, 282; first layman president, 316; under great strain, 325; and finances, 325–6
Brown, Rev. William, 7
Bruce, G. W., 191, 215
Bryce, Rev. Peter, 293, 311
Burnham, Mark, 2
Burns, Rev. R. N., 152
Burr, Miss Elizabeth, 31n.
Burt, A. L., 253, 296
Burwash Hall, 259
Burwash, Rev. John, 195, 204, 236
Burwash, Rev. Nathanael (Chancellor), 17, 60, 64, 97, 99, 100, 102, 105, 127, 129, 141, 144f., 147, 149, 155, 157, 163, 165f., 176, 180, 184, 193–5, 199, 200n., 201, 203f., 208f., 217n., 219, 222, 224, 227, 260, 265, 269, 270, 282, 292, 303, 310, 325; as a teacher of Science, 130; his attitude in 1868, 137; Dean of Theology, 143; his first thoughts on federation, 160–1; erred in diplomacy, 177–9; his vote against federation, 181; Chancellor, 187; inspects American colleges, 205; at laying of corner stone, 206; and athletics, 212; and the "row" of 1895, 215; his dispute with Walker, 218; and the Jackson controversy, 236–40; and Annesley Hall, 242–4; his resignation, 244; Hutton's tribute, 245; his death, 276–7; Burwash lectureship, 277
Burwash, Mrs. Nathanael (Margaret Proctor), 141, 241f., 266
Bush, J. Douglas N., 220n., 279–80, 304

INDEX

CAIRD, Rev. Edward, 231
Caird, Rev. John, 114
Calvin, D. D., 52n., 113
Cameron, C. M. D., 82
Cameron, Rev. M. A., 311
Campbell, Sir Alexander, 207
Campbell, John, 70, 82, 90, 102, 126
Campbell, Sir John, 19
Campbell, T. W., 153
Canniff, Dr. W., 142
Carman, Rev. Albert (Bishop), 72, 101, 167f., 175, 190, 208, 267; and Jackson controversy, 234–7
Carnegie, Andrew, 240, 266
Carroll, Rev. John, 8 and n., 10f., 23f., 29, 33, 103
Case, Rev. William, 16, 21, 23, 36
Caswell, Rev. W. B., 272n.
Caven, Rev. Wm. (Principal), 161f., 165
Cazenovia, N. Y., 23, 28f., 33, 69
Charbonnel, A. F. M. de (Bishop), 138
Chown, Rev. E. A., 215
Church, L. S., 15
Church Union, 284
Clarke, M., 135
Classics Club, 255
Cleaver, Rev. S., 238
Cleghorn, J. W., 15
Clergy Reserves, 3, 82, 111; prospective source of income for Victoria, 92
Coburn, Miss K. H., 294, 307
Cochrane, C. N., 264 and n.
Cocker, Rev. B. F., 145, 146
Cody, Rev. H. J. (President), 226, 311, 318, 328
Co-education, 23, 30–1, 255; in question, 281–2
Cohoe, B. A., 215
Colborne, Sir John, 5, 9, 10, 15; reproved by Goderich, 13
Coleman, A. P., 105, 150–3, 192 and n., 196, 200, 202–4, 209, 292, 320
Collegians' Debating Club, 252
Colquhoun, A. H. U., 226, 302
Columbian College, 247
Conference (Methodist), of 1829, 1; of 1830, 6; of 1831, 9; union with Wesleyans, 16; nine resolutions of 1859, 105; deduction from salaries for College, 123; federation debate of 1886, 178–81; decision reviewed in 1890, 189–90; of 1910, 237–40
Cook, Miss A. L., 294
Cook, Rev. John (Principal), 113
Conger, W. S., 15
Constitutional Act, 2; limitations imposed by, 5
Conversazione, 126, 150, 199, 252; attacked, 141; dancing at, 204
Cosgrave, Rev. F. H. (Provost), 311, 318
Cousland, Rev. K. H., 286, 321
Coutts, Rev. William, 248
Cox, George A., 204, 206, 216, 247
Cox, Mrs. George A., 206, 247
Cox, H. C., 269
Cox, L. C., 249
Coyne, J., 136
Crane, Edward, 15, 21
Croft, H. H., 110
Crooks, Adam, 121, 148, 158
Crossley, Rev. H. T., 155
Cruise, G. A., 296
Cullen, Miss Rose (Mrs. E. W. Wallace), 295
Cumberland, F. W., 135, 138
Currelly, C. T., 147, 305
Cutter, Mrs., 242
Czowski, C. S., 160

DALE, William, 215
Daly, Sir Dominick, 74f.
Daly, R. A., 150
Davidson, Rev. Richard (Principal), 278, 286, 307, 311, 318–19, 320
Dean, W. W., 76, 84, 88, 98
de Beaumont, Victor, 232, 321
de Montmollin, D. P., 322
Deeks, G. S., 193
Denison, Col. George, 216
Dennis, J. C., 32
Dewart, Rev. E. H., 153, 175f., 178f., 181, 185 and n., 193, 199, 203
DeWitt, N. W., 232–3, 305, 321
Dingman, R. G., 253, 257

Dingwall, Kenneth, 140n.
Dominion-provincial scholarships, 314
Donly, Miss M. E., 197f.,
Dorion, A. A., 124
Douglas, Rev. George, 145, 190, 199
Dow, Rev. John, 280
Dramatic Club, 255, 310, 323
Draper, W. H., 44, 56, 61, 64, 68, 74
Drury, E. C., 280
Duggan, George, 59
Dumble, J. H., 134
Dumble, Miss Martha L. (Mrs. A. R. Bain), 141
Dumble, Thomas, 104, 134
Durham, Lord, 36

EATON, Sir John, 269
Eaton, Mrs. Timothy, 242
Edgar, Sir James, 220
Edgar, O. Pelham, 220-1, 243
Educational Society, 156, 269, 298
Edwards, R. L., 316
Ellice, Edward, 19
Ellis, W. S., 152
Emmanuel College, 286-7, 301, 320, 327; Council of, 289
English, Rev. B. R., 306
Episcopal Methodists, 13, 77, 167
Evans, Rev. Ephraim, 20, 36
Evans, Rev. James, 32, 144

FALCONBRIDGE, Miss Dorothy, 284
Falconer, Sir Robert, 194, 224, 229, 246, 291, 297, 328; his meaning to Victoria, 230
Family Compact, 9, 14
Faraday Hall, 145-6, 188f.
Fenian raids, 129
Fennell, Rev. W. O., 326
Fenton, Rev. Hubert, 254
Ferguson, G. Howard, 291
Ferguson, Thomas A., 90, 98
Ferrier, James, 145
Field, C. C., 184
Field, G. W., 322
Field, H., 213
Fish, Rev. Charles, 123
Fisher, J., 307, 316

Fisk, Rev. Wilbur, 35, 40
Flag incident, 64-5, 70
Flavelle, Sir Joseph, 226, 247, 269
Flavelle, Lady, 283
Flint, Rev. C. W. (Bishop), 311
Ford, A. R., 253
Ford, H. E., 271
Ford, Dr. Norma, 302
Forward Movement for Missions, 221
Found, Dr. N., 249
Founders' Dinner, 292
Fowler, J. H., 150
Fraser, A., 135
French Revolution, 2, 56, 137
Frye, H. N., 220n., 254, 307
Fudger, H. H., 269, 295

GANDIER, Rev. Alfred (Principal), 304, 307; discussion with Bowles on relation of Theology to Arts, 285-6
Geikie, Dr. Walter, 102
General Course, 248, 291, 308
Geoffrion, C. A., 124
George, David Lloyd, 246
German refugees, 315-18
Gilchrist, Dr. John, 14f., 17
Glee (Music) Club, 257, 310, 323; British tour, 254
Glenelg, Lord, 19
Goderich, Lord, 13f., 18
Gooderham, Eliza, 247
Gooderham, William, 189, 247
Goodyear, H. J., 257
Gould, Dr. C. M., 187
Gould, S. H., 321
Gouinlock, John, 72
Graham, Rev. J. W., 296
Grammar schools, 3, 4, 75, 98, 125, 141-3
Grant, Rev. G. M. (Principal), 160, 162-4, 174, 209; rejects federation, 167
Grant, J. R., 321
Grantham Academy, 23
Greaves, W. H., 278-9, 305
Green, Rev. Anson, 1, 11f., 16, 21, 25, 60, 70, 103, 134, 155; his charge to Ryerson, 46

Green, Columbus, 22
Green, John Richard, 118n.
Greenwood, Lord, 216
Greenwood, Miss Nellie C. (Mrs. W. W. Andrews), 150, 197
Greer, Rev. John, 69
Grey, Sir George, 19
Griffin, Rev. W. S., 187
Griffith, Rev. J. E., 296n.
Guillet, E. C., 302
Guthrie, Rev. J. R., 321

HAANEL, Eugene, 145f., 155, 157, 192, 195ff., 200, 202, 303, 329; Dean of Science, 194
Haanel, Julia F. (Mrs. E.), 150
Haggen, G. L., 249
Hamill, Miss Velma (Mrs. E. W. Wallace), 295
Hamilton, considered as site, 103, 181
Hamilton Ladies' College, 195
Hardy, H. A., 65
Hardy, W. G., 279
Harcourt, Richard, 208
Hare, F. A., 306
Hare, R. B., 155
Harris, Elijah P., 100, 127, 129f., 140, 147
Harris, Rev. J. H., 6
Harrison, R. A., 124
Havelock, E. A., 293–4, 321
Hayden, Rev. William, 46
Hazen, A. C., 249
Head, Sir Edmund, 67, 111
Heck, Barbara, 224f., 241
Herrington, W. S., 292
Hickey, R. I., 98
Higginson, J. M., 62
Highet, Miss M. E., 197–8 and n.
Hincks, Sir Francis, 53f., 68, 91, 92–3
Hodgins, J. G., 50, 59f., 63, 76, 104
Hoeniger, F. D., 317
Hooke, S. H., 263
Horning, L. E., 193–4, 202, 215
Hough, Henry, 153, 184, 187f.,
Household Science building, 269
Howard, Rev. I. B., 48, 50, 57–60; his poem, 49

Howe, Joseph, 36
Hudspeth, Robert, 26f., 29
Hunter, Rev. J. E., 144
Hurd, A., 49
Hurlburt, Jesse, 22, 29f., 33f., 37, 41, 57, 70, 76, 84
Hurlburt, Mrs. Jesse, 47, 76
Hutton, Maurice (Principal), 222, 228, 229; his tribute to Burwash, 245
Hutty, W. E. W., 248
Huycke, E. C. S., 203, 292
Huycke, W. F., 249

INDIAN STUDENTS, listed, 33
Innis, H. A. (Dean), 12, 317, 330
Irving, J. A., 322
Irwin, Rev. A. J., 200, 202, 237

JACKSON, Rev. Clyo, 296
Jackson, Edward, 140, 143–4, 152
Jackson, Rev. George, 233; chair of English Bible, 234; Jackson controversy, 202, 233–40
Jackson, Lydia Ann, 143, 152
Jackson Society, 152, 155, 200f., 213
James, C. C., 204, 220, 253, 276
James, W. C., 276, 310
Jameson, R. S., 58
Jeffers, Rev. Wellington, 132
Jeffries, H. C., 258
Jenking, Miss R. I., 294, 322
Joblin, Rev. K. J., 320f.
Johnston, Rev. A. J., 270
Johnston, Rev. Geo., 321
Johnston, R. H., 240
Jones, Rev. Richard, 14, 134

KEENLEYSIDE, C. B., 204
Kemp, W. A., 269
Kennedy, W. P. M., (Dean), 317
Kent, Duchess of, 20, 32
Kerby, G. W., 199
Kerr, C. W., 200
Kerr, J. W., 102
Kerr, William, 59, 98, 124, 184, 188, 199
Keyes, G. L., 321
Kilpatrick, Miss Dorothy, 284

Kilpatrick, Rev. Thomas, 284, 285, 286, 287
King, W. L. M., 216
King's College, 4–6, 15n., 27, 36, 45, 52, 54, 56, 68, 71 and n., 75, 109, 121; Amendment Act of 1837, 51; offers 72 scholarships, 74
Kingston, William, 28, 33, 35, 38, 40, 47, 70, 76, 83, 89, 127, 129f., 140, 196
Kirkpatrick, Sir George, 208
Knister, R., 220n.
Knox College, 52, 75–6, 161f., 284–7, 294f., 300, 320, 327
Kono, T., 200

LACEY, Alexander, 279
Lafontaine, L. H., 62, 64, 91
Laidlaw, G. N., 321–2, 325
Lane, W. B., 267
Lang, A. E., 151, 219–20, 240, 265, 288, 304
Langford, Arthur L., 202, 210, 232
Langford, Rev. F., 202
Langford, Rev. F. W., 277f.; Dean of Emmanuel College, 320
Langford, Henry, 199, 201f.
Langford, H. E., 326
Langton, John, 108, 109–10, 111f.
Lasserre, H., 294
L'Assomption College, 139
Lauder, A. A., 134
Lavell, Rev. C., 87
Law, Faculty of, and Montreal branch, 124
Lawson, Rev. J. S., 323
Leitch, Rev. William (Principal), 107, 121f., 158; convenes public meeting at Kingston, 114; his speech, 115–17
Leslie, Rev. C. W., 307, 321
Libby, Miss M. F., 197
Library, 4, 57, 220; the new building, 240
Liddell, Rev. Thomas (Principal), 54, 56, 158; corresponds with Ryerson, 51–3
Line, Rev. John, 293, 320

Literary Association (Society), 102, 126, 193, 200f., 204, 210, 213, 246, 251f., 258, 269, 323; Union Literary Society formed, 213
Literary Society (Ladies', Womens), 197, 215, 252, 323
Little, Rev. W. J., 249, 293
Locke, G. H., 204, 311
London Missionary Committee (*see also* British Wesleyan Conference), 9, 16
Lord, Rev. William, 18, 20
Loudon, James (President), 165, 208, 216, 218f., 228
Lount, Samuel, 17
Love, C. C., 322
Lyon, James, 272 and n.
Lyons, James, 17

MACAULAY, L. (Chairman of Board of Regents), 327
McCabe, William, 124
McCarty, John, 15, 17, 64
McCaul, Rev. John (President), 51, 68, 74, 100, 109f., 120f., 148
McCullough, Rev. W., 71
Macdonald, Rev. D. Bruce, 226
McDonald, Donald (Senator), 134
Macdonald, Rev. J. A., 239
Macdonald, John (Senator), 123, 139, 147, 163, 180, 217, 247
Macdonald, Sir John A., 68, 74–5, 77, 113f., 118f., 121, 123, 132, 200; at Conference debate, 180
Macdonald, John Sandfield, 121, 132, 158, 225; his obstinacy, 133
Macdonell, Rev. Alexander (Bishop), 3
Macdougall, Rev. George, 147 and n.
Macdougall, Rev. John, 147n.
McDougall, William, 32, 48n.
MacDowell, T. W., 256; wins Victoria Cross, 275–6
McGill College, 104
Machar, Rev. John, 114
McHenry, D. C., 151, 160
MacInnes, C. S., 318
McKenzie, Dr. B. E., 151

INDEX

Mackenzie, William Lyon, 14, 57, 91, 102
Mackerras, Rev. J. H., 134
Mackintosh, W. A. (Principal), 328
Macklem, Rev. T. C. Street (Provost), 223f.
Maclaren, J. J., 176, 181, 184f.
McLaughlin, Rev. J. F. (Dean), 195–6, 201, 202, 230, 236, 240, 286, 288, 304
McLean, C. V., 321
McLennan, Sir John, 229
MacLean, K., 307
Macleod, Rev. John, 305
MacMahon, Hugh, 188
McMaster College (University), 16, 252, 311
Macmillan, Rev. J. W., 277–8
McMullen, Rev. George, 305
MacNab, Rev. Alexander, 28f., 46, 69, 71f., 74, 80, 83; Acting Principal, 66; Principal, 77–8; becomes rector of Darlington, 82
MacNab, Sir Allan, 77
MacNeil, Rev. John, 286
Macpherson, Miss Jessie, 302, 322
Macpherson, Rev. John, 322
Madden, Rev. T., 7
Managing Committee, 26–8, 34, 38f., 41, 83
Mann, Horace, 23
Manning, Miss Muriel, 284, 302
Mason, G. W., 327
Massey, Alice Parkin, 277
Massey, Chester D., 225, 259, 269
Massey, Eliza Phelps, 247
Massey, Hart A., 72–4, 188, 208, 217, 224, 247
Massey, Lillian (Mrs. Treble), 269–70
Massey, Vincent, 271, 277, 312; dean of residence, 259–60
Massey, W. E. H., 247
Masten, C. A., 154, 276, 292
Matheson, Rev. A. D. (Principal), 320
Matheson, Rev. Hugh, 286
Matthews, Peter, 17
Meacham, Rev. G. M., 79 and n.
Medicine, Faculty of, 98, 102, 124, 142; Montreal branch, 125

Meighen, Arthur, 293
Meredith, Sir William, 183, 226
Metcalf, Rev. Franklin, 1, 10
Metcalfe, Sir Charles, 56, 61f., 67, 69
Michael, Rev. Hugh, 263
Michie, James, 134
Mills, James (President), 148, 155, 187, 208
Milner, W. S., 214, 222
Misener, Rev. A. P., 230–1, 236, 305
Missionary Society, 197, 199, 204, 213, 221
Modern Languages Club, 204, 255
Moffit, L. W., 257f.
Moore, Rev. A. B. B. (President), 299, 328
Moore, Dennis, 195
Montgomery, R. A., 102
Morse, S. P., 70
Moss, Sir Charles, 161
Moss, C. M., 151
Mott, John R., 200
Mowat, Sir Oliver, 147f., 165, 175–7, 180f., 207
Moyer, J. W., 254, 258
Mulholland, J., 191
Mulock, Sir William, 110, 159, 161–6, 178, 180, 184, 208, 303, 311
Mumford, Rev. W. J., 248
Murray, Rev. Robert, 61, 67n.

NATURAL SCIENCE ASSOCIATION, 152
Nelles, Rev. S. S. (Chancellor), 12, 48, 50, 59, 70, 86, 91, 99, 101, 103, 107, 109, 114, 126, 129, 131, 133, 140f., 145, 148, 151, 157f., 160f., 163, 176, 178, 180, 184, 191, 196, 199, 200f., 203 and n., 246f., 279, 292, 303; his early career, 87; sole professor, 88; Ryckman's tribute, 89; opening address of, 1853, 94–7; assumes full responsibility, 104; speech at Kingston, 117; at Elm St. conference, 134; resigned to failure, 137; address to Teachers' Assn., 142–3; opposes dean's inclusion on Board, 155; and Goldwin Smith, 159; negotiations re federation, 164f.; and the authority of Confer-

ence, 168; becomes Chancellor, 169; his address at Convocation, 1885, 169–74; his increasing mistrust, 177; his vote against federation, 181; his death, 185–7
Newburgh Academy, 87
Normal School, 109

Oasis, The, 49
Odlum, Edward, 152
Odlum, Victor, 152, 246
Ogden, Dr. E. A., 102
O'Loane, James, 26
Ontario Agricultural College, 65n., 276
Ontario Ladies' College, 247
Ormiston, David, 125
Ormiston, Rev. William, 60, 70, 80, 185
Orton, Rev. A. S., 306
Osgoode Hall, 183, 252
Owen, Francis, 270–1

PACEY, D. E., 220n.
Paddock, W. McK., 76
Parke, Thomas, 17
Parker, Rev. W. R., 103
Paton, John, 114, 119
Patton, James, 113f., 118f., 121, 158
Pearson, Lester Bowles, 292, 315n.; welcomed as Chancellor, 327
Peltier, Dr., 125
Perry, Ebenezer, 7f., 15, 17
Petch, John, 195, 220
Phelps, A. L., 284
Philalethic (Literary) Society, 41, 48, 57
Philomath, The, 48, 49, 50, 57
Phoenix Association, 49
Pickthall, Miss Marjorie, 220n., 240
Pidgeon, Rev. G. C., 327
Portland, Duke of: his despatch, 3; 158
Potter, Rev. W. A., 305
Potts, Rev. John, 72, 137, 150, 184f., 188f., 199, 217n.
Pratt, E. J., 220n., 253, 275, 279
Pratt, Mrs. E. J., 248
Punshon, Rev. W. M., 137, 139, 141, 143, 145, 148; a mysterious offer, 147

QUEEN'S COLLEGE (University), 22f., 36, 41, 45, 51, 54, 56, 68f., 71, 74–6, 106–9, 114–16, 119–23, 136, 139f., 160, 162, 175f., 209, 219, 251; as between Act and Royal Charter, 37; prepared to surrender Arts, 52; and "residuarism", 63; sources of revenue, 111; rejects federation, 167
Queen's College School, 23

RAMSAY, W., 71
Ray, Miss M. V., 323
Rebel, The, 263
Reeve, Dr. R. A., 244
Regiopolis College, 54, 56, 68, 75, 107, 120, 134, 139
Reform Bill of 1832, 5
Reid, Dr. John, 102
Responsible Government, 62, 66
Retirement of professors, 300–1
Reynar, Rev. A. H. (Dean), 127–8, 141, 143, 147, 157, 186–7, 194, 203, 217–18, 220, 236, 270, 303
Rice, Rev. S. D., 99–101, 134
Richardson, Rev. James (Bishop), 1, 7, 13
Richey, Rev. Matthew (Principal), 21–7, 29–31, 33, 36, 77f., 82f., 164
Riddell, R. G., 322
Riddell, W. R., 148, 150, 154, 216, 247, 249, 292, 311
Riese, Miss L., 294, 322
Ritchie, Mrs. C. Fraser, 48n., 50n.
Roaf, John, 71
Roaf, Rev. John, 3
Robertson, H. G., 249, 279
Robertson, J. C., 213–15, 243, 273, 288, 304; on the working of federation, 222–3
Robertson, T. H., 90
Robertson, T. J., 102
Robins, J. D., 220n., 248, 254, 258, 270f., 307, 322; on Puritanism, 250–1
Robins, Mrs. J. D., 248
Robinson, Sir John Beverley, 14
Roblin, J. P., 18, 56
Robson, David, 154
Robson, D. O., 305, 321

INDEX

Robson, Mrs. D. O., 305
Robson, Rev. Ebenezer, 104
Robson, John, 105
Rodd, G. L., 256
Rolfe, Sir R. M., 19
Rolph, Dr. John, 14, 83, 98, 102, 124, 141–2 and n.
Rose, J. E., 169
Rose, Rev. S. P., 203, 244
Ross, A. C. M., 322
Ross, Sir George W., 165f., 175f., 178, 180, 183f., 204, 207, 225
Ross, Rev. J. S., 265
Ross, Mary Lowrey, 253
Rowell, Miss M. C., 279, 281
Rowell, N. W., 211, 244, 301, 311; and Jackson controversy, 236–9
Roy, Rev. James, 143
Royal Commission of 1862, 108, 113, 119–20; of 1905, 225–8
Rundle, Rev. R. T., 105
Rundle, W. E., 311
Ryckman, E. B., 200
Ryckman, Rev. E. B., 88, 101
Ryerson, Mrs. C. E., 302f.
Ryerson, Rev. Egerton, 2, 5, 8f., 17, 20, 22f., 28, 34–7, 41, 48, 50, 56–8, 60–3, 67, 69, 74, 76, 81, 83, 89, 92, 103–6, 112–14, 133, 139n., 140, 144f., 148, 155, 158, 165, 208, 247, 292; secures Royal Charter, 18–20; first address to students, 38; rights of faculty defined, 40; expounds reason for Royal Charter as vs. Act, 45; induction as principal, 45–7; corresponds with Liddell, 51–3; as teacher, 60; involved in Metcalfe controversy, 64; quells a disturbance, 65; resigns as Principal, 77; a curious emphasis, 79–80; titular President, 91; speech at Kingston, 117–18; views on grants, 133
Ryerson, Dr. E. S., 100n., 302f.
Ryerson, Rev. George, 2, 5, 9f.
Ryerson, Rev. John, 1, 6, 11, 16f., 23f., 29, 35, 58, 77f., 86, 87, 101
Ryerson, Col. Joseph, 11

St. Francis Xavier University, 229

St. Jerome College, 139
St. John, J. W., 215
St. Michael's College, 139, 161f., 257, 329; enters federation, 229
Sampson, James H., 69
Sanderson, Rev. G. R., 78, 80
Sanderson, Rev. J. E., 141
Scarlet and Gold, 323
Sclater, Rev. J. R. P., 287
Scobie, Hugh, 56, 64
Scott, A. M., 311
Scott, Mrs. C. V., 249
Scott, Rev. John: declines D.D., 82
Scott-Raff, Mrs. Ema, 242
Select Committee of Legislature (1860), 108, 111–13
Senior Dinner, 154, 202, 280
Senior Stick, 154
Separate Schools, 118, 132, 138, 139n.
Shenick, Miss A., 150, 152
Shepard, Alan, 213
Shepley, G. F., 154
Sheraton, Rev. J. P. (Principal), 208
Sherwood, Henry, 59, 74f.
Shore, Rev. R. A. A., 213
Shore, T. C., 306
Sicotte, L. V., 121
Sifton, A. L., 154
Sifton, Clifford, 153f., 217 and n., 329n.
Sifton, H. B., 249
Silverthorn, N., 80
Simcoe, Governor, 3, 5
Skinner, Miss M. H., 281
Small, J. E., 10
Smith, Rev. A. Lloyd, 248, 269, 313
Smith, Rev. G. M., 271, 277
Smith, Goldwin, 155, 158, 171, 208, 226
Smith, James, 150
Smith, Lyman C., 153
Smith, Sidney (President), 328, 330
Smith, W. Morley, 249, 257, 258
Smoke, S. C., 151
Snodgrass, Rev. William (Principal), 133–4, 136, 158
Snow, F. H., 271
Social Caput, 290
Sororities (and fraternities), 282–3

Sparling, Rev. J. W., 238
Spencer, A. C., 319, 327
Spencer, George B., 8, 189
Spencer, Rev. James, 26, 32, 58
Springer, Oliver, 32, 49, 59, 71, 76, 77n., 82; examined for degree, 70; his Latin diploma, 72
Sproatt, Henry, 276, 301
Squair, John, 69
Stanley, C. W. (President), 263–4
Stapleford, Rev. E. W., 313
Staples, W. E., 249, 305, 322
Starr, J. R. L., 199, 202, 243, 311
Steinhauer, Rev. Henry, 26, 32f.
Steinhauer, Rev. R. B., 32
Stephenson, Dr. F. C., 312n.
Sterling, J. E. W. (President), 296
Stinson, Rev. Joseph, 20, 29
Storm, W. G., 187
Stowe Gullen, Dr. Augusta, 197n.
Strachan, Rev. John (Bishop), 4, 5, 13, 36, 51f., 56, 75, 77, 107, 138, 199, 286, 312, 323
Stuart, Rev. G. O. (Archdeacon), 114, 117
Student Christian Movement, 263
Students' Council, 258, 265
Student Volunteer Movement (Missionary), 105, 200, 250
Students' Alma Mater Society, 251
Students' Parliament, 307, 323
Students' Union, 326
Sturgis family, 33
Subscription books, 8
Sullivan, R. B., 44, 59
Surerus, J. A., 294
Sutherland, Rev. Alex., 175, 179, 184, 188, 203
Swinarton, T., 138
Sydenham, Lord, 36f., 61
Sykes, W. J., 197

TABLES OF MERIT, 30, 59
Taylor, Rev. Lachlin, 86–8, 134, 147
Taylor, J. W., 249
Taylor, T. W., 161, 216
Taylor, Wilson, 273
Terpsichore, 290

Theological Union, 201, 203
Theology (at Victoria), not taught in U.C. Academy, 6; Ryerson's attitude to, 47; Liddell's mistake re, 53; the first D.D. offered, 82; not mentioned by Nelles in 1853, 95; Nelles on an educated ministry, 104; Punshon and, 137–8; course instituted in 1871, 143; Faculty set up in 1873, 143; at Montreal, 145; Dean not on Board, 155; authority of Conference over, 156; in 1900, 221; commingling with Arts, 250; appointments to faculty, 267–8; as affected by Church Union, 284–9; Emmanuel chosen as name, 286–7 and n.; graduate school is formed, 320
Thomas, D. A., 254
Thompson, Wattie, 202
Tolkein, Charles, 32
Toronto School of Medicine; *see* Medical Faculty
Torrington, F. H., 208
Toye, Miss Bertha, 210
Treble, Mrs. Lillian Massey, 269–70
Trethewey, W. H., 306
Trinity College (University of), 106, 108, 111, 119f., 134f., 139, 162f., 167f., 175f., 184f., 219, 229, 311, 320f., 329; enters federation, 223–4; and Religious Knowledge, 308; and German refugees, 318
Tucker, James A., 215
Tucker, Rev. W. B., 200
Tweedsmuir, Lord, 310; becomes a D.D., 311; his speech at Centenary Dinner, 312
Tyrrell, J. B., 31n., 150, 253

UNDERHILL, F. H., 12, 264 and n.
University at Kingston; *see* Queen's
University College, 93, 110, 112f., 117, 164, 167, 246, 300, 315, 329; so named in 1853, 92; fancied alienation of building, 178; religion in, 182; a separate head, 223
University federation, chap. VIII, 328–30

University of London, a model for Toronto, 92, 115; Goldwin Smith's opinion of, 159
University of Ottawa, 139
University of Toronto (*see also* King's College), 4 and n., 52, 74–5, 105–6, 108, 138, 140; "lethal" Bill (1843), 50, 53–4; Draper's bills (1845, 1846), 68, 74; Macdonald's bill (1847), 68; Baldwin's Act (1849), 81–2; amended (1850), 85; Hincks' Act (1853), 92–3; many Senate meetings, 109; extravagance of, 119; change of front in Senate, 120–2; the act of 1887, 181–4; financial relations with Victoria, 218; Act of 1906, 226–8; Council of Faculty of Arts, 226; appointments to staff, 227; intra-mural athletics, 256
Upper Canada College, 5, 10, 27, 51, 81, 183

VAN ALLEN, Miss Mary, 302
Van Dusen, Rev. Conrad, 83, 89; his "scholarships," 90–1
VanNorman, Rev. Daniel C., 28–30, 33, 35, 70; and Science teaching, 42
VanNorman, Mrs. D. C., 42, 47, 63, 80
VanNorman, Isaac, 29
Varsity, The, 202, 229
Varsity Christian Fellowship, 323
Victoria College (University), Acts: of 1841, 22, 37 and 43; of 1847, 76 and n.; of 1850, 85; of 1874, 149; of 1879, 156; of 1884, 169; of 1898, 218; of 1915, 267–8; of 1928, 288–9; of 1944, 319; of 1951, 306
Victoria College, Council of, 28, 289, 300, 309
Victoria Reports, 315n.
Vincent, Rev. Charles, 161
V. P. Society, 151 and n., 200f.

WAKEFIELD, GIBBON, 57
Walker, Sir Edmund, 218, 226
Wallace, E. W. (Chancellor), 15n., 251, 295, 300, 302, 307, 309–11, 316; advocates General Course, 308

Wallace, E. W., Jr., 316
Wallace, Rev. F. H. (Dean), 194, 222, 236, 261, 273, 300
Wallace, M. W. (Principal), 317
Wallace, W. S., 108, 178
Wallbridge, Lewis, 124
Watson, Dr. A. D., 238
Watson, G. H., 154
Webster, Robert, 63
Wesleyan Theological College, Montreal, 145, 155, 193
Wesleyan University, Middletown, 22, 35, 40, 48, 70, 72, 77f., 87
Whidden, Rev. H. P. (Chancellor), 311
Whitehead, Rev. Thomas, 6, 7, 21, 23
Whitlock, Rev. G. C., 99, 100, 127, 140
Whitney, E. C., 259
Whitney, J. P., 225, 259
Whittington, Rev. Robert, 153
Wiegand, W. B., 257
Williams, "Prof.", 213
Williams, A. T. H., 160
Williamson, James, 115
Willoughby, Miss K. K. I., 197
Wilson, Sir Daniel, 109–12, 123, 161, 163–6, 175–8, 181 and n., 183, 207
Wilson, Edward, 148, 194
Wilson, Rev. John ("Old Trinity"), 76, 83f., 90, 102, 131, 143, 151, 157, 191, 196, 303
Wilson, Miss Mary, 209
Wilson, R. W., 143, 151
Winter, F. W., 238
Women's Residence and Educational Association, 241
Wood, C. B., 249
Wood, E. B., 135
Wood, E. R., 269
Wood, Mrs. E. R., 283
Wood, Rev. Enoch, 86, 90
Wood, G. H., 269
Wood, J. S., 321–2
Wood, Miss Mary Bakewell (Mrs. S. S. Nelles), 90
Woods, Sir James, 301
Woodside, M. St. A., 306
Woodsworth, Miss C. M. (Mrs. G. J. Blewett), 231

Woodsworth, J. S., 221
Woodsworth, Richard, 231
Woodsworth, Rev. Richard, 231
Workman, Rev. G. C., 150, 191–5, 203, 303
Workman, Dr. J. J., 98
Wright, Rev. Daniel, 7
Wright, Dr. H. H., 98, 102
Wright, Rev. W. P., 59, 70, 80, 89
Wrong, G. M., 292
Wycliffe College, 161, 208, 320, 328
Wymilwood, 283, 326

Young, George Paxton, 140, 166, 231
Young, R. W., 60
Y.M.C.A., 155, 199, 200n., 210, 213, 250, 263, 278
Y.W.C.A., 250, 263

www.ingramcontent.com/pod-product-compliance
Lightning Source LLC
LaVergne TN
LVHW020417070526
838199LV00055B/3645